ONCE
Around the Bases

Bittersweet Memories of Only One Game in the Majors

RICHARD TELLIS

With a Foreword by
Jerome Holtzman

Triumph Books
CHICAGO

© 1998 by Triumph Books and Richard Tellis.

No part of this publication may be reproduced, stored in a retrieval system, or transmitted, in any form by any means, electronic, mechanical, photocopying or otherwise, without the prior written permission of the publisher, Triumph Books, 644 South Clark Street, Chicago, Illinois 60605.

Library of Congress Cataloging-in-Publication Data
Tellis, Richard, 1930-
      Once Around the Bases : Bittersweet Memories of Only One Game in the Majors / Richard Tellis
      p.   cm.
     Includes bibliographical references.
     ISBN 1-57243-277-2 (hc.)
     1. Baseball players—United States—Interviews. 2. Baseball—United States—History.   I. Title.
GV865.A1T43 1998
796.357'092'273—dc21   98-15934
                                                        CIP

This book is available in quantity at special discounts for your group or organization. For further information, contact:

Triumph Books
644 South Clark Street
Chicago, Illinois 60605
(312) 939-3330
FAX (312) 663-3557

Printed in the United States of America

ISBN 1-57243-277-2

Page xv excerpt from THE NATURAL by Bernard Malamud. Copyright © 1952 and copyright renewed © 1980 by Bernard Malamud. Reprinted by permission of Farrar, Straus & Giroux, Inc.

Photographs courtesy of the featured players.

Book design by Sans Serif.

To Bea, Larry, and Laurie,
who have provided me with years of joy,
and to the game of baseball which,
stubbornly, has done the same.

The run Otis Davis scored, in his only game in the majors, helped the Brooklyn Dodgers tie the St. Louis Cardinals for first place in 1946.

CONTENTS

The Expansion Years (1963–Present)

Foreword

In big league baseball it is often said that "There is nothing new under the sun." In other words, don't get too excited. What happened today has happened before. But there never has been anything even closely similar to Richard Tellis's *Once Around the Bases: Bittersweet Memories of Only One Game in the Majors*. In the vast storehouse of baseball literature, it's a first.

Tellis interviewed 40 of the approximately 150 living players who appeared in only one major league game. Lumped together, it could be said they were failed big leaguers but that isn't necessarily so. Many of their stories are heroic, as inspirational and fascinating as some of the superstars enshrined in the Hall of Fame.

Bert Shepard of the Washington Nationals, a fighter pilot during World War II, was shot down over Germany. His right leg was amputated below the knee. When he awoke he was in a German camp for prisoners of war. Shortly after returning to the United States, Shepard and other POWs met with Secretary of War, Robert P. Patterson, at the Pentagon.

"He asked me what I wanted to do," Shepard recalled. Before he had gone to war, Shepard had pitched in the minor leagues. "I told him I wanted to continue my career in professional baseball."

Patterson called his friend, Clark Griffith, then the owner of the Washington club, and Shepard was granted a tryout. His wooden leg barely affected his pitching motion, and he made the team.

On August 4, 1945, in the second game of a doubleheader, Shepard worked five and one-third finishing innings in relief against the Boston Red Sox, the only big league pitcher to take the mound with an artificial leg.

"I'm a competitor," Shepard said years later. "I was pitching a lot of batting practice and had developed a lot of confidence. I said to myself, 'Here's my chance!' I was awfully glad about it. I said 'Goddamn it, I'm in the ball game.'"

Manager Ossie Bluege summoned Shepard in a perilous fourth-inning situation: Two outs and the bases loaded. With a full count and the runners running, the one-legged Shepard struck out George Metkovich. The inning over, Shepard returned to the Washington dugout to a standing ovation. He allowed only one run on three hits the rest of the way.

Shepard never appeared in another big league game. It was a sensational debut, easily matching the performance of John Paciorek Jr. two decades later. John was the younger brother of Tom Paciorek who had an 18-year major league career. An eighteen-year-old outfielder with the Houston Colts, John departed with a perfect 1.000 batting average: 3 for 3, with two walks, and three runs batted in, against the Mets on September 29, 1963, the final day of the regular season.

After the game, a local sports announcer predicted he would be with the Houston club for many years. The *Houston Press* described him as a "cinch to make it as a big leaguer." But in spring training the next season a physical examination revealed he was suffering from a congenital spine abnormality. He sat out the next two seasons. When he returned, he was sent to the minor leagues and never made it back to the big time.

Pitcher Larry Yount, younger brother of the long-time Milwaukee superstar, Robin, also had his career cut short because of an injury. Technically, Larry got into a game on September 27, 1971 when he was also with Houston. Once he was announced, his name was automatically inserted into the box score.

While warming up in the bullpen, his elbow was inflamed. When he reached the mound he realized he would be risking his career. What he didn't know was that it was his first and last major league opportunity. He left the game without throwing a pitch. He played four more years in the minors in a futile comeback attempt.

We are only scratching the surface. There is much more wonderful reading ahead.

Jerome Holtzman

ACKNOWLEDGEMENTS

As then-Yankee-manager Casey Stengel once admitted after winning a pennant, "I couldn'ta done it without the players." Similarly, one does not put together a book such as this without the help of these former baseball players, who were so willing to share their experiences with me and who provided me with so many months of fun along the way. I thank them all, and I only hope they enjoyed reminiscing with me at least half as much as I enjoyed listening to them.

Outside of the forty players profiled here lie the stories of others I have interviewed. These men equally deserve my thanks and they have my sincere appreciation. They are Roman "Lefty" Bertrand, Morris "Buddy" Hancken, Hersh Lyons, Hank Schmulbach, Mike Kosman, Harry MacPherson, Rinaldo "Rugger" Ardizoia, Cal Ermer, Bob Mavis, Cal Howe, Chuck Daniel, Cal Browning, Bart Zeller, and Hank Small.

There were three other major sources that also were absolutely vital to the completion of this project and I am indebted to each.

The first is *The Baseball Encyclopedia*, published by Macmillan, which, although not absolutely perfect, is as close to it as anyone can reasonably expect. I used the ninth edition, primarily. I also wish to thank the *Encyclopedia*'s statistical director, Ken Samelson, for his help in pointing me in the right direction and for putting up with my notes about a few things that didn't jibe with what I was told.

The second necessary ingredient was the voluminous material supplied by the National Baseball Hall of Fame and Museum in Cooperstown, New York, and I am particularly indebted to the help provided there by research assistant Ralph P. Insinga and his associates, Scot E. Mondore, Thomas D. Craig, and Patty Gracey.

Finally, the seventh edition of *Sport Americana,* by R. J. "Jack" Smalling, published by the Edgewater Book Company, was responsible for allowing me to continue moving the project forward once it was under way. To all these people and organizations, I am deeply grateful.

Along the way, I received help and encouragement from a number of others who deserve my thanks. They include, in no special order, Gene Pemberton of the Houston Astros, Glen Serra of the Atlanta Braves, Mike Selleck of the Oakland Athletics, Michelle Baugh of the Texas Rangers, Craig Sanders of the New York Mets, Connie Bell of the

Detroit Tigers, Cindy McManus of the Baltimore Orioles, Shawn M.
Bertani of the St. Louis Cardinals, Connie Barthelmas of the Cincinnati
Reds, and Mary Jane Ryan of the Boston Red Sox.

In addition, the media and public relations departments of the New
York Yankees, Chicago Cubs, Minnesota Twins, Montreal Expos, Kansas
City Royals, Toronto Blue Jays, Milwaukee Brewers, Los Angeles
Dodgers, and California Angels all contributed to my knowledge.

I also owe thanks to individuals who provided other information or
who added their best wishes as I toiled to put this material together.
These included Phyllis K. Mehrige of the American League; Wally
Weibel of the Baseball Commissioner's Office; Bob Vanderberg, associate
sports editor of the *Chicago Tribune*; Glen Miller of the Fort Meyers,
Florida, *News-Press;* Naomi Thomas; and Kristin E. Wurm.

A number of books, newspapers, and magazines helped me obtain the
history of the teams and the times, as well as some leads to anecdotes
and player information.

These include the following, again in no special order: *The Boys of
Summer,* by Roger Kahn, Harper & Row; *The American League* and *The
National League*, both by Donald Honig, Crown Publishers, Inc.; *Dia-
monds in the Rough*, by Joel Zoss and John Bowman, Macmillan Publish-
ing Co.; *The Minors*, by Neil J. Sullivan, St. Martin's Press; *Our Game*, by
Charles Alexander, Henry Holt & Co.; *Baseball Anecdotes*, by Daniel
Okrent and Steve Wulf, Oxford University Press; *We Played the Game*,
edited by Danny Peary, Hyperion; *They Also Served*, by Bill Gilbert,
Crown Publishers; *Baseball in '41*, by Robert W. Creamer, Viking; *The
Era*, by Roger Kahn, Ticknor & Fields; *A Glimpse of Fame*, by Dennis
Snelling, McFarland & Co.; *The Second Fireside Book of Baseball*, edited by
Charles Einstein, Simon & Schuster; *Who Was Harry Steinfeldt?* by Bert
Raldolph Sugar, Playboy Press; *Bill Mazer's Amazin' Baseball Book*, by Bill
Mazer with Stan and Shirley Fischler, Zebra Books, Kensington Publish-
ing Co.; *Field of Screams*, by Richard Scheinin, W. W. Norton & Co.; and
Baseball Bloopers and Other Curious Incidents, by Robert Obojski, Sterling
Publishing Co., Inc.

Also: *Number One*, by Billy Martin and Peter Golenbock, Delacorte
Press; *Veeck As In Wreck*, by Bill Veeck with Ed Linn, G. P. Putnam's Sons;
I Had A Hammer, by Hank Aaron with Lonnie Wheeler, Harper Collins;
Behind the Mask, by Bill Freehan, The World Publishing Co.; *Strikeout*, by
Denny McLain with Mike Nahrstedt, The Sporting News; *My Favorite
Summer 1956*, by Mickey Mantle and Phil Pepe, Doubleday; *The Last
Yankee*, by David Falkner, Simon & Schuster; *The One and Only Bobo*, by
John Lardner, True Magazine, Fawcett Publications; *Judge Landis and 25
Years in Baseball*, by J. G. Taylor Spink, Thomas Y. Crowell Co.; the Ham-
tramck, Michigan, *Journal and Courier;* *The Boys of Summers Past*, by John
Moylan, *Irish America Magazine;* *Newsday;* the New Castle, Pennsylvania,

News; the *St. Petersburg Times*; *Baseball Digest; The Michigan State Journal*; *Hardball Magazine*; and *Baseball America*.

And, finally, of course, to my family and friends, who have put up with me and encouraged me as I traveled this path and gushed on interminably, I want you to know that I couldn'ta done it without you guys, either.

Richard Tellis
East Hills, New York

Ralph Gagliano (Chapter 32) says he "walked around naked a lot," as a direct result of playing in one game in the major leagues.

INTRODUCTION

"Sometimes when I walk down the street I bet people will say there goes Roy Hobbs, the best there ever was in the game."

She gazed at him with touched and troubled eyes. "Is that all?"

—Bernard Malamud, *The Natural*

During the past sixty or seventy years, if you asked any young American boy what he wanted to be when he grew up, the odds were that "major-league baseball player" would be at, or near, the top of his list.

Even today, if you ask men aged forty, fifty, or sixty what they wished they could have been—if they weren't what they had become—"major-league baseball player" would still rank high.

If you have any doubt about that, think about the fervor and excitement shown by those men who hoped to be named replacement players at the start of the strike-delayed 1995 season. And can you recall how Michael Jordan, considered the world's greatest basketball player, was willing to give it all up just for the chance to try?

But, obviously, very few of us ever made it to the major leagues. Those who did can be divided into four groups. First, there are those who received fame, if not fortune, and reached the pinnacle of their profession through election to the Baseball Hall of Fame—men such as Cy Young, Babe Ruth, Lou Gehrig, Ty Cobb, Walter Johnson, Honus Wagner, Joe DiMaggio, Ted Williams, Stan Musial, Hank Aaron, Jackie Robinson, and others of that stature.

In the second and much larger group are those who turned out to be good, solid baseball players, who played a number of years at the major-league level and carved out respectable careers for themselves over the years, but who didn't quite rate election into the shrine at Cooperstown. Most baseball fans would generally recognize and remember these players' names.

Then there are those whose talent allowed them to play one or more full seasons in the majors, but who never made much of a meaningful impact on the sport. These are the journeymen ballplayers whose achievements are remembered only by the most rabid of baseball aficionados and, perhaps, by friends and family.

And, finally, there are those who came to the majors, in the parlance of the sport, "for a cup of coffee." These are men who had an opportunity to play in the major leagues for less than a full year. Some of them made a good impression in spring training, started the season in the majors, but quickly returned to the minors when, as they say, "the pitchers started throwing curveballs." A few were able to hang on for a good part of the year. Others came to the big leagues from the minors only when rosters were allowed to expand late in the year. But all of them achieved their boyhood dream of becoming a major-league baseball player, even if briefly.

This book focuses on a particular few in this last group. They, like Ruth, Cobb, and DiMaggio, were once major-league ballplayers, but their careers were nothing like those former players'. They are men who were brought up to the major leagues once "for a cup of coffee," but hardly got a sip. Each of the men in this book played in one, but *only* one, major-league game and then, for whatever reason, never played in the majors again.

There are approximately 150 men living today whose entire major-league career consisted of *one game*. A number of them came to bat just once and didn't even get to play in the field. Some struck out. Others batted 1.000 in their one-game major-league career. Some played in the field and never got to bat. Some served only as pinch runners. Some pitchers were perfect in their only appearance. Some were winners while others lost or weren't able to retire a single batter. Some have earned run averages of infinity which will remain in the record book for all time. How would you explain that to your grandchildren?

I've reached approximately one-third of this group. Each was asked about his performance that day and to describe how he felt and how the experience affected the rest of his life. They all spoke about their teammates, managers, coaches, minor-league experiences, what it took for them to get to the big leagues, and what they did after they stopped playing.

Sometimes their recollections were faded or clouded with age, and sometimes they sounded as if they were fishermen talking about the big one that got away. Sometimes both. For example, Ed Wineapple, the first player profiled here, played in one game for the American League's Washington Nationals back in 1929. Originally, he told me he thought it was in 1926. He also thought he was the losing pitcher, but he wasn't.

When I asked Wineapple what he remembered most about that game, he said, "Striking out Hank Greenberg with the bases full." Well, that would be something to remember, all right. Unfortunately, Greenberg didn't reach the majors until 1930, a year *after* Wineapple pitched in the American League. When I pointed this out, he admitted his memory of the event was clouded. It may have happened in an exhibition game sometime later.

I cite that only as an example of how the memory may have played tricks on some of those who talked to me. For this reason, I obtained box scores of all the games in question as well as the minor-league records of each of the players. Where their recollections differ with the records, I attempt to point this out or to reconcile it. In minor points, for example when players claimed batting averages or pitching records which were slightly off (both in their favor or against them), or when someone said, "I think it was hit to short" when it was actually hit to third, I just made the numbers correct and took the liberty of changing "short" to "third."

There is the common denominator in their stories of having reached the major leagues. Practically every one of these men was a good baseball player, or a good athlete, by the time he reached his teens.

While they all had the ability and were talented enough to reach the majors, there are a variety of reasons why they didn't stay—why they played only one game once they got there. Some, of course, simply failed to perform well on that one occasion and were never given another chance. A number of careers were derailed by military service, and a few because the players lacked faith in their own abilities. Others were affected by injuries. And in a good number of cases, as one of them points out, careers depended simply on "somebody likes you or they don't."

These stories range from 1929 to 1989. I expected to find startling differences in salaries over the years, but I was surprised by the other things I learned along the way.

For one thing, as I reviewed these stories chronologically, I could almost see the game, as well as the attitude of the players, changing over the years. The Depression, the development of the farm system and the rebirth of the minor leagues, World War II, racial integration, television, geographic expansion, physical expansion, and the advent of unionism and free agency all had a profound effect on the game of baseball. These players, collectively, experienced all of these things.

As for attitude changes, in the earlier years most veteran players thought of rookies as job competition in an economically hard world and would do little or nothing to help them. Some of the older players interviewed said they would play when they were hurt simply to protect their jobs, and decry the "softies" of today.

In the later years, however, the older players accepted the rookies as teammates who could help put more money in *all* their pockets—as well as provide a welcome day off for a hurt or weary, but now economically secure, veteran.

Of course, the players' attitudes toward the game itself and to the fans also have changed. To the old-timers, it was a game they loved. The later players considered it much more of a business. In that regard, the oldsters often point to their better-known contemporaries who spent hours giving away autographs to adoring fans, and compare that to today's "make an appointment, see me at the show, and bring your wallet" approach.

Perhaps I should have expected to see these things, but certainly not with such clarity.

The best-known "player" with a one-game major-league career is not included here, but let me remind you of him.

He was Eddie Gaedel, the three-foot-seven, 65-pounder who, on Sunday, August 19, 1951, pinch hit for the eighth-place St. Louis Browns in the second game of a doubleheader against the fifth-place Detroit Tigers as part of a stunt cooked up by Browns' owner, Bill Veeck.

Veeck positioned the two teams differently on game day. In his autobiography, *Veeck—As In Wreck*, the former owner of the Browns says, "The day we chose was a Sunday doubleheader against the *last-place* Detroit Tigers, a struggle which did not threaten to set the pulses of the city beating madly. . . . The press, for the most part, took the sane attitude that Gaedel had provided a bright moment in what could easily have been a deadly dull double-header *between a 7th and an 8th place* ball club. . . ." The emphasis is mine.

The stunt was quintessential Veeck. He and sponsor Falstaff Brewing, supposedly celebrating its birthday on that date, had attracted more than 18,000 to the doubleheader—the largest crowd to see the Browns at home in four years. Upon entering the stadium, everyone received a can of the sponsor's beer, a slice of birthday cake, and a box of ice cream, along with salt-and-pepper shakers in the shape of Falstaff beer bottles.

Although the Browns lost the first game, the fans were treated to a festive Falstaff Beer birthday party between games, so they were still in a good mood when the second game started. The between-games festivities featured a parade of old-fashioned cars circling the field, men and women dressed in Gay Nineties costumes pedalling around the park on old-fashioned bicycles, and troubadours roaming through the stands. A band, featuring Satchel Paige on drums, played at home plate. A hand-balancing act took place at first base, a trampoline act was at second, and a juggler was on third. On the mound, the baseball clown-contortionist, Max Patkin, jitterbugged madly with a woman who had joined him from the grandstand, according to Veeck's account.

Finally, a seven-foot birthday cake was rolled out, shepherded by a hefty actor in Elizabethan costume representing Sir John Falstaff. At this point, public address announcer Bernie Ebert reported that "a brand-new Brownie" was being presented to the Browns' manager, Zach Taylor. Sir John put his sword to the cake and, on cue, out popped the tiny Gaedel, wearing a miniature Browns uniform. The crowd laughed, but it appeared to be an anticlimax.

Then came the second game—the one game of Eddie Gaedel's major-league career. After Detroit was retired in the top of the first inning, Ebert announced over the loud speaker system that Gaedel would pinch hit for the scheduled leadoff batter, center fielder Frank Saucier. "For the Browns," Ebert told the unsuspecting crowd seriously, "number ⅛, Eddie Gaedel, batting for Saucier." Suddenly the park went wild as Gaedel, waving three Little League bats and wearing the number ⅛ on the back of his uniform, bounced out of the Browns' dugout and strode to the plate.

A fifteen-minute delay ensued, during which the Browns had to convince plate umpire Ed Hurley that Gaedel actually was on the team's current active list and had a legitimate contract, and that league headquarters had been properly notified (by telegram that morning). Hurley waved Gaedel into the batter's box and shooed away the photographers who had rushed out for pictures. After the Tiger battery, pitcher Bob Cain and catcher Bob Swift, held a brief conference on the mound, Swift returned to his position behind the plate and got down on both knees. The stadium was in an uproar.

Cain, hardly able to believe this was happening, actually tried to pitch to Gaedel's strike zone (with Gaedel bent over, it was measured by Veeck earlier at one and a half inches). After two failed attempts, Cain softly tossed in the third and fourth balls about three feet over Gaedel's head. Gaedel trotted down to first base accompanied by the roar of the crowd. When Jim Delsing, the Browns' regular center fielder, came out as a pinch runner to replace him, Gaedel, imitating what he had seen, patted Delsing on the rump, waved to the wildly cheering crowd, and slowly returned to the Browns' dugout, stopping to bow and wave his hat happily every step of the way.

For his services that day, including jumping out of the cake, Gaedel was paid $100, according to Veeck. Oh yes, his pinch runner, Delsing, got to third base with one out that inning, but was left stranded and the Browns lost, 6-2.

Gaedel died ten years later at the age of thirty-six. Cain attended his funeral, although the two had never formally met. Cain was quoted as saying he "felt obligated to go." But no one else from the baseball world was there. And, according to Gaedel's mother, a man claiming to represent the Hall of Fame swindled her out of her son's bats and Browns' uniform.

Gaedel, however, was not the only nonprofessional to play in one major-league game. Equally as strange, if not stranger, was a game played in Philadelphia on May 18, 1912, between the Athletics and the Detroit Tigers. On that day, the Tigers were without their star, Ty Cobb, who had been suspended for going into the stands a few days earlier to chase a heckler.

To show their support for Cobb, the rest of the Tigers refused to play. When A's manager Connie Mack heard about it, he suggested that Hugh Jennings, the Detroit manager, use some collegians and sandlotters to take the players' places so the game could go on. That's what Jennings did. He hired the first replacement players in the major leagues (well ahead of his 1995 management brethren). These amateur replacements included a number of players from the St. Joseph's College team in Philadelphia and a few local sandlotters—and even two Tigers scouts, both former major-leaguers in their forties, were pressed into service.

This makeshift Tiger team made four hits and scored twice against the Athletics, but lost 24–2. Amazing as it may seem to today's fans, despite the score, the game was completed in one hour and forty-five minutes.

The Detroit pitcher, Aloysius Travers, who had just turned twenty years old four days earlier, allowed all 24 runs, an all-time single-game record that still stands today. Not all the runs were earned, however. While Travers gave up 26 hits and seven walks, his teammates made nine errors.

According to a newspaper account, "Detroit's pitcher, Travers, could do little but float the ball up to the plate, and the home players banged his delivery all over the field and ran bases recklessly. . . . The crowd of twenty thousand persons took the affair as a joke. At the end of the third inning there was a rush by a couple of thousand bleacherites who demanded their money back. When this was refused, nearly all returned to their seats. There was no disorder at the end of the game."

In addition to Travers, the other "Tigers-for-a-day" included college boys Bill Leinhauser, 19, the centerfielder who got to wear Cobb's uniform; Jack Smith (nee Coffee), 18, who played part of the game at third base; second baseman Jim "Red" McGarr, 23; and left fielder Dan McGarvey, 24. The sandlotters included Joe "Hap" Ward, 26, in right field; two other third basemen, Billy Maharg, 31 (he spelled his real name, Graham, backwards), and Ed Irwin, 30, who got two triples that day; and a 41-year-old shortstop, Pat Meany. Maharg got into one other game with the Phillies—four years later. For all the rest, it was their only major-league game.

The two Tiger scouts used were Joe Sugden, then 41, at first, and 48-year-old Jim "Deacon" McGuire behind the plate. McGuire, back in 1895, was the first man to catch in all 132 games his team—the Washington Senators, then in the National League—played that season. (Only two other catchers, Frankie Hayes—twice—and Mike Tresh, have ever caught in every game of a season.) McGuire, who had been in the major leagues twenty-five years, and Sudgen both had singles—and scored—to help account for Detroit's total of four hits and two runs that afternoon. Neither ever played again.

Even the manager, the forty-three-year-old Jennings, who hadn't played for three years, got into that strange game, pinch hitting for Travers in the ninth. It was his only appearance that year, although he came back again to appear in one more game six years later.

Neither Gaedel nor most of those representing Detroit that day in 1912 were legitimate baseball players. In contrast, most of the men included in this book spent years in the minors, working hard to reach that day they all dreamed about. Many toiled on the rough diamonds of the minor leagues for years afterwards, just hoping to return for a second chance. Even those who came to the majors directly from college—or high school—were really major-league baseball players.

For some, the day was joyous, for some miserable.

Then it was over.

Yet for a moment, only a moment, all of them achieved the dream of many American boys. They were all major-league baseball players.

Edward "Lefty" Wineapple

WASHINGTON NATIONALS, 1929

Ed Wineapple might well have been one of America's best-known multisport professional athletes. Unfortunately, he was born about forty or fifty years too soon and an injury cut his professional career short.

In the late 1920s, Wineapple was one of the nation's top college basketball players. He was a first-team All-American as an underclassman and went on to play both professional basketball and professional baseball at the same time. But just as with Bo Jackson, who also played two sports simultaneously, a football injury limited Wineapple's effectiveness in both sports.

He was born August 10, 1905, in Boston. Growing up in Salem, Massachusetts, Wineapple was what might be called a "phenom" today. At Salem High School, he excelled at all three major sports. "Basketball was my best sport," he says, "football second, and baseball was my worst sport, yet I went to the big leagues as a baseball player."

In one high school basketball game, he scored 57 points. "The average score of a game then was, maybe, 33–23, because in those days, we had a center jump after each basket. That's less than what I scored alone," he says. "And, remember, there were no three-point shots in those days. I could have scored a hundred if they had that."

"In football, I was a quarterback who stuttered and that's why the other team was offside all the time," he laughs. In one special postseason game against Portland, Maine, Wineapple, a left-footed kicker as well as a lefty thrower, punted the ball seventy yards. However, a leg injury sustained in one of his high school football games would eventually shorten his athletic career.

This picture was taken around the time Ed Wineapple played baseball in the Cape Cod League. The All-American (left) stands with an unidentified friend.

In baseball, he was the team's star pitcher. A number of years after graduating in 1925, Wineapple was named "the greatest athlete ever in Salem history" and was elected to the Salem High School Hall of Fame.

After high school, the young left-hander was heavily recruited by college athletic directors. He chose Syracuse University, where he quickly became the ace pitcher of the freshman baseball team. After his first year, however, he left Syracuse to enroll at Providence College in order to be reunited with Al McLennan, who was his Salem High School basketball coach.

Providence was a Catholic school, run by Dominican priests, with about 1,000 students. Wineapple is Jewish. "My mother came to visit me there one time and saw all the priests and couldn't understand what was going on," he laughs.

Primarily an athlete and not a scholar, Wineapple skipped a lot of classes. "When the Dominican priests asked about it, I'd say 'Father, it's a Jewish holiday.' One day, however, one of the priests came in with a Jewish calendar. 'Edward,' he said—they always called me Edward—'I can't find any of those holidays you told me about on this calendar.' So, from then on, I went to classes.

"I also remember they used to have special breakfasts for the team and usually someone would get up to make sort of a speech and most always it had something to do with religion. Well, one morning they asked me to speak and I didn't know how to make a speech, especially about religion, so I got up and I tried to make it sound religious, so I said, 'Hail, Mary, full of grace, four balls, take your base.' Well, they just all howled with laughter."

At Providence, Wineapple was the star of both the baseball and basketball teams. The school did not have a football team. "In baseball, I was mainly a pitcher, but I was always a good hitter, so I played the outfield once in a while and pinch hit." In his first game on the mound for Providence, Wineapple pitched a no-hitter against Lowell Tech. He quickly became the team's top pitcher, leading the Dominicans to a 19–3 season, its best in years.

In basketball, Wineapple says he "put Providence on the map. Nobody ever heard of Providence College until I was named to the All-American team in the 1928–29 season. I mainly used the two-hand set shot," he says, "but I also had a one-handed jump shot. I started that although Hank Luisetti got the credit for it."

The school went on to further basketball successes, and today Wineapple feels forgotten. Although he was elected to the Providence College Hall of Fame and was also a member of the All-Time Rhode Island Basketball Team, he says, "I could go back there today and no one would know me, I wouldn't know anybody, and nobody there today would have ever heard of me."

During the summers he was at Providence, Wineapple also was picked to play for Osterville in the Cape Cod League. "That was like a strong minor league," he says, "and you had to be invited. I really looked forward to that time. I could make about $100 a week playing semipro ball, which was about as much as the mayor of Salem was making then."

In addition to his bank account, his reputation was growing. A number of major-league teams approached him while he was in college, including the Giants, Tigers, Pirates, Dodgers, Yankees, and both Boston teams. On September 12, 1929, after two years at Providence, the lure of a cash bonus got him to leave school and sign a $400-a-month contract to play professional baseball for Clark Griffith's Washington Nationals of the American League.

Shortly after signing with Washington, he also agreed to play professional basketball with Harry Moskowitz's Syracuse Nationals of the American Basketball League. His basketball contract also was for $400 a month. "I couldn't get anybody to pay me more than $400 a month," he says, "but I didn't have a manager or an agent. I had to do it all myself."

Al Schact signed Wineapple for the Washington Nationals. "He was a Washington coach at the time. I think I got $5,000 in cash when I signed, and the first thing Schact did was take me to a haberdashery store in Washington to buy me a striped suit. I was a hick from a small town and I was wearing only a sweater or something. Schact said, 'I want you to look like Goose Goslin.' Schact made me buy this striped suit—I always hated that suit—and to this day, I think he was working for the store owner."

Schact and Washington shortstop Joe Cronin were Wineapple's closest friends in Washington. "I knew Joe Cronin from the Cape Cod League, and he was a dear, dear friend. He used to say to me, 'Oh, Eddie, if you could only control that fastball of yours.' I was a bit wild. But Cronin [later the president of the American League] was very nice to me. I remember he used to take me out of the hotel in Washington and take me to shows."

On September 15, 1929, shortly after he signed with Washington, he played in his one and only major-league game. It was in the nation's capital against the Detroit Tigers. "I was in the dugout just watching the game when Schact came over and said, 'Walter Johnson wants to talk to you.' Johnson was our manager. He never did say much; he was very quiet, and all he said then was something like, 'Kid, you're going in next inning.' I don't know how he became a manager. All he did was grunt.

"In those days, pitchers warmed up right in front of the dugouts, not down the outfield foul lines or in bull pens hidden from the fans," Wineapple recalls. "I warmed up and I remember it was [the first game of] a Sunday doubleheader against Detroit and I remember seeing all those white shirts in the stands. When it was time to go in the game, I didn't know where I was. I'm a very hyper guy anyway, even to this day, and I was really excited and scared. Al Schact walked to the mound with me to try to calm me down. He told me, 'Walter Johnson has faith in you.' Well, he left and I threw my first warm-up pitch over the catcher's head back to the screen. I was so excited, I'm surprised it didn't go over the grandstand. Muddy Ruel was the catcher and he tried to calm me down too, but after that first pitch the crowd got on me and I don't remember anything else. I don't remember going in or coming out."

When Wineapple came in to pitch in the top of the sixth inning, Detroit had already jumped on Washington starter Myles Thomas for six runs in the first inning. Then they had scored six more against him and his reliever, Bobby Burke, in the fifth. At the end of five, they led 12–2.

The Tiger lineup Wineapple faced that day included five hitters with batting averages over .300—catcher Pinky Hargrave (.330); rookie first baseman Dale Alexander (.343); Hall of Fame second baseman Charlie Gehringer (.339); rookie right fielder Roy Johnson (.314); and center fielder Harry Rice (.304). Defensively, Wineapple had three Hall of Famers behind him, Cronin at shortstop, Goslin in center field, and right fielder Sam Rice.

In both the sixth and seventh innings, the twenty-four-year-old Wineapple shut out the Tigers without a run. In the eighth and ninth, however, he gave up a total of four runs (one in the eighth and three in the ninth), two of which were unearned. He had an assist, but also made two of his team's eight errors that game. Overall, in his four innings, Wineapple allowed seven hits and three walks, and struck out one batter.

At the plate, Wineapple got to bat twice, going 0 for 2, and, like many

CLARK C. GRIFFITH   WILLIAM M. RICHARDSON   EDWARD B. EYNON, Jr.
PRESIDENT   VICE-PRESIDENT   SECRETARY

WASHINGTON AMERICAN LEAGUE
BASE BALL CLUB

OFFICES: 7th ST. AND FLORIDA AVE. N. W.
WASHINGTON, D. C.

TELEPHONES: NORTH

January 11, 1930.

Mr. Edward Wineapple.
391 Lafayette Street,
Salem, Mass.

Dear Mr. Wineapple:

       Enclosed you will find contract
for four hundred dollars per month for the coming
season. This is the same figure you signed for last
year and of course, I cannot raise you until you
show you are worth more money. Please sign and return
one copy to me at once.

       Hoping this finds you in the
best of health I beg to remain

       Yours very truly,

Clark Griffith

       President.

P.S. - I will advise you later about reporting.

Here's the letter Clark Griffith sent with Wineapple's contract for 1930, saying: "I cannot raise you until you show you are worth more money."

pitchers, all he really recalls today of his one time in the majors is one of his turns at bat.

"I was always a good hitter," he says, "and when I came up left-handed, most of the defense swung around toward the right field side. But for some reason, the left fielder [John "Rocky" Stone] moved over closer to the left field line. I guess he expected me to swing late. The left fielder played me perfectly because I lined the ball to the fence in left where he caught it. If he had played me normally, I would have had an extra base hit."

Shortly thereafter, the baseball season ended and Wineapple turned to his pro basketball assignment. While playing for Syracuse in the ABA, he received his 1930 baseball contract from Washington owner Clark Griffith, who wrote: "Enclosed you will find contract for four hundred dollars per month for the coming season. This is the same figure you signed for last year and, of course, I cannot raise you until you show you are worth more money. Please sign and return one copy to me." In a postscript, Griffith wrote: "I will advise you later about reporting."

But the fact was that Wineapple's major-league baseball career was over. "My leg was killing me," he says, "and I played on pure grit." The high school football injury was eventually diagnosed as lumbar neurosis, which continues to produce pain running down his back and through his leg. Today, although still spry at age ninety, he must hobble around with a cane. He says, "if I did what I did in the 1940s, '50s or '60s, instead of in the 1920s, or if I did it in a big media center like New York, I'd be rich and famous today. Someday," he adds, "I'm going to find my mother in heaven and ask her why I couldn't have been born forty years later."

After spring training in Biloxi, Mississippi, the team sent him to the Chattanooga Lookouts, their farm team in the Southern Association, for the 1930 season. For the next few years, he played for a variety of minor-league teams including New Haven; Harrisburg; Elmira ("Jake Pitler was the manager there and he liked me"); Buffalo ("Ray Schalk was a tough S.O.B. He worked me hard"); Wilmington; Toronto; and Wilkes-Barre.

Wineapple never achieved the kind of success in professional baseball that he had in high school or college, primarily because of his lack of control, but he nevertheless enjoyed playing, even at the minor-league level. He has many fond memories.

"One time, when I was with Chattanooga, we played the New York Yankees in an exhibition game," he remembers. "In those days, during the exhibition games, they used to have a buffet set up in the dugouts so the players could eat. I remember seeing Babe Ruth come out of the dugout and go up to the plate with a hot dog still stuffed in his mouth—and hitting one over the roof. I also remember pitching to Lou Gehrig in that game and he grounded it back to me and I threw him out. As he crossed the mound going back to his dugout, he said, 'I see you're still throwing that high school curveball,' and I laughed and said, 'Well, it's good enough to get you out!'

"In the minors, we traveled by bus with our uniforms on, and we stayed at hotels that had one bathroom to a floor. Think about that—one bathroom to a floor! We got $1.75 a day for meals, but down South you got to eat as much as you could for fifty cents, and I hated to leave that. I loved the South."

Back when he was pitching high school ball in Salem, and even at Providence, the local papers often referred to Wineapple as a "Jewish" player. When asked if he had run into any prejudice during his professional career, he said, "No, never. I had a New England accent and 90 percent of them didn't know what I was."

In the years following his athletic career, Wineapple held a number of jobs. He owned and operated a theater in Milton, Massachusetts, and spent a number of years selling insurance. During World War II, he tried to enlist, but his leg wouldn't allow him to pass the physical, so he worked in a navy yard for the duration. After the war, he joined the sales staff of Russ Togs, a major producer of sportswear, and spent seventeen years there before he retired. "I was a good salesman," he says, "and that's where I was able to make some money."

Today, after moving from his former home in Scarsdale, New York, Wineapple lives in a posh, beautifully decorated co-op apartment on New York's fashionable Park Avenue, where he has resided for the past thirty years with his wife of fifty-five years, Maxine. Their son, John, and their daughter, Patricia, along with her son, James, all live nearby in Manhattan.

"I just was born forty years too soon," Wineapple sighs. "Look at all the attention Michael Jordan got for trying to play professional baseball after being a basketball star. Never mind the money. That could have been *me*."

Merritt Marwood "Mem" Lovett

CHICAGO WHITE SOX, 1933

For only one month during 1933 and a couple of months during the following season, "Mem" Lovett played professional baseball. He doesn't think it affected his life at all, though he accomplished something extremely rare. He hit the one and only pitch ever thrown to him in the major leagues, a claim very few can make.

Born in Chicago in 1912, Lovett grew up in suburban Oak Park, after his family—including a younger and an older sister—moved there in 1919. "My father was in the banking business in Chicago—until everything folded up [in the Depression]," he says somewhat sadly. "Then, for a while, he ran a gas station and later became a bookkeeper."

In high school, Lovett played four years of varsity baseball and three years of varsity basketball and football. In baseball, he played at shortstop, second base, and third base. He was a quarterback in football and captain of the team in his senior year. In basketball, "I played forward, guard, whatever they needed." He says he played all three of those sports "okay."

People started calling him Mem in high school. "The name Merritt seems to give people a lot of trouble," he says, "even today. I've been called Merrill, Milton, Marshall, everything. Now, most people just call me 'Coach.'"

Following his graduation in 1931, Lovett enrolled at the University of Chicago in a general education curriculum. "In those days, they had a system where you sat in an auditorium with five or six hundred others and listened to all kinds of speeches on a variety of subjects, and then at the end of the semester, you took a six-hour test." As a freshman, he played all three major sports. "To help defray expenses," he says, "I worked in the athletic department and also waited tables in a frat house."

During his freshman year in 1932, however, at the height of the Depression, the bank in which his father worked closed its doors for good, and Lovett left the university after his first year. "That was only part of why I left," Lovett says. "My college coach, Kyle Anderson, had recommended me to the Chicago White Sox and they sent scouts over to see me play a couple of games. They asked me to come down to the ballpark and work out for them. I remember Lew Fonseca was the manager, but I don't remember seeing much of him at the time. Harry Grabiner, the general manager, signed me to a contract. I think it was for $200, or maybe $250, a month. I don't remember and I don't have the contract anymore. I gave it to one of my grandchildren who was doing an essay for school one time.

"The White Sox had a very poor ball club that year. They had [Al] Simmons and [George 'Mule'] Haas, [Jimmy] Dykes, and [Luke] Appling—a lot of name players, if you know what I mean—but the team wasn't very good," Lovett says.

"I joined them [Chicago] on September 1, 1933," Lovett says, "and took the eastern swing to Detroit and Washington and then back to Chicago. I roomed with Ted Lyons, who was just great. Lyons kind of took me under his wing and kept me out of trouble. I remember one night we went out to dinner and he said, 'Listen, kid, they gave me $35 expense money so you keep your money in your pocket.' Well, I think the $35 was supposed to last a week, but back then you could get a real good meal for a dollar. But Lyons was a real class guy, a college graduate, a fine man and no bull about him, not like some of the others. I couldn't believe the kind of language I heard Simmons and Haas use in the dugout in Washington, especially with a lot of the spectators so close by."

On Labor Day, September 4, 1933, with more than 50,000 in attendance, the White Sox played a holiday doubleheader against the Tigers in Briggs Stadium, Detroit. In the first game, Lovett, who then stood almost five-foot-ten and weighed 165 pounds, came up to bat for the only time in a major-league game. It was only three days after he had joined the team and almost three months after he had celebrated his twenty-first birthday.

By the time Lovett got his chance, the game was lost. With two out and nobody on, Detroit had scored four runs in the top of the first, highlighted by Hank Greenberg's three-run homer off Sam Jones, and four more runs in the second off his reliever, Chad Kimsey.

Leading 8–0 going into the top of the ninth, Vic Sorrell, the Tigers' right-handed pitcher, had limited the White Sox to just four hits all game. "Detroit had a hell of a team that year," Lovett remembers, "with [Charley] Gehringer and Greenberg."

"The first man up for us in the ninth was a pinch hitter, I can't remember his name or who he was hitting for, but he struck out. The next batter was [rookie outfielder] Milt Bocek, who also was pinch hitting. Somebody in the dugout tapped me on the shoulder and told me I would pinch hit next. I don't know who it was. It might have been one of the coaches or it might have been Fonseca himself. I got a bat and somebody else told me to start swinging when I left the dugout because Sorrell was really throwing fast. I went out on deck and was absolutely scared to death. I mean I was shaking. I know how these guys feel today when they go up there. I know what Michael Jordan went through. I hoped he'd make it, but, I tell ya, it's *hard*.

"Anyway, Sorrell struck out Bocek. Two pinch hitters, two strikeouts. I was the third pinch hitter. I don't recall exactly who Bocek or I were hitting for, but either he batted for Haas and I batted for Simmons or it was the other way around. I know they were good hitters, our third- and fourth-place hitters, and I couldn't understand it, but that's what Fonseca did. I guess he thought the game was over and was giving the rookies a chance. When I went up, I was shaking. I really felt as if I were swinging coming out of the dugout, and I hit the first pitch and popped it up in the infield, to the first baseman [Greenberg], I think."

Simmons and Haas were good hitters. Simmons hit .331 that year and had 119 runs batted in; Haas hit .287 and had 51 RBI—and Fonseca did not send in a pinch-hitter for either. According to the record of that game, Bocek batted for the pitcher, Chad Kimsey. Lovett batted for right fielder Evar Swanson, the leadoff batter, who hit .306 that year and had a lifetime major-league batting average of .303. Haas batted second in the order that day, Simmons fourth, but neither came up after Lovett, whose popout ended the ball game and, ultimately, his major-league career. In the second game of the doubleheader, Detroit won again, 5–4, giving rookie Eldon Auker his first major-league win.

"Later, I remember riding back to Chicago on the train from Washington with a pitcher named [Ed] 'Bull' Durham. I have no idea what ever happened to him. When we were in Washington, he pitched about five or six innings of no-hit ball, a really strong game, when Fonseca pulls him out—something about a sore arm or something. I'm not sure he ever pitched again. [He didn't.] In my opinion, Fonseca was a very poor handler of men. I mean, I know he [Fonseca] was a good hitter and all, but he even had *Appling* crying. Appling was in his first year [actually fourth], and Fonseca had him crying! Fonseca was just a terrible manager as far as I was concerned."

When the 1933 season ended, Lovett returned home and, with a group of his friends, formed a basketball team called the Chicago Circus Clowns. They toured, playing town teams throughout the Midwest during the winter of 1933–34. "We'd travel wearing clown suits," he says, "and we played a lot like the [Harlem] Globetrotters do today. We traveled in Michigan, Wisconsin, Indiana, even down to Little Rock, Arkansas, and

Tupelo, Mississippi. We didn't make much money, maybe $5 or $10 a game apiece, but back then, that was pretty good."

In 1933, as the Depression wore on, only fourteen minor leagues remained in operation—just one-third of those that had operated three years earlier. Salaries in the minors had fallen about 40 percent in four years and players at the Class D level, the bottom, were averaging about $50 a month.

Prior to the start of the 1934 baseball season, the White Sox, who had Appling at shortstop and Dykes at third, told Lovett they wanted him to play that year for their farm team in Longview, Texas, for $100 a month. "I told them I didn't want to go, so they released me," he says. "But I knew another scout, who worked for the Cincinnati Reds, had seen me play and liked me, and he came around and signed me up to play for the Cincinnati farm in Bartlesville, Oklahoma, in 1934.

"They sent me a bus ticket to go down there and try out. I was only there a few weeks, and they assigned me to the team in Lincoln, Nebraska, in the Nebraska State League, I think. They gave me $15 to get up to Lincoln, but I just put it in my pocket and thumbed my way there." He stayed in Lincoln until June. "I just didn't like the playing conditions in the minors—some of those fields were awful—and I guess I could see the handwriting on the wall as far as my playing was concerned, so I just left and went back to Chicago." At the time, he was not yet twenty-two years old.

Back home, he went to work for the Oak Park Trust and Savings Bank and also played some semipro baseball around Chicago. "I made $65 a month at the bank," he recalls, "and I also earned extra money playing semipro ball with a local team called the Duffy Florals. On holiday weekends, I'd go over to play with a team in LaPorte, Indiana, because they would pay me even more. All together, I did as well as I would have in the minors."

After about a year and a half at the bank, he was offered a job at a local sporting goods company, Gregory Sports, for $125 a month, provided he run what Lovett calls "the company's 12-inch baseball team," or what's better known today as softball.

In 1936, a spectator at one of the team's games approached Lovett and asked if he would be interested in a sales job. Lovett expressed interest and in 1937 joined the Glidden Company, one of the nation's leading paint producers, as a trainee. "I stayed there forty years, selling industrial coatings all over the country until I retired in 1977."

Today Lovett reports he gets an average of two or three requests a month for autographs as the hunt for major-league signatures intensifies. "Some people send checks, but I send them back. I don't charge for signing my name," he says. A few fans ask for pictures as well, but Lovett can't accommodate them. "I don't think I ever had my picture taken in a baseball uniform," he explains.

William Paul "Dutch" Fehring

CHICAGO WHITE SOX, 1934

Many sports fans recognize "Dutch" Fehring's name, perhaps because he was the head baseball coach at Stanford University for more than fifteen years, and helped develop such future major leaguers as Jim Lonborg and Bob Boone. Perhaps it's because he earlier was on the football coaching staffs for the University of Oklahoma, UCLA, and Stanford. Some also may recall that he spent more than fifteen years on the Board of Directors of the U.S. Olympic Committee, and still others will remember when he was elected to the Indiana Basketball Hall of Fame.

But few people remember Dutch Fehring as a major-league baseball player who competed in one game for the Chicago White Sox less than a year after Mem Lovett did (see Chapter 2).

Growing up in Columbus, Indiana, Fehring was a top student and president of his high school class. In sports, he played everything well— baseball, football, and basketball. "I got the nickname Dutch in a high school football game," he says. "Somebody blocked a punt or something that fell into my arms, and since there was nobody in front of me, I ran about sixty-five yards for a touchdown. The local paper called me 'the Flying Dutchman.' Later, that was shortened to Dutch."

After graduating from high school in 1930, the eighteen-year-old entered Purdue University to major in chemical engineering. "Everett Dean, the coach at Indiana University, offered me an athletic scholarship to go there, but I chose Purdue because my older brother, Ray, along with one of my best friends, had gone there ahead of me. Besides, I thought it had a better football program," Fehring recalls.

At Purdue, he lettered in all three major sports and was named All-Big

*"Dutch" Fehring will never forget tagging out Lou Gehrig as he slid
into home plate trying for an inside-the-park home run.*

Ten in basketball and football. "They didn't choose an All-Big Ten baseball team in those days," he says, "and I honestly don't know if I would have made it if they did." In basketball, he became the starting center his sophomore year; in football, he played both offensive and defensive tackle and was captain of the team; and in baseball, he was a solid switch-hitting catcher.

"I became a catcher when I was about seven or eight years old," Fehring says. "One day Ray, my brother, was throwing some rocks and one of them hit a telephone wire and bounced back and hit me in the mouth, chipping my tooth. I didn't tell anybody about it for weeks, but when my father finally found out about it, he bought me a catcher's mask as a joke. Since I was the only kid in the neighborhood with a catcher's mask, I got to be a catcher growing up."

At Purdue, chemical engineering proved a bit too overwhelming for Fehring to handle. "What with all the lab work I needed to do, and the practice schedules for the various athletic teams, I found I was only getting about four hours sleep a night. Finally I called my father and told him I just couldn't make it. He told me to talk to my football coach, Noble Kizer, before doing anything. Coach Kizer finally worked it out with the academic office so I was able to switch to the School of Science at Purdue without losing any credits. This let me reduce the number of hours I had to spend in class each week. It was a big help."

After the football season ended in his sophomore year, Fehring joined the basketball team, which had already begun its season. "I wasn't supposed to make the first road trip to Columbus to play Ohio State because my name wasn't on the roster that was originally submitted. But one of our players, a fellow named Bizjak, number 34, couldn't go, so I went in his place and wore his number. I played in the game, and we won by one point. I don't remember whether I scored or not.

"But what I really remember most about that trip," he says, "was when we were going home. We were in a railroad sleeping car stopped on a siding, waiting to be picked up by the train that was going to take us home. I was in an upper berth, and the guy in the bottom berth, one of our seniors, started talking to me about the basketball team. He told me what we needed to do to be successful, he told me what each player on the team needed to do to contribute, and he told me what I needed to do to improve my game. He was absolutely right about everything. I was so impressed with his knowledge and understanding of the game, I knew right then that this guy was going to be a great coach some day. His name was John Wooden.

"As a matter of fact, years later, when I was an assistant football coach at UCLA, I read in the papers that we were looking for a new basketball coach. I went in to see Wilbur Johns, the athletic director, and I said, 'I hear you're having trouble finding a basketball coach. Well, I know one who'd be perfect for you: John Wooden.' Well, Wilbur called him up, and

John came out and was interviewed and was offered the job. John accepted, and he was one of the best college basketball coaches ever."

After final exams at Purdue in June 1934, Fehring and his roommate, Jack Grady, attended a dance at a country club near Chicago. "Al Simmons, who was then with the White Sox, walked in, and Jack, who knew him from previous affairs at the club, introduced us. I mentioned that I was interested in professional baseball, and Simmons told me to get hold of Harry Grabiner, the White Sox general manager, because the team was scheduling tryouts very soon. Jack's brother knew where he lived and he took me there. I introduced myself to Grabiner, and he arranged for me to go for a tryout at Comisky Park.

"An older man, I can't remember who it was, worked me out, and he must have thought I was okay because afterward I got a call from Harry, who asked me to come over and sign a contract. I signed for $700 a month and a $500 bonus." (This was less than a year after Grabiner had signed Mem Lovett for $200 or $250 a month.)

"But I couldn't join the team right away," Fehring says, "because Purdue had a rule that if you didn't attend graduation ceremonies, they held up your diploma. So I had to go back to school for graduation. When that was over, I returned to Chicago and, with Luke Appling, took the train to Washington, DC, to join the White Sox there. Appling was recovering from some sort of injury," Fehring recalls.

"We had a three- or four-game series in Washington, and we stayed at the Wardman Park Hotel. After the first game was over, I didn't want to bother anyone, so I left the park and went downtown to eat by myself and then went to a movie. When I got into a cab to go back, I couldn't remember the name of the hotel. So I mumbled, 'Mummum Park Hotel.' The driver said, 'What?' and I said, 'Mummum Park Hotel.' Of course the driver still couldn't understand me, so he pulled over and turned around. I said, 'I want to go to the hotel where the White Sox are staying.' He said, 'Oh, you mean the Wardman Park Hotel,' and I said, 'Yes, that's what I've been saying!'

"After Washington, we went to Philadelphia for four games, to Boston for four games, and then New York for four more. During this time, I was primarily a batting-practice catcher, with some infield practice at first base. During the games, I was a bullpen catcher."

Of his teammates, he recalls Hall of Fame pitcher Ted Lyons (Mem Lovett's former roommate) as the ultimate Mr. Nice Guy. "Teddy would hit pop fouls for twenty minutes a day for me to help me," Fehring says. "There aren't many people who could, or would, do that for a rookie like me. And he was a great pitcher. While he won a lot of games [260], he would have won a lot more with a better team.

"I felt I knew Luke Appling fairly well," Fehring says, "primarily because of that train trip we took together when I joined the team. 'Old Aches and Pains,' we called him, but he was pretty much an introvert."

On June 25, 1934, approximately two weeks after joining the team, Fehring got into his one major-league game against the New York Yankees at Yankee Stadium. "I was sitting in the bullpen when the phone rang, and I remember Burleigh Grimes, who was then with the Yankees, answered it. Don't ask me why we were in the same bullpen."

Fehring remembers Grimes answering the phone and saying, "Perry? Perry? There's no one here named Perry." "He hung up," Fehring continues. "A minute later the phone rang again, and I knew they meant Fehring. I had no indication at all that I was ever gonna get in a game. I hadn't even taken batting practice. It just never dawned on me that I would play, and I was kind of numb.

"When I got the call, I really didn't know what to do. After infield practice, I usually went back to the clubhouse and put on a dry shirt and then walked underneath the stands to the bullpen. I didn't know whether to go back to the dugout the same way or to go straight out on the field. The dugout looked like it was forty miles away. Anyway, I went out across the field, and I had the feeling that everybody in the park was watching me. I walked out and then started to trot a bit, and I was really nervous.

"When I got to the dugout, Muddy Ruel, one of our coaches who used to catch Walter Johnson and who was always real nice to me, helped me put on the shin guards. 'Just calm down,' Ruel said, 'I know you're nervous, but there's nothing to worry about.'"

It was the top of the seventh inning, with the Sox losing 10–2. "Jimmy Dykes," Fehring continues, "who had replaced Lew Fonseca as manager earlier that year, was putting me in to catch one of my roommates, right-hander Harry Kinzy."

Fehring replaced Merv Shea behind the plate. Kinzy was pitching in relief of Phil Gallivan who, in turn, had replaced George Earnshaw earlier. At that point, New York had already collected 14 hits to go along with their 10 runs. "Kinzy was a great college pitcher at Texas Christian University and it was his first [and only] year, too. I don't remember what pitches I called or what pitches were hit," Fehring says, "but I do recall Kinzy was having arm or elbow trouble because he had pitched a 23-inning game in college earlier that year, so I believe he was throwing only fastballs. Anyway, [left fielder] Earle Combs, the first man up, led off with a home run. I really felt sorry for Kinzy then."

According to the box score, the next batter was Yankee third baseman Jack Saltzgaver, followed by Ben Chapman, the center fielder. "Now Ben was from back home in New Albany, Indiana," Fehring says, "and I told him that Red Mackey, a mutual friend from Purdue, wanted to be remembered to him. Ben said something like, 'Oh, yeah?' and then smacked a single. Chapman was a good base stealer, and I remember thinking, 'I hope he steals, I'll throw him out.'"

The next batter was first baseman Lou Gehrig, and his at-bat is what Dutch Fehring remembers most about his one game in the majors.

"First, Gehrig hit a foul ball directly over my head back toward the screen. I moved back to the stands as close as I could get—I remember putting my knees against the stands—and watched the ball coming down. I never saw a ball act like that, almost like a knuckler, and I didn't get close to it. Fortunately, it went into the seats.

"Then, on the next pitch, he connected solidly and hit it way over the right field wall, but just foul. He was halfway to second when the ump called it, and when he returned to the plate, he was really hot. 'You blind so-and-so,' he yelled at the ump, 'what are you trying to do, don't you know I'm going for a record, how can you call that foul,' and things like that. It shook me up to hear him use that kind of language, because he was so admired by the public. But the umpire, I think it was [George] Moriarty, never said a word.

"Finally, Gehrig hits one to deep center field over the head of Mule Haas." The hit scored the speedy Chapman all the way from first, and Gehrig had the idea of turning it into an inside-the-park homer. "Haas picked the ball up and relayed it to Al Simmons, our left fielder, who relayed it to my other roommate, Joe Chamberlain [at shortstop in place of Appling that day], and he threw it towards me," Fehring says. "I remember trying to gauge the throw as I saw Gehrig steaming in. I caught it and I thought, 'Oh, oh, he's really gonna let me have it,' but he didn't. He slid in and I tagged him out at home and he never did touch the plate. There was a photo of my tagging out Gehrig in one of the New York daily papers the next day and I kick myself for not keeping a copy."

Gehrig eventually won the Triple Crown that year, leading the league in batting average (.363), home runs (49), and runs batted in (165). Tagging him out at home as he was trying for an inside-the-park home run, as might be expected, was something that clouds Fehring's memory. "I just don't remember how the other outs that inning were made," he laughs.

But he does remember his only time at bat. "It was the top of the ninth, one out and none on and I think the score by then was something like 13–4 [13–2]. I went up against a Yankee right-handed pitcher, John Broaca.

"As I got into the batter's box, batting left-handed," Fehring says, "[catcher] Bill Dickey asked: 'First time in the bigs? Fastball down the pipe.' I watched it for strike one. Dickey said again, 'Right down the pipe.' I watched strike two. Dickey said, 'I'm not fooling you—same pitch.' Even Moriarity, the umpire, said something like, 'He's not fooling you. Take your cuts.' I fouled a fastball back to the screen. Both Dickey and the ump said, 'That's the way, good swing.' Dickey said, 'Same pitch.' It was a fastball, high and outside. I swung and missed." And so, in his only time at bat as a major leaguer, Dutch Fehring struck out.

After the Yankee series, the White Sox went to Detroit for four more games before returning to Chicago. "All the traveling was by train," Fehring remembers. "In Chicago, we stayed at the Brevoort Hotel, downtown, and paid 50¢ per night each. On the road, we were given $11 per day for meals, except in Boston, where we could sign checks at the Copley Square Hotel restaurant. That's where I had my first taste of scrod, which I still enjoy when I can get it."

In July, about a month after joining the White Sox directly from college, and without getting an opportunity to play in another game, Fehring was sent to the White Sox farm team in Dallas, Texas. "When I was sent out, that was only about the second time I ever heard Jimmy Dykes speak," Fehring says. "The first time was right after I joined the White Sox and we were sitting around after breakfast one day. Dykes was a player-manager that year, playing third base, but that morning, the subject was golf. He was betting somebody that he could break 100 using only a putter on a certain course.

"Now, however, we had just finished the road trip and we had lost something like 14 out of 19 games and Dykes told me he had to make some changes and, since I was the youngest and newest player, he was gonna send me down. But he said he wanted me to come to spring training next year. Those were the only two times I ever heard him talk."

Fehring was sent to Dallas, in the Texas League, and stayed two or three weeks but never got into a game. He was then sent down to a Class D team in Longview, Texas, where he finished out the season—and his professional baseball career. "It was strange in Dallas," he says. "One day in batting practice, I hit one out, and after that, I never got a good pitch to hit. There were twenty-four guys on the team, but only about four Northerners. The rest were Southerners, and I had the feeling they were still fighting the Civil War.

"I don't recall who the manager was, but he had a rule that every player had to report to the clubhouse at 10 A.M. every day regardless of what time the game started. And because it was so hot down there, we often didn't start 'til late. But the reason for this rule was that a lot of these guys were fairly heavy drinkers and he wanted to make sure they were all sobered up before the game started. You can imagine the impression this made on a young college boy like me."

When the season ended, Fehring returned to Purdue where, during his junior year, he had been offered a job as head coach of the freshman football, baseball, and basketball teams upon his graduation.

"The job paid $2,200 for a ten-month contract. This was in the middle of the Depression, and I had the choice of this sure thing at Purdue or taking my chances in spring training with the White Sox. I took Purdue."

Fehring spent the next ten years coaching baseball, basketball, and some football at Purdue, while serving as an associate professor of physical education and hygiene. In 1936, he earned a masters degree in physical education at Purdue and in 1937 he was named the school's head baseball coach. To further his teaching and coaching career, Fehring began taking courses leading to a doctorate in education.

"Only three schools in the country offered the degree, Columbia and New York University, both in New York, and Stanford in California," he said. "I started at NYU but my younger brother, Theodore, was getting married in the state of Washington and wanted me to be his best man, so in 1938 I transferred to Stanford to be closer to him."

In 1939 Dutch Fehring married his own childhood sweetheart, Edna Rose Suverkrup, and in 1942 their daughter, Susan, was born. By then, Fehring had completed almost all the requirements for his doctorate. Unfortunately, World War II interrupted his plans.

During the war, from 1943 to 1946, he served in the U.S. Navy, primarily on an aircraft carrier where pilots trained in carrier takeoffs and landings. Before that, at the Iowa preflight school, he was in a class with other college coaches including Jim Tatum and Bud Wilkinson. "For a while, before we were reassigned, Bud Wilkinson and I roomed together in San Diego," Fehring says, "and became fairly close friends." In 1944, while he was still in service, Fehring's second daughter, Ann, was born.

Upon discharge, Fehring received a call from Jim Tatum, who was then the head football coach at Oklahoma, offering him a job as an assistant coach along with Bud Wilkinson. "I was there in 1946 and '47," Fehring says, "and they were two of the happiest years of our lives. Jim Tatum left at the end of the first year to take the head coaching job at Maryland and wanted me to come with him, but I stayed at Oklahoma to assist Bud Wilkinson, who was named head coach.

"About that time, my daughter, Ann, began having asthma attacks, fairly bad ones, and the doctors said the climate in Oklahoma was not good for her. They suggested more of an ocean climate. Well, it just so happened that I went on a recruiting trip in Texas around that time and bumped into Bert LaBrucherie, the coach at UCLA. Well, one thing led to another, and in 1948 I joined the coaching staff at UCLA."

Fehring was only there one year. Unbeknownst to him, the man he replaced was a former All-American at Nebraska who had had a falling out with LaBrucherie. According to Fehring, one of the newspaper writers in Los Angeles at the time was a fellow Nebraskan and a friend of the fired assistant. This writer constantly criticized LaBrucherie in the paper and called for his job. "I went to Bert and asked him if there was any problem, and he told me not to worry. He said Wilbur Johns, the school's athletic director, would never be swayed by a newspaper columnist. Unfortunately, a fellow by the name of Bill Ackerman soon became the new Head of Associated Students and Wilbur ended up firing us all."

Fehring had a two-year contract and was able to get by while considering a couple of jobs selling sporting goods. "Then, all of a sudden, I got a call from Everett Dean—the coach who had offered me a scholarship to go to Indiana University when he was coaching there. Everett said he wanted to talk to me. He was now coaching basketball at Stanford and was going to take over as head baseball coach. Since the seasons overlapped, he was looking for someone who could take over the baseball job from January until the basketball season ended in late March and then assist the football coach, Marchie Schwartz, with spring football and stay with football season right through the following fall."

Fehring moved to Stanford in 1949 and from then until 1977 was a mainstay of the university's athletic department. At the start, he helped coach both football and baseball. His third daughter, Carol, was born in 1950, and in 1952 Fehring finally completed his doctorate in education. He served as head baseball coach from 1956 through 1967, when he received the Lefty Gomez Award as Coach of the Year of the American Baseball Coaches Association. For a number of years, he was also the university's director of intramural and club sports. In addition to Jim Lonborg, a Cy Young winner, and Bob Boone, who caught the most games in major-league history, Fehring sent a number of other Stanford players to the majors, including ten-year man Frank Duffy, pitcher Darrell Sutherland, and another player who played in only one major-league game, Harvey Shank (see Chapter 34).

During his tenure at Stanford, not only did Fehring serve as a director of the U.S. Olympic Committee, but he also conducted baseball coaching clinics for U.S. armed forces in Europe, Hawaii, Japan, and Korea. As a result of his work in the Far East, Fehring became the United States' prime negotiator in establishing an annual U.S.–Japan baseball series. Later, he was the chief delegate for the United States, arranging for amateur teams to play in Hawaii, Japan, Korea, Colombia, Nicaragua, the Dominican Republic, and Italy.

At various times in the 1970s, he also served as president of the U.S. Baseball Federation, the International Baseball Association, and the American Baseball Coaches Association's Hall of Fame.

After stepping down from his position at Stanford in 1977, Fehring went into semiretirement. "I still conduct Stanford sports tours," he points out.

How did being a major leaguer affect his life? "I wasn't up there long enough to be affected," he says, "but I shall always cherish the association with Ted Lyons, Muddy Ruel, Al Simmons, and the others. And I will never, ever, forget putting that tag on Gehrig."

Manuel Dominguez "Curly" Onis

BROOKLYN DODGERS, 1935

When the Boston Braves played the Brooklyn Dodgers at Ebbets Field on April 27, 1935, two players made their National League debut. One was "Curly" Onis; the other was Babe Ruth.

In that game, Ruth went 0 for 3 for the Braves and Onis 1 for 1 for the Dodgers. Ruth played in only 27 more games and then ended his career with a .342 batting average after making more than 2,500 major-league appearances.

Onis ended his major-league career that same afternoon with a batting average of 1.000.

Onis, pronounced "Oh, niece," was born in Tampa, Florida, on October 24, 1908, the only child of a tobacco wetter in a local cigar factory. "The tobacco came in dry, and he wetted it and fixed it so you could handle it," Onis explains his father's job.

The young man attended George Washington High School in Tampa, but the school had no baseball team. "I played outside school in pickup games, you know, sandlot ball," Onis says. "That's when I got the nickname Curly," he says. "I had a thick, black, curly head of hair, and you know how it is. We all had nicknames. One kid started calling me that and then another one and soon everybody was calling me Curly."

Onis left high school before graduating to help support his family. "I went to work for Tampa Electric," he says. "They had a four-team league, and they told me they'd give me a job driving a streetcar if I would catch for them. So, since jobs were scarce, I took it and played ball for them. We won 24 out of 25 games.

"I was raised with Al Lopez," Onis says, speaking of the Hall of Famer

21

who also was born in Tampa the same year, "and he got me into professional baseball. He was with the Dodgers, and he told Mr. Wilbert Good
about me. Mr. Good was the manager of the team in Johnstown, Pennsylvania, and Al told him to sign me."

In 1931, Onis, then a twenty-two-year-old catcher, played for Johnstown that season, but they released him. "I played for the Cuban Stars in
1932. We played against the colored league," Onis recalls, "but in 1933, I
don't know where the hell I played. In 1934, I was with Jacksonville, in
the Florida-Georgia League.

"That's when I got a call from Lopez in Brooklyn. He asked, 'Can you
come up here?' I told him I had no money, so he sent me a train ticket. So
I went up to Brooklyn in 1934 and spent about two months there warming up pitchers." That was the season New York Giant manager Bill Terry
asked if the Dodgers, who were playing poorly, were still in the National
League.

"I didn't play or anything," Onis continues. "At the end of the season,
Al had a little car, and I rode home with him to save money. They didn't
pay for that in those days.

"A few weeks later, I got a letter from the secretary in Brooklyn, saying,
'We're sorry, but we forgot to sign you for 1935 before you left. Here's a
contract. Please sign it and return it.' Well, I signed it real fast and sent it
back right away. I think it was for $400 a month."

Onis reported to spring training camp with the Dodgers in 1935.
"That spring I was playing regular and hit .350," he says. "I caught about
19 games, most of the games we played. Al didn't catch that much in the
spring. You know, I still have a picture of that 1935 Dodger team in spring
training. It must be worth about two or three hundred dollars now.

"I was very excited about being there," he says. "I remember we played
the Yankees with [Lou] Gehrig. Ruth had gone to the Braves that year.
We barnstormed up home, and I remember playing in such places as Atlanta and Cincinnati.

"The first time I saw Babe Ruth was in Boston, in an exhibition game
just before the season started," Onis says. "His first time up he hit a home
run off Ray Benge."

The early season game in which both Onis and Ruth made their inau-
gural appearances as National Leaguers came less than two weeks later, on
April 27, 1935. The Dodgers had won five games in a row and started the
day leading the league with eight wins and two losses, one game ahead of
the Giants, who had six wins and two losses. The Braves had lost five in a
row, had an early season record of 2–7, and were only half a game ahead of
the last-place Phillies.

For the full year, the Bill McKechnie–managed Braves would win only
36 more games and would finish last, 61½ games behind the pennant-winning Cubs. The following year they would change their name to the
Boston Bees and play under that nomenclature through the 1940

*Manuel "Curly" Onis has a major league career batting average of 1.000
and played in the game in which Babe Ruth made his National League debut.*

season—still without notable success—before changing back to Braves. Brooklyn, meanwhile, would finish fifth in 1935, 29½ games out.

On this day, however, Babe Ruth had not yet played for Boston because of a heavy cold he had developed coming from Florida into the colder weather up north. But now he was scheduled to start, and 21,600 fans paid their way into Ebbets Field on a cold day to see him. While the park had a capacity of about 33,000, this attendance—especially for a Depression year—was much higher than normal.

Brooklyn started the game with Benge, a small right-hander who had won 14 games the prior year. On the mound for the Braves was a tall lefty, Ed Brandt, a 16-game winner for the Braves in 1934. Ernest "Babe" Phelps started behind the plate for the Dodgers instead of Lopez, the club's regular catcher that year.

Ruth, "wrapped up like an Eskimo," according to a press account of the day, was the third batter up in the top of the first. "He grounded out to [Tony] Cuccinello at second," Onis says, "and cussed at him all the way to first. See, Cuccinello played him back on the grass because he was slow. When he fielded the ball, Tony sort of walked a few steps toward first and then lobbed the ball over, teasing Ruth. The same exact thing happened his second time up, and he ran down the line cursing at Tony all the way."

For the first five innings, it was a pitchers' duel. Benge allowed the Braves only one hit during that time, and both teams remained scoreless. In the top of the sixth, however, the Braves broke out with four runs. Braves' shortstop Bill Urbanski and first baseman Baxter "Buck" Jordan opened the inning with consecutive singles. Benge, perhaps remembering the homer Ruth hit in the exhibition game less than two weeks earlier, walked the Babe to load the bases with nobody out.

Wally Berger, the Braves' center fielder and cleanup hitter, who would go on to lead the league in home runs that year, then doubled. The hit scored both Urbanski and Jordan and sent Ruth to third. At this point, Dodger manager Casey Stengel brought in Frank Lamanske, a rookie left-hander, to relieve Benge.

Lamanske retired the first batter he faced, the Boston third baseman Arthur "Pinky" Whitney, without Berger moving off second or Ruth off third. The Boston right fielder, Randy Moore, then hit a grounder that became a fielder's choice when Ruth tried to score and was tagged out by Phelps at the plate. So with two runs in, two out, and two on, the Braves' second baseman, Les Mallon, came to the plate. Mallon banged out another double, scoring both Berger and Moore, who was running from first at full speed. Finally, Lamanske got the Braves' catcher, James "Shanty" Hogan, to end the inning, but Boston led, 4–0.

In the bottom of the sixth, however, the Dodgers came back to score two runs off Brandt. Brooklyn center fielder Len Koenecke walked, and first baseman Sam Leslie doubled, putting runners on second and third. Cuccinello singled to center, scoring Koenecke and Leslie. When Berger threw home trying to get Leslie, however, Cuccinello tried to go to second. Brandt alertly cut off the throw and got the Dodger second baseman with a quick throw to Mallon, cutting off the rally. The Dodgers still trailed, 4–2.

Neither team scored in the seventh. In the top half, Ruth came up for the fourth time, struck out, and retired to the clubhouse for the day, to be succeeded in left field by Hal "Sheriff" Lee. In the bottom half, Stengel sent out pinch-hitters, utility men Bobby Reis and Jim Bucher, for Phelps and Lamanske, the catcher and the pitcher. Both pinch-hitters were unsuccessful.

"I was sitting on the bench with two guys between me and Stengel," Onis says. "I remember Casey leaned forward and turned to me and said, 'Hey, kid. Wanna play?' I said, 'That's what I'm here for.' So he says, 'Okay, get yourself ready and go on in there.' So I got on my shin guards and my gear and I went in to catch the top of the eighth." The new Dodger pitcher was another rookie, left-hander Bob Logan.

"In that first inning I was in," Onis says, "I didn't know the ground in front of home plate was frozen. I don't know who it was, but one of their batters that inning took a full swing and just topped it in front of the plate, a swinging bunt you'd call it. I ran out to pick it up and slipped and fell down. When I tried to throw it to first, I threw it away, into right field. I could hear our right fielder, [Ralph] Buzz Boyle, cussing as he came over to get it. 'Goddam rookie!' I could hear him yelling. The batter went all the way around to third, but they didn't score in either the eighth or the ninth."

The rookie pitcher Logan, pitching to his rookie catcher Onis, gave up no hits and no runs in his two innings, while walking one man and striking out one. Onis was credited with his only big-league putout on the strikeout to go along with his one error.

In the bottom of the ninth, with the Dodgers still behind 4–2, Onis came up to bat against Brandt, who had given up only five hits, including the three the Dodgers got when they scored twice in the sixth.

"I couldn't stand up, I was so nervous," Onis says about facing Brandt. "The first pitch was a strike and I took it. I was so nervous. I stepped out of the box and walked away from the plate about five feet and stooped down and picked up some dirt and rubbed it on my hands. The umpire [Bill Stewart] sort of walked by me and said, 'Get up there, kid, and hit that ball.' Well, that sort of pepped me up and I went back. The next pitch was a curveball and I hit it right over third for a single. Oh, man! I got to first and I knew they couldn't pick me off. I didn't leave the base! I can't tell you how I felt. I felt great, just great."

It was the last hit Brandt gave up that day, and the game soon ended with Boston winning by the 4–2 margin.

"I felt great just to be there," Onis says. "You know something? In those days, nobody gave you any help. They were afraid if they helped you that you'd take their job. Nobody would tell me anything—except Al. They wouldn't even talk to me. Hack Wilson [who had been with the Dodgers when Onis first arrived in 1934] was the only other one I remember. 'Hang in there,' he'd tell me. 'You're gonna make it.' Koenecke was nice, too. He'd encourage me."

Other Dodger teammates Onis remembers include outfielder Stanley "Frenchy" Bordagaray. "He was a little guy, and we called him the man who could outrun a horse." In 1936, Bordagaray reportedly came to spring training wearing a mustache and a Vandyke, which Stengel ordered him to shave. Teammates recall Bordagaray losing his hat while going after a fly ball that year and trying to retrieve the hat before resuming his chase for the ball.

Among the pitchers, Onis recalls Van Lingle Mungo ("He could really throw that potato") and Emil "Dutch" Leonard, then in his third year. "Dutch was just beginning to throw his knuckleball then," Onis says. "I was the only one who could catch him. Phelps couldn't catch him and even Al had trouble. But Brooklyn sold him to Washington the next year, and he finally mastered the pitch and got better and better.

"Then there was Boom-Boom Beck," Onis laughs. Beck, whose given name was Walter, supposedly was given his nickname because so many of his pitches ended up being hit off the wall. (*Boom* off the bat and then *boom* off the wall.)

A few weeks after the game in which Onis appeared, the Dodgers optioned him to Allentown, which was doing poorly, in the New York-Pennsylvania League. There he batted .263 but appeared in only 27 games. "I got in a fight and they suspended me," he says.

The fight was with an umpire.

According to Onis, when he was catching for Allentown in Wilkes-Barre one day, he felt the umpire behind home plate should have called a pitch a strike instead of a ball. "It would have been a strikeout," Onis says, "and I complained. We got into an argument and finally he says to me, 'You get back down there and catch or I'll throw you outta here,' and I said, 'If you throw me outta here, I'll hit you in the head with my mask.' So he threw me out and I hit him with my mask. They suspended me for thirty days and fined me my salary for that whole time.

"I was ready to play after thirty days, but they sent me back to Brooklyn, and they released me," Onis says. "They didn't want me. Nobody wanted to hire me. They were scared of what the umpires would do if I played. I couldn't get a damn job. That year I rode home again with Al."

Apparently, time heals all wounds, and Onis was able to resume his career the following year. He returned to Allentown for the 1936 season, where he batted .293, and then played most of 1937 at Sioux City in the Three-I League after starting the season in the Texas League at Fort Worth. "Fort Worth wanted to cut my salary, to give me less than $400 a month, and I wanted at *least* that. We diddled around and finally they gave me the $400."

It was not a particularly meaningful year for Onis in either place, and his batting average slumped. But there was one memorable moment. "One time in Fort Worth, I think it was in an exhibition game," he says, "I hear somebody screaming my name from the stands. 'O-nees, O-nees!' I look over and who do I see waving at me from the stands but the umpire I had the fight with in Wilkes-Barre. He was smiling and waving at me." (The umpire was Bill Grieve, who later worked in the American League.)

"In 1938, Leesburg [in the Florida State League] bought my contract from Fort Worth," Onis says. "For some reason, the owner there liked me." Onis played in 116 games that year, hit .255, and returned to play there again for most of 1939, raising his average almost 20 points. At the tail end of the year, he was conditionally assigned to Hartford in the Eastern League, where he appeared in only 14 games.

Shortly before the 1940 season began, Leesburg sold Onis to Orlando, also in the Florida State League, where the thirty-one-year-old catcher became the team's player-manager. "It was pretty hard managing," he says. "We had three or four Cubans on the team who couldn't speak any English, and it was difficult for the others to communicate with them. One of them, Luis Minsal, was a very good shortstop, but he couldn't speak English and didn't like it here, so he eventually went back to Cuba."

Managing, however, did not seem to affect Onis's playing adversely. At Orlando that year, player-manager Onis was in 139 games, hit .284, and was named the league's All-Star team catcher.

The right-handed pitcher named to that All-Star team came from the Daytona Beach team. His name was Stan Musial. "He also played third base that year when he wasn't pitching," Onis says. "I recommended to our management that we buy him, but St. Louis owned him and they told us he was not for sale. Lou Klein was his friend, and I heard that Musial told the Cardinals he wouldn't sign with them unless they also signed Klein."

Despite playing in 139 games that year, Onis had to end his season early. "Lou Klein slid into home and broke my right knee," he says. "I was holding the ball and had him by about ten feet. But instead of sliding in to try to touch the plate, he came straight into me. He was a mean son of a gun. I had to have my knee operated on twice to have some cartilage removed, and I still can't walk right today.

"Washington bought my contract, and I was supposed to go to Charlotte and be a player-manager, but I couldn't squat. I wrote Washington and told them I couldn't play and I retired.

"I went back to Tampa Electric and asked for a job, and they made me a streetcar motorman again," Onis says. "I stayed there until 1942, when I became a City of Tampa fireman." He stayed with the city's fire department, eventually becoming a fire inspector in the Fire Marshall's Division, until he retired in 1960. Three years later, he came out of retirement and worked as a clerk for Hillsboro County. "I retired for good in 1975," he says, "and it's fantastic."

In 1942 when he first became a fireman, Onis married Zoraida Diaz, a girl he had known since they were youngsters, when she played softball. "I really didn't have a job until then, and I didn't want to marry her until I got a job where I could support her. So when I became a fireman, we got married." Today they still reside in Tampa. Their daughter and grandson, who is about to enter law school, Onis says proudly, live in Lexington, Kentucky.

"Today my friends still call me Curly, and there ain't many of them left," Onis laughs. "But even people who write me for autographs now want me to put Curly in there."

And he does.

Harry "Choz" Chozen

CINCINNATI REDS, 1937

Harry Chozen once hit in 49 straight games, the sixth-longest consecutive game hitting streak in the history of professional baseball. But he played only one game in the majors.

Replying to an initial request for information about his career, Chozen said he preferred to be interviewed on the phone or in person. He explained, "I talk better than I write." But after hearing his story, it becomes apparent that his writing of a few letters played a major role in his becoming a professional baseball player.

Chozen was the son of a Russian immigrant, a foreman in a tannery in that country, who came to make a new life for himself and his family in America as a junk dealer. "I was born September 27, 1915, in Winnebego, Minnesota, and we were just about the only Jewish family in a Swedish town that was named for Indians," he says, laughing. "I was the next to the youngest of seven children. Actually, my oldest brother, Morris, and my sister, Ann, were born in Russia. The rest of us were born here."

Harry was sandwiched between his brother Meyer ("Mike") and the family's youngest, Robert. His other two siblings born in this country were older sisters. The three youngest boys all played professional baseball, but only Harry reached the major leagues. "Mike was a second baseman and shortstop for Portland in the Pacific Coast League," Chozen says, "and it's funny, but my brother, Bobby, played for me in 1942 when I was managing Newport News."

The family's eldest son, Morris, left home when Harry was just a toddler to move to Long Beach, California, and seek his fortune there. "My mother begged him to come back, at least once in a while, but he never

Harry Chozen hit in 49 straight games in the minors—
only four men in baseball history ever did better.

did come back. So my mother made my father sell everything and move the whole family out to California just to be closer to my brother. That was in 1923, when I was seven years old, and it took us fourteen days to get there," Chozen remembers.

Eventually the family ended up in nearby Pasadena, where Chozen went to school and was a catcher for his high school and American Legion teams. Why a catcher? "I was five-nine and two hundred pounds," he chuckles. "It was the only position I could play." One of his classmates there was Mack Robinson, the older brother of Jackie Robinson, who was a few grades behind them. "One of my teammates on the Pasadena American Legion Post 13 team was Don Ross, who later played for Detroit."

Baseball ran in the Chozen family for a reason. "My father loved the game," Harry says, "and wanted us to play. He always encouraged us. I remember him telling us that he had read in the Jewish newspaper that

[Giant manager] John McGraw was looking for a Jewish player. He wanted us to play professionally, and he sent my brother Mike, who was three years older than me, to a baseball school in Los Angeles.

"In 1932, I remember my brother-in-law and I went to Wrigley Field in Los Angeles. It was an exact replica of the one in Chicago and the New York Giants trained there. We saw McGraw and Carl Hubbell, and my brother-in-law talked his way in and got a tryout. I just kept trying and trying and trying."

The next year, however, a St. Louis Browns' scout, Willis Butler, signed Harry to a contract with San Antonio, a Browns' affiliate. "I went to training camp with them in 1933," he says, "but I didn't make it." He was seventeen years old.

"I went home, and sometime in 1934, I read in the paper that a fellow named Ray Doan, from Iowa, was running a baseball camp in Hot Springs. Doan was someone I heard of, because he also operated a couple of the House of David teams. Anyway, the cost was $250. Well, I didn't have any $250, so I wrote him a letter telling him what a good ballplayer I was and asking him if I could come free."

By writing this letter, Harry Chozen began what turned out to be an 18-year career as a professional ballplayer.

"Mr. Doan recognized my name because my brother, Mike, had played for one of his House of David teams, and he wrote back and said I could go free. Well, that was great. The instructors there included George Sisler; Grover Alexander; and the Dean brothers, Dizzy and Paul. There was even a third Dean brother there, Elmer."

Another instructor, John "Josh" Billings, a catcher who had played 11 seasons in the majors, signed Harry to a contract to play the following year for Lake Charles, Louisiana, in the Evangeline League, which had a working relationship with the Cincinnati Reds.

In Lake Charles, Chozen batted .321 in 1935 and also fell in love with the area, which he made his home shortly thereafter. He also met Ruth Nelson there, who became his wife three years later. Harry's successful season in Lake Charles earned him a promotion to Fort Worth of the Texas League at the tail end of that season.

In 1936, he went to spring training with Fort Worth, but ended up playing that year and the next with El Dorado of the Cotton States League. "A couple of my teammates there, Harry Craft and Lloyd 'Whitey' Moore, also went to the big leagues," he said. In El Dorado in 1936, the twenty-one-year-old catcher had a so-so season, batting just .261. But the following year, he broke loose, hit .339, and was voted the league's most valuable player as his team won the Shaugnessy Plan Playoffs. This earned him an immediate, albeit short-term, ticket to the major leagues. (The Shaugnessy Playoffs were devised to help the struggling minor leagues maintain attendance during the Depression. At year end, the first-place team in each league played a series against the fourth-place team, while the second- and third-place finishers faced each other. The winners then played for the league "championship.")

After the playoffs, Cincinnati called Chozen up for the final few weeks of the 1937 season. "On the day I got there they had fired Chuck Dressen as manager," Chozen recalls, "and they gave me his uniform number. When I went out on the field, I got booed." Dressen was succeeded by Bobby Wallace for the last 25 games of the season, of which the Reds won only five. "Wallace had been a scout, I think, and wasn't too close to the team," Chozen says.

A few weeks after Chozen joined the Reds, Wallace told him he would be starting the second game of the following day's doubleheader against the Philadelphia Phillies. "Nervous" is the way Harry describes feeling at the time. "I guess they just wanted to see me play. I was always nervous before something like that. In all the years I played and managed, I always got nervous on opening day."

He doesn't recall much about the first game of that twin bill on September 21, 1937, "except Morrie Arnovich, the Phillies' left fielder, hit a home run." The Reds' regular catcher (and eventual Hall of Famer), Ernie Lombardi, sat out the doubleheader between the seventh- and eighth-place teams that day, and Dee Moore caught the first game. Lombardi did pinch hit in the second game, however.

According to the record, Cincinnati won the first game, 6–3.

Then came the second game, the game that would make Harry Chozen a real one-time major leaguer.

"Our starting pitcher was 'Wild Bill' Hallahan, who had already pitched in four World Series with the Cardinals and who I remembered reading about just a few years earlier," Chozen says. "Before the game, Hallahan told me we'd use the indicator system to call pitches. I didn't know what the indicator system was. I had always used a flat hand for the fastball and fist for the curve. Well, it was funny, but I got through it. In the shower after the game, he told me, 'Son, you called a good game. I didn't have to shake you off once.'"

The box score of that game shows that Hallahan did not start the game but, instead, relieved the Cincinnati starter, Joe Cascarella. Regardless, it wasn't a particularly good game for the Reds, who lost, 10–1. It was one of the 20 games the team lost—out of 25 played—under Bobby Wallace at the end of that 1937 season. The team eventually finished last.

The record shows Chozen caught all nine innings, had four putouts, one assist, one error, and went 1 for 4 at bat. "You know, on defense, I was very good at catching foul pops behind the plate," Chozen says, "and don't you know, around the fourth inning, the first one that was hit, I dropped. That was the error. I caught one later for one of the putouts. I think I got the other three outs on strikeouts."

As for the assist, "I threw out a guy trying to steal, their third baseman, [Arthur] Pinky Whitney."

He remembers his plate appearances vividly. "[Rookie lefthander] Wayne LaMaster was the Philadelphia pitcher," Chozen recalls. "My first time up was with the bases loaded and two out. I pulled a long ball down the left field line that just went foul. Then I lined out to right center.

"The second time, I hit a foul behind first base that [Dolph] Camilli just plucked out of the stands, and the third time I hit a long fly to left center field."

The fourth time was the charm. "I hit a single right by the third baseman," he said. "I was very excited."

This was about a week before his twenty-second birthday. "I remember thinking to myself that it probably would take me a long time to reach the big leagues," he says, "but here I was, in my third year, playing in the majors. I was just plain excited. I really didn't think beyond the moment. I thought it would always be this way."

Instead, it lasted just those few weeks. He enjoyed the time, however, rooming with his former El Dorado teammates, Harry Craft and Whitey Moore. Chozen also remembers other Red teammates fondly, such as Paul Derringer, Kiki Cuyler, and most of all, Lombardi.

"He was so nice to me," Chozen says, speaking of Lombardi. "He bought me a new mitt just before my birthday. Not only was he a great player, but he was always a very nice person. He led the league in hitting that year [actually it was the next year] and he was the highest paid player, but you know what he was making then? Just $17,000!" (Chozen's earnings that year came to $2,500.)

In 1938, the year he and Ruth Nelson got married, Chozen went back to spring training with the Reds but was optioned to Albany in the Eastern League, where he eventually spent the next three seasons. And that's where the second letter comes in.

After his first year in Albany, Chozen was expecting to be recalled by the Reds at the end of the season, but it didn't happen. "I saw in the paper the list of those who were being recalled and I wasn't on it," he said. "I was disappointed, especially because [general manager] Warren Giles promised me, when he optioned me out, that he'd recall me at the end of the year.

"So I called Giles and asked about it. He got mad and told me that if I wanted to make trouble, he'd recall me and ship me to Durham, North Carolina, where their Class D team was.

"So I wrote a letter to [baseball commissioner] Judge Landis, asking him to declare me a free agent. I wrote that when I signed my original contract, I was too young to sign—you had to be twenty-one then—and, therefore, the contract wasn't valid. I felt I was a valuable property then, having had that most valuable player award at El Dorado the year before, and I figured I could make a better deal for myself. Well, Judge Landis sent my letter on to the minor-league czar, a Judge [William] Bramham, I think it was. That was in the off season.

"That spring [1939] I get a wire from Giles saying, 'Lombardi holding out; need you right away,' and telling me to report to the Reds' training camp in Tampa. Well, no sooner than I got to the hotel, the room clerk says, 'Mr. Giles told me to tell you to go right up to his room the minute you get in.' So I go up to his room and he's sitting there with Gabe Paul, who was his assistant, and he jumps all over me about the letter. Well, I was scared; I had no money to get back home or anything and they made me sign a letter which I guess took them off the hook. It wasn't really 'til years later that I got to wondering if that letter ever got me blackballed from playing in the majors again."

No one will ever know. Chozen was optioned outright to Albany, where he played two seasons and then moved over to Williamsport, in the same league, in 1941.

In his four years in the Eastern League, Chozen never batted above .274. "I guess it was becoming apparent that I wasn't going anywhere, but Tommy Richardson, who was the president of the league, liked me, and he helped arrange for me to go down and be the manager of Newport News, an affiliate of the Philadelphia A's, the next year."

Before that 1942 season began, however, Chozen wrote still another letter, this time to the legendary Athletics' owner-manager, Connie Mack. "The A's were going to be training in Anaheim, California, that year, and I wrote Mr. Mack saying that I had family close by in Pasadena and I didn't have to be down in Newport News until late April. I said maybe I could come by and play in spring training with the Athletics and it wouldn't cost him anything. Well, he said okay, and I ended up playing most of the exhibition games with the A's that spring as [Frankie] Hayes and [Hal] Wagner weren't ready. I almost thought Mr. Mack was going to keep me at the start of the season, but one day he said simply, 'Harry, I'm not going to use you anymore. I want you to pick up your players and go to Newport News.'"

Chozen served as the player-manager at Newport News in the Virginia League in 1942, hitting .312, and the team finished fourth in a six-team league. At the end of the season, he was only twenty-six years old. "An *old* twenty-six," he laughs.

As World War II heightened in intensity, Chozen returned home to await his expected call-up for military service. "I didn't do anything about baseball for 1943 because I thought I was going into the service," he says. "While I waited, I took a job at the M. W. Kellogg Company refinery in Lake Charles [where he, his wife, and young son were living]. People kept getting in touch with me about baseball jobs, but I figured I'd be drafted any day. But all of 1943 went by and I was never called.

"Then Mr. Edgar Allen, the owner of the team in Knoxville [in the Southern Association], called me and asked me to play for them. Finally I decided to accept, so he sent someone down, and I signed a contract. As soon as I started playing that spring [1944] at Knoxville, that's when I was called for my physical," he says.

Chozen was turned down by his draft board. "They said I had a moderate enlargement of something or other near the heart, so I went back to playing ball with Knoxville." A few weeks after the season began, the entire franchise was moved to Mobile, Alabama, and Chozen played the 1944 season there, batting .266.

Mobile wanted him back for 1945, but in the spring of that year, he was reexamined by the military doctors. "I went from 4-F to 1-A just like that, and I didn't know what my situation would be," Chozen says. "I was awaiting induction every day." To entice him back to Mobile, a Brooklyn Dodger farm team, Allen promised to let him be a free agent at the end of the season.

Returning to Mobile, Chozen went on a hitting rampage. He batted .353 for the year and hit in 49 straight games, a new league record. "I wasn't much of a home run hitter," he admits, "but the hit that broke the record was a homer. The previous record was 46, set by Johnny Bates."

The difficulty of Chozen's feat becomes apparent when you realize that only four players in all of baseball history have hit safely in more consecutive games. In 1919, Jo Wilhoit got hits in 69 straight games for Wichita in the Western League, and in 1922, Otto Pahlman hit in 50 straight for Danville in the Three-I League. Joe DiMaggio, of course, set the major-league record of 56 in 1941, but also had a 61-game streak when he was with San Francisco in the Pacific Coast League in 1933. In 1954, at Waco in the Big State League, Roman Mejias hit safely in 55 straight games.

A date for Chozen's Army induction was finally set. "I caught a doubleheader, and then I was going to go home for a week before induction. I was supposed to take a train to Chattanooga, but before I left, my roommate, who happened to be the batboy, came in with the mail, and there was a notice in there for me from the draft board saying my induction had been canceled. By that time, the war was ending, and they had stopped drafting so many people."

Despite Chozen's record-breaking season, Allen kept his promise and gave the now thirty-year-old catcher his freedom. "He just didn't offer me a contract," Chozen says. "I thought I could make a good deal with some team after that year, but the best deal I could make was with Doc Prothro, who gave me a bonus to play for him at Memphis. I think I got $5,000 in cash. [Dodger owner Branch] Rickey wanted me to come for nothing."

Chozen played for Memphis in the Southern Association in 1946, and then Prothro asked him to be the player-manager of Memphis's Class C affiliate in Greenville the following year, which he did. "I'll tell you about playing and managing," he says. "Your own batting and fielding can erase a lot of mistakes you make as a manager. A manager is just no better than the players he has."

The following year he became player-manager at Miami Beach in the

Florida International League, hitting .288. "That's the only time I ever got fired," he says. "Joe Ryan, who later on was president of the American Association, was the business manager and fired me with 11 games left. One time that year, we had a 17-game losing streak.

"I came home that winter and decided to hang them up," he continues, "but then I got a call from Pine Bluff, a St. Louis Browns farm team, and they wanted me to join them."

For the next two years, Chozen was player-manager at Pine Bluff, batting .287 and .289, and winning the pennant in his second year there. "We had a great team there," he says. "One of my pitchers was Ryne Duren."

While at Pine Bluff in 1950, Chozen also was part of a group back home in Lake Charles that was establishing a reorganized franchise there, and in 1951 he returned as part owner, general manager, and player-manager. "I did everything because that was a way I could justify getting more money," he laughs. As a nearly thirty-six-year-old, part-time player, he still hit .300.

An offer to do all those jobs for even more money brought him back to Greenville, the Memphis affiliate, and he closed out his career there in 1952.

"After 1952, I retired," he says. "I had just built a new house and I just wanted to stay home and enjoy it." Chozen became an independent insurance broker. "I knew a lot of people and I can say I made a nice living," he says. In 1962, his wife of almost twenty-five years passed away. Ten years later, he married the former Ruth Sternberg, whom he met on a visit to Tulsa.

A review of Chozen's career statistics shows he had a remarkable ability to make contact with a pitched ball. He rarely struck out. In round figures, in all his years of playing, he struck out slightly more than 100 times in approximately 5,000 times at bat!

Despite the unpleasant episode with Giles, Chozen maintains, "I have no regrets at all about my career." Remembering his one-time major-league appearance, he says, "It was all a thrill just being there."

John Joseph Leovich

PHILADELPHIA ATHLETICS, 1941

In grade school, John Leovich was part of a double-play combination with another eventual major-league player and a future state governor. In college, he played football in the Hula Bowl. And in the major leagues, he lined a double off Bob Feller in the one game he played.

The youngest in a family of five children, Leovich describes his youth: "I grew up around north Portland [Oregon]. My father was the foreman in a lumberyard, but he died when I was five years old. In school, I played everything: football, ice hockey, baseball, and a little basketball."

And the famous double play? "I was the shortstop, Johnny Paveskovich was the second baseman, and Michael Stepovich was the first baseman. Later, Stepovich became the governor of Alaska."

Paveskovich, his best friend, also became well known in professional baseball, although under another name. "When we were still in grade school, Johnny and I got jobs with the Portland Beavers of the Pacific Coast League," Leovich says. "I was a clubhouse boy and Johnny was the batboy.

"Johnny was just a little kid and one day L. H. Gregory, a sportswriter at the [Portland] *Oregonian*, brought a team in to Vaughn Street Park [where the Beavers played] to play a pickup game against the kids who worked in the ballpark. Gregory himself was pitching and here comes Paveskovich up to bat and the bat was bigger than he was. Gregory called me over and says, 'What's this? How do I throw to this little guy?'

"I said, 'Just throw it and duck.'

"Well, he didn't quite believe me. Anyway, Johnny hit four terrific line

In his only game in the majors, John Leovich doubled off Bob Feller
and claims he faced high school and college pitchers who were just as fast.

drives and went 4 for 4. After the game Gregory said, 'What's that kid's name?'

"'John Michael Paveskovich.'

"'*What?*' he says. 'He's a pesky hitter, so his name's Johnny Pesky from now on as far as I'm concerned.'"

In the clubhouse and around the field at Portland in the early 1930s, Leovich got to see many of the great players of the Pacific Coast League during that era. Among those he particularly remembers are Smead Jolley, Oscar "Ox" Eckhardt, Arnold "Jigger" Statz, Frank Shellenback, and one of his future Philadelphia teammates, Bob Johnson. He also saw a seventeen-year-old San Francisco Seals' outfielder, Joe DiMaggio, during his 61-game hitting streak in 1933.

In the winters, Leovich and Pesky headed for the skating rink where they enjoyed practicing with hockey players from the minor-league Portland Buckaroos. Pesky was an especially good player, Leovich says, and both boys were offered professional contracts. But Leovich preferred to go to college.

In 1938, he enrolled at Oregon State University, where he played both baseball and football. By then he had become a catcher. "I was a shortstop in my first year in high school," he says, "but the next year we needed a catcher, so I shifted to catcher and Johnny [Pesky] moved from second to shortstop."

So Leovich becoming a catcher led to Pesky becoming an All-Star shortstop? "I guess you could say that," Leovich laughs.

"In 1939, I played [offensive and defensive] left end on the football team," Leovich says. "We went to Hawaii on Christmas Day and won. I don't remember who we played, but then we played there again the next week, on January 1, 1940, in the Hula Bowl against the University of Hawaii, and we beat them, too."

Leovich stayed at Oregon State until early 1941, then left school after receiving contract offers from both the Detroit Tigers and Philadelphia Athletics. He accepted the latter. "I knew more people there," he says. "Tom Turner, the owner at Portland, had a working relationship with Philadelphia and I was familiar with them." There was no bonus, only an annual salary. "I think the minimum that year was $7,500," he says.

Reporting directly from Oregon State to Philadelphia after signing his contract, Leovich was installed as the A's third-string catcher behind Frankie Hayes and Hal Wagner. Generally, he worked on his catching with coach Earle Brucker and warmed up pitchers between innings and in the bullpen.

In that job, Leovich remembers trying to catch the knuckleball of fellow rookie Luman Harris. He recalls studying the ball and trying to determine where it would break. But if Harris was throwing into a stiff wind, nothing helped. "I was out there one day, and he threw one that started in about the middle of the plate. It ended up fifteen feet high on the back of the screen. Later I asked him, 'What the hell are you trying to do, *decapitate* me?'

"I just got a letter from one of Luman Harris's children," Leovich interjects. "He had to have both legs amputated and isn't able to get around very well. I'm writing to him now, and I'm planning to be in Dallas soon, and I think he lives around that area now so maybe I can give him a call. He was a wonderful person."

With the Athletics, there were few men Leovich admired more than his manager, Connie Mack. "He was a great gentleman. That's all you can say. He was *Mister* Mack. He had a nice sparkle in his eyes, and he looked right at you when he was talking to you. Anything he told you, you could bet it was right. I really enjoyed having met the man.

"I remember one time Connie got mad at me and [outfielder] Sam Chapman," Leovich recalls. "We were clowning around in the outfield one day and were showing a kid out of Purdue, Felix Mackiewicz, how we did it in the Coast League. We lined up in a football stance, and we knocked him down a couple of times. Well, I guess the old man was watching us and he got the word to us: 'Quit that football stuff.'

"Well, the very next week there was an article in *The Sporting News* where they asked Mr. Mack about Leovich. He said, 'As a baseball player, he's a hell of a *football* player.' That was his way of letting me know he didn't like it."

On Thursday, May 1, a few weeks after the start of the season and four days before Leovich's twenty-third birthday, the Athletics were in Cleveland to face the Indians and their ace, Bob Feller. This was the year after the "Cry Baby" Indians had lost the 1940 pennant to the Tigers, and Roger Peckinpaugh had now taken over as manager, replacing Ossie Vitt.

For five innings, Feller kept Philadelphia from scoring while Cleveland rapped out ten hits against the A's starter, Jack Knott. Finally, in the bottom of the fifth, the Indians knocked Knott from the box. They led 8–0. Feller himself was a key contributor, hitting a home run (he would get two of Cleveland's 18 hits that day) while recording the 1,000th strikeout of his career along the way.

In the top of the sixth inning, Philadelphia finally scored when a single by Frankie Hayes, the starting catcher, drove in a run. "That Hayes, he wouldn't get out of a *doubleheader*," Leovich recalls. "He was a hell of a guy, but that was his job, and he wasn't gonna let anybody else in there. Which, you know, you can understand. He was a competitor."

Behind 8–1, manager Connie Mack told Leovich to go in and catch the bottom of the sixth. "I was sitting next to him in the dugout, or one man away," Leovich recalls. "See, if I wasn't in, and we got a man on base, it was my job to flash the signal to the coach about whether to steal or not. So I had to be close to him. I guess he just wanted to give Hayes a rest."

Today, Leovich has forgotten most of the details of the game. According to the box score, when he entered the game in the bottom of the sixth, the Indians scored another run off Adam Johnson, who had relieved Knott, to move ahead 9–1. In the top half of the seventh, the Athletics scored twice against the tiring Feller, but the Indians banged the third Athletic pitcher, Herm Besse, for four more runs over the next two innings and led 13–3, going to the ninth. Feller, coasting, gave up homers to second baseman Benny McCoy and left fielder Bob Johnson, whom Leovich knew at Portland. The A's scored five times, but Feller finished the game a winner, 13–8.

"One of the big injustices is Bob Johnson never making the Hall of Fame with the records he achieved," Leovich says. "He was the center fielder. He always hit .300, or close to it, and 20 or more home runs a year. He used to hit a lot of doubles and triples." Johnson also drove in 100 or more runs seven seasons in a row and retired with a career slugging average of .506, topping players such as Ernie Banks, Johnny Bench, and Reggie Jackson. "He had a great arm," Leovich continues, "and could run like a deer. He did it all out there. Of course, he played for the Athletics, the bottom of the league. He did it without fanfare. If he'd have been playing on a contender, hell, he'd have gotten a lot of publicity."

As for Feller, Leovich definitely remembers his two at-bats against the Cleveland fireballer. "I had faced kids in high school and in college who were just as fast as Feller," he claims, "although they didn't have the good curve he had. He was a hell of a pitcher. But I'd been around baseball and baseball players a long time and I knew them. I was not overawed and was able to relax. The first time up, I lined out to Lou Boudreau at short, and the next time, I hit a double to right field, right center."

That was Leovich's major-league career—one hit, a double, in two times at bat against Bob Feller, for a batting average of .500. Neither of his plate appearances affected Philadelphia's scoring. Despite his success, Connie Mack never called on him again.

He continued working in the bullpen and warming up pitchers during that historic 1941 season in which DiMaggio hit in 56 straight games and Ted Williams batted over .400. Leovich admires them both but feels Williams was the better, more disciplined hitter. "He also was a very gracious person," he says of the Boston slugger. "If a person on the other ball club was having trouble hitting, he'd meet them out at the ballpark at ten o'clock and straighten them out. That was a side that nobody knew about because he was always fighting with those Boston writers."

During the middle of the summer, with Hayes catching regularly and getting spot help from the more experienced Wagner, the Athletics sent Leovich to their International League affiliate in Toronto. "I was only in Toronto a couple of weeks," he recalls, "because their catcher got hurt. When he got better, they sent me to Wilmington [in the Interstate League]." He got into 54 games there that summer, but hit only .190 before returning to Philadelphia to finish the season.

In 1942, the following year, Leovich went to spring training with his hometown Portland Beavers (the team was still affiliated with the Athletics) and became the starting catcher. "Frank Brazill [a former Athletic infielder] was the manager there," he recalls. "The bumps and bruises I suffered from football didn't help me in baseball that year," he says.

Nor was he helped by two accidents during the year. First, he injured his shoulder badly in a collision while blocking the plate, but he returned to the lineup "as soon as it quit throbbing." Then he was beaned. "I got hit in the head by [Eddie] Stutz, who was a hell of a curveballer. He threw a curveball that didn't break. First one he'd thrown in nine years that didn't break. They didn't even give me a pinch runner, so I had to stay in until the game was over. I tell you, I felt that for quite a while."

Despite his injuries, Leovich played in 117 games that season but again batted only .190. His team finished in last place.

The two Portland players he remembers best were minor-league veterans Ted Norbert, a home run hitter, and a thirty-six-year-old submarine pitcher, Ad Liska. "Norbert was a real gentlemen at all times, a serious hitter, and had a good sense of humor," Leovich recalls. Despite leading the league in homers for four years, however, Norbert never made the majors.

Liska, on the other hand, had already been there, having pitched for the Senators and the Phils between 1929 and 1933. But he was primarily a minor-league star, eventually winning 248 games, most of them with Portland. "Liska was a fierce competitor," Leovich says. "He hated to lose at anything. He was a pleasure to catch. It was like sitting in a rocking chair; he was always on target. His control was perfect, and he didn't dilly-dally around on the mound. Ad pitched fast and you had better be in position to receive his pitch when you returned the ball to him. He *fired* the ball right back, as soon as he got it. Most of his games were over in an hour and a half."

In June 1942, he married Janet Goresky, a local girl who, he says, "lived right next door to my sister in Portland." With World War II under way, the newly wed Leovich joined the Coast Guard after the 1942 season and, for the next three years, was stationed near Seattle, from which he and his shipmates patrolled the Alaskan coastline.

Upon his discharge, Leovich, then twenty-eight, just didn't want to play anymore, so in 1946 he joined his sister and brother-in-law in their Seattle tavern business. "My priorities had changed quite a bit," he says. "I was not really interested in going back to baseball then. I started in business, liked it, and didn't want to leave it. I wasn't going anyplace in baseball. It was like an avocation to me, and I wanted to get on with my life."

He did come back a couple of times, but only briefly. The first time was soon after his discharge when he was asked to play in an exhibition game and got an opportunity to catch the legendary Satchel Paige.

"You just put your glove there and he'd hit it and he had a lot of fun while he was doing it," Leovich says of Paige. "He'd talk to you before the game and tell you what he'd like to do. And then he'd put on a little show, that [hesitation] pitch. He'd give the sign when he was gonna take the step and then throw it later. He knew what he was doing out there all the time.

"He had tremendous control of his curveball. He'd get two strikes on you most of the time. Depending on the situation, he'd throw that curve by them, a slow curve, this and that. Then when he wanted you out of there, he'd throw one that'd break right off the table. He could *fire* that ball when he wanted to. He was a very smart man. He knew what he wanted to do out there."

At the start of the 1946 season, Leovich returned to baseball once more. "I promised Sam Gibson [a former major-league pitcher], who was the manager at Bremerton, that I'd help him out. I had known Sam in Portland when he was with the San Francisco Seals. So for a little while that year, while I was in business in Seattle, I'd travel to Bremerton at night. But that just lasted a short time," he says.

Over the ensuing years, Leovich branched out from the tavern to the restaurant business, opening restaurants in Seattle and later in Lincoln City, Oregon, a resort area ninety miles west of Portland. He retired a few years ago; he and his wife still live in Lincoln City, in a house right on the Pacific coast. "I look out my window, and I can see the ocean for miles and miles," he says. "It's just beautiful."

After his retirement, Leovich suffered a stroke that temporarily left him unable to walk or speak. "I had a rough couple of years," he says, "but I'm getting along real good now. I'm back on my feet walking, even though it took me about two years to work up to a mile. I had to start with just one block at a time. I use a cane to help me now, although I don't need it all the time. It's getting better."

As for regaining his speech, Leovich says, "I feel very fortunate to be able to talk again, although sometimes it's difficult. I remember when I was going through therapy, seeing so many people having a bad time of it. It's really a difficult thing when you're unable to talk."

Leovich still follows sports actively. When asked his opinion on the current state of baseball, he says, "I don't like to say things like this, but when I was playing, we loved to play. Now it seems like it's just the big dollar sign that counts. I thought we had more camaraderie then than they have today. Back then, we made friends, friends for life. I met a lot of great people in baseball, which I cherish. I met a lot of nice people. That's what I enjoyed the most.

"It was a great experience, playing ball. I enjoyed being part of it," he says, "even if I *was* just sitting there."

Charles Anthony Marshall (Marchlewicz)

ST. LOUIS CARDINALS, 1941

Charlie Marshall's remembrances of his one game with the Cardinals are a bit faded. His major-league career began and ended before his more famous 1941 rookie teammate, Stan Musial, arrived near the season's end.

Born in Wilmington, Delaware, in the late summer of 1919, Marshall, whose real surname was Marchlewicz, was the second son in a family of three boys and a girl. As a youngster, he went to the Wilmington Trade School to study carpentry and was the catcher on the school's baseball team. "That was the only sport they had," he says, "and I was a catcher since I was eight years old."

Outside of school, he also played American Legion baseball. "My older brother also played American Legion ball and people had trouble pronouncing his name and so they just started calling him Marshall, and then me, too. It was easier. But in American Legion ball, you had to use your right name. I can show you eight box scores where they screwed up my name eight different ways," he laughs. "So I became Marshall." (Today, even *The Baseball Encyclopedia* misspells his original last name.)

In 1937, his American Legion team from Wilmington made it to a tournament playoff game in North Carolina. "It was a one-game elimination tournament, and we were eliminated right away," he says. "But a scout named Pat Crawford, from the St. Louis Cardinals, walked up to me at the dinner we had at the end of the tournament and asked me to go outside for a walk with him. He asked if I had any interest in playing professional ball. Well, I didn't have enough money for another pair of Jockey

*Charlie Marshall, here in a Rochester Red Wings uniform, was ready to slug
opposing manager Leo Durocher after entering his only big-league game.*

shorts then, and I said 'Sure.' He signed me to a contract and sent me a check for $150." At the time, Marshall was seventeen years old.

"They sent me to Cambridge, Maryland, in the Eastern Shore League," Marshall continues, "and I got the magnificent sum of $70 a month." He laughs again.

Marshall played at Cambridge in both 1937 and 1938, hitting .246 and .248 in 88 and 92 games respectively. In 1939, he moved up to Portsmouth, Ohio, in the Middle Atlantic League, where he had a good season, raising his average to .280 and playing in 119 games. He recalls Dain Clay, later an outfielder with Cincinnati, as a teammate, but more clearly remembers that "Springfield had some team that year. They had Allie Reynolds pitching and Bob Lemon played shortstop and that catcher who played with them—Jim Hegan."

In 1940, the Cardinals sent him to play in Houston, in the Texas League, under manager Eddie Dyer, who later managed the parent team for five years and became one of only six managers to win the World Series in his first season. "That was a good team," Marshall says of the Houston squad. "We won the pennant that year by 17 games." Members of that team included such future major-leaguers as Howie Pollett; Howie Krist; Johnny Antonelli; Sam Narron; Sam Nahem; and Danny Murtaugh, who had his skull fractured by a Sal Maglie pitch in 1950 and later managed the Pirates for fifteen years, winning two World Series. "Murtaugh was my roommate for five years, at Cambridge, at Houston, and later at Rochester," Marshall says, "and we were good friends."

Later in 1940, shortly after turning twenty-one, Marshall returned to Wilmington and married Jenny Syvy, a girl he had met while in high school there.

In 1941, he got to play in his one game in the major leagues, but in looking back, Marshall describes the year as a whole as a "nightmare." Even so, he laughs about it now and obviously enjoys describing it.

"At the start of the season, I get a telegram from Branch Rickey [Cardinal general manager] to report to Sacramento in the [Triple-A] Pacific Coast League. They told me that the catcher there had drowned. Pepper Martin was the manager. Well, one morning, I get a call from Pepper Martin and he said, 'Come down to the lobby, and with your bags packed!' Well, he was the kind of guy who got into a lot of horseplay and everything, practical jokes. It's six o'clock in the morning, and I thought it was a joke. So I said, 'C'mon. Don't do this to me.' But he said to do it, so I packed up and met him in the lobby. He told me I had to go to St. Louis because Walker Cooper, who was the second-string catcher, had hurt his shoulder, so they wanted a backup for [Gus] Mancuso."

Marshall and his wife took the train from Sacramento to St. Louis. "We traveled by Pullman in those days," Marshall says. "I told my wife that when we got to St. Louis, we were gonna go straight to the hotel and go to sleep and that I wasn't gonna report to the ballpark 'til the next day.

"But when we arrive at the station in St. Louis, who is waiting for us there but Branch Rickey. He says, 'C'mon, son. I need you in Cincinnati.' Well, I'm sick about this. He asks my wife if she'd like to join me on the plane to Cincinnati, but she says she'd rather go to the hotel. Well, Rickey and I get on this little four-seater plane and fly to Cincinnati and when we get there, it's got to be like 110 degrees. We get to the ballpark and [Cardinal manager Billy] Southworth says, 'Kid, put your stuff on and go catch batting practice.' Well, I'd like to die."

A short while later, when the Cardinals were back in St. Louis on June 14, 1941, Marshall actually got into his one major-league game. That day the Cardinals were hosting their chief rival for the National League pennant, the Brooklyn Dodgers, in a rain-threatened Saturday afternoon doubleheader.

The first game looked promising for the Cardinals as they jumped out to a 4–0 lead at the end of five innings. That changed suddenly in the top of the sixth when the Dodgers clobbered Cardinal starter Harry Gumbert and his successor, Clyde Shoun, for seven runs, and then went on to score five more during the next two innings. At the end of seven-and-a-half innings, they led 12–5.

In the bottom of the eighth, Mancuso led off with a single. As Marshall relates the story, "Southworth says, 'Hey, kid. Go run for Mancuso.' I go in. Now Terry Moore is the batter and Terry hits a shot to deep left center and I take off and round second and head for third. All of a sudden I see Mike Gonzalez, the third base coach, waving and yelling, 'Go back! Go back!' So I go back around second and get back to first. I thought the ball that Moore hit was going over the wall, but [Dodger center fielder Pete] Reiser caught it. I get back to first and [Brooklyn manager Leo] Durocher comes out to argue. He gets into it with [umpire George] Magerkurth. He started arguing, 'That S.O.B. never touched second on his way back. Didn't ya see that?' I said, 'Who you calling an S.O.B.?' I was gonna go for him, but the first base coach held me off."

In any event, Marshall then went out to catch the top of the ninth inning, replacing Mancuso. The new Cardinal pitcher was Ira Hutchinson. "We had a set of signs then," Marshall says, "that allowed us to call a pitch 64 different ways. I walked out and asked him, 'You want to use the 64 combination signs? He says, 'Fuck it. Let's just use one and two.'

"I don't remember who it was, but the first batter hit the first pitch thrown, and it was a high foul ball in front of the Dodger dugout. Well, I went over and made the putout, and I'll never forget them [the Dodgers] calling me all kinds of names as I was going over there."

The game ended shortly thereafter with the score still Dodgers 12, Cardinals 5. The second game that day was rained out.

"I lived a block or two from the park in St. Louis," Marshall continues, "and one day sometime later I get a call from the secretary at Rickey's office to come over and see him. I figure I'm going back to Sacramento on the Pullman again.

"I get over to his office and he says, 'Son, we're gonna send you to Syracuse.' Well, I blew my top. When I left Sacramento, they were only a game behind in the pennant race, and now St. Louis was only a half a game behind the Dodgers, and they're sending me out. I said, 'What are you doing to me? Goddamn it, I'm not reporting!'

"Well, Rickey raised hell with me for using the G-d word. Finally, he left and one of the scouts told me to just report to Syracuse and don't worry about it. I said, 'But I'm gonna lose playoff money.'

"I didn't report to Syracuse 'til three days later," he goes on. "I got a call from the Syracuse president. 'Where are you?' he asks. I said, 'You called me. You gotta know where I am.' The twenty-one-year-old Marshall remained angry and hit only .186 in 27 games at Syracuse.

"Then I get another telegram from Rickey. 'Return to Sacramento,' it says. So I get on another train and go all the way across the country and get back to Sacramento and finish the season there. At the end of the season, I'm getting ready for the playoffs when the Sacramento president, Phil Bottomley, calls me in his office. He says, 'I want to thank you for your work here this year, but you're not eligible for the playoffs.' I just said, 'Oh, no.'

"And that's why I call the '41 season a nightmare," he says. But he laughs heartily.

From 1942 through most of 1945, Marshall, like many, served in the military during World War II. "I was a corporal in the combat engineers," he says, "and was in the invasion in France." He returned to professional baseball in 1946 and was assigned to Rochester, the Cardinals' Triple-A farm team in the International League. "Burliegh Grimes was the manager there, and he told me, 'Kid, I don't think you're gonna make it. You have trouble hitting the high fastball.' So he sent me to Houston. A month later, I'm back in Rochester and Grimes had been fired. Benny Borgmann was the manager.

"I stayed at Rochester five years," Marshall says. In the late forties, following World War II, the International League was one of the strongest minor leagues in the country, if not the strongest. During those years, Marshall played with and against a huge assortment of players who later went to the majors. In 1946, for example, Jackie Robinson made his debut in organized baseball with Montreal.

During his tenure at Rochester, Marshall was never that much of a hitter. His batting average ranged over those years from .203 to .260. In 1950, his last season there, he turned thirty-one years old.

"After five years there, we had a disagreement," he says. "All I wanted was to be able to take my wife and daughter on the train, but they wouldn't agree." Evidently, a light-hitting, aging catcher didn't have much clout at that point.

"The Cardinals sent me to Columbus, Ohio, for the 1951 season," he says. Columbus was in the American Association, another strong Triple-A league. Both Willie Mays and Mickey Mantle played there briefly that same year, Mays at Minneapolis and Mantle at Kansas City. Marshall's Columbus team, however, was the doormat of the league, losing 101 games out of 154 and finishing dead last. But their player-manager, Harry "The Hat" Walker, led the league in hitting with a .393 average. "All he cared about," Marshall says glumly, "was getting base hits. He didn't care about winning."

At year end, the Cardinals offered Marshall a job as player-manager at Omaha, Nebraska, for the 1952 season. "I wouldn't take that job for nothing," he says. "That was too hot a place for me." Instead, he accepted a similar job from an independent team in Augusta, Georgia. The team he managed finished seventh, and at age thirty-two, Marshall got into 47 games and hit .262. "The money wasn't bad in those days," he says. "I was making around $1,100 a month then and my brother, who was a hell of a good carpenter, was making $80 a week."

But after that year, Marshall returned home to Wilmington and left professional baseball for a career in the post office. "But I caught six years of semipro ball after that, and I coached American Legion ball for eighteen years," he says.

In 1982, after twenty-nine years at the post office, he retired. Two years later, his wife, Jenny, passed away. "I still got my daughter, though, four grandkids, and four great-grandkids," he says, "and never had it better. I got a good pension, and I'm really living.

"Listen, I had a hell of a time playing baseball. I wouldn't exchange it for anything else."

Pinson Lamar "Phil" McCullough

WASHINGTON NATIONALS, 1942

World War II prematurely ended "Phil" McCullough's career as a ballplayer.

Born in Stockbridge, Georgia, on July 22, 1917, McCullough was the second of three sons born to John and Jessie McCullough.

At Stockbridge High School, he played both basketball and baseball. "I played center in basketball," he says. At six-foot-four, 204 pounds, "I was tall and lanky." As a basketball player, he "played fair enough to make the team, but I was much better at baseball. In baseball, I was a right-handed pitcher, but on days I wasn't pitching, I played first or the outfield. In those days, you played where you were needed. We didn't have that many kids on the team.

"They didn't have American Legion ball in that area then," McCullough says, "but they did have amateur ball, which was sponsored by business people, and they set up leagues. I played that when I was in high school."

After his high school graduation, McCullough entered Ogelthorpe University in Atlanta in 1934. "That was known as an outstanding baseball school," he says, "and I played there all four years—one year freshman ball and the other three on the varsity. I think I had three good years out of four." At Ogelthorpe, McCullough majored in physical education and recreation, specializing in athletic injuries and therapy. He received his degree in 1938.

"While I was in college, I also played ball in a mill league in Alabama," McCullough recalls. "In those days, you couldn't get paid for playing ball or you'd lose your college eligibility, so you had to have a job. The mill gave us a job painting houses. In most of those towns, the mills owned all the houses, so we painted houses three days a week and got paid for that, and then played ball three days a week."

Following his graduation, McCullough signed to play professional base-ball with an independent team at New Bern, North Carolina, in the Class-D Coastal Plain League. "Doc Smith, an ex-catcher and former manager of the Atlanta Crackers, was managing at New Bern, and he got word to me, through another ballplayer, to come up there and play for him. He knew about me from when he was in Atlanta. I was a starter—I was always a starter—and my main pitch was the fastball. I think I got $147 a week. There were a lot of good players in that league, a lot of good players. I remember the Yankees and the White Sox had farm teams in that league."

At New Bern in 1939, McCullough won seven and lost eight, although he says he thinks he won more. One possible reason he might not remem-ber correctly was a girl named Mary Ruth Oliver, whom he had met a year earlier on a blind date. They were married that year.

"Washington bought my contract after that season," McCullough says. "I found out about it when I was planning to go back to New Bern the next year and they told me to go to Kinston instead."

Kinston was in the same league, and in 1940, McCullough's record was 7–12. "Washington had a working relationship with Kinston," he says, "but it wasn't one of their farm teams. The next year, though, they sent me to Greenville in the Sally [Southern Association] League, which was one of their farm teams.

"I seem to remember two managers there in 1941," McCullough says. "One was Cliff Bolton, an ex-Washington catcher, and one was Gus Brit-tain, who was also an ex-catcher.

"That was an interesting team at Greenville," McCullough continues. "It had a lot of old ballplayers, major-leaguers on the way down, and I was able to learn a lot from them. I remember a pitcher named Link Berry who taught me how to throw a slider, although we didn't call it a slider then."

At Greenville, McCullough won 14, lost 16, and posted a 3.10 earned run average. He also led the league in hit batsman that year, with 14. "I started throwing a knuckleball that year," he explains, "and it was a hard pitch to control. It's funny, but Washington had a lot of knuckleballers around then—'Black Jack' Wilson; Dutch Leonard, whom I knew well; Johnny Niggling; Roger Wolff; and that guy from the brother pitcher-catcher team—the Ferrells, Wes Ferrell."

In 1942, Washington invited McCullough to his first major-league spring training camp in Orlando, Florida. "I remember the crowd there— guys I had played with or guys I had heard about on the radio. There was George Case, Ben Chapman, the Ferrells, Jake Early, Al Evans, Sid Hud-son, all of the other players.

"It was quite an education to watch these guys," he says. "After a while, you realized they weren't any better than anyone else, but they were good at it. They were good at what they did. They practiced and they developed consistency. That's the key—consistency. I watch Greg Maddux pitch today. He's got great consistency. I think he's the best pitcher around today. Anyway, I was just amazed at being there with them.

"That spring, all the rookies would sort of hang together," McCullough remembers. "They knew better than to mix and mingle with the rest of them. All the rookies and the second-line players stayed at a boarding-house a couple of blocks down from the park, while the rest of the team stayed at a hotel closer to the park.

"Well, back then, just as they do now, the umpires would also come down and go through spring training, too. That year, Cal Hubbard, who was a peach of a guy, was there with us. Now Cal was about six-foot-seven and about 270 pounds—all muscle. He was a former football player, with the Green Bay Packers I think, and he had hands like shovels. He came by the boardinghouse one day and says to a bunch of the rookies, 'C'mon, I'll buy you something to eat.' So a few of us went out with him to one of the nice restaurants they had there.

"Now, in Orlando at that time, they had a big air base, and the town was filled with a lot of young guys who were going through flight school there. They were all in uniform, and they wore these peaked hats—we used to call them 'go-to-hell' hats. Anyway, at this restaurant we went to, they had four pretty girls who were cashiers, sort of in the middle of the restaurant, and these fly-boys were always hanging around them. Well, we finished our meal, and Hubbard picked up the check and went over to pay it.

"The cadets were all around the cashiers, about four deep, so Cal just reached over the crowd and laid the check and his money on the counter. As he did, he accidentally knocked one guy's hat sideways. This guy thought somebody was deliberately messing around with him, so he spins around angrily and yells, 'Who in the hell. . . .' His nose came about even with the second button on Cal's shirt. Then he looks up at Cal and says quietly, 'Who in the world are you?' I'll never forget the look on that kid's face."

McCullough pitched well enough in spring training that year to land on Washington's opening-day roster. "I went up north with them, and the biggest thrill I got was pitching against the Atlanta Crackers in Atlanta, my hometown," he says. "I have no idea how that game turned out. I think I went about four or five innings."

McCullough recalls the team opened the season in Washington and then took a short road trip, which included Boston, before returning to Washington. "When we came to Washington," he remembers, "we had to find a place to live and I remember that [pitcher] Bobo Newsom had a suite in one of the hotels and he let a couple of the rookies stay there 'til they could find a place.

"In addition, they set up cots in the clubhouse," McCullough continues. "With the war on, it was hard to find housing, and so players slept in the clubhouse. Finally Newsom, who had a big convertible—I don't remember if it was a Caddy or a Lincoln—drove me out to the outskirts of Washington one day, and I found a place to stay. My wife came up then. I remember Newsom drove us around Washington in that convertible, just before the season started, to show us the town.

"That reminds me of something else that happened in spring training that year," McCullough says. "Newsom was driving that car down Orange Avenue, which was the main drag in Orlando, and a cop pulled him over for speeding. The cop asked him his name. 'Bobo Newsom,' he answered. 'What do you do?' the cop asked. Bobo says, 'You don't know?' The cop told him the ticket would cost him $25. Bobo, who had a low, kind of raspy voice, says 'Well, I'm gonna give you $50, 'cause I'm gonna go back just as fast!'"

After the first two weeks of the season, Washington, under manager Bucky Harris, was 5–9. They had won three of their games against Philadelphia and lost five. They had been swept in a three-game series by New York, but had won two and lost one against Boston.

On Wednesday, April 22, 1942, the Red Sox were in Washington to play the Nationals, and Phil McCullough made his only appearance in a major-league baseball game.

"The main thing I remember about that game," McCullough says, "is that it was cold. It was sleeting—freezing rain. It was just a terrible, terrible day. We were in the bullpen, behind the fence. I remember ['Black Jack'] Wilson was there, and we tore up chairs and benches and furniture and made a fire in the bullpen to keep warm. It was so cold."

While the weather may have been cold that day, the Red Sox were hot. They pounded out 12 hits against three Washington pitchers, Early Wynn, Alejandro Carresquel, and Walt Masterson, and led 9–2 at the end of five and a half innings. In the bottom of the sixth, the Nationals were able to score two more runs off Boston's pitcher, Oscar Judd, to make the score 9–4 at the end of six. Bruce Campbell pinch hit for Masterson in that inning, and that's when McCullough learned he would be going in to pitch the top of the seventh.

"I was in the bullpen trying to stay warm when the telephone rang from the dugout," he says. "Our bullpen catcher and coach was Bennie Bengough. He was a class guy, and I got to be pretty good buddies with him. He answered the phone, and when he hung up, he took a brand-new baseball out of his pocket and gave it to me and said, 'You've got two minutes to warm up.' I said, 'In this weather? My God, I'll need a stove!'

"When I was called in to pitch, it wasn't any big thing," McCullough says. "It's real hard to say how I felt, but I wasn't too scared. I looked around and here was the stadium about half-full, maybe 20,000, and then who do I see ready to come to bat but Ted Williams. I thought, 'Here I am

from Stockbridge, Georgia, and I'm in the big leagues." Williams had hit
.406 the year before and would win the Triple Crown that year, leading
the league with a .356 average, 34 home runs, and 137 runs batted in.

McCullough recalls a moment later that Williams was actually the second batter he faced. "The first was another lefty batter, [Johnny] Pesky."

McCullough managed to retire the Red Sox in the top of the seventh
without any runs being scored. "I remember going back to the bench after
that first inning," McCullough says, "and I thought, 'Hey, this is easier than
I thought it would be.' I had a positive outlook. Yes, I was a rookie, but I
had good stuff. I told myself, 'You just don't make a mistake, because
they'll hit your mistakes.' I remember one of the Washington coaches
came over and sat down beside me and said, 'Nice going. See, it's not
hard.'"

McCullough went on to pitch the eighth and ninth innings as well.
Boston scored a run off him in the eighth and three more in the ninth.
Two of these runs were unearned, though, the result of an error by Washington second baseman, Jose "Chile" Gomez.

"When I came back after the eighth inning and they had scored, the
same coach came back over and said, 'That's all right. Remember, there
were three [pitchers] before you.'"

The Boston lineup McCullough faced that day had not yet been affected by World War II. It included center fielder Dom DiMaggio; Pesky,
then a rookie shortstop (see Chapter 6); Williams, the left fielder; first
baseman Ted Lupian; third baseman Jim Tabor; right fielder Pete Fox; second baseman Bobby Doerr; catcher Johnny Peacock; and pitcher Judd.

In the three innings he pitched, McCullough gave up five hits, walked
two, and struck out two. He was also credited with an assist and went 0 for
1 at bat against Judd, as Boston finally won the game, 13–4.

"I don't think Williams got a hit off me," McCullough says. "I remember throwing him a knuckleball, and I heard from someone after the game
that he said he wished I had thrown him another one, but I didn't. I remember Tabor got one of the hits off me, and either Pesky or Doerr got
one. I don't know who else. I'm pretty sure the catcher [Peacock] was one
of the guys I struck out, but I don't remember the other."

One of the walks he issued went to Doerr. "He had an amazing stance,"
McCullough says. "He faced you. It was a completely open stance, and it
kind of threw me off." His recollection of the rest of the game is hazy
today, including his one time at bat. But he does remember how he felt
when the game was over. "I thought, 'This is going to be good.' It was
kind of like anything else in life. I made some mistakes, but everybody
makes mistakes. But you can learn from them and you can correct them.

"You know, you don't walk into your first major-league game with
butterflies just in your stomach," McCullough says. "You got them all
around you. I know what it's like and I know what the guys today are
going through. But the key is consistency. Pitchers can't throw the ball by

them. You have to be able to control your location and make them hit your pitch."

McCullough has good memories of his time in Washington. "I guess the people I was closest to included [infielder] Bob Repass—we lived together for a while; [pitcher] Sid Hudson; Benny Bengough; and Dutch Leonard, of course. I had played with Dutch in the minors, and he helped me with the knuckleball. He was really the master knuckleball pitcher."

Other teammates he remembers include first basemen George Archer and Roberto Ortiz, and the catchers, Al Evans and Jake Early. "I think both Evans and Early were North Carolina boys, and we used to joke a lot about how banged up they both were from trying to catch all the knucklers," McCullough recalls. "Evans was a good pool player. [Outfielder] Stan Spence was also from North Carolina, and he spoke so slowly we used to say by the time he ordered a meal in a restaurant, the food had gotten cold. I also remember the Ferrells and 'Black Jack' Wilson. He was a clown. [First baseman] Mickey Vernon was real nice.

"Another thing that impressed me," McCullough says, "were the people, the fans. It was an old park, but the people seemed to be regular attendees. The same ones came every day. And then the kids who wanted autographs. That was nice. I felt that if they wanted your autograph, that meant 'I like you.' We would stand out there thirty or forty minutes giving autographs. We would sign and it felt good. Not like they do today."

About a week or so after he pitched, McCullough was informed he was being sent down to Washington's farm team in Chattanooga. "Benny Bengough told me," he says. "He was sort of a go-between for Bucky Harris and the players. Bucky was quite a different type of guy. He was sort of hard to approach. I felt he was always mad at the world. He always seemed to have a sour look on his face, and he didn't joke around.

"Benny came over to me one day and says, 'Mac, they're gonna send you to Chattanooga, and I just wanted you to know about it before Bucky tells you.' Sometime later on, in the clubhouse, Benny came over and says, 'Okay, go see Bucky now.' I remember I was still in uniform. Bucky told me, 'We're gonna have to pick up another relief man, someone with experience, and a couple of boys are gonna have to be let go.' He said he thought his starters would be better than they had been, but that he didn't need more starters. He needed relievers. He said, 'We need real help.'

"The next morning, I went to the ballpark around 10 A.M. and they gave me a train ticket for me and my wife and we left Washington around 3 P.M. for Chattanooga. I think it was May 1 when we got there, and the traveling secretary at Chattanooga, Sandy Sandelin, met us at the train and took us to the hotel. He was very nice."

McCullough pitched for Chattanooga for the rest of the 1942 season, recording 8 wins against 14 losses. Among his pitching teammates there, he recalls Rae Scarborough, and John "Ox" Miller.

At the end of the season, as World War II expanded, McCullough took a job at the Hercules Power plant in Atlanta. "But I expected I'd be drafted," he says, "because I was twenty-five years old and we didn't have any children. So I volunteered for the navy."

After boot camp at Norfolk, Virginia, McCullough spent three years in the South Pacific. "I spent about a year in Alungapu in the Philippines," he says, "but I was in Manila when FDR died. I was a chief petty officer, and I was in charge of registering people in, and I ran some recreation programs. I remember running into Dom DiMaggio one time in the South Pacific, one of the guys I pitched to on the Red Sox."

Discharged in November 1945, the now twenty-eight-year-old Mc-Cullough returned home. McCullough never gave returning to baseball another thought after having been away from the sport for three years. He had a college education and a wife to support .

"We were living in Atlanta," he says, "and I needed to do something, but I didn't want to start right away. I wanted to sit on the porch and rock a while. But my wife was teaching Sunday school at church, and I went with her one day and met another guy who was teaching there with her. He was the principal of a boy's school in Atlanta, which was set up to handle delinquents, truants, and slow learners. He was looking for a teacher for his school and asked me if I'd be interested. It was set to open on January 3."

McCullough spent the next thirty-four years in the Atlanta school system. "In that first school," he explains, "we sort of coerced them to come to school. We recycled kids, but we saved a lot of them and got them back on track.

"After about seven years, I became principal of a new elementary school for about three or four years, then to a high school and then back to elementary. I was a principal for twenty-three years and retired in 1980, and I'm enjoying it," McCullough says from his home today in Atlanta's suburbs. "My daughter followed my footsteps and also became a teacher."

William Frederick Webb

PHILADELPHIA PHILLIES, 1943

During 1943, Bill Webb got into his only major-league game, with the Philadelphia Phillies. The twenty-nine-year-old pitched only one inning and, in that inning, gave up a hit, a walk, a run, and had an earned run average of 9.00.

It would be easy to dismiss him as one of those people who got an opportunity to play in the major leagues only because the "good" players were away during World War II. But that, like the walk on his record, could be a big mistake.

Bill Webb happened to be an all-around athlete and an excellent pitcher who probably would have reached the majors years earlier, but he steadfastly refused a number of opportunities to play professional baseball (except for one month at the end of the 1941 season). When he played for the Phillies in 1943, he may have been just past his prime.

As a youngster, his family definitely did not encourage him in sports. "There'd never been an athlete in the family, and they didn't think much of sports," he says. "They was all hard-working people. Matter of fact, my daddy told me that if I got hurt playing sports, he'd whup me. I hate to say this, but I was the star baseball and basketball player in high school, and in all the time I played, they never came to see me play one game."

It was the mid-1920s, and the Webbs were living in East Point, Georgia, near Atlanta where Bill was born in 1913. With six children to feed (two others had died earlier), Webb's father was a textile mill worker in a mill town. Most of the boys in town were destined to follow their fathers into the mill, but young Webb's athletic talent eventually allowed him to break that pattern.

Bill Webb, shown here at Mobile, once won a minor-league game with only one pitch.
In another, he hit a man three times in one inning, but not when the player was at bat.

As a youngster, Webb was an athletic dynamo who showed his skill early. "When I was ten years old, I could beat everyone in the town throwing horseshoes," he says, "and I mean all the men—I could beat all the men.

"I was good at all sports," Webb says. "It just seems like if it was a sport, I could do it easy." At Russell High School, as a pitcher, he once led the city in strikeouts. His excellent control, even as a youngster, allowed him to go 44 straight innings without issuing a walk. (Not many major-leaguers can do that today.)

When summer ended, Webb turned to basketball. "I played something all year round," he says, "basketball in the winter and baseball in the summer." In basketball, he earned All-State honors as a six-foot-two center. Later, while playing professional baseball, he continued to play semiprofessional basketball for fifteen years.

After high school graduation, however, earning a living took first priority. "I went to work first for $13.60 a week at a steel plant in Atlanta," he recalls, "but then I moved up to Anderson, South Carolina, to play ball there, and for three years, I was the village plumber. I didn't know anything about plumbing, but I could fix toilets and take care of most repairs. That's where I met my wife," he says.

"I had played ball with a friend in the neighborhood, and he and another guy, Reese Adler, were playing for a mill team over in Manchester, and they were always coming over, trying to get me to join them there, but I wasn't interested. Anyway, this Reese Adler went up to play for a mill in Anderson and the manager there asked him if he knew of any good pitchers and he mentioned me. Now the thing is that Reese had never *seen* me pitch, he had only *heard* about me from my friend from the neighborhood. But when the manager asked him if I was really any good, he said, 'Listen, if he don't work out, then you can fire me.'

"They offered me $25 a week to come to Anderson, which was about double what I was making in Atlanta," Webb says. "I got $12 a week for working in the mill and another $13 for playing ball. It wasn't professional ball, but they had a bunch of good ballplayers there. They had an eight-team mill league, and I played with a number of guys there who played in the majors later—Art Mahaffey, Bob Bowman, Ike Pearson, and a number of others.

"In 1938, we moved back to Atlanta. Atlanta offered me about the same money I was making to come back, and I had my family there, so we went back and I played for the mill there."

Over the next few years, Webb had a number of opportunities to turn professional, but spurned them all. "One time Branch Rickey's brother, Frank Rickey, came down and saw me pitch and wanted to sign me up, but I just wasn't interested in leaving home," he says.

Finally, in 1941, he succumbed for just over a month. "There was a pitcher for Mobile named Abe White who broke his arm near the end of the season in a tight pennant race," Webb says. "He come around and asked if I'd be interested in going down and pitching for Mobile. I said, 'What kind of pay would I get?' and he says, 'Around $200 a month.' I said I'd do it *if* I could get a leave of absence from the mill *and if* Mobile would promise to release me at the end of the season so I could get my job back at the mill.

"My boss at the mill gave me the leave of absence, and White sent me to see the Mobile [Shippers] owner, who signed me. And he gave me his promise that he'd release me at the end of the season.

"I joined Mobile in August, near the end of the season, and won four and lost one. I hit .464 and we made the playoffs. When the season ended, they released me just like they promised and I went back to the mill."

In 1942, with World War II under way, Webb, like most American men his age, received a notice to appear for an army physical exam, but was classified 4-F, physically unqualified for military service. "I had broken my back when I was about twelve, when I was running through the woods and tripped over a tree root," he explains, "although it don't bother me. The doctor who examined me for the army asked if I had ever broken any bones, and I told him I had broken two ribs playing football and broke my ankle playing basketball, and I told him that I once broke my back. He asked me to turn around so he could look at it and of course I'm stark naked and he could see the knot I still got there. He asked if it ever gave me any trouble, and I said, 'No, except if I stay stooped over for a while, it takes me a little while to get up.' He says, 'You're not physically qualified for military service. 4-F.' So I stayed at the mill."

That year, Webb finally realized that professional baseball could offer him some advantages. "I felt pro ball was easier to play—at least based on what I did at Mobile—and for playing in about one game a week, I could earn as much as I did working sixty hours a week in the mill.

"So I wrote to all the ball teams, telling them about what I did at Mobile and telling them to check my record with the people at Mobile and, if they was interested, to let me know. Well, about five of them wrote back, but only Philadelphia [Phillies] would come up with any money. They offered me a $1,500 bonus and $500 a month, which was like a fortune to me at that time."

Webb was invited to the Phillies' training camp in 1943 and pitched exceptionally well during the exhibition season. He threw three scoreless innings against the Chicago White Sox, three more against the Philadelphia Athletics, and another three against Mitchell Field, a service team outside of New York City. "[Phillie manager] Bucky Harris kept telling me I was doing good, and I knew I was, 'cause nobody could score off me."

The season started with Webb on the active roster. "But from then on, I never even threw batting practice," he says. "All I did was shag flies in the outfield. Looking back, though, I can understand. He [Harris] had about seven pitchers with major-league experience, and he had to pitch them. But I sure wish he would have let me pitch."

The problem was that the Phillies couldn't hit. Third baseman Pinky May led the team with a .282 average, and he was in the twilight of his career. In fact, it was to be his last active season in the majors.

Bill Webb finally got his chance to pitch on May 15, 1943. The first-place St. Louis Cardinals were playing the third-place Philadelphia Phillies in Shibe Park in Philadelphia. The Cards would go on to win the pennant that year—their second straight—by 18 games over Cincinnati, their nearest rival, while the Phillies would fade and finish seventh.

Though losing such stars as Enos Slaughter, Terry Moore, and Johnny Beazley to the military, the Cardinals were not hurt as badly as some of the other teams. Stan "The Man" Musial was still with the team (he claimed many dependents and was not drafted until early 1945), and that year he led the league with a batting average of .357. Max Lanier and the Cooper brothers also remained. Lanier won 15 games that year, and Mort Cooper tied for the league lead with 21 wins. Walker Cooper chipped in with a .318 batting average.

On this particular afternoon, St. Louis was leading 5–2 in the ninth inning, with the Cardinals' Cooper outpitching Charlie Fuchs of the Phils.

In the top of the ninth, Bucky Harris brought Webb in to pitch. Although Webb was then twenty-nine years old ("I told them I was twenty-seven"), it was his first game ever in the major leagues. "I felt good going in," he says. "I always felt like I could win."

The first batter he faced was the Cardinal pitcher, Mort Cooper, the league's most valuable player the previous year. Cooper was known as a good hitting pitcher. "I figured that with me being a rookie and all, and him never seeing me before, that he'd take the first pitch, so I figured I could get ahead of him by firing it right down the middle," Webb remembers.

So Webb wound up and threw the first real pitch of his major-league career right down the middle of the plate. Cooper swung and the ball landed in the left field seats for a home run. Cooper trotted around the bases, and Webb got a new ball from Mickey Livingston, his catcher. "Nobody said anything," says Webb, "but I was embarrassed for just laying it in there like that." It was one of only six home runs that Cooper hit during his eleven years in the majors.

The next three Cardinal batters coming up were second baseman Lou Klein; centerfielder Harry "The Hat" Walker; and finally, rightfielder Stan "The Man" Musial, who not only led the league in hitting that year but also would be named its most valuable player. "I knew I was in the big leagues when I saw those good hitters," Webb says, "but I knew I was good, too. I didn't give them anything good to hit, and I got them all out on groundouts, one, two, three."

Klein grounded to Babe Dahlgren, who was playing shortstop; Walker grounded to second baseman Danny Murtaugh, Charley Marshall's minor-league roommate (see Chapter 7); and Musial bounced out to first baseman Jimmy Wasdell. That was it.

The box score of that game indicates that Webb also walked a man that inning. But Webb denies it. "I did not walk anybody," he says emphatically. The box score shows that Klein, Walker, and Musial batted directly behind Cooper in the Cardinals' lineup that day, which would indicate Webb is correct.

After his stint on the mound, Webb reports, "I went back into the dugout, still embarrassed by the home run, and Bucky Harris says, 'Son, you done all you could. He should have been taking that pitch.' I said, 'That's what I thought, too, Skip. I thought he'd at least take one pitch.' " And so the Phils lost, 6–2, not 5–2.

Webb got one more chance to pitch later that year. "On June 6, we had an off-day, and we went down to Baltimore to play Camp Holibird, another service team. On the way down, Bucky told me I was gonna pitch, and I was glad about getting another chance."

Webb again pitched well, giving up only two runs in seven innings. The Phils won the game, 11–2. "My roommate, Andy Lapihuska, finished up, and we both felt real good after the game. I thought, 'Now maybe I'll get to pitch some more.' "

It didn't happen. The next morning, he was gone from the Phillies, and although he didn't realize it then, his days as a major leaguer were over.

"That next morning we were packing to go back home," Webb remembers, "and the phone rang. It was the Phillies' general manager, I don't remember his name, and he said, 'Don't catch the train. Come up and see me in my room.' Well, I knew right away something bad was up, and I felt real low. When I got there, he told me that I had been traded to the Brooklyn Dodgers for [pitcher] Newt Kimball." Kimball went on to lose six while winning only one for the Phils in what turned out to be his last major-league season.

"I was really disappointed," Webb recalls, "'cause I just knew I could win if they let me pitch."

Webb was told to remain in Baltimore and wait for the Dodgers to call him to let him know where to report. He waited five days before hearing from the Montreal Royals, the Dodger farm team in the Triple-A International League. He was told to report to the Royals, who were then playing in Rochester. With the Royals that year, he compiled a 7–4 record.

"I set some sort of record when I was with Montreal," he laughs. "One time I hit a man three times in one inning, but never hit him when he was at bat. I don't remember his name," Webb goes on, "but he was a left-handed batter with Rochester. He bunted down the first base line and I went over to field it and the ball had gotten wet from the dew on the grass and, when I tried to throw him out at first I hit him in the back.

"Well, I see him leading off first and I throw over there trying to pick him off and again I hit him in the back. The ball bounces off him and he goes to second. This time he takes a good lead off second, so I turn and throw to second, trying for another pickoff, and hit him again. The ball goes into center this time, and he picks himself up and runs on to third. Well, you may not believe this, but it's true. I walk off the mound and go over to him at third, and I said, 'If you move off this base, I'm gonna hit you again.' And he says, 'You go to hell! I got this far by myself, and if they can't knock me in from here, I'm gonna stay right here!' "

Soon thereafter, the Montreal general manager called Webb in. "I remember *his* name; it was McDonald," Webb recalls. "He says, 'Bill, you don't have to do this if you don't want, but I'd like you to go down to New Orleans [another Dodger farm team]. They're in a pennant race right now and we're not going anywhere and they could use you.' I said I didn't mind as long as they paid me the same money.

"He said that if New Orleans paid me less, then the Royals would make up the difference, so I wouldn't lose anything. So I went to New Orleans, and instead of being a starter, they made me a relief pitcher. I won 2 and had 16 saves, and we won the pennant and got into the playoffs. In the playoffs, I remember striking out the cleanup batter for the other team with the bases loaded and us leading 2–1. They also had what they called the Shaughnessy Playoffs in those days, and we beat Pensacola four straight and I won the fourth and final game."

After the excitement of playing for Philadelphia, Montreal, and New Orleans during the 1943 season, Webb played for nine more years with such teams as Minneapolis, Minnesota; St. Paul, Minnesota; Carrollton, Georgia; Lakeland, Florida; Gadsden, Alabama; Idaho Falls, Idaho; and Baxley-Hazelhurst, Georgia, before retiring from the game at age thirty-eight.

He remembers one game in 1946 when he became the winning pitcher for the Minneapolis Millers after making only one pitch. With the game tied in the top of the ninth, Kansas City, the opposing team, had men on first and third with two out. The runner on first tried to steal second base on Webb's pitch. "It was a strike," Webb remembers. The catcher unleashed a throw toward second, and Webb speared it in midflight, whirled around, and picked off the runner who had strayed from third and was heading home.

When Minneapolis scored in the bottom of the ninth, "I was the winning pitcher and only threw one pitch."

In another game that season against Columbus, Webb came up to bat five times against five different pitchers and got four hits and a walk. "I don't know of anyone else who's ever done that," he says.

The next year, with the Carrollton Hornets in the Georgia-Alabama League, he pitched 26 complete games in 27 starts, compiling a 22–5 record and at one point winning 14 in a row. His winning percentage of

.815 that year led the league, and he also batted .406. The league's book of highlights that year called Webb "a one-man team."

Today, Bill Webb has difficulty accepting player salaries. "Nobody's worth a million dollars," he says, "and they don't even play half the time. If they have a hangnail, they won't even play. I've seen people play with broken fingers and everything else because they knew if somebody got in their place, they might not get back in."

Webb knows what it means to play hurt. In 1949, on the night before his basketball team was to play a championship game, Webb broke his foot. "I went down [the next day] and had my leg put in a cast from my toes to my knee." At his coach's insistence, he still suited up for the championship game, even though he would sit on the bench. With the opposing team leading by one point and only thirty seconds left in the game, the coach asked Webb to go in. "'What for?' I said. 'I can't move.' The coach says, 'Just go out and stand there, and if we get the ball to you, shoot it.' Well, I went out there and, as luck would have it, they passed the ball to me and I threw it through the hoop and we won 37–36. I bet I'm the only guy who, at age thirty-five, ever won a basketball game with a broken leg."

After leaving baseball, Webb joined the Atlanta Fire Department and served there for twenty-seven years, retiring with the rank of captain. He and his wife of almost sixty years, Martha, now live in nearby Powder Springs.

From 1954 through 1966, Webb also scouted high schools and colleges for the San Francisco Giants and returned to his old love—horseshoes. According to Webb, he won five single and twelve double state championships during those years. Until recently, he also was an avid bowler and golfer. Today he's more involved with camping and fishing.

Of his baseball career, Webb says, "I don't regret playing for so long in the mill leagues and not turning pro earlier. That's how I met my wife, and that resulted in two children, five grandchildren, and eight great-grandchildren—a lot of Christmas presents. Listen, I came from a mill town, and by being a ballplayer, I got to see and play in places I never even dreamed I would see. I played in Cuba, Puerto Rico, Venezuela, and most of the United States. I didn't make much money at it, but I got a liberal travel education."

LeRoy Everett "Roy" Talcott Jr.

BOSTON BRAVES, 1943

From 1942 through 1945, as the majority of American athletes marched off to World War II, the pool of skilled, able-bodied manpower left available to play professional baseball shrank sharply. This shortage of manpower not only led to the elimination of a number of minor leagues but also caused major-league teams to resort to using players such as Pete Gray, an outfielder with one arm, and Bert Shepard, a pitcher with one leg (see Chapter 15).

It also gave LeRoy Talcott, a twenty-three-year-old medical student with a torn rotator cuff, a chance to pitch in the major leagues.

Talcott, the younger of two sons, was born in Brookline, Massachusetts, in 1920. When he was nine, his family moved to New York City, where the young Talcott attended George Washington High School for three years before his family moved to West Hartford, Connecticut.

"I didn't play much baseball at George Washington," Talcott recalls. "It was an urban school, so most of our playing was done on the sandlots and in Van Cortland Park. I caught for three years and played some shortstop, but then one day we needed a pitcher and I pitched. I did well, and from then on, I was a pitcher. But because I was a good hitter, I also played in the field when I wasn't pitching."

When he arrived in West Hartford in 1938, the teenager attended William Hall High School for his senior year and was immediately installed as the team's top pitcher. "For some reason," he says, "the coach and I clicked immediately, and we had a good year and got into the state championships. I don't recall how it worked then; I know today they have district and regional playoffs before the state tournament, but I remember we lost in the semis.

"I had decided by then that I wanted to study medicine and become a doctor," Talcott continues. "You see, I had a grandfather who owned an inn in Bermuda, and I used to spend my summers there with him. We used to fish together and were pretty close. Well, that year, the year we moved to West Hartford, he came to visit us on vacation and had a stroke and died in three days. It hit me very hard. I know now that nothing could have been done to save him, but it made me believe then that I should become a doctor and help see if that sort of thing might be prevented.

"When I graduated from high school, I applied to attend Princeton, but they told me I was one credit short, and a school like Princeton wasn't going to make any exception to its admissions policy, even for one credit. So I went to prep school that year, Pawling Prep, in Pawling, New York, to make up the credit and then entered Princeton in 1939. I signed up for pre-med. In those days, you had to say right away what you wanted to study, not like today where you have a couple of years to make up your mind."

During his years at Princeton, Talcott was an all-around student-athlete. "I learned to fly while at college," he says, "and joined the ROTC in the artillery. I pitched and played in the outfield on the baseball team, and in my sophomore year, my record was something like 17 and 2." Both the Boston Braves and the Brooklyn Dodgers showed interest.

"Now in those days," Talcott says, "we used to begin playing in March or April, and in the Northeast, the weather was cold. Very early in my junior year, I was playing center field and I tried to throw a guy out going from first to third and hurt my shoulder. I wasn't sure then what it was, but I have no doubt now it was the rotator cuff. After that, I just couldn't pitch as I could before. I couldn't throw as hard, and the longer I'd go, the weaker I'd get. I got worn out after just a few innings. In those days, nothing could be done about it. Now, of course, all kinds of stuff can be used to provide remedies."

The Dodgers lost interest, but not the Braves. "Boston kept coming around almost every month or so after my sophomore year," Talcott says. "They knew my arm was bad, but I hit well enough, so they thought if I couldn't make it as a pitcher, maybe I could make it as a fielder. In my senior year at Princeton, I played mainly in the infield and outfield, and I won the Ivy League batting championship."

After graduating from Princeton in the spring of 1943, Talcott applied to medical school at Duke University via the navy's V-12 program. That summer, before going off to become a doctor, LeRoy Talcott got his chance to be a major-league pitcher.

"I really don't remember what happened," he says. "I couldn't pitch. I remember I threw for them [the Braves] before I signed, and one of the scouts who knew me said, 'What the hell happened to your arm?' My father handled most of the negotiations with Bob Quinn, and I think the deal was that they were going to send me to their farm team in Hartford [in the Class-A Eastern League] to see if I could pitch and, if not, maybe play the infield.

"I was told I would get my major-league salary even though I would be playing at Hartford. I don't remember how much I got, maybe $500 a week. The key was that it was a 'major-league' salary. There may have been a bonus. It may have been $4,000, but it had something to do with the first month or something."

That "first month" may well have had something to do with Talcott's opportunity to play in a major-league game. Instead of shipping him to Hartford immediately after they signed him, the Braves kept Talcott with them for about thirty days.

"I remember going on the road with them to Philadelphia, New York, St. Louis, and Chicago," he says, "and the game I played in was at home at Braves Field in Boston, so I was with them for a while. My roommate was [catcher] Phil Masi. The coach [manager] was Casey Stengel, and he was a tough guy. He had a broken leg or a cracked hip or something, and he was miserable. He was in a big, massive cast, which was almost like a body cast; it went up around his waist. He couldn't sit, he couldn't walk, he felt just awful. I think it was a femoral [thigh bone] fracture."

On June 24, 1943, in the middle of World War II, the sore-armed medical student appeared in his only major-league game. Talcott's memory of the experience is extremely clouded. He thought the game was against the Chicago Cubs, but it was actually against the Philadelphia Phillies.

Neither team was much good that season. Boston finished in sixth place, 36½ games behind the Cardinals, who ran away from the rest of the league. Philadelphia was seventh, 41 games out. That afternoon only 1,585 fans had come to the ballpark. They saw the Braves jump off to a 1–0 lead in the bottom of the first against Philadelphia's thirty-six-year-old pitcher, Si Johnson. But the Braves rookie starter, Dave "Porky" Odom (he carried 220 pounds on his six-foot frame) could not hold the lead for long. In the top of the third, the Phillies teed off on him. Talcott recalls warming up in the bullpen with catcher Clyde Kluttz. "I wasn't feeling well," he says. "I wasn't nervous or anything; it was just that I knew I had no pop in my arm. I was not in command physically."

The Phils scored five runs off Odom that inning and were threatening to do more damage. After giving up six hits and three walks in only two and two-thirds innings, Odom was removed, and the right-handed Talcott was called into the game. "It wasn't Stengel who was at the mound when I came in," Talcott says. "It was one of his coaches, but I don't remember who. He [Stengel] just couldn't move in that cast. Masi was there, and he said something like 'Just take it easy, kid.' "

There were two outs and a man on first, according to Talcott. "I don't remember who the runner was," he says, "but I picked him off, but we lost him in a rundown and he ended up on second.

"I think I gave up a scratch hit in the infield," he says, "and then got the next batter on a grounder to third to get out of the inning without a[nother] run scoring. When I got back to the dugout, the guys said, 'Hey, kid, great job.' They were very nice."

Today he remembers neither the name of the runner he picked off first nor the batters he faced. The Phils' lineup that afternoon included second baseman Danny Murtaugh leading off, followed by the slugging right fielder Ron Northy, center fielder Buster Adams, first baseman Jimmy Wasdell, third baseman Babe Dahlgren, left fielder Coaker Triplett, a truly short (five-foot, eight-and-a-half-inch) rookie shortstop named Charlie Brewster, catcher Mickey Livingston, and the pitcher, Johnson.

In the bottom of the third, the Braves made two runs to bring the score to 5–3. Talcott went out to start the top of the fourth.

"I think I got the first guy out," he says. "It may have been a come-backer to me. Either that or he grounded to third and the comebacker was in the previous inning. I know they only hit easy grounders. [Talcott was credited with an assist during his time in the game.] But I walked the next two guys, both on three-and-two pitches, and they removed me."

Again it was a coach who came to the mound, not Stengel. "I don't remember what he said, but it was something nice. Again, something like, 'Hey kid, nice job.' But the next pitcher allowed a home run and the two walks were [runs] charged to me. That's why my earned run average was so high (27.00)."

The pitcher who relieved Talcott was thirty-eight-year-old Allyn "Fish Hook" Stout, who had last pitched in the major leagues eight years earlier. After Stout came in, Philadelphia scored two runs, not three (which would have been the case if a home run had followed the two walks). Nobody on the Phils had a homer that day. Most likely the hit off Stout was a double, since the Phillies hit five of them that day.

Talcott is correct in remembering Stout got "clobbered." After getting two outs to retire the side in the top of the fourth (after the two runners Talcott had walked had scored), Stout allowed two more runs of his own in the top of the fifth and got nobody out in the sixth, when Philadelphia scored three more times. Altogether, Stout gave up six hits and two walks in one and two-thirds innings before rookie first baseman Kerby Farrell came in to pitch, holding off the Phillies the rest of the way. The game concluded with Philadelphia winning 12–5, ending a three-game losing streak. The Boston pitchers who appeared in the game included three rookies—Odom, Talcott, and Farrell, who wasn't primarily a pitcher—and the over-the-hill Stout, who never pitched in the majors again after that year. Such was the state of major-league manpower in 1943.

Because of the lack of manpower and talent, four members of the Braves' pitching staff—Jim Tobin, Nate Andrews, Al Javery, and John

"Red" Barrett—each had to pitch more than 250 innings that year, with Javery capturing the league lead with 303.

"I wasn't very close to anyone on the team," Talcott notes. "I guess I was closer to Barrett than most of the others. He could have pitched a million innings a year because he never threw the ball more than sixty-five miles an hour. He'd just toss it up there, but he was tricky and had pretty good control and could put it where he wanted it. I thought everybody on the team was very nice."

In early August, the Braves shipped Talcott to the minors to see whether his arm would be strong enough to pitch. "I was sent down to Hartford, where Del Bissonette, a former Brooklyn Dodger first baseman, was the manager—hopefully to rehabilitate, but it never worked," Talcott says. "At that time, Warren Spahn and I were considered 'the future' of Boston's pitching staff." Spahn had pitched for Hartford the previous year but was in the military service in 1943.

"The first game I started at Hartford, they made five errors in the first inning," Talcott laughs. "I figured that was an omen."

It was quickly determined that his arm was not going to allow him to pitch. "I played third base and pinch hit," Talcott says of his days at Hartford. Eastern League records indicate he got into 10 games and had a single and a double in nine official trips to the plate (plus five bases on balls). "I don't remember the pitcher, but I hit that double off the right center field fence," he says proudly. Talcott also believes he played a few games at the end of the season at Pawtucket in the New England League.

When the season ended, Talcott entered Duke Medical School in Durham, North Carolina. In his second year at Duke, he married Josephine Sorota, a girl he had known for about three years, and their daughter was born a year later.

Talcott also played ball at Duke, even though he had already played as a professional. "That was because of the war, I guess," he explains. "I did quite well. I remember one time around 1944 or '45 we played an exhibition game with one of the service teams in Norfolk against Johnny Vander Meer. My coach asked me if I could give him a few innings on the mound, and I said, 'Sure, I can give you a few innings.'

"Well, I went five innings, and I got progressively worse each inning as my arm tired, but I had an extremely good [pickoff] move to first, and I remember in five innings I picked off four guys.

"To supplement my income while I was at Duke, I also played some minor-league and semipro ball with the Durham Bulls at third base," Talcott says. "It was fun and I enjoyed it. Baseball's not like that today. I don't like what I see now."

After graduating from medical school in 1947, the newly minted *Dr.* Talcott spent the next few years as an intern in residency at Columbia Presbyterian Hospital in New York City, but developed a bad sinus problem, which hampered his ability to breathe. "I was getting $25 a month and room and board, and working eighty hours a week," he says, "and after a while I was *in* the hospital as much as I was *working* in it." He took a six-month leave of absence and moved to Miami where the climate was more helpful to his condition. Before completing his residency there, Talcott also served as ship's surgeon on cruise ships between Miami and Argentina.

In 1956, after serving in the naval reserves during the Korean War, he began his private practice of medicine and general surgery in Miami, a practice that continues today, although on a limited basis.

In 1963, Talcott's wife perished when a fire destroyed their home in Miami. He was remarried in 1972 to Myrtis Ascar, to whom he was introduced at a party. They have a daughter and a son. Talcott also has a teenage granddaughter as a result of his first marriage. "She's a pretty good softball player," he says enthusiastically.

"Today I'm semiretired," Talcott reports. "I only go in a couple of days a week, and I only do the easy operations," he laughs. "I guess I've lost some of my interest in baseball, but I enjoyed my time in the game. I just wish when I pitched in Boston and Hartford that I had been able to pitch like I had before I hurt my shoulder."

Talcott is one who thinks today's ballplayers don't measure up to those of his era. "I see these hitters today batting .300 with helmets. Let me tell you," he says, "Ted Williams is a friend of mine and was a former patient. He hit .404 [.406 in 1941] with a soft hat. I remember one time at Durham, I got hit by a pitched ball I absolutely didn't see and was in the hospital two months. If some of today's players had to go up there with a soft hat against pitchers who didn't hesitate to throw inside, they'd be *non-baseball players!*"

Christopher Francis "Bud" Haughey III

BROOKLYN DODGERS, 1943

Chris Haughey was an absolute pitching sensation, perhaps the best teenage pitcher in the United States at the time. One major-league team wanted to sign him when he was only sixteen years old, and half of all of the major-league teams made offers to him in the following year. (Brooklyn's general manager, Branch Rickey, who was never known for his largesse, gave the right-handed youngster a sizable bonus to sign a *no-cut* major-league contract when he was just seventeen.)

On his eighteenth birthday, Haughey pitched, and pitched fairly well, in a major-league game. But by the time he was twenty-four, having played in only one big-league game, Haughey was finished with professional baseball, his career killed by World War II.

Growing up in the Astoria section of Queens, New York, where he was born in 1925, the third child and only son of an operating engineer, Haughey attended St. Agnes High School, a private Catholic institution in nearby College Point on Long Island. "St. Agnes had about 400 students, total," Haughey says, "both boys and girls. They had twenty-five baseball uniforms, and when they had baseball tryouts, only twenty-five kids showed up, so that was the team.

"We played both Catholic and public high schools in the area. In the two years I pitched, I had two losses," he says, "and was something like 12 and 1 in my senior year. My first game that year was a no-hitter. I could throw in the upper nineties, and I could throw it all day," he says. "And my fastball moved. It jumped up and in to a right-handed batter and up and away from a left-hander. When I sliced it, and threw off-center, it would act like a screwball, going down and away from a left-hander."

72

As a teenager, Chris Haughey pitched for the Brooklyn Dodgers in a game he says Leo Durocher was not managing to win.

While in high school, Haughey also played in the Catholic Youth Organization (CYO) Leagues in the area. "In my junior year in high school [1942], I played for the Bayside Rangers in the junior league, which was up to sixteen years of age. I won every game I pitched and was batting cleanup in the lineup and hit .526.

"That year we won our division, and the finals for the New York City Federation championship were played in Yankee Stadium. I pitched six hitless and runless innings and had scored the only run 'til that time when the assistant manager let our other pitcher finish the game. We lost 2–1.

"Two weeks later, I pitched for the unlimited division in the second game and went 13 innings. A scout for the Pirates, his name was King Lear, just like in Shakespeare, wanted to sign me at age sixteen. But my mother said, 'No, he's not going to sign anything. He's only sixteen and he's going to college.' "

At that time, the Pirates were not the only team interested in Haughey. Haughey was considered a bona fide prospect, war or no war. "When I was sixteen years old, I would pitch batting practice for the Yankees, Senators, Red Sox, Athletics, Dodgers, Pittsburgh, Cincinnati, and the Braves," he said. "The out-of-town teams would invite me to come to Yankee Stadium or Ebbets Field when they came to town." Eventually, all these teams—half of the major-league teams then in existence—made him offers.

"The following year, at seventeen, in CYO ball, I threw three no-hitters in a row," Haughey says. "I struck out 56 of 69 batters in 23 innings. Then I threw two subsequent one-hitters, so in five games, I had given up only two hits. I averaged something like 22 or 23 strikeouts a game. And during this time, I was also winning in high school against some of the best teams in the city."

When Haughey graduated from St. Agnes in 1943, the New York Yankees made the best financial offer, but they wanted him to play for Newark, their Triple-A farm team in the International League. "But I didn't want to play Triple-A ball," Haughey says, "so I told them I wanted to go to college instead. Paul Kritchell, their head scout, asked me what college I wanted to go to, and I said, 'Fordham University.' So he introduced me to the athletic director at Fordham, and he offered me an athletic scholarship to play baseball and basketball." Haughey had played some basketball in high school, but his accomplishments on the court were in no way comparable to what he did on the diamond.

"Because the war was going on, Fordham was running continuous sessions," Haughey says, "so I was able to start there in June, right after my high school graduation. But I only stayed there two or three months because I decided to play professional ball."

It was then that Dodgers general manager Rickey signed Haughey to a no-cut major-league contract. "I don't remember the bonus I got,"

Haughey says. "I think it was around $7- to $10,000. The salary was $7,500, I think. It was a standard contract."

Haughey joined the Dodgers in September and stayed with them for the remainder of the season, but did not get a chance to pitch. "The thing was," Haughey remembers, "the Dodgers were fighting for third-place money that year and [manager Leo] Durocher didn't want to use rookies."

But on the last day of the season, Oct. 3, 1943—Haughey's eighteenth birthday—the time came.

That day the Dodgers were playing the second-place Reds at Cincinnati's Crosley Field. "I never expected to play," Haughey says. "The race still hadn't been settled, and I remember the Phillies had to win the game they were playing to ensure the Dodgers of third place. If the Phillies won, it wouldn't matter what the Dodgers did in Cincinnati. But if the Phillies lost—I think they were playing the Pirates—then the Dodgers would have to win this game."

The Pirates, who were still battling the Dodgers for third place, were playing a doubleheader against the seventh-place Phils. To finish third, the Pirates would need to win both games while the Dodgers lost.

Reds manager Bill McKechnie was not going to make it easy for the Dodgers. He started his workhorse, Johnny Vander Meer, whose earned run average was 2.87. Durocher countered with his ace, Whitlow Wyatt, who had an even better 2.49 ERA. At the end of the first inning, it was 0–0.

"During that first inning," Haughey recalls, "we got a wire or something that the Phillies had won their [first] game, meaning the Dodgers would finish third no matter what, and so our game didn't mean anything. Durocher then told me to start the second inning.

"I had mixed emotions. I was excited and very nervous," Haughey says. "I was seventeen [actually eighteen that day], and this was my first game in organized ball. To be perfectly honest, when I first took the mound against the Reds, I was nervous, but once I threw the warm-up pitches and once they put a batter up there, it just felt like any other game. I just had the confidence that I could throw hard and challenge anyone."

Haughey does not remember much about the Cincinnati hitters he faced. "It didn't make any difference," he says. "They were all nonentities to me. In my first inning, I threw five pitches to register the first three outs. I faced Mike McCormick, Gee Walker, and Dain Clay. They all popped up. I threw a real live fastball in the upper 90-miles-an-hour register, and I got a lot of movement on the ball. I threw a very heavy ball, and I was wild enough to be effective. They wouldn't dig in at the plate against me," Haughey says.

The box score of the game indicates that the batters Haughey faced that inning were McCormick, Walker, and Steve Mesner. (Clay did not play until later when he replaced center fielder Walker.)

The record also indicates that Haughey finished the game, going seven full innings. (The Reds, ahead 6–1, did not bat in the bottom of ninth.) Haughey gave up only five hits, three earned runs, and three others which were unearned. But he also gave up 10 walks. He was credited with an assist, debited with an error, and at bat, was hitless in three times up.

When asked about the specifics of his performance that day, Haughey remembers his assist came on a sacrifice bunt and the error on a throw over the first baseman's head. As for the 10 walks, Haughey says, "The difference in umpiring from sandlot ball to the majors is a fine line. In sandlot ball, you'd get the strike call. In the majors, it had to be perfect. I wasn't really wild. I was just missing, maybe a half an inch or so.

"We were ahead 1–0 when Howie Shultz drove in a run in the second," Haughey says. "I gave up a bunt single to Vander Meer in the third and a single to Ray Mueller in the fifth. I had a two-hit game 'til the seventh [eighth] inning. Then I gave up a double to Mesner, the only extra base hit of the game."

According to the box score, the Reds scored twice in the bottom of the fifth to lead 2–0. The Dodgers then scored once in the top of the seventh and were behind 2–1. In the bottom of the eighth, the Reds broke the game open, scoring four more times on two singles, Mesner's double, two walks, and an error.

"That's when they scored the *unearned* runs," Haughey says. "[Catcher Bobby] Bragan tried a pickoff at third base and threw the ball over [Gil] Hodges's head into left field and two runs came in. By the way, that was the only game that Gil Hodges ever played third base in the major leagues."

The game was Hodges's major-league debut as well as Haughey's. Hodges and Haughey roomed together on the road that year, along with catcher Mickey Owen. "Hodges was only about a year older than me," Haughey recalls, "and we got very close. As a matter of fact, my number was 14, and, when I left, he took it and wore it the rest of his career." Hodges that day went 0 for 2 at bat, but walked once and stole a base. He also made two of the Dodgers' four errors, with Haughey and Bragan making the others.

In his own three times at bat against Vander Meer, Haughey flied to left fielder Eric Tipton twice and struck out. "I hit him [Vander Meer] pretty good," he says, "but not enough to do any damage. He was throwing hard, and to face him was quite a revelation," Haughey says. "I mean, I was just a kid, and he had pitched two no-hitters. I was just gratified to meet the ball. He threw a real live fastball, a good change, and had good direction. He was a professional. It was a real experience to bat against him."

On the bench between innings, the manager and the coaches were supportive. "Most of the team let me alone pretty well during the game," Haughey says. "I remember John Corriden and [Chuck] Dressen, the coaches, kept saying things like, 'Hey, they're not doing nothing with you. Just throw strikes and let the other guys get the outs for you. Just keep throwing strikes.' Durocher had a big mouth, but he was always good to me. He called me 'son.' "

But Durocher was also playing games that day. "McKecknie was going for a double-play record that year," Haughey says, "and Durocher, who had no particular love for McKechnie, did not want McKechnie to break the DP record, so every man we would get on base would try to steal second, so they wouldn't get the record. Resultantly, we had no chance to win the game."

The Dodgers got nine men on base that day, four on hits (including two doubles by Shultz), four on walks (including Hodges's), and one on an error. It wasn't until two runners were erased in double plays, bringing the Reds close to the record, that Durocher had his team run. Although only two Dodgers were thrown out stealing, Durocher successfully foiled McKechnie. The Reds recorded 193 double plays that year, barely missing the National League record of 194 originally set by Cincinnati in 1928 and tied by the same team in 1931.

How did it feel to pitch in the major leagues for the first time on his eighteenth birthday? "When it was over," Haughey says, "I couldn't believe it. I had gone all the way. I had what I thought was a great game. I thought, 'How lucky can one guy get?' "

Asked to recall specific teammates on that Dodger team, Haughey started with his other roommate, Mickey Owen. "He was awfully nice. He was older and treated me like a son. He tried to guide me and tell me what to do and what to expect. A very nice man. Another awfully nice man was [coach] Johnny Corriden. He was just a *nice* person.

"Dolph Camili was a real pro, a hard worker. He was all business. And if you asked, he would help you a lot. Frenchy Bordagaray was a lot of fun. He loved people and he played to the crowd. Billy Herman was an excellent fielder, excellent. There was no one better at second base. He didn't have a great arm, but he was able to 'cheat' and get in good position. He would watch the signs, so he knew what was going to be thrown and get in the right location. He was a lot like Durocher in the way he played his position.

"Paul Waner was near the end of his career then," Haughey continues. "We used to call him 'Shutter Eyes.' He used to use a bat where the width at the handle was almost as much as the rest of the bat, and he would just punch the ball over the infield. He was such a good hitter because all he would try to do was meet the ball.

"[Joe] Ducky Medwick was also near the end of his career. I classify him as a mechanic. Arky Vaughn was another one who was at the very last stages of his career, but he was a good competitor. No matter what, he would hang in there. He would never give up.

"Luis Olmo was from Venezuela, a hustler, a good ballplayer. Durocher used to do a number on him all the time. Olmo would be in the clubhouse, playing cards, and Durocher would come along and take the other guy's hand and play it against Olmo. Durocher loved to play cards and was an excellent gambler. Olmo could never win."

In 1946, when major-league players asked for—and were refused—minimum annual salaries of $5,000, shorter spring schedules, and a limit on salary cuts, Olmo was the first Dodger to jump to the newly formed Mexican League. (That's why Haughey's 1943 salary of $7,500, as he indicated, was not "standard.")

As for Dodger pitchers that year, Haughey remembers, "Whitlow Wyatt was a real gentleman. His legs were in terrible shape. I'll tell you, if the other teams knew how bad his legs were, they would have bunted him silly. He used to have both legs taped up to the groin. But he was a real competitor, and he gave me a lot of insight into the game. He was one of my favorites.

"Kirby Higbe was our 'Southern belle.' He traveled first-class. He had more luggage than anyone on the team. He loved to dress. He had more clothes than anyone. Everyone else had suitcases. He had trunks. We used to sometimes call him 'Skinhead' because he didn't have much hair, and we were always poking fun at him.

"Bobo Newsom pitched for the Dodgers earlier that year, before I got there, but I knew him when he was with the Senators, when I used to pitch batting practice for them. He was a strange individual, a vindictive kind of person. He was always chewing tobacco, and if the fans behind the dugout were getting on him, he would let loose a stream of tobacco juice over the dugout roof. He had utter disdain for people, for the fans, and would use terminology that wasn't exactly suitable. He was just hard to get along with. And he didn't care what the catcher called for. He threw whatever pitch he wanted to. That's why he was traded so much. He might get four or five wins in a row but couldn't get along with the manager, so they traded him."

After the game—and the 1943 season—had ended, Haughey returned home for the winter. "It's funny, but I got my 1944 contract in the same mail that brought my draft notice," he recalls. "I called Mr. Rickey to tell him about being drafted, and he said, 'Don't do anything. Let's just see what happens. Maybe we can do something to see if you might be able to play ball in the service.' Or something like that. I don't recall exactly what happened, but I remember something about a request for transfer to Fort Benning, Georgia."

As it turned out, when Haughey entered the army in February 1944, he was assigned to Fort Riley, Kansas. "We had a really formidable major-league team there," he says. "We must have had seven or eight major-league pitchers on that team. There was Rex Barney, who was also a teammate of mine in Brooklyn; Ken Trinkle of the Giants; John Lanning of Pittsburgh; Alpha Brazle and Murry Dickson of the Cardinals; and me. Our catcher was [Joe] Garagiola, and we had guys like Pete Reiser and

Harry 'The Hat' Walker. There were also two or three Double-A and Triple-A players.

"Well, the team got so much publicity and notoriety that Washington finally had to break up the team and send guys overseas. I stayed at Fort Riley and was a noncom and spent the rest of my time in the basic training of recruits. I was discharged in April of '46."

Haughey reported back to the Dodgers. "I was wilder than a March hare," he says, "especially not having pitched for almost three years. Then [Eddie] Stanky was with the club, and it was difficult. See, I hit him one time in batting practice and he didn't like it. Now, with my contract, I was entitled to spend a full year in the majors, but the Dodgers asked me if I would mind going to the minors so I could play regularly. I said, 'Sure,' because I knew I needed playing time. So they sent me to Cambridge, Maryland, to relocate the plate, and then to Asheville, North Carolina, in the Tri-State League, and then to Zanesville, Ohio, in the Iowa State League."

At Asheville that year, Haughey pitched only four innings in three games and ended with an 0–2 record. In those four innings, he gave up five hits and five walks, hit two batters, and threw two wild pitches. Of the fifteen outs he recorded, five were strikeouts.

Later that year at Zanesville, Haughey improved. "I remember we played an exhibition game against Rochester [a St. Louis Cardinal farm team] and I struck out 13 or 14 and I won 1–0. The Cardinals then bought my contract from the Dodgers," he recalls.

In 1947, the Cardinals assigned the twenty-one-year-old Haughey to St. Joseph, Missouri, in the Western Association. "I went 17 and 4 there and pitched a no-hitter in the playoffs," he says. (The records say it was actually 15–7 with eight shutouts and a 2.64 earned run average.)

In 1948, he moved up to Columbus in the Triple-A American Association, but didn't stay there long. "I was sent to Omaha, where I was 3 and 0, but then one night in Denver, I hurt my arm throwing in a game that was called because of snow. That just about ended my season."

Haughey spent the rest of 1948 at Allentown, where his record was an undistinguished 4–7. In 1949, he played in the Colonial League at Bridgeport, Connecticut, and later at Liverpool, Nova Scotia, where Jimmy Foxx was his manager. "I just about had it with baseball at that point," Haughey says. "I had hurt my arm and I just didn't feel like playing anymore." He gave it one more chance in Venezuela and Puerto Rico in 1950, but, at age twenty-four, he was all done with baseball. "I think it was a matter of my looking at things as they *are* and not as we *hope* they'd be," he says. "I saw so many guys in the minors who were looking for that one good year to get back to the majors, and I just didn't want to be like that.

"And there was the politics. I remember at Columbus we had a third baseman at spring training at Daytona Beach who had played in the Texas League the year before. He had a great spring. He hit around .350, had a lot of RBIs, and had a great arm. But just before the end of spring training, he was told to go back to the Texas League. 'Why?' he asked. 'Because I don't think you can move to the left well enough,' the manager says.

"'Oh yeah, well, how many balls have I missed going to my left?' the guy asked. 'Let me tell you something,' he says, 'I ain't going back to the Texas League. I'm going home. I quit!' And that's what he did. He's the only guy I ever saw do that. It was politics," Haughey says.

"Looking at this kind of thing, there's a lot of politics involved. Take Al Campanis as an example. I don't mean anything against him, but he kept being brought along and brought along by the Dodgers because he was a politician. Every time Durocher would fly into New York, Campanis would meet him at the airport. I wasn't gonna be like that, and I think I was looking at things as they were."

After leaving baseball, Haughey joined the Sinclair Refining Company in New York where he worked first in sales, then as a heating engineer, and finally as an operations manager. He remained with the company for fifteen years until a vacation took him to California. "I fell in love with the place," Haughey says. "I saw the mode of living, and I said, 'That's it, we're moving out here. My wife said, 'You're crazy,' and I said, 'Maybe so, but that's what I'm doing.'

"In New York, I was living in New Hyde Park on Long Island, and I used to drive to work in Long Island City," Haughey says. "It seems to me it was somewhere like eleven miles away, but it took me an hour and a quarter to drive every morning. I saw there were other ways to live. I came home and put my house up for sale and moved to California."

In Salinas, California, Haughey invested in a retail menswear establishment and then opened his own business, which he operated for fifteen years. After selling that, he spent thirteen years with two other men's clothing retailers and, late in 1993, joined the menswear department at Macy's in Pleasanton, California, where he works today. He currently lives with his second wife, Karen, in nearby Hayward, California.

Today Haughey believes the three years he was away from baseball while in the military service effectively killed his career. "If I was sixteen today," he says, "I wouldn't have anything to worry about. Now I understand I had a God-given talent to throw hard and throw all day."

But yet, looking back on his baseball career, Haughey isn't bitter. He says, "You know, I had more fun doing what I did then, and I really treasure all the stories and all the times I had."

Gene Tunney Patton

BOSTON BRAVES, 1944

Gene Patton is convinced. "If I wouldn't have gotten hurt in the U.S. Army, I know I'd have made it big," he says with certainty.

Patton was born in Coatesville, Pennsylvania, on July 8, 1926. "I think that was the year of the 'long-count' fight between [Gene] Tunney and Jack Dempsey, and my father named me after Tunney," he says. He was the youngest of fifteen children, nine of whom were boys. "We had a family ball team," he says.

Growing up during the Depression as the youngest in a large family meant hand-me-downs. "I never had any clothes or shoes of my own," Patton says. "Everything was patched-up stuff. But it was always clean. Everything was always clean. I can't ever remember my mother doing anything but cooking, sewing, and taking care of her kids. And not one of us ever got into any trouble.

"My father was a blast-furnace foreman for Bethlehem Steel, and he got transferred to a town a number of miles away. My mother liked Coatesville and didn't want to move, so she stayed there with the kids and he came home on weekends. We lived in a three-bedroom house, a row house, and we'd sleep four and five in a bed," Patton laughs. "Since I was the youngest and my father was away during the week, I slept with my mother when I was young and didn't have to share a bed with my brothers.

"But I remember sometimes, when we'd pass around the pot of bean soup at dinner time, by the time it came to me, there were only a couple of beans left. I'd yell and complain to my mother, and she'd say, 'Well, just put a lot of crackers in it.' He laughs recalling the story.

Having a large family had benefits, too. "It was fantastic," Patton says.

Gene Patton, one of the best high school hitters in the country, signed this picture for his girlfriend, Jane Verbiski, who soon became his wife.

"They made me what I am. I was the smallest, and they made me a fighter. They were always beating on me and picking on me, but they were helping me and teaching me, too. Some of my brothers were good ballplayers, too, and I was able to play with older guys, and that helped me a lot."

Patton, though not imposing physically at five-foot-ten and 165 pounds, was an extraordinarily talented athlete. At Coatesville High School, he lettered in four sports and was named to All-State teams in baseball, football, and basketball. "In basketball I was a set shooter," he says. "Back in those days, we'd score 39, 40 points a game, and I'd get 31 of them. I was a gunner. In football I was a halfback, but I called the signals. We ran from the single wing," he says, "and only had about fifteen or twenty plays, mostly traps and such. And in track I ran the 220 and the 440, and did the broad jump."

But in baseball he excelled most. If Chris Haughey (see Chapter 11) was one of the country's best high school pitchers of the era, Patton, playing at shortstop, was one of the best hitters. "I hit .710 or .712 in 30 games at Coatesville High School," he says. "I held the consecutive straight-hit record of any high school player. I hit safely 13 consecutive times. The 14th time, the center fielder trapped my line drive, but the umpire didn't see the complete play and called me out. I then hit safely in the next nine times at bat. If the umpire had been on the ball, I'd have hit safely 23 consecutive times.

"When I was fifteen years old, I played ball outside of school, under another name, for Herb Pennock, the old Yankee and Red Sox pitcher, over at Kennett Square. He'd give me $50 a game. He was trying to hold onto me for [Tom] Yawkey [owner of the Boston Red Sox]. I'd bat against guys who were thirty-one years old, and I'd hit something like .485. I was just gifted."

In one memorable high school game, Patton recalls, "When all the scouts were there, I had six hits in six at bats. I had two home runs and seven RBIs *in one inning*. I was scouted by sixteen major-league scouts and," he points out, "there was only sixteen teams in the majors at that time.

"In my senior year, I had about forty-eight scholarship offers to play football in college," he says, "and all of the major-league baseball teams were interested." He chose to sign a professional contract with the Boston Braves.

In 1943, Patton's junior year in high school, the Braves had invited him to tag along on one of their road trips to New York, and he took advantage of the opportunity. "One of their scouts, John Ogden, used to bring me new bats all the time. He was one of the Ogden brothers that used to pitch in the majors."

But it wasn't the trip or the bats that finally influenced Patton to go with the Braves. It was what he calls "a very nice" bonus. "I chose the Braves because they came up with 35,000 bucks," he says simply.

"See, my favorite team when I was a kid was the Detroit Tigers. Charlie Gehringer, their second baseman, was my favorite player, but I liked them all—Tommy Bridges, Hank Greenberg, the whole team. I was hoping to sign with them, but all they could offer me was ten grand. They had made a huge investment in Dick Wakefield out of the University of Michigan a couple of years earlier. I think they gave him something like $56,000. My high school coach was advising me, and he kept telling me, 'Get the money, get the money.'

"I was signed at seventeen years old, right out of high school. John Ogden of the Braves signed me that evening [following his graduation] at 2 A.M. in the morning," Patton says. "In addition to the bonus, I also got $12,000 a year, $1,000 a month. They took me to New York to meet Judge [Kennesaw] Landis [the baseball commissioner] at the Commodore Hotel and sign my contract in front of him. Since I was under eighteen, he had to approve it, and I met him and he talked to me for a while about it.

"Then they put me on a plane to Logan Airport in Boston, and I stayed at the Charles Hotel, right on the Charles River. I had never flown before or stayed overnight by myself before, and I was really scared of that airplane ride, I tell you. When I got to Boston," Patton says, "they told me to see Bob Coleman [the Braves' manager] out in Brookline, and I took the trolley car over there to Braves Field.

"Oh, in addition to my bonus, the Braves said they'd give me a new car, too, but I didn't want a car. So they said, 'What do you want?' and I told them I want all new clothes. I never had any clothes of my own before. I wanted my *own* hand-me-downs. I got about ten new suits, all gabardine, and about ten pairs of new shoes, and I was the best dressed rookie you ever saw! I was really dressed to kill.

"I only kept $5,000 of the bonus and gave the rest to my folks to help them out, and they got a new house. But houses only cost about $3,000 in those days."

Patton joined the Braves in the early spring of 1944. Boston was a mediocre team that year with only one legitimate major-league star on the roster, center fielder Tommy Holmes, a lifetime .302 hitter. For much of the season, Max Macon, a converted pitcher, played first base while their leading pitcher, Jim Tobin, was used as a pinch-hitter.

Other "mainstays" of the team that year were thirty-one-year-old catcher Stew Hofferth; first baseman Buck Etchison; infielders Frank Drews, Damon "Dee" Phillips, Mike Sandlock, Warren Huston, Whitey Wietelmann, and Connie Ryan; third baseman/outfielder Chuck Workman; and two other outfielders, thirty-eight-year-old Albert "Ab" Wright and Butch Nieman. They were all typical wartime players, and most were gone when the regulars returned in 1946. Two other catchers on the team, Phil Masi and Clyde Kluttz, had longer careers in the majors.

The Brave pitchers in 1944 included Jim Tobin and Nate Andrews, both thirty-one-years old, Charlie "Red" Barrett, twenty-nine; Stan Klopp, thirty-three; Macon, twenty-nine; Ira Hutchinson, thirty-four; Al Javery, twenty-six; and Ben Cardoni, twenty-four.

Fresh out of high school, Patton clearly was an outsider. "When I first got to the Braves, I was in awe of all these older guys," Patton says. "Jim Tobin used to go down to the end of the dugout all the time when he was pitching and I didn't know what he was doing. One day, Carden Gillen-water said, 'It's okay. Go take a look.' So I went down, and what Tobin was doing was taking a shot of whiskey between innings whenever he was pitching! I tell you, it frightened me.

"They wouldn't even *talk* to me," he recalls. They were all older and they said, 'Why should this kid play? We spent years getting here and he's coming right from high school! That's not right.' I remember Tommy Holmes telling me to get out of here all the time. He was a good hitter, but he'd talk like a girl. He had this high-pitched voice. Later, though, we became good friends.

"I had to wait and wait to get up in batting practice," Patton says. "I re-member we had an old batting practice pitcher and he'd call me, 'Hey,

Bush! Hey, Bush!' That was for 'Bush Leaguer,' which Tommy Holmes started calling me. It was Bush this and Bush that.

"Whitey Wietelmann, the shortstop, was real nasty. He hit about .088 and was afraid I'd take his job. I'd be in the shower, and he'd come in and yell, 'Get the hell out of here.' Well, one day I called him on it and challenged him to fight. He backed off and never said anything again."

It was said that when Casey Stengel managed the Braves a few years earlier, he kept Wietelmann around as a reserve infielder only because he would also sweep out the clubhouse. When this was mentioned to Patton, he says, "He used to squeal on people, too."

Under Coleman, the Braves were never in contention in 1944, finishing sixth, 40 games behind the league champion St. Louis Cardinals, whose lineup had not been quite so depleted as others.

Despite the Braves' need for hitting, Patton sat on the bench. "I remember getting into one City Series game against the Red Sox," he says, "and I went 2 for 3." Then Saturday, June 17, 1944, Patton became a real major-league player when the New York Giants, led by Mel Ott, their outfielder-manager, came to Boston to play a doubleheader.

In the first game that day, with about 5,000 fans in the stands, there were only nine hits altogether, but the affair was settled with home runs. With two out in the first inning, Ott hit his 18th homer of the year. This was offset later by a pair of two-run clouts by the Braves, one by Kluttz and one by Workman. Boston went on to take the game, 5–1, as Javery hurled a four-hitter for his third win of the season, against eight losses.

Then the second game started. Boston's Hutchinson was on the mound, facing Ewald "Lefty" Pyle of the Giants. In this game, there were decidedly more base runners, and one of them was Gene Tunney Patton.

In that game, Boston rapped out eleven hits while the Giants managed seven. The New Yorkers also took advantage of nine walks given by Hutchinson and two Brave relievers, Klopp and Cardoni. Going into the bottom of the ninth, Pyle and the Giants were holding on to a 6–2 lead.

In that inning, Macon, who had come in to play first base for Etchison, led off with a single. The next scheduled batter was the shortstop, Mike Sandlock, who had replaced Wietelmann after Kluttz had batted for him earlier in the game. Stew Hofferth, the club's third-string catcher, batted for Sandlock and was walked by the tiring Pyle.

"Hofferth wasn't much of a hitter," Patton says, "and wasn't much of a runner, either." So Patton was sent in to run for him. "I was nervous," he says. "Let me tell you something. Every game I ever played—baseball, football, whatever—I used to get extremely nervous when I first started. It would go away right after the first play or so. It was a cocky nervousness, I guess. I thought if I ever *wasn't* nervous like that, I wouldn't be any good."

With Patton on first and Macon on second, the next batter was another pinch-hitter, reserve outfielder Butch Nieman, batting for the pitcher, Cardoni. "Nieman was no outfielder," Patton says. "He was mainly a pinch-hitter. I think he had some sort of a disease or something, like he was punch-drunk from football. Every once in a while his eyes used to roll up in his head.

"They threw over to first a couple of times," Patton continues. "They wanted to see how I'd react, I guess. As I recall, the first-base coach was Tom Sheehan, and I think Bennie Bengough was coaching at third. Coleman gave the sign for a double steal or a hit-and-run. I remember him always telling batters that even if the steal was on, not to let a strike go by."

Nieman hit a slow hopper to Giant shortstop Buddy Kerr who flipped to second baseman George Hausman to force the sliding Patton. "I almost made it," he says. "I thought I might have been in there, since I was running on the pitch. When I got back to the dugout, Carden Gillenwater said, 'Atsa way to go. I thought you beat the ball in there.'"

After Patton was forced at second, the next hitter, Tommy Holmes, hit a three-run homer to make the score Giants 6, Braves 5. If Patton had made it safely into second, it would have tied the score. "Holmes wasn't much of a home run hitter," Patton says. "He was more of a spray hitter. But they had just put a new, short right field fence in there, and he hit it over that."

The Giants then brought in Ace Adams, the league's premier fireman during the war years. Adams halted the uprising, getting the final two outs.

Gene Patton never played in the major leagues again.

"In July, when I turned eighteen, I got my draft call," he says. "I told the club, and [owners] Mr. Quinn and young John Quinn said that, if I wanted, they'd check with the governor and see if they could get me sent to Fort Devens, which was right nearby, so I could still get to play in home games. Well, most of my brothers were in the service then, one was even missing in action at the time. I couldn't see myself going into Special Services while they were risking their lives, and I told them I didn't want to do that. They said something like 'Who do you think you are? We only do this for stars. You're a nobody and we're trying to help you out.' I said, 'Let me think about it for a day,' but the more I thought about it, the more I felt that if anything happened to any of my brothers in service, that I'd never be able to live with myself if I were in Special Services. So I said no and ended up in the infantry.

"I went home and found out that I'd have thirty days before I had to report," Patton says. "The Braves had paid me off for the year, but I called them and said I had another thirty days. They said, 'That's okay, Gene. Just stay home and relax. We weren't gonna use you anyway. Just take it easy and we'll see you in spring training when you get out.'

"Then I get a call from Herb Pennock. He says, 'How'd you like to make $1,000 for a month playing at Wilmington?' Wilmington was in the

Interstate League, and he had some sort of interest in it. He told me he
had been in touch with the Braves, and it was okay with them. They were
willing to loan me to Wilmington for that last month before I had to go
in the army. He said I could live at home and commute to the ballpark.
Now, Wilmington is in Delaware, just twenty-four miles from where I
live, but I didn't want to commute, so Pennock put me up at the DuPont
Hotel in Wilmington. And I played actually two months, August and September, for them before I went in the army and made $1,000 a month."

At Wilmington, Patton appeared in 48 games and collected 50 hits, including ten doubles, three triples, and a home run in 189 times at bat, for a
.265 average.

On October 1, 1944, he was inducted into the U.S. Army and sent to
Camp Wheeler, Georgia, for sixteen weeks of infantry basic training.
"During basic, I used to get a lot of sore throats," he says, "but every time I
went on sick call, they'd say, 'Aw, you're fine. Go on back to your unit.'
They thought I was kidding them.

"At the end of basic, we went out on bivouac and we were out in pup
tents and one morning I woke up with a very bad throat and I couldn't
move. I said to one of the guys, 'I can't move. I can't feel anything.' He
starts kicking me in the leg and says, 'Can you feel that?' and I say, 'No, I
can't.' Well, they rushed me to the hospital, and I was paralyzed. I had
rheumatic fever, which came from a strep throat.

"I remember a doctor there, a doctor from Brooklyn. He said, 'I don't
know what we can do for you, Gene. It's gotten into your chest, you've
got a continuous fever, your legs are like lead, and you're not responding
to any medication. It may be a matter of time.' I was paralyzed for about
two or three months, but then they tried penicillin, which was new then,
and that worked. They used to give it to me a few times a day, and little by
little, I got better. I guess I was in the hospital about six months."

In the spring of 1945, Patton was discharged and given a 100 percent
disability pension. "I was told I'd never play ball again," he says. "But I
went up to Boston to see a doctor there, and Dr. Paul Dudley White, who
was Eisenhower's doctor, was the Brave's team physician at that time. He
checked me out, and he gave me permission to work out with the Braves'
farm team in Hartford during the year. After the season, I went with him
to Florida and worked out there. All that time, the Braves were paying my
contract. I was still getting $1,000 a month.

"When everybody else came down for spring training in 1946, I was
already in good shape. Billy Southworth was managing the Braves then
and a lot of guys were just coming back from the service, so all we did all
spring long was concentrate on fundamentals. Over and over. We'd practice sliding, bunting, relays from the outfield, and basic things like that.
They had me playing third base that spring, and I got into about twenty-
one intersquad games.

"One day we were playing the Giants in Miami, and I batted third.

Their pitcher was a big left-hander, Monte Kennedy. Southworth pulls me aside and says, 'Listen, I had this guy in the minors and I can tell you he dips his glove when he throws a curve and he points his glove when he's gonna throw a fastball.' I said, 'Wait a minute, Billy. I don't hit that way. I watch the pitcher and react to what he throws.' Billy says, 'Look, Gene. I know what I'm doing. If I call out "Gene," it'll be a straight ball. If I say, "C'mon Patton," and use your last name, it'll be a curve.'

"Well, I go up to bat, and Billy yells, 'C'mon, Patton.' I look for the curveball, and sure enough, it's there. I swing and hit it over the fence for a home run. Well, I'm rounding the bases, and as I get right past second, here comes Kennedy, cursing me out. 'You S.O.B.,' he yells. He follows me around third and almost to home, hollering at me all the time. I just ignore him and go into the dugout.

"Later in the game, I come up again against Kennedy. Billy yells out again, 'C'mon, Patton.' Well, either the Giants got wise to him picking up their pitches or something, but I'm standing there looking for another curve. It comes in straight and hits me right behind the ear, knocking me cold for a day and a half. I woke up in the hospital. It had bruised a bone in the back of my ear.

"You know, it's hard to hit a guy. Oh, you can throw at him, but it's not easy to hit him because he can move out of the way. The only way you can hit him is if he freezes. That's what I did. I froze because even though it was coming at my head, I was expecting it to curve.

"After I got out of the hospital, the first time Billy put me in to hit, who do you think was the pitcher? It was Kennedy. This time I fouled out. Billy told me later he put me in to face Kennedy on purpose. It was like getting back on a horse after you've been thrown.

"After spring training, they told me they were gonna farm me out. I think it was Rip Collins who told me, but it could have been Southworth," Patton says. "At that time, the team had been sold to the Three Steam Shovels [the Perini brothers, who were in the construction business], and Collins told me, 'Look, Gene, there's no question you're gonna be back. We're shooting for third or fourth place this year, but the Three Steam Shovels are gonna improve the team and make some deals so we can go for the pennant next year. And right now, you're so damn young.'

"Well, after that, of course, they got Bob Elliott from Pittsburgh to play third, and that finished me.

"The Braves were going to send me to play at Milwaukee, their Triple-A team," Patton says, "but little Dutch Dorman, who was managing their Double-A team at Hartford [in the Eastern League], asked for me. He was about five-foot-three and was like another Southworth. I didn't know it then, but Dorman had scouted me in high school and was instrumental in getting the Braves to sign me originally. I found that out later."

Patton went to Hartford for the 1946 season. "By going back to play baseball, I gave up my army pension," he says. "I was getting $900 a month disability, but I gave it up to play ball. Then I never could finish a season. I got sick again. Whenever the weather changed, when the seasons changed, I had a hard time breathing. I had a leaking heart from the rheumatic fever." He played in only 41 games that year, hitting a weak .208.

In 1947, he started the season at Hartford again, but after hitting only .239 in 12 games, was sent to Evansville, in the Three-I League. "Bob Coleman was managing there," Patton says. "He lived in Evansville and must have managed there about twenty-five years." Patton's illness again prevented him from playing well. He appeared in only 16 games and batted .209.

"The next year, I went up to Branford, Ontario, in Canada and played in an outlaw league there, the Provincial League," Patton recalls. "It was great," he says. "I was named the MVP of the league, and they had some good ballplayers there. Oscar Judd was there, and Jim Bagby. We played three days a week, and I got paid $1,000 a week in American money. They invited me back for the following year to be a manager, at a cut in salary, but I didn't want that."

Patton applied for, and was granted, reinstatement in organized baseball in the United States, and his contract was purchased by Raleigh in the Carolina League. He played there in 1949, but again was limited by his health. "The weather was just too hot and changeable for me," he says. He had 43 hits in 47 games, but hit just .254.

In 1950, he returned to a cooler climate, playing again in the Provincial League, this time for the Mayo Clinic team based in Rochester, Minnesota. "I enjoyed playing there," Patton says. "It's hard to believe, but we used to get crowds of eighteen to nineteen thousand a game. That year, I got beaned again. I guess my eyes were going. But that finished me." After managing the Branford team in 1951, Patton left professional baseball.

He returned to Coatesville and went to work full-time for the Lukens Steel Company as a time-study man in the industrial engineering department. "I used to work there during the off-seasons," he says. He remained with the company for almost thirty years before retiring.

During this time, Patton's interest in baseball never waned. In 1952, he formed Coatesville's first American Legion team and coached it for about eighteen years. In 1970, he was elected to the Legion's Pennsylvania Hall of Fame.

He and his wife, Jane, whom he met in Coatesville in 1945 and married five years later, are the parents of two daughters and have four granddaughters. Despite his physical problems, Patton, until recently, was an active bowler, and he follows the nearby Phillies as well as the Braves on cable television. "I also like horse racing," he says. "Delaware Park is only twenty-three miles away, but I don't get over there now as often as I used to."

Patton is a repository of baseball stories, sharing them readily. Talking about baseball is still a favorite pastime. "I look at the players today and I don't begrudge them a nickel," he says. "But back then, the players just *loved* the game. Even the owners loved the game. It was a hobby for most of them. Life is so different today."

Carl Mac McNabb

DETROIT TIGERS, 1945

Carl McNabb spent more than a dozen years playing professional base-ball, and in ten of those seasons, he played regularly, usually as a slick-fielding second baseman, in anywhere from 111 to 140 games a year.

Small at five-foot-nine and 155 pounds, he was still a decent hitter. During his ten years as a regular in the minor leagues, he hit over .300 four times and between .274 and .299 three times. In the season prior to his becoming a major leaguer, he batted .283 in the strong Triple-A Inter national League.

"But I never liked to pinch hit," he says. "Pinch hitting is a hard job, and I don't think it's fair to let one time up as a pinch-hitter determine a man's career." Yet that's what happened to him when he got his one chance to play in a major-league game.

"I doubt if you could print what I think about my one time at bat in the majors," he says. "After a good year at Buffalo in the International League, I was only given one chance. What a pity for a young fellow."

The youngest in a family of ten children, including seven boys, McNabb was born on a farm in Stevenson, Alabama, on January 25, 1917. Soon the family moved across the border to Jasper, Tennessee, where his father ran a small country grocery store. "I don't exactly know when we moved to Jasper," McNabb says, "but that's the first place I remember see-ing the light of day." Later, during his professional baseball career, McNabb would return to Jasper each winter to help out at the store.

He grew up in a community of approximately 3,500 and attended nearby Marion County High School, where football was the major sport.

Carl McNabb, in a Buffalo Bisons uniform,
still remembers every one of the pitches that struck him out.

"There was no baseball team there," he recalls, "but I played a little football, tried to play basketball, and ran track, mostly in the relays.

"Around 1935, when I was still in high school, I played baseball on an amateur or semipro kind of team, and a guy from the Cleveland Indians, a scout, saw me and asked me to go to Zanesville, Ohio, for a tryout," McNabb says. "My brother and I—he was a pitcher—both went. I remember seeing Tommy Henrich at that tryout camp, too."

The Indians were interested in the young infielder and in 1936, after his high school graduation, signed him to play at Tyler, Texas, then in the East Texas League. "Wally Dashiell was the manager at Tyler, and he signed me," McNabb recalls. "I got $125 a month, but I would've played for my board if truth be known." When asked if he received any bonus, he laughs and says, "They didn't have such things back then.

"I only stayed twelve days [at Tyler]," he says, "and then went to play [at Ozark] in the Alabama-Florida League, I believe. I played third base, and I was the youngest player in the league." He was nineteen at the time.

In 1937, McNabb returned to Tyler and was thrust into the shortstop position. "A fellow named Gene Ater was the shortstop there, and he broke his jaw, so they put me there, but I didn't like it. One day, Wally Dashiell said he had Frank Waites, who was a better shortstop, and he shifted me to second base. That's what I played the rest of my career."

As Tyler's regular second baseman, McNabb hit .279 in 1938 and earned a promotion to start the following season at Wilkes-Barre, Pennsylvania, Cleveland's Class-A farm team in the Eastern League.

"With Wilkes-Barre, I remember we took spring training in Suffolk, Virginia, and an old catcher by the name of Eddie Phillips was the manager. I remember we started off good and had 15 double plays in the first five games. But in the twelfth game of the season, I got hit while at bat and busted my thumb. Then I developed shoulder trouble by trying to play before my thumb got well. I had a calcium deposit. They sent me to Springfield, Ohio [in the Mid-Atlantic League], where Earl Wolgomat was manager."

Wolgomat told McNabb, "You're my second baseman, whether you hit or not." A number of other Cleveland prospects were on the club that year, including Jim Hegan, Allie Reynolds, Jack Conway, and Bob Lemon.

In 1940, McNabb again started the season at Wilkes-Barre, where he was joined by many of his former Springfield teammates and by Wolgomat, the manager. But McNabb started poorly. After 22 games, he was hitting only .194.

This time Wolgomat was not so forgiving. "That second year at Wilkes-Barre I just couldn't get going," McNabb says, "and was sent to Sunbury, Pennsylvania [in the Interstate League], where I hit .300 [.305 in 96 games] and had 20 home runs, mainly because of a short left field fence. I was a little guy, but I was a good pull hitter. A fellow by the name of [Arnold] Greene hit 21 home runs and beat me out [for the league lead] by one. But," laughs McNabb, "his were honest home runs."

In 1941, the Sunbury club (managed by Dutch Dorman) was moved to Hagerstown, Maryland, and McNabb played there for the next two years, although his hitting fell off. Playing 135 games in one year and 125 in the other, he hit only .252 and .259, respectively.

In his first year at Hagerstown, the twenty-four-year-old McNabb met a local girl, Maebelle Miller, and the following year they were married. "She's been with me ever since," he laughs.

In late 1942, shortly after his marriage, McNabb was drafted into the army and, after basic training at Fort Gordon, Georgia, he was shipped out to North Africa, and assigned to the Eighty-third Chemical Batallion. "I remember I spent Easter Sunday [1943] in Boston, where we were sailing from, and it was about the loneliest time of my life," he says.

"After about six months in North Africa, I got sick. You see, I told them when I got drafted I had stomach ulcers, but they didn't believe me. So, naturally, after eating C-Rations or K-Rations, or whatever it was, for six months, I started getting sick and I started passing blood. They sent me to a doctor and he spotted the ulcers right away and they sent me home.

"They sent me to recuperate at a hospital in White Sulphur Springs, West Virginia. That is the most beautiful place I've ever seen in my life. It was like a resort."

Discharged in 1943, McNabb planned to return to Hagerstown in the Interstate League for the 1944 season, but received a telephone call from the Buffalo team in the Triple-A International League, which, unbeknownst to McNabb, had acquired his contract. "John Steigelmeyer, the general manager at Buffalo, called and asked me to come play for them," he recalls. "I wanted more money than he was offering, but he said, 'If you come and you stay for thirty days, I'll pay you what you want.' Well, I wasn't sure about him, but I asked some guys I knew and they said he could be trusted, so I went to Buffalo. After I was there a month, we were playing in Baltimore, and I got a note in the mail from him saying, 'Keep up the good work.' There was a check in the envelope for the difference in salary. That was nice."

Although finishing in fourth place, the Buffalo team, managed by Bucky Harris, led the International League in hitting that year with a collective .271 average, eight percentage points higher than its nearest rival. McNabb, with a .283 average, was the team's fifth leading hitter behind the league's batting champion, outfielder Mayo Smith (.340); outfielder Ed Kobesky (.328); third baseman Bob Maier (.298); and outfielder/first baseman Otto Denning (.288). "Andy Seminick was on that team, too," McNabb points out.

"Bucky Harris was the best manager I ever played for," McNabb says. "When that season ended, Detroit [Buffalo's parent team] bought the contracts of [pitcher] Walter Wilson and Bob Maier, and Bucky Harris told them to buy mine, too. That's how I got to the majors in 1945.

"I went to spring training with Detroit at Evansville, Indiana, that year [1945], as the war ended the travel to Florida," McNabb recalls. "At first I was awestruck to see the major leaguers, but then I found they were just guys, guys just like the ones in the minors. I done my job in the spring and played all their spring games. We played the Chicago White Sox most of the time. I had 2 for 4 off Eddie Lopat in one game. Most of the time we played intrasquad games. [Hal] Newhouser pitched for the side I was on, and Dizzy Trout pitched against us. I got a base hit off of Dizzy one game that won the game. He told me later he didn't know how I hit it 'cause it was his best pitch. Dizzy was my best supporter; in fact, on a local radio program there, he gave me a big boost."

Just after the season began, Carl McNabb got his opportunity to play in the major leagues against his former employers, the Cleveland Indians. It was in the third game of the year, on April 20, 1945.

"The game I was in, in the regular season, was at Briggs Stadium in Detroit," he says, "in early spring, and it was a cool day. I pinch hit for the pitcher, Walter Wilson, with the game already lost, in the [bottom of the] ninth inning. There were two out and nobody on."

Cleveland led Detroit 4-1 at that point. Their four runs came in the first three innings against the Tiger starter, Stubby Overmire. Wilson, a six-foot-four right-hander from Georgia, then came in to relieve him and gave up only three hits the rest of the way. But it was too late. The Indians' pitcher, Steve Gromek, had allowed just one run (in the sixth inning when Tiger third baseman Don Ross doubled in first baseman Rudy York) while scattering six hits through the first eight innings.

In the bottom of the ninth, the Tigers sent up three pinch-hitters to face Gromek. Batting for shortstop Joe Hoover was Hub Walker. Ed "Red" Borom batted for catcher Paul Richards, and finally, McNabb came up in place of Wilson.

According to McNabb, it wasn't until the second out of the inning had been recorded that he was told to pinch hit, so he didn't have much time to get loose properly in the on-deck area. And, he emphasizes, "I just didn't like pinch hitting.

"Paul Richards was managing that day, since [Tiger manager] Steve O'Neill had the gout, and he told me to take a pitch. I never did talk to Steve O'Neill. He had the gout all spring," McNabb recalls. "Steve Gromek was the pitcher, and [Jim] Hegan was the catcher [actually it was Hank Ruszkowski]. I had known Hegan before because we were on the same ball club. When I walked up to the plate, he tried to talk to me, but I was nervous and awestruck by my first time at bat in a ball game and I didn't answer him. He said something like 'Ah, there you are.' I didn't know the rules, see. I didn't think we were allowed to talk to players on the other team.

"I took the first pitch," McNabb continues, "then for some reason—until this day I can't figure why—I took the second one right down the middle. I know I could have hit it 'cause I saw it as big as a softball. Then he threw a change-up, and I just jumped at it and struck out." The game was over and so was McNabb's major-league career.

"After the game, I didn't feel too good. Back then, they'd razz you about something like that, but I didn't go for it. I remember in spring training, I was facing Eddie Lopat and he threw me a curve on a 3 and 2 pitch, and I took it for a third strike. They kidded me about that, saying, 'You got to remember they'll curve you on 3 and 2 up here.' Well, that's the game I went 2 for 4 off Lopat, and there was no mention of it no more after that. Anyway, with all due respect to Gromek, I had seen better pitches in the minors than those that he threw me, and I said so."

After striking out as a pinch-hitter in his only at bat in the major leagues, McNabb never got another chance to play. "I stayed with Detroit for about thirty days until cut-down day," he says, "and went on the road with them to Cleveland, St. Louis, and Chicago." When asked why he never got a chance to play again during this time, McNabb says, "Paul Richards had his favorites. I'm not saying that to criticize; it's just a fact. I owe Paul Richards and Steve O'Neill my regards for their interest in me."

Of the Tigers, McNabb felt closest to Dizzy Trout and Hal Newhouser. "Ol' Dizzy was real down to earth and," McNabb continues, "if you know Dizzy, well, he borrowed some money from me. Hal Newhouser used to sit in the hotel lobby all the time and talk to all the rookies, just talk for hours. He was a prince of a guy." (Newhowser's nickname was "Prince Hal.")

When asked about his own nickname, "Skinny," which is listed in *The Baseball Encyclopedia*, McNabb responds: "I was never known in all my years playing as 'Skinny.' I thought someone there at Detroit came up with that. No one ever called me anything other than 'Little Mac' or just plain 'Mac,' which is, by the way, my middle name."

The year McNabb was with Detroit, the Tigers went on to win the American League pennant by one and a half games over Washington, and then beat the Chicago Cubs in the World Series, four games to three. They were led by Newhouser, who had a spectacular season, leading the league's pitchers in wins, complete games, shutouts, earned run average, innings pitched, strikeouts, and the fewest hits allowed per nine innings. For the second year in a row, he was named the league's most valuable player. The Tigers also were helped by the late-season return of Hank Greenberg, who hit what turned out to be a pennant-winning home run in the last game of the year. In the World Series, Greenberg hit .304, knocking out two singles, three doubles, and two homers in 23 plate appearances.

But about a month into the season, when the major-league teams had to trim their rosters, McNabb was optioned back to Buffalo. "The general manager at Detroit, I can't remember his name, was the one who told me," McNabb says. "He told me Bucky Harris had been calling every day to get me back. I don't know if that was true or whether he said that just to make it easier. He told me if Detroit won the pennant or anything like that, 'We'll see you get your part.' Well, they got into the Series that year, and I guess I had *no* part 'cause I got nothing."

McNabb finished the 1945 season as Buffalo's regular second baseman, hitting .274 in 122 games. In the field, he made only 20 errors in 672 chances. But before the 1946 season began, as many veterans returned from the war, the Tigers, who had been successful enough to win the world championship without McNabb, sold the twenty-eight-year-old in-fielder to Dallas in the Texas League.

But McNabb never played for Dallas—or anyone else—in 1946.

"I just sat at home all year," he says. "They wanted me to play for less money than I was making at Buffalo, and I wouldn't do it. My daddy had retired by then, but we just opened the country store up again, and I worked there that year. They [Dallas] wrote me that summer and wanted to send me to Seattle [in the Triple-A Pacific Coast League], but I said no 'cause I didn't want to go there after the season had started without having gone through spring training, while everyone else was in midseason shape."

McNabb, then thirty years old, returned to baseball in 1947 when he agreed to play with Tyler, Texas, his first professional team. He played there for the next three years, except for a brief time when he attempted to manage in Greenville, Texas. With Tyler, he hit .308 in 116 games in 1947; .299 in 140 games in 1948; and .261 in 135 games in 1949.

At second base during 1948, he also led the league's infielders in field-ing and tied for participating in the most double plays. His partner at shortstop that year was the slick-fielding Roy McMillan, who later spent sixteen years in the majors with Cincinnati, Milwaukee, and the New York Mets.

After starting the 1950 season at Lubbock, Texas, in the West Texas-New Mexico League, McNabb decided he had played enough, even though he was hitting .316 at the time. "I came back to Jasper to the little grocery store. My brother was running it and had built up a good trade. But after a while, he married and moved away, and I ran it," he says.

Eventually the store was sold, and McNabb began a new career. "I got a job as a rural mail carrier and did that for twenty years 'til I retired in 1987," he says. In recent years, he has had a number of serious eye opera-tions, including cornea transplants, and has difficulty seeing and recogniz-ing people. Today he uses a six-power magnifying glass to read and write, but otherwise is in good health. He and his wife (they have no children) still live in Jasper, where he continues to follow baseball, especially Atlanta in the National League and Baltimore in the American.

"I really enjoyed playing," he says, "but I know today in my own heart I could have played major-league ball. I never did have any trouble with my fielding and making the double play. In fact, I had two—or one, at that time—good years at Buffalo, so I thought, and still do, that I should have been given a chance to play. And, you know, even today I can still see that second strike from Gromek and wonder why I took it. To this day, I kick myself for not swinging at that second pitch."

Joseph Christopher "Fire" Cleary

WASHINGTON NATIONALS, 1945

Joe Cleary was a tough little Irish kid from New York City who wouldn't take crap from anybody. Not even a big-league manager. And that was one of the reasons why his first major-league game was also his last.

Born in Cork City, Ireland, December 3, 1918, Cleary came to the United States when he was almost ten years old, after his father, a carpenter who had come here earlier, finally earned enough to send for his wife and five children.

The year was 1928. The family settled on the Upper West Side of the melting pot which was then New York City. Before long, the youngster, who had already developed his athletic ability by playing hurling, soccer, and football in Ireland, was heavily involved in schoolyard basketball and sandlot baseball games.

But his nickname, "Fire," had nothing to do with sports. "A kid at the local candy store started calling me 'Fire' 'cause I was always ready to fight," Cleary says. "He would yell, 'Here comes Fire,' every time I came down to the candy store."

Cleary fell in love with America's pastime. "I remember my aunt buying me a glove, a ball, a bat, and a uniform," he says, "and my mother had to drag them off me at night, you know. I slept with them.

"In those days," he recalls, "baseball started and ended with Babe Ruth. My uncle roomed with us at the time. He was a baseball fan, and I was always waiting for him to say, 'What do you say we go up to the stadium and see the Babe today?' That was my big thrill. I can still see one of his homers leaving the bat, a line drive into the right center field bleachers."

Cleary attended the High School of Commerce in Manhattan and quickly became one of the school's star basketball players. Although standing only five-foot-nine and weighing just 145 pounds, he was named to the All-Manhattan–Bronx team. As a result, he almost had his choice of going to Harvard, Yale, or Princeton for an education.

During his senior year, after the high school basketball season ended but before the baseball season began in the spring of 1939, Cleary was invited to visit an exclusive New York college preparatory school, Trinity Prep. "The people there were very straightforward with me," he says. "They told me that their basketball team was very bad and that they'd like me to come and play for them for a year. They said, 'We're getting a lot of complaints from our alumni and parents about being the doormats of our league. Now, if you come and play for us for one year, we'll *guarantee* you can go to Princeton, Yale, or Harvard.' I don't think they knew what kind of courses I was taking in high school, you know, typing and commercial courses. But they said, 'If you don't want to go to college, we'll get you a good job, probably in Wall Street. Think about it and let us know.'

"Then they gave me a tour of the place, you know, and I saw all these kids walking around with their blazers on and all, and I knew it wasn't for me."

When he was a high school freshman, Cleary tried out for the baseball team. "I pitched and the coach said, 'In a couple of years, you'll be the best pitcher in the city.' But the school dropped baseball for a while, so I only played basketball my first years there. Later, when they started playing baseball again, I played the infield until my senior year, see, because by then I was pitching semipro on Sundays and I wanted to save my arm for that."

Cleary's strong right arm aided such semipro teams as Bay Parkway, the Belltones, and the Puerto Rican Stars. At age sixteen, traveling around the city by subway or trolley car, he was earning $50 or $100 a week. "I gave it to my mother," he says. "It was during the Depression and my dad was out of work and a dollar was hard to come by. We used to play all the black teams you heard about. I played on one team there with that one-armed player, you know, Pete Gray.

"In 1937 or 1938, I was pitching either for or against the House of David. Grover Cleveland Alexander was sort of a side attraction for the other team, and after he saw me pitch, he said, 'You got a hell of an arm there, son. Take good care of it.' That sure gave me a lift."

First, however, came his senior year of high school baseball. "My coach didn't know for sure I was playing semipro at the same time, but he probably had a good idea, 'cause I was starting to get a name for myself, starting to pitch." Cleary pitched for his high school team in 1939 and was named to the All-City team before graduating that June. He says he received "about fifteen scholarship offers to play either baseball or basketball, at a time when such offers weren't common."

He continued playing semipro baseball because "dollars were scarce.

Excluding pitchers who never retired a batter, Joe Cleary (shown here at Chattanooga) has the highest earned run average in big-league history.

Semipro ball then was high-quality baseball—maybe equal to Double-A ball. Nobody traveled in those days, and there were a lot of good, hungry ballplayers around. Ex–minor-leaguers could make more in semipro than in Triple-A, where they might make only $200 a month. In semipro, the good ones could make $100 a game while holding steady jobs. You often saw fifteen or sixteen thousand people in the stands when the House of David played the Bushwicks in Brooklyn.

"In those days, winning ball games at any level was important because it meant more money. But it was wild and woolly. I've seen some fights in the minor leagues that were bloody—bats, fists, everything. I was even in a few. I mean, when I knocked a guy down, I expected him to come out after me. Umpires got flat tires. Sometimes the cops or the sheriff had to escort them out of town after a bad call or a call that went against the home team. You met some good friends but you met some rats, too.

"In those days," Cleary continues, "teams had ringers for all sorts of reasons. When I played for the Puerto Rican Stars, I had to play under the name of Jose Hernandez 'cause I was also still pitching for Commerce High. One night at Roosevelt Stadium in New Jersey, I was warming up on the sidelines to pitch against the Union City Reds, and the public address announcer says, 'And pitching for the Puerto Rican Stars, number such-and-such, Jose Hernandez.' Now Al Schact was managing Union City; you remember him, the comedian, and he was standing right next to me on the field. And here I am, red-haired, blue-eyed, you know, Irish all over, and Schact looks at me in disbelief and says, '*Jose Hernandez!*' "

Normally, during the winters Cleary played basketball, primarily in local church-sponsored leagues. In 1939, however, he pitched winter ball for Guayma in Puerto Rico, where one of his teammates was Satchel Paige.

In 1940, he returned to pitch for the Danbury, Connecticut Cubans. "I think I was the only American on the team," says Cleary, the Irish immigrant.

Late in the season, Joe Cambria, a scout for the Washington Nationals, invited Cleary to work out with the team's Springfield, Massachusetts, farm team in the Class-A Eastern League. Soon, he was signed to a Springfield contract.

"I only pitched a couple of games there," he says, " 'cause it was late in the year." Nevertheless, with a good fastball and a biting curve, he was able to handle the opposition fairly easily in his first few starts as a professional. "I had a great curveball," he recalls, "even though my hands are small. Even when my curve hung, they couldn't hit it because it dropped so fast."

Washington purchased his contract at the end of the season, and he was invited to the team's 1941 spring training camp in Orlando, Florida, where owner Clark Griffith gave Cleary a choice. "He asked me where I wanted to play that year, Charlotte [in the Class-B Piedmont League] or Orlando [in the Class-D Florida State League]. I chose Orlando 'cause I was already there and had gotten familiar with the town. But I was upset that they weren't keeping me, because I thought they liked me."

Cleary reported to the Orlando manager, Bucky Harris, and proceeded to post a 2.35 earned run average and rack up 19 wins during the 1941 season. "They had me try for 20 on the last day of the year with only two days rest," he remembers, "but the game was rained out."

In 1942, Cleary was inducted into the military and spent the next two years in the U.S. Army infantry, serving in North Africa and participating in campaigns around Casablanca and Oran. "I lost some friends" is about all he cares to mention of those years. While in service, he was notified that Washington had transferred his contract to the Chattanooga Lookouts in the Double-A Southern Association.

When he was discharged, Cleary joined Chattanooga for the 1944 season, but he was wild after being away for two years and won only 6 while losing 14.

The following year, however, he moved up to Charlotte, won 10, and lost 5 by the time the league's All-Star team was selected in July. "They didn't play an All-Star game that year because of the [wartime] travel restrictions, but they did select a team," Cleary says. Despite being selected, the twenty-six-year-old Cleary was upset with the way things were going and left the team to go home. "I was upset because they told me if I did good, they'd call me up, but they didn't," he says.

Clark Griffith telephoned him at home and asked him to come down to Washington to talk. "Would you still like to play?" Griffith asked him. Cleary still wanted to play. So in the last week of July, for a salary of $500 a month, he joined the Washington Nationals as a member of the big-league team that was, surprisingly, in an extremely close race for the pennant.

A year earlier, in 1944, the Nats had finished dead last, 25 games out of first place. In 1945, despite losing their leading hitter, center fielder Stan Spence to the military, Washington was fighting tooth-and-nail with Detroit for first place. It was one of the most amazing turnarounds in baseball history. The fight would not end until the last two days of the season, with the Tigers winning by only one and a half games, thanks to a ninth-inning grand slam by Hank Greenberg, who had just returned from military service in midseason.

Washington's pitching staff that year featured four knuckleball pitchers, Dutch Leonard, Johnny Niggeling, Roger Wolff, and Mickey Haefner. Their fifth starter was an Italian-born rookie, Marino Pieretti. Offensively, they were led by veterans Joe Kuhel, George Myatt, Rick Ferrell, and the speedy George Case. In July, just before Cleary joined them, the team also was bolstered by Buddy Lewis's return from military service.

On August 4, 1945, about a week after he joined the team, Cleary got into his only major-league game, into the record book, and nearly into a fight with his manager. Cleary today refers to it as "that day of infamy."

The Nationals were playing the Boston Red Sox in a doubleheader in

Washington. According to the recollection of another team member, it was one of a number of doubleheaders the team had been forced to play over a short time, and the pitching staff was wearing thin.

In the first game, according to Cleary, the Nats' pitcher was Emil "Dutch" Leonard, and, Cleary says, he was shaky from the start. The call went out early to get somebody ready in the bullpen. Cleary says he got up and, in getting ready for what might be his major-league debut, warmed up fast and hard. Meanwhile, Leonard settled down for a while, then got shaky again. So Cleary was up again and throwing in the bullpen. Finally, Cleary says, Leonard worked himself out of trouble and won the game.

According to the box score, the pitcher in that first game was actually Wally Holborow, not Leonard. And although Cleary may have been up and down in the bullpen during that game, the box score shows Holborow pitched a two-hit shutout, issuing only three walks along the way, hardly a "shaky" performance. Washington scored twice in the very first inning and once more in the second and led all the way in a 4–0 victory.

The second game, Cleary says, was almost a carbon copy of the first one, with the Washington starter, Cuban-born Carlos "Sandy" Ullrich, on the ropes from the early going. Again, Cleary kept warming up steadily in the bullpen. Finally, after the Red Sox had taken a 7–2 lead, scoring five runs in the fourth inning off Ullrich, Cleary was called into the game, having, he says, already pitched the equivalent of nine or ten innings while warming up.

"There was one out and men on first and third," Cleary says. "I don't remember who the first batter was, but he hit a beautiful double-play ball to second base, and I thought, 'Hey, I'm out of the inning.' But the ball takes a big hop right over the second baseman [Myatt] and goes into the outfield for a hit. Well, I don't have any excuses for what happened after that. I just got bombed."

Cleary was able to strike one man out, but gave up five hits, three walks, and seven more runs, as the Red Sox batted around and eventually scored 12 runs in the inning. Not counting a few pitchers who gave up runs without retiring a single batter, Cleary's earned run average of 189.00 today stands as the highest in baseball history. He left the game with the bases still loaded, and if Bert Shepard (see Chapter 15), who came in to relieve him, had not gotten the next man out, it could have been even higher.

Cleary's experience did get worse, however, before he left.

"Someone threw me the ball and I'm standing on the mound rubbing it up," Cleary says, "and I look over at the dugout and I see [Washington manager Ossie] Bluege waving at me. He's got one leg up on the step of the dugout and he's waving at me to come out. I thought, he's got to be kidding. What the hell can he be thinking? No manager takes his pitcher out that way. You go to the mound. You don't embarrass him. So I stood there rubbing the ball and waiting. [First baseman] Joe Kuhel came over and he said he never saw anything like that and he'd been around a long time. He called it bush league. I told Kuhel, 'I'm not leaving.' Finally, the umpire came over and said, 'Son, I think you better go,' so I left."

Cleary walked into the Washington dugout and took a seat on the bench. "I heard Bluege say, 'Pitcher, my fucking ass!' and I yelled back at him, 'Go fuck yourself!' We went for each other, but the other players got between us and shoved me down the stairs into the dressing room.

"I thought, who the hell does he think he is, Joe McCarthy or something, and what am I, a bum or something? I just got out of the army, I didn't need that. I had a very good reputation in the minor leagues. Every manager I played for knew I put out all the time. Sore arm or not, I was always ready to pitch, always ready to go into the second game of a doubleheader if they needed me for an inning or two. You know, I could get them out with my curveball. He had no right to do that.

"I got dressed and left before the game was over," Cleary says. "I never gave it a thought until recently, but I was pissed off because I knew I could get these guys out. I'd been hit hard before, but then delivered.

"The next morning I'm in the dugout, and Bluege yells over, 'Hey, you!' I don't answer, and he yells again, 'Hey, you!' I say, 'I got a name!' So he says, 'Okay, *Mr. Cleary*, go see Mr. Griffith.'"

Clark Griffith sympathized with Cleary, but told him, "You can't act like that in the major leagues."

"So I says, 'Mr. Griffith, Bluege didn't act like a major leaguer, either.' I told him, 'I was never trouble. People used to fight to room with me. I was always ready. Any manager will tell you that.'"

But Griffith told Cleary it was over. "He told me Bucky Harris would like to have me at Buffalo [in the Triple-A International League] where he was managing then, so I finished the season at Buffalo. I won three or four games for a last-place team." His record there was 3–3.

The following season, Washington, with undertones of retaliation, tried to send Cleary to their Class-B team in Charlotte at $200 a month. But the interim baseball commissioner, Leslie O'Connor, stepped in and declared Cleary a free agent, having determined there had been a secret deal between Washington and Detroit to send Cleary up to Buffalo, a Detroit affiliate, after his altercation with Bluege.

O'Connor had worked with baseball commissioner Judge Kennesaw Landis for twenty years. In the 1930s, O'Connor's investigation of the minor-league system of the St. Louis Cardinals resulted in Landis's declaring seventy-four players to be free agents and fining a number of teams that had cooperated with St. Louis to violate the principles of competition. In the mid-1950s, O'Connor was named president of the Pacific Coast League.

Washington appealed O'Connor's decision on Cleary. "The old man [Griffith] said they sent me to Buffalo 'cause my mother was sick in New York and I could be near her. Well, that was a lot of bull. Buffalo is no closer to New York [City] than Washington."

Cleary reported to Charlotte and was offered the contract that paid him less than half of what he had earned the previous year. "I said, 'What is this?' and the general manager there, Phil Howser, said, 'Mr. Griffith told me not to give you anymore.'" Cleary refused to sign.

"One day, I came into the office there, and I heard Howser talking on the phone with Griffith. He said, 'Are you sure, Mr. Griffith? Are you sure?' When he hung up, he looked up at me and said, 'Mr. Griffith said to just give you your free agency.'"

In 1946, Cleary pitched for the Jersey City Giants back in the Triple-A International League where his teammates included Bobby Thomson and Don Mueller. Over the next few years, he continued to pitch in such places as Palatka and Gainsville, Florida; Anniston, Alabama; Augusta, Georgia; and Charleston, South Carolina. He continued to win his share of games, reaching nearly 100 in his overall professional career. In 1947 and 1948, his earned run averages were 2.16 and 2.17, respectively.

After the 1950 season, which included some time in the semipro Southern Minny (Minnesota) League, Cleary returned home to his bride of almost two years and retired from baseball. "She was tired of me being away so much and was expecting our second child and she said, 'That is it.' So that was it, and I just packed it in."

After clerking on Wall Street for about three years, Cleary purchased a bar three blocks from his old West Side neighborhood home. He operated it for more than twenty years with his wife, Mary, and opened a second similar establishment. After both places were sold, Cleary continued working as a bartender for a few years before finally retiring in 1982 at the age of sixty-two.

When recounting his experiences today, Cleary speaks without rancor and holds no grudges. "I spent ten years in the bushes, and there were many wonderful experiences I had playing minor-league baseball and, of course, many happy events," he says.

But, like many former ballplayers, Cleary does not feel today's players are the equals of his contemporaries. "They don't play the game now near as hard as they did when I played," he says. "They hurt the game. I don't even watch them anymore unless I'm in a bar and I can't escape the television. I don't care how much money they make, they're always crying. Every little thing—the rotator cuffs, a hangnail—is a major operation. After the fifth inning, if they're leading, they're looking down to the bullpen for relief. Then there's drugs. They didn't do that in my day and I never looked to the bullpen. I wanted to stay in there.

"Like they say, you got to have heart. But heart and courage don't mean 'let's go out on the street and fight.' It's so easy to stand out on that mound, when things are going against you, and quit, without anyone knowing it. That's where the heart shows up—on the mound. When the chips are down and things are going against you and you just grit your teeth and bear down harder."

Robert Earl "Bert" Shepard

WASHINGTON NATIONALS, 1945

Before Eddie Gaedel came along, Bert Shepard was probably the most publicized one-game major-leaguer in history, when he became the only man ever to pitch in the major leagues with an artificial leg.

Shepard, the second oldest of six sons, had been born healthy on June 28, 1920, in Dana, Indiana.

His father had a "delivery business"—a horse and a wagon—until the Depression forced him to become a farmhand for $50 a month plus housing for his family. It was a transient existence, and the Shepard family resided in a number of different communities in the area as Bert was growing up. He played a little football and basketball in high school, but the school didn't have a baseball team.

In 1930, the first full year of the Depression, Shepard went to live with his grandmother in Clinton, Indiana, and learned about baseball and baseball players by listening to her radio. He especially recalls listening to the 1931 World Series when Pepper Martin of the St. Louis Cardinals got 12 hits in 24 times up and stole five bases against the Philadelphia Athletics.

Soon Shepard began playing pickup baseball with boys his own age and shagging flies for the neighborhood teams. As he moved into his teens, he became a fairly good player and starred in the local sandlot games in and around Clinton.

Shepard loved the game and heard that California was the place to go if you wanted to be a baseball player, so at the end of his junior year in high school in 1937, he and a friend hopped some freight trains and hitchhiked out to the West Coast, working as busboys along the way to get their meals and enough money to finance the next leg of their journey.

In California, Shepard supported himself by working in a tire retread plant while playing baseball on every playground and in every league he could find. In 1938, he came across a copy of *Life* magazine that featured pictures of Cincinnati's Johnny Vander Meer who, that year, had become the only man ever to pitch two consecutive no-hitters. From the pictures of Vander Meer in action, Shepard taught himself the elements of a left-handed windup in front of the mirror in his room.

At eighteen, Shepard began playing semipro baseball and, in 1939, was spotted by Chicago White Sox scout Doug Minor, who signed him to a contract for $60 a month. Shepard was sent to the White Sox minor-league spring training center in Longview, Texas, but in his eagerness to make an impression, he threw too often and developed a sore arm.

"It's amazing the lack of coaching they had then," he says. "Shoot, they'd let you just pitch every day if you wanted to. Then, after you were injured, they'd say, 'Well, he *said* he was all right.'"

The White Sox released him and Shepard returned home to let his arm recover. In 1940, the following year, he played for Wisconsin Rapids in the Wisconsin State League, where he appeared in nine games, winning three and losing two before being released. He was having control problems; in 43 innings, he walked 48 batters.

"I walked a lot of batters because I didn't have the right coaching and theory," he says. "Everybody said, 'Pitch to the corners.' The corner's what, three inches wide? So you're throwing a ball three inches outside. That's still accurate throwing, but it caused me to walk a lot of people. As I look back now, I wasn't wild. My problem was where I was trying to throw the ball."

After going back to Clinton to get his high school diploma in the summer of 1940, Shepard answered a newspaper ad the following February to drive a new car across the country to Seattle, Washington. He got the job and then worked his way down the Pacific Coast to Anaheim, California, where the Philadelphia Athletics were training for the upcoming 1941 season. Shepard talked his way into a tryout with the A's and got to meet their legendary owner-manager, Connie Mack. He pitched well enough to be offered a contract to pitch for the A's minor-league team in Anaheim.

But the same problem with control plagued him there, and he was quickly released. Shepard then traveled to Bisbee, Arizona, where he hooked on with the Arizona-Texas League team.

After an undistinguished summer, he was released again, but Shepard was encouraged by his performance that year. Although his pitching wasn't what he would have liked it to be, he felt his control was getting a little better. Furthermore, his hitting also continued to improve. It was good enough, in fact, to keep him in the lineup at first base on days when he wasn't pitching. Since he always was a fast man on the bases, Shepard

Bert Shepard was one of the most highly publicized players of his day, and was an inspiration to other amputees returning from the war.

thought he might be able to make it professionally as a first baseman instead of as a pitcher.

But the minor leagues were one of the early casualties of World War II, with the lack of players causing many teams to fold. At the start of 1942, there was no team for Shepard to play on. Within two years, only ten minor leagues would still be in operation. But it made little difference. He was drafted that May.

Shepard went to Daniel Field near Augusta, Georgia, and applied for pilot training, although he knew absolutely nothing about it. "I'd never been near an airplane. Hadn't been within a mile of one," he says.

Before being sent out for flight training, however, Shepard played first base for the Daniel Field baseball team and even got started on a brief football career, which he remembers happily. Although he'd never played football before, outside of an occasional pickup game, Shepard tried out for the base team. When asked where he was from, the young recruit replied, "Indiana," which was taken to mean Indiana *University*.

"I made first-string fullback and all the rest of the team were college players," recalls Shepard. "I went behind the barracks that night to practice the Notre Dame shift. I didn't want people to know I didn't know much about it.

"So I played one game against Clemson and got a rib hurt. Then two games later, we played Jacksonville Naval Training Station. They had six of their starting eleven out of the pro league. I intercepted three passes, made eleven clean tackles, and even gained a few yards even though we got the hell beat out of us.

"So I get back and my orders are there to go to flight training school. And the newspaper said, 'Daniel Field will miss the valuable experience of Shepard.' That's the first whole game I ever played," he laughs. "But you don't tell people all those things. It's a good example of how people often overrate the opponent."

At flight school, Shepard began training as a fighter pilot. "I go out with five other students to our instructor, and they've all flown before. The instructor gets to me and he says, 'Have you ever flown?' I said, 'This is the closest I've ever *been* to an airplane.' He said, 'Well then, I'll take you first.'

"I was getting into something I didn't know anything about. But I said, 'Well, I'm gonna give it a try.' I found I had some skills as a pilot, and I wanted to fly. I wanted to pursue it to the fullest extent, and the more I pursued it, the more I liked it. I enjoyed flying tremendously. You're the boss. You're in a fighter aircraft, a P-38, and in a dive we could get it up to about 525 miles an hour. We could go up to 46,000 feet. And I've rolled it fifty feet off the ground in front of the tower and been grounded for a couple of days," he laughs.

After completing his training, Second Lieutenant Shepard, P-38 pilot, took a train from Los Angeles to New York, where he boarded the troop ship *Aquatania* and landed in Scotland two weeks later.

After six more weeks of training, Shepard began flying combat missions with the Fifty-Fifth Fighter Group of the U.S. Eighth Air Force and piloting a fast, new P-38 Thunderbolt. On his thirty-fourth mission, he flew in the first daytime bombing raid over Berlin.

As the weather improved that spring, the base decided to organize a baseball team, and Shepard volunteered to manage. On the morning of the first game, May 21, 1944, another mission was scheduled to bomb Berlin. When he heard about it, Shepard volunteered, even though he wasn't due to fly until the next day. "I'd flown four out of the last five days, but it was going to be a rough mission," he says. "We were scheduled to do low-level bombing and strafing, so I knew we'd need as many pilots as we could get. Besides, [I thought] we'd be back in time for the ball game. But I never got back for that first game.

"I was going in to strafe an aerodrome, and I'm probably a mile or two away, about twenty feet off the ground. When you go in to strafe an aerodrome, they've got 100 or 200 automatic weapons, and they're just setting up a crossfire. Some airplanes had already strafed the field, and there were some German planes burning, so I had a good column of smoke to line up on. I didn't have to raise up to see the field.

"I'm probably a mile from the field, and they shoot my right foot off. You can just feel the foot coming loose at the ankle. I called the colonel and told him I had a leg shot off and I'd call him back later. In the meantime, I get hit in the chin and that caused me to slump over the controls and the next thing I know, I'm just ready to hit the ground. I pulled back. but I couldn't make it. The airplane crashes at 380 miles per hour, explodes, and burns.

"I wake up in a German hospital two or three or four days later. They had the leg amputated, and the gunsight had mashed in my skull over my right eye. They had removed about a two-inch-square piece of the frontal sinus bone over the right eye.

"I woke up fat, dumb, and happy," he says. "They talked to me a little bit, gave me a shot, and I went back to sleep."

After recovering from his injuries, Shepard was held in a prisoner-of-war camp and worked himself back into shape. A fellow prisoner crafted a crude artifical leg on which he could walk surprisingly well, and the two played catch every day. Shepard began to test his limits. He pivoted, practiced covering first base, and fielding bunts. He quickly discovered he could do a lot more than he had originally thought. A German doctor was so impressed he brought his hospital staff out to watch the American prisoner.

While Shepard explored his potential, the Red Cross came through the camp to interview injured detainees and identify those unable to return to combat. He was examined and cleared for repatriation in the next trade of POWs between the Allies and the Axis. In February of 1945, after eight months as a prisoner of war, he sailed into New York harbor aboard a Swedish Red Cross ship.

"I landed in New York and then went down to Walter Reed Hospital to get a new artificial leg," Shepard recalls. "While we're waiting, Secretary of War [Robert] Patterson asked two officers and two enlisted men that just returned from prison camp to come to his office. So he sent the staff car out, and I happened to be one of the prisoners that was chosen to go.

"He asked each of us what we wanted to do, and one old farm boy from Arkansas, he says, 'All I want to do is go home and get my shotgun and shoot some ducks.'

"Patterson [asked] me, and I said, 'Well, if I can't fly combat, I'd like to play professional baseball.' Patterson said, 'Well, hell, you can't do that on that leg, can you?' and I said, 'As soon as I get a new leg, I'm pretty sure I can.'"

Patterson telephoned Clark Griffith, a friend of his and the owner of the American League's Washington Nationals. He told Griffith, "We have a prisoner of war that just came back from Germany and lost his leg. He says he can play pro ball."

Griffith, perhaps sensing the publicity to be gained, replied, "Well, after he gets his new leg, have him come out."

On March 14, four days after receiving his new artificial leg, Shepard arrived at the Nats' spring training complex. Only as Shepard was getting dressed did the players and Bluege realize he was an amputee. When he walked to the mound, it was nearly impossible to tell he wore an artifical leg, and when he threw, he threw *hard*. It was obvious he was serious about playing. Soon, reporters, photographers, and newsreel cameramen were overrunning the camp to see this twenty-four-year-old war veteran amputee pitch.

One day a newsreel cameraman asked Shepard if he could field bunts. "Sure," said Shepard. "Just let me know when you're ready." Everyone stopped and watched as Shepard pitched to backup catcher Al Evans, who bunted the ball six feet in front of the plate. Shepard came in, scooped it up, pivoted as left-handers must, and fired to first. Then he did it again. The Washington players were abuzz. Bluege, in a choked-up voice, yelled, "Atta boy, Shep."

Shepard's artificial leg did not affect his play much. "You pitch off your back foot," he explains, "and I was left-handed and it was my right leg that was off. So I was coming down on the right leg. And as far as batting, well, I batted left-handed, and Mel Ott could have had his right leg off and still hit 510 home runs." The fact that the amputation was below his knee, not above, also helped his agility.

Shepard became an immediate celebrity and his workout was featured in newsreels across the country. *The Sporting News* called him "The baseball man of the hour—or the afternoon or evening." He became the only left-handed batting-practice pitcher for the Nats that spring, and also worked out at first base and took batting practice.

"One day after our workout, I was over at Secretary Patterson's office," Shepard remembers, "and Larry MacPhail of the Yankees, who was on his staff, came in. He says, 'Bert, we got a lot of amputees over at Atlantic City. How about coming over tomorrow and work out with the Yankees? If the Senators don't sign you, I will.'"

Shepard went to Atlantic City, but unbeknownst to him, Griffith had scheduled him to pitch for Washington that same day. When Griffith discovered that Shepard had gone with MacPhail, he exploded.

In an effort to defuse the situation, Patterson's office told Griffith that the trip had been for the morale of the soldiers and that it had been *their* idea, not MacPhail's. Satisfied, Griffith quickly signed Shepard as a coach, but gave every indication that the young man would get a chance to pitch or pinch hit in a game during the 1945 season. The *Washington Post* quoted Griffith as saying, "We certainly welcome Lieutenant Shepard to the club. This boy is a symbol of the courage of American youths. The same spirit that carried him into combat with our enemies is with him in baseball. He believes in himself and we believe in him."

That spring, Shepard pitched in several exhibition games, especially against various armed forces teams, whose lineups were often more formidable than those of the wartime big-league teams. The ex-fighter pilot was heavily publicized to inspire other disabled veterans returning from the war. In one game, when he pitched two innings against Fort Story, he gave up a run in the eighth inning, but struck out the side in the ninth. Against the New London Naval Base, one of the better armed forces teams, he went five innings, allowing only one run on three hits against a lineup that included Yogi Berra.

Although anxious to go on the active roster, Shepard was pleased to be where he was. "I was so happy to be with a major-league ball club. I was pitching batting practice almost every day, so I was gradually developing myself all the time. I used to take infield at first base. After Joe Kuhel would take the first two rounds, I would take the next two. And I've had people tell me that they didn't know when we changed. So that gave me good practice as far as the footwork was concerned. I bided my time. I was just as happy as the devil to be there."

Pitching batting practice regularly also helped Shepard solve his control problems. "I would pitch to good hitters, and I'd throw the ball right down the middle. They *didn't* get a hit every time. They *didn't* hit it out of the park. And so it gave me confidence in not being afraid to throw the ball over."

One day in Boston, fans who arrived at the park early to see batting practice saw something they would never forget.

"I had been doing some running in the outfield in Yankee Stadium in the series before Boston, and I heard a little crack [in the artifical leg]," Shepard recalls. "But the leg still felt solid, and we moved on to Boston. I was pitching batting practice that day, and after a few pitches, I came down on it and it cracked a little bit."

Shepard just kept pitching. "I made another pitch, and the leg turned sideways. So I straightened it up and threw another pitch, and by now the leg is almost at a 90-degree angle. So I straightened it up again and made another pitch, and this time the foot broke completely off inside my sock."

The fans in Fenway Park saw Shepard's foot, still in its sock and shoe, dangling loose as the batting-practice pitcher went into his next windup, brought his leg up, kicked back toward center field to get his momentum, and began his pivot toward the hitter—only to have the shoe and the foot fly off and head toward center field.

"I just turned around casually and made another pitch," Shepard says, "and the players were lying around on the ground laughing. But think of the fans! They didn't know I had an artificial foot." Catcher Rick Ferrell also remembered the incident. "The crowd gasped," he said. "They thought it was his real foot."

Another of Shepard's memories from that summer concerns the occasional Griffith Stadium appearances of Washington's biggest baseball legend, Walter Johnson, who had managed Ed Wineapple (see Chapter 1) in 1929.

"A wonderful man. Gentle as they come," Shepard reports. "He came out there to the ballpark, and of course, everybody's in awe of him. He just threw a few on the sidelines in his street clothes, and Bluege, the manager, said, 'I bet he could still fire them if he had to.'

"Walter Johnson never swore and his catcher, Muddy Ruel, never swore," Shepard says. "And Joe Judge, who used to play first base with them, told me they'd be out on the mound in a tight situation, and Walter would say, 'Well goodness gracious, Muddy, I don't know what to do!' And Muddy would say, 'Well, dadgummit, Walter!'"

In 1945 there was no major-league All-Star game because of wartime travel restrictions. Instead, a series of exhibitions between different American and National League teams was set up across the country to benefit the war-relief effort. On July 10, Washington was matched with the Brooklyn Dodgers in Griffith Stadium.

Two days before the game, Bluege told Shepard he would start. "Having not started a game in almost four years, I felt the pressure, and I knew there were an awful lot of people who thought I couldn't do it," he remembers. "And there were things that could happen out on the field—if I messed up a bunt or slipped like any other pitcher fielding a ground ball, they'd say it was because of the leg. If that happened to me, it would be lights out. Mr. Griffith gave me a chance, but there was much more pressure on me because everybody else was afraid I'd fail.

"But I was willing to give it a good try and see what the hell happened," he continues. "Like your first mission in combat. It's what you've trained for."

Shepard tossed and turned the night before, but expected he would. "I don't think anybody sleeps good in situations like that," he says. "If you sleep good, you're in trouble. I don't think anybody going into an important game has ever felt really good. You don't sleep too good, you warm up very carefully, you can't wait for the game to get started, and then you settle down."

More than 23,000 fans showed up that night. In the pregame festivities, Shepard met with the press and kibitzed with Brooklyn manager Leo Durocher.

"Leo and I were standing there talking while the press was taking pictures and interviewing both of us," Shepard says. "A reporter asked Leo if they were gonna bunt against me. Leo says, 'I'll fine anybody $500 that bunts tonight 'cause we need the batting practice.' But the sportswriters wrote it up as, 'Leo Durocher, the Good-Hearted Manager, Agrees Not to Bunt Against Shepard.' So everybody thought I couldn't field bunts."

The pressure took a toll right away. Shepard walked Durocher to lead off the game. "I think I walked the first two batters on eight pitches," he says. "I said to myself, 'Oh, my God. You've got a house full of people here, and you'd better get this straightened out pretty soon.'" He knew another walk or two could spell disaster and admits he "was pretty concerned."

His catcher, Ferrell, resisted the temptation to go to the mound to talk, which might have made Shepard even more nervous. "My pitches were close," Shepard says. "I told myself, 'Damn it! I know I can get it over the plate.'"

And he did. He retired the side without further problems and then shut out the Dodgers on just one base hit through the first three innings. Shepard asked Bluege if he could pitch another inning. In the fourth, he gave up two runs on four successive singles, but left with the Nats leading 3–2 and was eventually declared the winning pitcher.

How did Shepard feel about it? "I was just happy as hell that it turned out that way," he says. Following the game, Shepard was rewarded by being placed on the team's active roster, which made it possible for the one-legged pitcher to appear in a real major-league game a few weeks later.

The day was August 4, 1945, the second game of the doubleheader against the Red Sox. In front of 13,035 fans, Bluege waved Joe Cleary off the mound and into the dugout. The Red Sox had just scored 12 runs in the top of the fourth inning.

From the way the game was going, Shepard thought he might get called in. "When we fell way behind, Bluege told me to get ready," he says. "They were fighting for the pennant," he says of his team, "and they had used up all their pitchers." Soon he was the only one warming up.

Washington's pitching staff was depleted from a heavy dose of doubleheaders, the game was out of reach, and Bluege, fuming from Joe Cleary's poor performance, was not about to use another pitcher he felt might help him down the pennant stretch. So he waved in the one-legged Bert Shepard from the Nats' bullpen down the right field line.

After almost being put to sleep by Boston's marathon inning, the fans stirred awake and applauded as Shepard walked from the bullpen in foul territory, down the right field line, across the foul line, and to the mound. Shepard does not recall Bluege or anyone else being there to greet him, and says he was unaware of the near-fight in the dugout between Bluege and Cleary (see Chapter 14). "I can understand Bluege being upset about how that inning went, though," he says.

Shepard took his warm-up pitches, throwing to Senators' catcher Mike Guerra. When Shepard was ready, Guerra didn't talk to him, except to go over the signs, and none of the infielders came over to help him relax with a few reassuring words. "I guess they figured I could handle it," he said. "Besides, there's not a hell of a lot you can say in a situation like that."

Unlike his exhibition game against the Dodgers, Shepard didn't have the night before to get nervous. So how did he feel?

"I'm a competitor," he says. "I was pitching a lot of batting practice and had developed a lot of confidence. I said, 'Here's my chance.' I was awful glad about it. I said, 'Goddamn it, I'm in the ball game!'"

There were two outs, and Cleary had left the bases still loaded. The hitter was a left-hander, George "Catfish" Metkovich, Boston's center fielder, who was in the third season of a 10-year big-league career. Shepard pitched carefully. "I got the count to 3 and 2, and I said, 'Hell, now you got to throw the ball over. You don't want to come in here and walk him.'"

With two out and the count full, the three base runners took off as soon as Shepard went into his windup. He threw a fastball, above the waist and on the inside half of the plate. Metkovich swung. And missed.

Bert Shepard, the only man in the history of baseball to pitch in the major leagues on an artificial leg, had struck out the first man he faced— with the bases loaded. With the inning over, he walked to the Washington dugout to a standing ovation.

Shepard wasn't finished. Bluege sent him back out for the fifth inning, and the sixth, seventh, eighth, and ninth. Shepard wasn't surprised. He knew the game was his to finish. He pitched five and one-third innings, held the Red Sox to one run on three hits, and struck out three men in a batting order that included veteran hitters Pete Fox, Leon Culberson, Dolf Camilli, Eddie Lake, and Tom McBride.

While pitching, Shepard also threw out two batters on ground balls back to the mound and walked only one man. "I was enjoying it," he says. "I felt that I could get them out." At the plate that day, he went 0 for 3 against the Red Sox's rookie ace, Dave "Boo" Ferris, who won 21 games that year. Shepard doesn't recall much about it. "I think I hit a fly ball off of him."

After the game, Shepard thought he'd done a "pretty good job" and might get the opportunity to pitch more often. But the closeness of the pennant race forced Bluege to stay with his veteran pitchers as the Senators drove to overtake the Tigers. Shepard never played in another game that season and never asked why.

"That's a question you wouldn't ask. We were fighting for the pennant and being very successful, and we had some pretty good pitchers," he says. "It's hard for the manager to imagine that his best chance of winning today is a guy with his leg off. You just can't imagine that. It didn't bother me, but I can see where the other person would have a problem believing that could happen."

Going into the final days of the 1945 season, Washington was still in the race with Detroit, but their season was ending early with a doubleheader against Philadelphia. The Tigers and the rest of the American League, meanwhile, would continue a week longer. In the first game of that doubleheader, Washington's pennant hopes were dealt a severe blow when they lost to the A's, 4–3, in 12 innings, on a fly ball that outfielder George Binks lost in the sun.

But the Tigers were not playing particularly well either, and they went into their final two games against the defending champions, the St. Louis Browns, still needing a victory to capture the flag. Because of rain, the two games had to be scheduled as a doubleheader on the final day of the season. If the Tigers lost both games, they would face the rested Nats in a playoff game in Washington.

In the first game, the Tigers went into the ninth inning trailing 3–2, but loaded the bases against St. Louis screwballer Nelson Potter. That's when Hank Greenberg hit his grand-slam homer into the bleachers, just inside the foul pole, to give Detroit the pennant. The second game that day was rained out.

Washington had come close to going from last place in 1944 to first place in 1945, which no team had ever done before. If the game on August 4, in which Joe Cleary and Bert Shepard both made their only major-league appearances, had ended differently, they might well have done it.

During the off-season, Shepard visited veterans' and children's hospitals and made a training film for leg amputees back from the war. He also barnstormed with the American League All-Stars and then reported for spring training with the Nats in 1946. Though he pitched in a couple of exhibition games and threw well, he wasn't given a serious chance of making the team, since the prewar stars were returning en masse. "There were so many good pitchers in that camp," he says, "that the handwriting was on the wall for me. There was no way I was going to make that staff, with Dutch Leonard, Sid Hudson, Walter Masterson, Bobo Newsom, Mickey Haefner, Roger Wolff, and Rae Scarborough. They even had a future Hall of Famer, Early Wynn." So Shepard remained with the team as a coach.

He remembers his roommate, Jeff Heath, who joined the club that year. "He was a lot of fun, and we did a lot of kidding around. I remember one time feeling his muscle and telling him he was as strong as a bull and thinking to myself, 'And damn near as smart,'" Shepard laughs. "When he broke his ankle so badly later on [in 1948], I sent him a note and said that if he needed one, I had a spare."

Later in the year, however, at Shepard's request, Griffith assigned him to the Chattanooga Lookouts, Washington's top farm team in the Southern Association, so he could get to pitch once in a while. "I wasn't getting to play, and I didn't get on the regular active list, so I asked to go down to Chattanooga and finish the season," he says. Shepard won two and lost two on the mound there, and surprised everyone one time by hitting a double and scoring from second on a single to left field.

He barnstormed again during the winter of 1946 with the American League All-Stars, playing in the Pacific Northwest. He pitched occasionally (once striking out Stan Musial), but actually preferred playing first base so he could play every day. He was having a successful tour and looked forward to playing against Bob Feller's All-Stars, probably the top barnstorming team that winter.

"We were playing Feller's All-Stars in Seattle," he recalls, "and I saw I wasn't in the lineup. I said, 'Hey, wait a minute. How come I'm not playing tonight?' They said, 'Well, Feller's out there and he has to bear down and we're afraid you might get hurt.'

"I said, 'Look, you guys, I've done everything I'm supposed to do up 'til now and, by God, I'm *playing!*' So I played first base, made a couple of pretty good plays, and I got 1 for 2 off of Feller and I got 1 for 2 off of Johnny Sain."

In November 1946, Shepard checked into Walter Reed Hospital for additional reconstructive surgery on his leg. The doctors in the German hospital had done the preliminary work, leaving the remaining surgery to be completed on Shepard's return to the States. The reamputation should have had a recovery time of six weeks, but there were complications that led to four more operations.

Shepard was on crutches for two and a half years before receiving medical clearance to play again, and by that time, his shoulder muscles had tightened so much that his arm never fully recovered. As a major-league pitcher, he was finished. In 1949, Shepard took a job as a player-manager with the Class-B team in Waterbury, Connecticut.

In addition to pitching and managing, Shepard also played nearly fifty games at first base, hitting four home runs, and driving in 21 in 131 times at bat. Two of his home runs came in one game on July 6 against Bristol. He also stole five bases during the year and excited the crowd by beating out a bunt for a base hit. "I had an advantage," he says, "because not only was I pretty fast, but nobody *expected* me to run. Even when pitchers were looking over at me when I was on first, I often could tell they were concentrating on the hitter and not on me." On the mound that year, he won five and lost six.

Shepard remained in Waterbury for only one season before deciding to retire. "The team was not winning, and when you're not winning, the board of directors gives you a lot of advice," he says. "One day we got back home from a road trip at three in the morning, and I was told to schedule a workout for the next morning. I asked why, and was told it would impress the fans. I said no. I wouldn't do it because it wouldn't help the team. So I left after that year." He spent two years selling typewriters for IBM.

In 1952, Shepard attempted a comeback and, primarily as a gate attraction, played for four different teams, St. Augustine in the Florida State League, Paris in the Big State League, Corpus Christi in the Gulf Coast League, and Hot Springs in the Cotton State League. Later, he took a job managing a semipro team in Willistown, North Dakota, where he met his wife, Betty, a school teacher in nearby Grand Forks. They were married in 1953.

At Corpus Christi, Shepard remembers hitting a home run halfway up the center field flagpole, but laughs when he tells the story of what happened after he left that city. "When I left Corpus Christi," Shepard says, "I called the owner of the Hot Springs club and told him I was looking for a job and said I had pitched for Washington, and he hired me sight unseen. About a week after I got there, he had the team over his house for a barbecue and came up to me and said, 'I have a confession to make. After I hired you over the phone, I went over to the sports department of the local paper, hoping to generate some publicity, and told them I had just hired a guy who used to pitch for Washington in the American League. One of the reporters there said, "Oh, that's that one-legged ballplayer." Well, I was so upset when I heard that, I tried to call you back to cancel the deal, but I couldn't get a hold of you.'"

Shepard still wasn't finished as a professional baseball player. Dividing his time between the pitcher's mound and first base, he played a couple of more years in the minors. At Tampa in the Florida International League in 1953, he played for manager Ben Chapman, a former major-league outfielder and manager. "We used to have a lot of exhibition races in Tampa," Shepard remembers, "and with my artificial leg, I was still able to win races going from home to first."

In one game in the minors, the other team's hitters became so frustrated at being unable to hit Shepard's pitches that they resorted to bunting. They laid down nine bunts against him, and he threw them all out. "If they had done that all game long," he chuckles, "I would have had a perfect game."

In 1955, Shepard was offered a contract by the Modesto Reds of the California League. Pitching in the first game of a doubleheader against Reno the day after his signing, Shepard surrendered two runs in the first inning, then settled down. No Reno base runner advanced past second base after the first inning. While he was being interviewed after his complete game victory, the fans crowded around him and urged him to pitch the second game, a plea Shepard good-naturedly brushed aside, saying, "Perhaps later in the season."

Later didn't come. In two more starts, he was hit hard and allowed 12 runs in two and one-third innings. That complete game victory proved to be his last hurrah. Hanging up the spikes for good, Shepard finally headed into private life, working as a safety engineer at Hughes Aircraft, and then for several southern California insurance companies. He also worked in the same capacity for Fluor Construction in both Saudi Arabia and Venezuela before retiring in 1982.

He is a two-time National Amputee Golf Champion, winning the title in 1968 and 1971, and still plays extremely well, walking on an artificial ankle he developed himself. Today, he and Betty reside in Hesperia, California, about forty miles north of San Bernadino. They have four children and eight grandchildren.

Shepard doesn't consider losing his leg a misfortune. "I've always en-joyed the situation of competition," he says, "I've never been afraid to fail. While I've had a couple setbacks, losing a leg and so forth, I found that wasn't as bad as I thought it would be. I felt that I could've done a pretty good job [for Washington] had I had the opportunity, but I'm sure a lot of ballplayers feel the same way.

"I remember when my daughter, Karen, was ten, she and I were sitting on the bed and I had the [artificial] leg off, and she said, 'Daddy, I'm sorry that you lost your leg.' I said, 'Well, Karen, I'm not. If I hadn't lost my leg, I wouldn't have met your mother and I wouldn't have you. And I wouldn't take anything in the world for you.' And that's the way to look at things."

Shepard's philosophy on life remains compelling. "When the Germans interrogated me," he recalls, "they asked me to answer some questions and I wouldn't do it. I said, 'When I went into pilot training and came over here to combat, I was willing to accept whatever consequences happened.' You take whatever happens and do the best with it that you can."

Otis Allen "Scat" Davis

BROOKLYN DODGERS, 1946

The run Otis Davis scored—in his single major-league game—helped the Brooklyn Dodgers finish the 1946 season in a flat-footed tie for first place in the National League with the St. Louis Cardinals. That year Davis was on both those teams, although he only got to play for one of them.

Davis was born on September 24, 1920, and grew up in Charleston, Arkansas. His mother died when he was eight, and his father, Cleve, was a coal miner. At Charleston High School, Davis played basketball and football, and ran track. "They only had a baseball team one year when I was there," Davis says. "We played about twelve games, but didn't even have any uniforms." As for his athletic ability, he says, "I was pretty good in all of them, but not outstanding."

Playing high school football, however, he injured his right knee. "I stretched some tendons, you know, and some cartilage got loose in there and it would swell up every once and a while," he says.

Although there was little high school baseball to play, Davis did play semipro ball in Charleston twice a week for a couple of years, and he played American Legion baseball in Fort Smith. "One of the guys I played against in those days was [Elwin] Preacher Roe," Davis recalls. Roe later spent twelve years in the majors.

In 1941, when Davis was twenty, Bob Kuykendall, who managed Davis's younger brother on another American Legion team, sent both boys to play amateur baseball at Marysville, Kansas, in the Ban Johnson League. "Clarence Mitchell, the old spitball pitcher, was the manager there, and he was a big help to me. I really learned a lot from him," Davis says.

As a left-handed batter, the tall, slim youngster (six feet and 160 pounds) played center field and hit over .300 at Marysville. His speed soon earned him the nickname "Scat." Asked why he batted left-handed although a right-handed thrower, Davis says, "Lots of guys did that. It was just natural. I just did it that way without thinking. I think people are born that way, to hit either right-handed or left-handed. It's natural. It's not something you learn."

At Marysville, "The scouts saw me, and I signed with the St. Louis Cards at the end of the season." The scout was Wid Matthews, and Davis received a $250 bonus for signing. "Can you imagine that?" he says. "Most people signed for nothing."

The Cardinals sent Davis to their New Iberia farm team in the Evangeline League to start the 1942 season. "The league folded early that year because of lack of attendance," Davis says.

"They sent me to Williamson, West Virginia, in the Mountain States League," Davis continues, "and I hit .285 or .290 [.283]. I played there with Del Rice and 'Hoot' Rice—Hal Rice—no relation, and they both made it to the majors. Toward the end of the year, they sent me up to Hamilton, Ontario, to play in what they called the Pony League."

As the 1942 season was drawing to a close, Davis, like many ballplayers throughout the country, received his army draft notice. "Once you were drafted," he says, "they gave you a little time to enlist in another branch if you wanted, so in August I enlisted in the navy."

Davis was sent to San Diego for Navy boot training, but after marching and drilling for a week, the knee he had injured in high school became heavily swollen. "I thought maybe they'd operate on it," he says, "but instead they discharged me." He was out of the Navy within three months.

In 1943, Davis started the season with Lynchburg, Virginia, in the Piedmont League. "I was only there a couple of weeks," he says, "but that's where I first got to play with [Albert] Red Schoendienst. Then they sent me to Jamestown, New York, back in the Pony League, and I spent the year there.

"The Cardinals had closed their farm team in Hamilton and moved it to Jamestown that year, so it was really the same team," Davis says. "I batted over .300, maybe .328 to .330, and stole 30 bases. [He hit .329 and stole 32 bases.] Despite my leg, I could still outrun most guys in the league. In those days, we didn't steal as much as they do now. We used to run only when we needed to, when it was necessary. We got into the four-team Shaughnessy Playoffs that year, but lost in seven games to Wellsville, New York, a Yankee farm team."

In 1944, Davis was assigned to Rochester, New York, the Cardinals' Triple-A team in the International League. "I played the full year there," he says, "and hit about .270, but I was around second in the league in fielding." In addition to Schoendienst, his teammates included Walter Alston, who later managed the Dodgers from 1954 to 1957.

After the season, another teammate, catcher Del Rice, suggested that Davis stay in Rochester and join him working at a Bausch and Lomb plant (where Rice had worked in the previous off-season) and play basketball for the company in a local industrial league. Davis agreed, and decided he liked Rochester enough to make the city his home.

He started the 1945 season in Rochester as the center fielder and part-time shortstop, but by July was hitting only .195. Rochester manager Burleigh Grimes suggested he might have a better chance of reaching the majors if he became a full-time infielder. "I wasn't hitting," Davis says, "and he [Grimes] thought if I could play shortstop every day, I could make it, so they sent me down to Allentown in the Interstate League to play shortstop regularly," Davis says.

At Allentown, Davis started out as a shortstop. Throwing as an infielder, however, he soon developed a sore arm and eventually was moved back to center field. His hitting picked up, however, and he batted .350.

In 1946, Davis went to spring training with the St. Louis Cardinals at Al Lang Field in Florida. "We played against clubs that spring that had a lot of future Hall of Famers," Davis says, "and I saw them all—DiMaggio, Dickey, Rizzuto, Ted Williams, Bobby Doerr, Bob Feller, and there might be others that I can't recall. I missed meeting Hank Greenberg with Detroit. Also, Bob Lemon was a third baseman with Cleveland that spring. All the players had come back from service, and I was with Musial, Slaughter, Marion, Schoendienst, Rice, and Harry Walker. The pitchers on that club were [Max, father of Hal] Lanier, [Harry] Brecheen, [Howie] Pollet, and [Ted] Wilks.

"St. Louis was mostly down-to-earth guys, small towners—Musial, Marion, Brecheen—mostly just ordinary guys," Davis says. "They were all easy to talk to. Slaughter was generally quiet. He didn't mingle with the rookies much, but [Terry] Moore and Musial made the rookies feel part of the team.

"Musial, in my estimation, and I've said this before, was the finest gentleman to ever wear the uniform. You may have heard that. I know some reporters say they don't like to interview him because he doesn't say anything bad, but nobody ever said a bad thing about him."

During training camp, Davis's closest friends were Del Rice, his roommate and friend from Rochester; Earl Naylor; and lefty pitcher George Dockins. "Dockins and I would play some pool and pinochle together," Davis remembers.

Despite the talented outfield competition that included Musial and Dick Sisler (both of whom also played first base), Slaughter, Walker, and veterans Terry Moore, Erv "Four Sack" Dusak, and Buster Adams, Davis made the Cardinals' opening-day roster.

St. Louis opened the 1946 season at home with three games against

Pittsburgh. Opening day marked the major-league debut of a Pirate out-fielder named Ralph Kiner. "And if the Cardinals needed someone to pinch run that day," Davis says, "it would have been me." But he stayed on the bench.

Two days later, on Thursday, April 18, 1946, another debut took place during the season opener of the Jersey City Giants of the International League. Before a sellout crowd of more than 20,000 in Jersey City's Roosevelt Stadium, Jackie Robinson played his first game for the Montreal Royals, a Brooklyn Dodgers farm team. Robinson beat out three bunt singles, hit a home run, stole two bases (one of which was home), and Montreal won 14-1.

The following day, three days after the National League season started, Davis was sold to the Dodgers for the waiver price of $7,500. He joined his new team the following day and watched from the Brooklyn dugout as the Dodgers completed a three-game sweep of the Giants on Saturday and Sunday, April 20 and 21. He was earning $500 a month.

"I knew a few people there from playing against them in the minors," Davis recalls. "There was Jean Pierre Roy, who had pitched for the Montreal Royals. I think he's now an announcer for the Expos. And there was Gene Hermanski and Ralph Branca and the little coach, Jake Pitler. And George Dockins, who had come to Brooklyn with me." Davis also recalls Dixie Walker, "a quiet kind of guy," and rookie outfielder Carl Furillo, "a good player with a *great* arm."

On Monday, April 22, just three days after he got to Brooklyn, the twenty-five-year-old Davis played in his first and only major-league game.

The Dodgers were facing the visiting Boston Braves at Ebbets Field. After six innings the game was tied, 2-2, with Jim "Lefty" Wallace of the Braves pitching against the Dodgers' Branca. In the top of the seventh, the Braves broke out with two runs to take a 4-2 lead, sending Branca to the showers.

The Braves took that lead into the bottom of the ninth. The first batter to come up in the Dodgers' ninth was Eddie Stanky, pinch hitting for Hank Behrman, who had relieved Branca on the mound. Stanky walked.

With the Dodgers down by two runs and Stanky on first with no outs, manager Charlie Dressen made two moves. He sent right-handed Bob Ramazzoti in to pinch hit for rookie left fielder Dick Whitman, a left-handed swinger who had gone 0 for 4 so far against the left-handed Wallace. Then, as Davis remembers it, "Dressen was coaching third, and he came down over to the dugout and told me to run for Stanky. Then he went over to the umpire and told him I was pinch running." (Dressen was managing in the absence of Leo Durocher who was in court for allegedly attacking a heckling fan. He was later acquitted.)

Davis explains the move. "I can run faster than Stanky, and we're down two runs. We don't score and the ball game's over. So he sent me in to run for Stanky. I heard my name and went out there.

"I didn't think, 'Okay, now I'm in the majors.' Nobody cheered for me. If anybody cheered, it was for Stanky 'cause he got something going. Running onto the field, I didn't think, 'This is where it starts,' or anything like that. I don't think anyone ever thinks that way."

Ramazzoti also walked, and Davis moved to second. Right-hander Bill Posedel was brought in to pitch against the Dodgers right-handed second baseman, Billy Herman. Herman tried to bunt the runners over. "He lays the ball down. I take off for third, go sliding in," Davis recalls. "The ball rolls foul. I go back to second. He bunts again. I go into third again. The ball rolls foul again. This time I hurt my knee [the same one he injured in high school]. Didn't hurt it too bad this time. I go back to second."

Finally, Herman popped out, and Davis and Ramazzoti held their bases. So, with one out and two on, third baseman Pete Reiser came to the plate. "Pistol Pete," who became a switch-hitter two years later, was batting only from the left side at this point in his career and was already 3 for 4 so far that day, including a double. So Braves manager Billy Southworth brought in a new left-handed pitcher, Robert "Ace" Williams, to face Reiser, who promptly lined an opposite-field double into left center, his fourth hit and his second double of the day.

Davis scored easily and Ramazzoti followed him around the bases to tie the game as the announced crowd of 24,902 (or what was left of them) cheered. "The place went wild," Davis says. "I ran across the plate and headed to the dugout and sat down. I was excited, but there was nobody there to greet you like they do now, no high-fiving. I scored a run, sat down, and flexed my knee."

When Williams then walked Dixie Walker, the Dodgers' cleanup hitter, he was removed from the game and never pitched in the majors again. His successor, Don Hendrickson, got out of the inning without any further scoring, sending the game into extra innings.

In the bottom of the tenth inning, however, Hendrickson gave up a one-out single to Pee Wee Reese and, after retiring Don Padgett, who hit for Dodger reliever Hugh Casey, he gave up another single to Goody Rosen. Rosen, and not Scat Davis, replaced Whitman in the Dodger outfield in the top of the inning. "I never thought about going in to play the outfield after I scored," Davis says. "It never came up and I didn't think about it. I guess Rosen was more of a veteran, and Dressen felt safer that way."

With two on and two out, Billy Herman, who had failed to bunt the runners over in the previous inning, then singled in Reese with the winning run, giving the Dodgers their fifth victory in a row, 5-4.

Little did anyone realize at the time, but not only did the run that Davis scored help the Dodgers win that game, it also helped them finish the season tied with the Cardinals for first place.

After that game, however, Davis's knee stiffened up, and he did not play in the other games in that series against the Braves. He wrote his father about playing in the majors. "People didn't call people much back then. Fact is, Dad didn't even have a phone," he says.

The Dodgers then went on the road to play the Philadelphia Phillies at Shibe Park and the Giants at the Polo Grounds. But the knee was not getting any better, and Davis was not able to play. A week after Davis ran for Stanky, Durocher called Davis into his office and asked if he could run. "He wanted to know if he could use me if he needed me. I told him, 'No, I can't.'"

Davis knew this might mean being sent back to the minors, but says today, "I wouldn't tell him I could if I couldn't. It wasn't that important. I didn't think about it. I knew if I went down, I'd be back." Or so he thought.

After just ten days with Brooklyn, Davis was sent to the Montreal team for which Jackie Robinson was playing. "Herman Franks also was there, and Chuck Connors," Davis says. "I got to know Chuck pretty well. We used to bum around some nights there."

But Davis played in only a few games before damaging the knee even more. Thinking that warmer weather would help, Montreal sent him to Fort Worth in the Texas League. "Ray Hayworth, the old catcher, was the manager there," Davis reports. "He was soft-spoken and was the best batting-practice pitcher I have ever seen. He used to throw every pitch right down the middle, belt-high." But at Fort Worth, Davis hurt the knee again, this time so badly that he went on the voluntary retired list and ended his season in August. He returned home to Rochester, and within the next month he married Ann DiMabro, whom he met while working at Bausch and Lomb.

By the time spring training camp opened in 1947, Davis's knee was feeling much better, and he let the Dodgers know he would like to be reinstated. "The season was getting started, and they sent me down to Greenville, South Carolina, in the Sally League," Davis says. "I didn't have any spring training that year, and they sent me there to play my way into shape. I was getting blisters all over. Little Frenchy Bordagaray was the manager there, and he worked me hard, but I did pretty good.

"Then they sent me up to Nashua, New Hampshire, in the New England League it was, for the rest of the year, and I was the only .300 hitter on the team. But I think I only hit like .302 or something. It was a good team, though," he recalls. "Don Newcombe was there and Bob Milliken was a rookie, and we won the Governors Cup championship against Manchester, New Hampshire, a Giants farm team."

Davis started the following season at Pueblo, Colorado, in the Western League, but stayed there only until July. "The Dodgers offered me a job as player-manager in Abilene in the West Texas-New Mexico League, so I went there." In Abilene, Davis inherited a second-division ball club made up primarily of young Dodger rookies, while most of the other teams in the league were composed of minor-league veterans. "But we did pretty good," Davis says. "We got to the top of the second division."

Davis says he generally liked managing. "It was easy making decisions," he says. "The problem was to keep all the players happy. You'd run into problems with pitchers. You know, if they weren't going good, they'd tell you their arms hurt. Keeping them happy, keeping them motivated, *that* was the problem, not strategy. Listen, if you have the talent, you can win."

Late in that season, Davis suffered a severely sprained ankle that stopped him from playing. "I couldn't even walk," he says. At the end of the season, he went home and started working at a local Buick dealership. "That's when I decided not to play anymore," he says. "I had a son coming [Otis Jr., who was born in 1949], and I was tired of constantly moving around. And I had no property or anything, so I thought I'd get a regular paying job." He was twenty-eight years old.

The Abilene team wrote asking him to return in 1949 as a player but not as manager, which served to strengthen his decision to leave baseball. However, the general manager of the team in Waterbury, Connecticut, wrote offering Davis a player-manager position. "I told him I really hadn't decided to play anymore," Davis says, "and we corresponded a while, but finally I said no."

Davis continued to work at the auto dealership, but then took a course in blueprint reading and machining at the Rochester Institute of Technology. "I went about half a year," Davis says, "and I think the course cost me about thirty bucks, the best thirty bucks I ever spent.

"I became a machinist and was gainfully employed for thirty years," he says.

Davis retired in 1982 at age sixty-two, and he and his family moved to Florida. Today, he and Ann reside in a golfing complex in Tarpon Springs, although Davis doesn't play golf.

"I'm a retired machinist," Davis says, "not an ex-major leaguer. Look, there's a romance to baseball. I know that. And I'm not belittling what I did, nor am I polishing myself as something I wasn't. I wasn't a major-leaguer. Oh, according to the book I was. But not really. Baseball was great, but it's not the greatest thing in my life. That moment in Brooklyn, it's not really very special. There are far more important things.

"I can understand those guys who say, 'I'd give up my career for that one game in the major leagues.' I can see that. But is it rational? No. When you get down to it, was it worth it to me, being in that one game? Yes, because that's what I was doing at the time—playing baseball. I didn't have to give up something to do it. Most people, they'd have to give up something else," he points out.

"When you're doing it, it's something you love to do, but you don't think, 'This is the greatest thing in the world.' You're not putting the emphasis on it that a spectator does. You don't think that much about it," Davis says.

"When I was sitting on the bench or shagging flies or something, talking to guys and playing catch, I wasn't thinking, 'This is history.' Since the years have gone by," he admits, "I suppose it means a little more to me now because I can look back on it and say I was actually there.

"What baseball did for me was give me something to talk about in my old age," Davis says. "It gave me another identity. I didn't gain anything from it toward making a living." Davis admits that he'd like to have batted. "But I don't feel I missed anything. I could've gone 1 for 1, or I could've struck out like Walter Alston did.

"And think about this," he adds. "What if Eddie Stanky had struck out?"

John Joseph Perkovich

CHICAGO WHITE SOX, 1950

John Perkovich was always a tough kid. His toughness allowed him to hit the beach at Normandy on D-Day, to pitch in the major leagues with a torn rotator cuff, and to fight back against a crippling disease.

Born March 10, 1924, Perkovich grew up during the Depression on Chicago's South Side in the same neighborhood as the city's (1955–1974) mayor, Richard J. Daley. "We were both elected to the Tilden Tech High School Hall of Fame," he says, "and we both got the same plaque."

While at Tilden Tech, Perkovich concentrated on basketball. He also was a member of the school's swimming team, but played baseball only in 1942, his senior year. As a pitcher on the baseball team, Perkovich says, "I think I only lost one game that year and went 8–1. But basketball was my sport," he adds. "I averaged 30 points a game in my senior year and made the All-City [and All-State] basketball team. I lost out on the scoring championship by four points. I went into the last game needing a few points, but I got five fouls and fouled out before I could get enough."

After graduation in 1943, he enrolled at the American College of Physical Education. "That's now part of DePaul University," he says, "but then it was a school that trained physical education teachers and coaches." In his short stay at the school, Perkovich played freshman basketball.

As World War II intruded into his life, as it did into the lives of so many others, Perkovich decided to enlist. "They were probably gonna draft me anyway," he says with a short laugh.

During the war, he served in the U.S. Army Medical Corps, landing at Normandy and accompanying the frontline troops as they moved through France and eventually into Germany. It's a period he prefers not to talk

Pitching with a torn rotator cuff, John Perkovich gave up three home runs in his only game in the major leagues. He says, "Only one hit was hit good."

about. On Christmas Day, 1945, he was discharged and returned to Chicago.

"A cousin of mine signed up with the [Chicago] Cubs, and I knew I was a much better athlete and ballplayer than he was, so I called up a scout I knew on the [Chicago] White Sox and asked for a tryout. Doug Minor, the head scout, signed me. [Minor also signed Bert Shepard—see Chapter 15.] They sent me down to the Wisconsin Rapids in a Class D league, and I played there in 1946.

"I led the league in strikeouts [229] and earned run average [2.72]," Perkovich says, "and won my first 13 games in a row. The first game I lost was 1–0." He finished the season with an 18–5 record. "And I could have won more, but I was out for a month with a sprained ankle," he adds.

He remembers one game that year when he came in to relieve and struck out five batters in one inning. "The catcher had a couple of passed balls," he explains, "but the best thing was in that game I struck out 12 in four and two-thirds innings. For this, I was elected to the Wisconsin Base-ball Hall of Fame."

In 1947, the following year, he played for the Waterloo (Iowa) Hawks in the Class B Three-I League, and again led the league in strikeouts [207] while compiling a 17–9 record. "I had a good overhand fastball with a nice, big hop," he says. "I was probably second or third in earned run aver-age [2.50]. I think it was [Carl] Erskine who beat me out in earned run average."

Perkovich was then promoted to the Memphis Chicks in the Double-A Southern Association and played there in 1948 and 1949. The first year was one of the most eventful of his life. On the field, he pitched well and had a 14–8 record. For the third year in a row, he also limited the opposi-tion to less than three runs a game and struck out more than 150 batters. Off the field, he became engaged to Nell Coto, the sister of a teammate, and they were married the following January.

In the fall of 1948, however, while playing semipro basketball in the off-season, he suffered an injury that was eventually diagnosed as a torn rotator cuff. "They didn't have an operation for it then," he says. "It just meant the end of pitching for most people. With that kind of injury, after I pitched, I couldn't lift my arm above shoulder level."

But Perkovich wasn't "most people" and continued to pitch even with the bad arm. In 1949, after going to spring training with the White Sox, he was sent to Memphis, where his strikeouts fell to only 67 and his earned run average rose to 4.28. Still, this gave him 656 strikeouts in four years, an average of 164 per year. He ended the season with a 6–6 record and was invited again to join the White Sox for spring training in 1950.

Despite his sore arm, he was comfortable in the White Sox camp. "There were a lot of fellows there that I had played with in Memphis, and I knew many of them fairly well," he says. He also recalls a number of spring training episodes. "I remember [infielder] Hank Majeski almost beaned me. I was pitching batting practice, and he asked me to throw fast-balls straight down the middle. Well, I did and he hit one back at me that almost took my head off. That's the closest I ever came to being beaned, and I'll never forget it.

"Another time, I remember Bill Wight was pitching for us in a spring training exhibition game. He had one of the best pickoff moves I ever saw. Well, in this game, some rookie had gotten on first base, and I remember the coach going over to him and telling him, 'Stay close; this guy's got a good pickoff move.' Then the coach turns around to go back to the coach's box, and before he gets there, Wight picks the kid off first. That was really something."

Another teammate was second baseman Nellie Fox. "He was very nice," Perkovich says. "We used to get a kick out of that big chaw he used to keep in his cheek, but he was one of the nicest people I ever met. In those days, we used to leave our gloves out on the field when we went in to bat, and one day, a good friend of Nellie's took Nellie's glove and put a big wad of spit into it. Boy, Nellie was mad when he put his hand in it."

The twenty-six-year-old Perkovich found himself on the White Sox roster starting the 1950 season. "[Manager] Jack Onlsow knew me 'cause I had pitched for him a couple of years in the minors. I felt good to be there. I knew I wouldn't last long with my arm," he said, "but I didn't want to give up that major-league salary [$900 a month]."

He was right; he didn't last long.

In the one game in which Perkovich appeared, on May 6, 1950, Chicago was being thoroughly dismantled in the early innings by an extremely powerful Red Sox contingent in Boston's Fenway Park before nearly 13,000 fans.

Boston had an amazing offensive team that year. Although the Red Sox finished third (by just four games), they led the league that year with a team batting average of .302, a slugging average of .464, and they scored more runs than anyone else. Walt Dropo, their first baseman, hit .322, had 34 home runs, tied for the league lead in runs batted in with 144, and was named the league's Rookie of the Year. The man who tied him for the RBI title was his teammate, shortstop Vern Stephens, who also chipped in with 30 homers and batted .295. The other two infielders were Johnny Pesky and Bobby Doerr. That year Pesky worked out 104 walks and Doerr tied (with teammate Dom DiMaggio) for the league lead in triples with 11. Birdie Tebbetts was behind the plate, and the outfield consisted primarily of DiMaggio, Al Zarilla, and Ted Williams. But if that wasn't enough, they were backed up by utility men Billy Goodman and Tom Wright.

"The thing I remember most about that game," Perkovich says, "is that the [Chicago] pitchers before me just could not get them out." Ken Holcombe started the game and, after giving up four runs, was relieved by Luis Aloma, who also was hit hard.

The Red Sox led 7–1 when Perkovich got the call. "Onslow told me to go to the bullpen, and I kind of thought this was the kind of game where he'd let me try out my arm and see how it was. It was still hurting. But after you throw a while, you don't feel it because it gets numb.

"I came in at the fourth inning and finished the game," he says. "All I felt at the time was that I was glad to get in a game. I wasn't awed by them 'cause I had pitched to many of them in the minors. Like I knew Dropo couldn't hit a high fastball. He was weak upstairs, especially if you threw real hard. He couldn't touch me. But I just wish somebody told me that Bobby Doerr was a high fastball hitter. Then I would never have thrown one to him."

Perkovich finished the game, pitching five innings, giving up one walk, four runs (including three solo homers) on seven hits, and striking out three.

"Dom DiMaggio hit a cheap home run over the green wall. I had Vern

Stephens fooled on a curveball, and his home run just made the foul line
in left field, about 250 feet. The other home run Bobby Doerr hit. This
was the only home run hit good," he claims.

"Ted Williams was up first in one inning, and while I warmed up, he
stood behind the umpire at the plate to see how my curve broke," he recalls. "Williams got one single for three at bats [after homering previ-
ously]," Perkovich says. He believes Goodman and Tebbetts also were
among those who got hits, but does not remember who got the other one
or how the fourth run scored. "I struck out Pesky twice, and Stephens was
the other one."

Perkovich did get to bat once, grounding out weakly to shortstop. He
faced Chuck Stobbs, who went all the way, giving up only four hits (one a
homer by Gus Zernial) and winning his second game of the year against
no losses, 11–1.

"Overall," Perkovich says of his performance that day, "I think I did
pretty well, considering the circumstances of having a torn rotator cuff."

But the arm was just not good enough for him to pitch at the major-
league level and two weeks later, Onslow told him he was being sent back
to Memphis. "Onslow knew me and he knew the condition of my arm,"
Perkovich says. "I knew I was there on a trial basis, and I didn't mind
going to Memphis. I had played there the previous two years, and we were
living there then, so it was sort of like going home."

Bad arm and all, Perkovich finished the season with Memphis, winning
six and losing nine. After the season, the White Sox traded him to Atlanta.

"I knew the arm was sore, but I felt that with a new team, I might
make a new start," he says. In 1951, he went to spring training with Atlanta. "Dixie Walker was the manager there, and I stayed there 'til the end
of spring training. I remember pitching in an exhibition game against
Billy Pierce [a former teammate on the White Sox], and I thought I was
pitching okay, despite the arm hurting. I thought they would keep me, but
when spring training ended, they gave me my walking papers."

So ended the professional baseball career of John Perkovich. Returning
to Memphis, he went to work for a friend who owned a photo-finishing
establishment. "I worked there for a couple of years, but my family was
growing and he couldn't afford to pay me more, so I asked him for a rec-
ommendation to Eastman Kodak. He recommended me, and I joined
Eastman Kodak in 1953 as a technical representative."

Perkovich remained with Kodak for twenty-five years, selling technical
photographic equipment in various areas of the country. For a number of
years, he was based in Milwaukee. Later he and his wife moved to Dallas,
and in 1965 he was assigned to Little Rock, Arkansas, where he and his
wife still reside. In 1979, however, he was forced to retire as a result of
medical problems.

"I came down with a rare disease called scleroderma," he says, "which
basically cuts off the blood flow to the extremities. As a result, they've had

to amputate most of my fingers, and I can hardly walk now, but sometimes the pain killers work, and I can still go out and rake the leaves."

How did baseball affect his life? "I met my wife because her brother played on the same team I did, and we're still married after forty-five years, with three daughters and three grandsons," he reports.

And the three boys, Joseph, Cody, and Jason, read the clippings about their grandfather's baseball career, and know that, one time, he was a major leaguer.

Harley Parnell "Jim" Hisner

BOSTON RED SOX, 1951

What "Jim" Hisner remembers most of his one-time appearance in the major leagues is this: "I struck out Mickey Mantle two times and Joe DiMaggio got his last regular-season hit off me." It was in 1951, the only year Mantle and DiMaggio ever played on the same team together.

Hisner (pronounced "Highs-ner") was born in Maples, Indiana, in early November of 1926, the fourth and last son of a local farmer.

"I was fourteen pounds when I was born," Hisner says, "and the doctor said he delivered thousands of babies, but I was the heaviest. When I was growing up, the doctor used to call me 'Jimmy Binooster,' and I couldn't say it. I used to say, 'Yimme,' and the nickname 'Jimmy,' stuck with me.

"My high school didn't have a baseball team, but I played basketball," Hisner says. "I was pretty good. They didn't have any Little League then, but I played in a league for fourteen-year-olds in Fort Wayne. A Red Sox scout saw me when I was fourteen, and he followed me all the way through high school. My brothers all played there, too, and two of them also signed with the Red Sox. One of them was released in spring training, and the other one played two months for one of their farm teams but got homesick and quit."

Hisner graduated from high school in 1945. "I had an offer of a baseball-basketball scholarship to MSU [Michigan State University], but I wasn't that good of a student and I wanted to play ball," he says. "I was an average student."

The Red Sox scout who had kept his eye on Hisner was Fred Hunter, then based in Columbus, Ohio, and he signed the young right-handed

Harley Hisner gave up Joe DiMaggio's last regular-season hit, but struck out Mickey Mantle twice when Hisner pitched his only game in the major leagues.

pitcher. "When I signed in 1945, I got $5,000 for signing," Hisner says, "and I was supposed to get $200 a month. But I went into the Army before I could play."

Hisner was drafted in June 1945 and sent to Fort McLellan, Alabama, for infantry basic training, and then to school at the Army Finance Center in Fort Harrison, Indiana. "The war ended in Japan just after I finished basic training," he says, "so since I had some clerk training, they sent me to the Jefferson Barracks in St. Louis to help process discharges for other soldiers. After about six months, they sent me back to Fort Harrison, and then I was able to play Army baseball and keep in shape."

Hisner met his future wife, Anna Cain, while playing ball at Fort Harrison. "She was working in Special Services," he says, "and used to write up the games for the post newspaper." They were married a little more than a year later.

In December 1946, Hisner was discharged from the military service and shortly thereafter reported to the spring training camp of the Scranton Miners of the Class A Eastern League, a Red Sox farm team.

"I started my first pro game on opening night of the season against Mike Garcia, who was pitching for the Wilkes-Barre Barons," Hisner recalls. At Scranton, Hisner won two and lost six for a team that included players who also would be his teammates when he later reached the major leagues. "Mickey McDermott and Jimmy Piersall were there, along with a couple of others," he says.

But his stay at Scranton in 1947 was relatively brief. Boston sent him to play at San Jose in the California League, managed by Marv Owen, a former American League third baseman. "I sat on the bench for thirty days without pitching," Hisner says, "because Williamsport, back in the Eastern League, had claimed me before I was sent to San Jose. So I couldn't play until that was straightened out." When he finally was allowed to pitch, Hisner won five and lost eight for the West Coast team that year.

Following his marriage in January 1948, the twenty-one-year-old Hisner went to spring training with Louisville, Boston's Triple-A team, but was assigned back to Scranton again at the start of the year. There, under new manager Mike Ryba, a former Cardinal and Red Sox pitcher, he won 11 and lost only 3, while compiling a 2.48 earned run average. "That was all before the Fourth of July," he says. "I got a sore arm and didn't pitch at all after that. I probably would have won 20 that year if I didn't hurt it. They said it was chronic bursitis in the shoulder."

After resting the arm, Hisner again went to spring training with Louisville in 1949 and once more was sent back to Scranton. "The arm still wasn't right in the spring," he says, "and the pain moved down from the shoulder to the elbow. I got off to a late start that year." For the season, he had a 6–10 record.

In 1950, Hisner followed the same pattern. "In spring training, I had arm trouble again," he says. "But this time they sent me to a doctor who had been with the Mayo Clinic or something, and he examined me and said my tonsils were infected. I had them taken out while we were in spring training, and eight days later, I was back. But Louisville was just breaking camp then, so I stayed with Scranton to pitch myself back in shape.

"I finally got to Louisville and made my first start on the first of June. I think I was 5 and 6 that year, but I remember I pitched a one-hitter against Toledo," he says.

"In 1951, I had my first year without soreness, and I had a wonderful spring with Louisville," Hisner says. "I went 15 innings without giving up any walks or any runs. I remember on a Wednesday before opening day, we played an exhibition game against the Red Sox. I pitched five innings and Ted Williams hit a two-run homer off me and we lost 2–1.

"I started on opening night in the American Association, but then spent most of the year in the bullpen," Hisner continues. The team was loaded with starters, including Dave "Boo" Ferriss, Leo Kiely, Jim Atkins, Tom Herrin, Bill Evans, and Jim McDonald, all of whom made it to the majors. "My record that year was not too good," Hisner says of his 7 wins and 13 losses, "until the last five weeks of the season when I won my last four starts and the first game of the playoffs.

"When the playoffs were over, Pinky Higgins, the manager, came over to me and said, 'Since you're the hottest pitcher in the Red Sox organization now, the Red Sox want you to get on the first flight to Boston and report to them.'"

By then it was mid-September and the Red Sox were in a three-way pennant race with the Yankees and Indians. "When I got there, [Boston manager] Steve O'Neill asked me where I was from, and I said, 'Fort Wayne.' He said, 'Oh, I was born in Butler, Indiana. [*The Baseball Encyclopedia* lists O'Neill's birthplace as Minooka, Pennsylvania.] Do you know where that is?' I said yes, and he called over a photographer and said, 'Take our picture.'

"While the picture was being taken, he said, 'I'd sure like to start you, but we're in a pennant race and the older veterans would raise hell. But I'll tell you, once we've got a position sewed up, you'll be my first starting pitcher.'"

Hisner's recollection of the last two weeks of the season differs somewhat from the records. "When I got there, I think we were only one or two games out of first place," he says. "The first game I was there, we won from the Yankees at Fenway Park. Mel Parnell pitched and Ted Williams hit a two-run homer and we won 2–1. Then we lost the next two games to them.

"Then we went on the road and lost all five games in Washington and went to New York for the last five games of the year against the Yankees and lost all of them. So we lost the last 12 games of the season," he says. "Four other guys had been recalled, including Norm Zauchin, whom I roomed with, and none of us could believe how we were losing."

On September 29, 1951, the day before the last day of the season, Allie Reynolds of the Yankees pitched a no-hitter against the Red Sox, his second no-hitter of the season. "That was the game that, with two out in the ninth, Ted Williams hit a foul pop behind the plate and [Yogi] Berra dropped it," Hisner says. "The next pitch, Williams hit in almost the exact same spot, and this time Yogi caught it. I was warming up in the bullpen that day, and Steve O'Neill had told me I would start the following day, the last day of the year. But because I had warmed up, I didn't know for sure he would keep his promise to give me a start. I wasn't real sure. But he kept his word. After the game, he said, 'You're starting tomorrow.' I was on cloud nine. Actually, I was on cloud nine just to be in the same ball field with all these guys."

So, on September 30, 1951, twenty-four-year-old Jim Hisner was the starting pitcher for the Boston Red Sox against Frank "Spec" Shea of the New York Yankees in their last game of the season.

"What they had done," Hisner recalls, "is dig up the pitching rubber from Reynolds's no-hitter the day before, and had all the players from both teams sign it. In those days," he continues, "the starting pitchers warmed up in front of the dugouts near home plate, not out in the bullpen. So, while I was warming up, they were having a presentation there at home plate, and Mel Allen was presenting the rubber to Reynolds. That's the same rubber you'll see in Cooperstown today. If you go look at it, you'll see my name in the lower right-hand corner."

Since it was the last game of the year and third place was clinched, O'Neill started an almost all-rookie lineup. Sammy White was the catcher instead of the regular Les Moss or the veteran Buddy Rosar; Norm Zauchin, Hisner's roommate, was at first in place of Walt Dropo; Mel Hoderlein played second instead of Bobby Doerr; Al Richter was at shortstop in place of Johnny Pesky; and Fred Hatfield played third, replacing Vern Stephens. In the outfield, Charlie Maxwell was in left field, not Ted Williams, and Bob DiPietro was in right instead of Clyde Vollmer. Vollmer moved over to center field, so Dom DiMaggio could take the day off.

Hatfield and Maxwell were both in their first full year with the club, but had seen relatively limited action. Hoderlein was playing in only his ninth major-league game; Richter and Zauchin their fifth; and White and DiPietro were in just their fourth major-league game. For Hisner, it was his first and only.

Meanwhile, the Yankee lineup that day was all regulars. Mickey Mantle led off and played right field. Phil Rizzuto was at shortstop, Hank Bauer was in left, Joe DiMaggio was in center, Johnny Mize was at first, Bobby Brown was at third, Jerry Coleman was at second, and Yogi Berra was catching for Shea, the pitcher.

It was a formidable group. Mantle, Rizzuto, DiMaggio, Mize, and Berra made the Hall of Fame, as did Johnny Sain, who relieved Shea after five innings that day. Stengel became a Hall of Famer, too. Bauer, Berra, and Coleman later managed in the majors while Brown later became the league president.

Hisner pitched six innings that day and gave up three runs on seven hits, all singles. He walked four, struck out three, and had an assist. He gave up one run in the second inning and two in the third, although today he says he thought all the runs were scored in the first two innings. "I was shaky and wild the first couple of innings because I never pitched before a big crowd [nearly 36,000], in such a cavernous place. I walked the four guys and gave up a few hits in the first couple of innings. That's how they got their runs.

"I walked Mantle, Bauer, [Archie] Wilson [a rookie who replaced DiMaggio later in the game], and Coleman," he says. "I struck out Mantle two times, and he hit a dribbler back to me with a man on first. I threw to shortstop and on to first for a double play." It was one of four double plays the Red Sox recorded that day. Hisner does not recall the third strikeout victim.

"Rizzuto got a bunt single off me. Berra [who knocked in two of the Yankee runs that day] got two hits off me," Hisner continues. "Both times I had two strikes on him. He took two curves for strikes each time, and then he hit bad balls for line drive hits. They were both outside.

"Before the game, [Boston pitcher] Harry Taylor, another Indiana boy, told me, 'As hard as you can throw, you can pitch DiMaggio in on the hands. He can't get around on the inside fastball anymore,' he said. Well, the first pitch I threw to him I got out over the plate, and he hit it in the upper deck, foul. The second pitch I did get inside, and he hit it on the fists. He hit it between third and shortstop and beat it out. The shortstop fielded it but couldn't throw him out. That was the last regular-season hit Joe got," Hisner says.

Despite their youthful lineup, the Red Sox out-hit the Yankees that day, nine to eight. (The eighth Yankee hit came off of Taylor, who relieved Hisner in the seventh.) Hoderlein went 2 for 2 with two walks, and Richter got what would be his only major-league hit. But Boston was not able to score off either Shea or Sain.

Hisner remembers his own two at-bats against Shea clearly. "I struck out the first time up," he says, "but the second time up I hit a soft liner over Mize's head into right field. I felt like I was on cloud nine again. In the paper the next day it looks like a hard line drive," he laughs. When his third turn to bat came in the top of the seventh inning, this time against Sain, Johnny Pesky pinch hit for him. The final score was 3–0, Yankees.

Hisner did not have much time to think about his performance. "Right after the game that day, I rode in the same taxi with Bobby Doerr to La Guardia Airport to catch a flight home. He was leaving around the same time for Oregon," Hisner recalls. "I didn't see anyone until the following spring."

But before spring training began in 1952, the Red Sox fired Steve O'Neill as manager and replaced him with Lou Boudreau, who had been a utility player with them the previous season. "I liked Steve O'Neill," Hisner says. "I feel that if he managed in '52, I would have had a better shot of making the team. Boudreau was for all the veterans. Not many rookies would make the team with him.

"It was my first spring training with the Red Sox," Hisner recalls. "Pinky Higgins, who was my manager at Louisville in 1951, was helping out there in spring training. On the first day, he says to me, 'Lou is gonna ask all the pitchers if they'd be willing to pitch batting practice the first day. With your history of arm trouble in spring training, say no.' So, when Boudreau went around to all the pitchers asking if they'd be willing to pitch batting practice right away, I said no. Well, I don't know if he held that against me or not, but I think he might.

"That spring, I got a chance to pitch three innings against the Phils, the middle three innings of a game, and I gave up one run. The pitcher who followed me, Walt Masterson, gave up eight runs in the last three innings.

But three days later, he's back on the mound, but not me. All I did was pitch batting practice. I even went down to St. Pete when we played the Cardinals, but all I did was pitch batting practice. I never got back on the mound.

"I was cut two hours before the end of spring training," he says, "and sent back to Louisville. Boudreau called me and Bob DiPietro in together and told us he was sending us down for 'more seasoning.' I remember him telling DiPietro he wanted him to learn how to hit. That was silly. DiPietro had played five years in the minors before then and never hit below .300."

Despite his bitterness toward Boudreau, Hisner has some nice memories of his teammates. "That was the spring they tried to make Piersall a shortstop," Hisner says. "He hated that. He was a wonderful center fielder. He didn't have a good arm and he wasn't especially fast, but he got the best jump on a ball of anybody living," Hisner says. "And I should know. He played behind me for three years in Scranton and Louisville."

Hisner also remembers Dropo playing Class A baseball at Scranton in 1948 and 1949, when he was right out of the University of Connecticut. "In the minors, he was just a so-so player, nothing special," Hisner says. "Then when Billy Goodman got hurt, they called him up, and he had a phenomenal rookie year, with 144 runs batted in or something."

"The pitchers I remember there," Hisner continues, "were Harry Taylor, a former Dodger pitcher; Mickey McDermott and Leo Kiely from the minors; Rae Scarborough; Randy Gumpert was there; and Willard Nixon. I remember they signed Nixon right out of Auburn, and he played at Scranton in 1948. I think he got a $40,000 bonus. He was a good pitcher and turned out to be a Yankee-killer later."

"For six weeks in spring training in 1952," Hisner says, "my locker was next to Ted Williams," he says. "Williams was a great guy and the best hitter I ever saw.

"I remember one time a good friend of mine, Jim Suchecki from Chicago, used to pitch batting practice for the Red Sox, and one day before I was with the Red Sox, they played an exhibition game against Pittsburgh. The Pirates had [Ralph] Kiner then, and before this game, they had a home run–hitting contest between Kiner and Williams. Well, Ted hit the most out, and they gave him a Longines wristwatch as a prize. He went into the clubhouse and went up to Jim, who had thrown batting practice to him earlier, and said, 'Hey. Here, you just won yourself a watch.' He gave the watch to Jim."

Remembering Louisville in 1952, Hisner says, "Pinky Higgins decided to turn me into a relief pitcher. I threw hard and did well." His earned run average there was 2.95.

"In July, they traded me to San Diego in the Pacific Coast League," Hisner says. "San Diego was an independent team. Lefty O'Doul was the manager, and Jimmy Reese was one of the coaches. I think the owners were friends with some of the people in the front office of the Red Sox, so Louisville sort of loaned me to them for this season. They traded me and Richter, the shortstop, for Al Benton, another relief pitcher.

"I started a game the day I got there and then relieved for the rest of the year. I think I was in about 42 games for both teams that year, but only started once for each of them.

"At the end of the year," Hisner says, "I was recalled by Louisville, and I went to spring training with them in 1953. Then they optioned me to Syracuse in the International League, but I was only there about three weeks. The manager there was Bruno Betzel [a Cardinal infielder during World War I], and one Saturday he told me I would start the second game of a doubleheader against Baltimore the next day. I told him I hadn't pitched in a while. Well, he said something about me either pitching or leaving, so I pitched about six or seven innings and we lost 5–3.

"I didn't like that kind of treatment, so I got on the phone to Louisville and told them I'm on my way back," Hisner says. "They said there was no use my going anywhere, so I said I'm going home. Pinky Higgins got on the phone and said, 'Dutch Meyer at Dallas wants you. Go on down there.' So I went to Dallas and was there a couple of nights in the bullpen. One night I'm called in, in the first inning with the bases loaded and two out and the leading home run hitter in the league at bat. I get a 3 and 2 count on him, and he hits a home run off me.

"Dallas sends me right back to Louisville, and they turn around and send me to Greenville in the Big State League," Hisner continues. "I won about three games in one week there, but my wife and I were fed up with all the moves. I asked for a release, and they said they would send me back to Louisville. I called up the Red Sox to quit. I spoke to Johnny Murphy, who was the farm director then, and he said, 'Look, Bobby Goth, the general manager at Wichita Falls, wants you bad. He wants you so bad, he'll even make up any difference in the contract you have with Louisville.'

"Wichita Falls was in the Texas League, with Dallas. My wife says Wichita Falls is the hottest place on earth," Hisner laughs. "But they paid me under the table. You talk about a salary cap today. They had one then in the Texas League. Because of that, they couldn't pay me what I was supposed to make, so they paid me under the table and they paid me in advance. Whitey Wietelmann [a former Boston Braves infielder] was the manager, and when I joined them, they were 10 or 11 games out of first place. But we won the pennant, and I went 14 and 5 and won two games in the playoffs.

"After the season, they sold me to Corpus Christi," Hisner continues. "Corpus Christi sent me a contract for the 1954 season calling for $350 a month. I sent it back and told them there was no way I was going to play for that. I had made $800 a month the year before. They wrote me back and said they had my contract with Wichita Falls, and it said I only got paid $250 a month. See, what happened was that, with that salary cap, Wichita Falls evidently wrote in my contract that I was getting $250, while they were really paying me $800 under the table.

"Well, I must have sent six contracts back to Corpus Christi," Hisner says. "Their last offer was up to $600 a month. Well, the season was about to start and I was still home. So I wrote them a 'voluntary retired' letter, and after a couple of days, I went up to Canada and played ball there for $800 a month. I only stayed about six weeks, though.

"I came home and played on a national championship semipro team in Fort Wayne. In 1956, we won the National Championship in Wichita and then won the Global World Series in Milwaukee's County Stadium. In 1957, we finished second in the nationals. In the national tournament that year, I pitched 38 innings in eleven days, and I won four and lost one, which tied a record that was set by Satchel Paige in that tournament in 1935.

"But back in 1954, after I quit playing pro," Hisner says, "I was supposed to pitch an exhibition game against the Phillies, but my manager came up to me and said there was just one problem. 'You're on the restricted list,' he told me.

"Evidently, when I went up to play in Canada instead of signing with Corpus Christi, Corpus Christi had put me on the restricted list. I called up George Trautman, who was the head of the minor leagues, and told him that I had written a 'voluntary retired' letter. He said, 'How come you didn't go to Corpus Christi?' and I told him the story about the money and said, 'I got the check stubs to prove it.' I told him I wanted him to clear up this thing within two days so I could pitch against the Phillies, or I would take legal action. He said he'd check into it and call me back. Well, he called me back a couple of hours later and told me he'd put me on the 'voluntary retired' list and it was okay for me to pitch against the Phillies. After I pitched, one of the Phillie coaches, Earle Combs, a Hall of Famer, said I quit too soon."

Hisner continued playing semipro ball through 1961 before hanging up his glove for good.

Following his discharge from the army back in 1946, Hisner had worked every off-season as a machinist at the Rea Magnet Wire Company in Fort Wayne. He joined them full-time in June 1954 when he left professional baseball, and retired in 1987, shortly before turning sixty-one.

Today, he and Anna live about twelve miles outside of Fort Wayne, "and I drive a fertilizer truck part-time," he says. They have three children and nine grandchildren.

"You know," Hisner says, "I didn't think people would remember a guy who only pitched one game in the major leagues, but here it is forty-six years later and I still get requests for autographs."

Leonard "Len" Matarazzo

PHILADELPHIA ATHLETICS, 1952

L en Matarazzo was a big, tough guy who came from an old railroad family and loved to play baseball. Eventually he had careers in both areas and thus considers himself "twice-blessed."

Matarazzo and his two younger sisters were born and grew up in New Castle, Pennsylvania. "They didn't have a baseball team at New Castle High School," he says, "only track. So I ran track. I was a miler—and a mediocre one at that," he laughs.

"But," he says, "the whole neighborhood played baseball. We spent our summers on the ball field. I thought nothing of spending eight or nine hours a day playing ball. I also played American Legion ball. I played and managed. I was only about seventeen, but they didn't have enough guys around during the war [World War II], so I managed, too. In our last year, we went undefeated. We won it all, and there were eight Legion teams in the city that year." Matarazzo says the team did not go on to play in the state tournament, however.

"I graduated high school in 1946," he says, "and went right into the service. I almost had to. See, I had gotten into a fistfight about a week before school ended, and they wouldn't let me graduate unless I paid the kid's doctor bills, made an apology to him and his parents, and promised to go into the service.

"So I ended up in the U.S. Navy. After boot camp, they selected me as one of about twenty-seven guys there to be a candidate for the U.S. Naval Academy. I went through a whole lot of exams and did okay, except for advanced math, which we didn't have in my high school, but then I realized it would mean a seven-year commitment. I said, 'What the hell do I

Len Matarazzo held the Red Sox scoreless in his first game,
but a case of food poisoning prevented him from pitching in the majors again.

want that for?' and just dropped the idea. So I ended up at the Naval Air Station in Quonset Point, Rhode Island.

"For most of my two years there, I played on the baseball team, playing first base and pitching a little. I even played on the football team there, although I was third string. But I had a lot of fun," he says. "The baseball team was a traveling team, and we went all over—to places like Pensacola; Quantico; and Fort Riley, Kansas, among others."

He was discharged in May 1948, "at the convenience of the government," Matarazzo says, "two months early, so I was only in twenty-two months." Matarazzo returned to New Castle and played semipro baseball. There, a White Sox scout, Fred Shaffer, who recently retired from the Braves organization, told Matarazzo to abandon first base and concentrate on pitching. Matarazzo is a right-handed thrower, which is not desirable for a first baseman. So he became a pitcher.

"A couple of months later, in July, I think, the Youngstown team [in the Class C Mid-Atlantic League] was having trouble with their pitching. One guy broke his leg, one guy hurt his arm, one guy had another kind of problem. Whatever it was, they were short of pitching. A local guy from my neighborhood, Babbo Orlando, was playing shortstop for Youngstown, and he recommended me."

Matarazzo had a problem, though. He had intended to go to college at the University of Southern California that fall, but if he turned pro, he'd lose his college eligibility. "So," Matarazzo explains, "when I went to Youngstown to sign a contract with one of the co-owners, Mike Andolino, I signed my uncle's name, Joe Frigone, and used his social security number. My uncle was out of work then, getting disability. I got $175 a month. I didn't get a bonus."

Playing under his uncle's name, Matarazzo, now known as Frigone, finished the season at Youngstown and in September boarded a train for California. "I was gonna go to college under the GI Bill," he says, "but when I got to Southern California, the military records weren't complete. By the time I got it all straightened out, I found I would have to wait until the new semester started in January or February.

"In Christmas week," he says, "I got a telegram from my father, saying that someone had exposed me. It seems that at the winter meetings, a guy by the name of Mike Canovino, who owned the Erie team, wanted to acquire my contract from Youngstown, and when he asked about Frigone, the Youngstown player-manager, Shine Richardson, said, 'Oh, that's Len Matarazzo.' That put the kiss of death on me."

After the scheme was exposed, minor-league czar George Trautman banished Matarazzo from playing. In addition, because Matarazzo had played professionally, he would not be allowed to play college baseball. "I was considered an outlaw," he recalls.

"But then I got a letter from Connie Mack," Matarazzo says. "He had bought the Youngstown team for the [Philadelphia] Athletics—the team had been a Cleveland affiliate—because he wanted to acquire four players, John Kucap, Bob Gardner, Shine Richardson, and me. He said that if I would agree to sign with his new Youngstown team, he would do everything he could to get me reinstated. Of course I agreed, and about two or three weeks before the 1949 season started, I was reinstated.

"That season," Matarazzo reports, "I threw bullets. I was a three-quarter overhand flamethrower." He was also wild. While he struck out 74, he walked 114 batters, hit five, and had nine wild pitches. He won his first four decisions, but then lost eight in a row, finishing up with a 6.67 earned run average.

"Ed Morgan was the playing manager that year, playing first base," Matarazzo says. "He had replaced Richardson when Philadelphia took over the franchise from Cleveland. We had some young pitchers that year who had been sent down to us—'bonus babies'—and they were on the staff. When the troubleshooters from the A's came around, they insisted to Morgan that he put them [the bonus babies] in the starting rotation 'cause they were there to be developed. The A's had invested a lot in them. The rest of us, who hadn't cost them a cent, were treated like excess baggage.

"One thing I remember specifically about that year," Matarazzo says, "we had a split season. When it came down to the last two games of the first half of the year, we were half a game behind Johnstown, and we were gonna play them a doubleheader for the championship. If we won both games, we'd win.

"Well, the first games in minor-league doubleheaders were seven innings. Kucap started the first game and did well up to the sixth inning and then got in trouble. The bases were loaded, one out, and he had a two-ball, no-strike count on the batter. I get called in the game. Now, I hadn't pitched in maybe two or two and a half weeks because we had to use the bonus babies. But I come in and I strike the first guy out on three pitches. Then I strike the next guy out to retire the side.

"In the top of the seventh, I strike out the side, and we win the first game. In the clubhouse between games, Morgan tells me I'm gonna start the second game," Matarazzo continues. "Well, I go out and I get by the first inning okay. Then I'm struggling in the second, and in the third inning I'm real wild and I'm pooped out. I come out, and we lost 5–2.

"After that game," Matarazzo says, "we had a little altercation. Morgan accused me of choking up, and we went at it. For the rest of the season, I was on his shit list."

In 1950, Matarazzo was assigned to Lexington in the Class B Carolina State League. The manager was Homer Lee Cox. "In 1948, a couple of years earlier, Homer was the manager of a team in Ohio that was in a bad bus crash and had sixteen or seventeen players killed," Matarazzo says, "and he had sat out all of 1949, recovering both physically and emotionally. This was his first year back."

At Lexington that season, the twenty-one-year-old Matarazzo appeared to improve his control, striking out more men than he walked (103 vs. 68). But he still threw eight wild pitches that year and hit a league-leading 18 batters. When asked about this, he says, "I wasn't that wild. A lot of those hit batters were intentional. I had a reputation as a guy who would retaliate, and I threw at guys. And they didn't wear batting helmets in those days," he laughs. As a starter and reliever for Lexington, he won 5 and lost 11.

Probably the most significant event for Matarazzo that year was an accident. "I was standing behind the mound, taking throws from the fielders and giving the balls to the batting practice pitcher," he recalls. "One of the batters, who was supposed to be bunting, swung away and hit a liner straight back over the mound. The batting practice pitcher ducked, but I wasn't looking and it hit me right in the shoulder.

"I was out for a couple of weeks, and when I came back," he says, "it hurt me to throw overhand, so I started throwing more underhanded and became what they call a 'submarine' pitcher. That didn't bother my arm, and I was able to get some good movement on the ball."

In 1951, Matarazzo was promoted to Fayetteville in the Carolina League and pitched there the next two years. In the first year, Matarazzo was used heavily as a relief man, appearing in 56 games, winning 8 and losing 13, with a 3.18 earned run average.

In 1952, everything somehow came together, and Matarazzo had an incredible year at Fayetteville. He began the season as a reliever and accounted for the team's first six wins. At one point, he won four games in five days, including both ends of a doubleheader. He then started 25 times and won 22, including nine shutouts, while losing only eight. He pitched 252 innings, compiled a 2.21 earned run average, and was named the league's most valuable player while on a team that finished seventh.

How did this transformation come about? "I just started getting the breaks that year," Matarazzo says. "Everything seemed easier. I had a lot of luck and a lot of good support. I used to finish games in an hour and a half, an hour and twenty-five-minutes, and once, even in an hour and twenty-three minutes."

At the close of this super season, Matarazzo was called up to join the Athletics for the last month of the American League campaign. "I think I got there on the Sunday before Labor Day," he recalls. "I roomed with another pitcher they had just brought up, Frank Fanovich."

A few days later, on September 6, 1952, the Athletics were in Boston's Fenway Park to play a doubleheader against the Red Sox. The two teams, along with Washington and Chicago, were in a four-way fight for third place. At the start of the day, they were all even in the lost column with 64 apiece, but they had each played a different number of games. Washington had won 76, Philadelphia had won 71, Chicago had won 70, and Boston had won 69.

The first game started with Carl Scheib (10–5), pitching for the A's against Boston's left-hander, Mel Parnell (11–8). Before a crowd of almost 18,000 fans, the Red Sox wasted no time. A three-run homer by out-fielder Hoot Evers put them up 3–0 in the bottom of the first inning. In the third, outfielder Clyde Vollmer tripled in a fourth run, and in the fifth, after the Athletics had scored once (during a double play), successive homers by Vollmer and shortstop Vern Stephens gave Boston a 6–1 lead.

In the sixth inning, A's manager Jimmy Dykes replaced Scheib with an-other pitcher just called up from the minors, a right-handed curveballer named Marion Fricano. Fricano, who had won 17 and lost 8 for Ottawa in the Triple-A International League earlier that year, pitched both the sixth and seventh innings and held Boston scoreless although he gave up three hits and a walk.

Meanwhile, the A's managed to score another run in the top of the sev-enth and two more in the top of the eighth, making the score 6–4 in favor of Boston. During the two-run rally in the eighth, Fricano was removed for a pinch-hitter, Kite Thomas.

Matarazzo, a week shy of his twenty-fourth birthday, was then called in to hold off the Red Sox in the bottom of the eighth. "It was surprising," he recalls. "Somebody else was warming up with me, and I really didn't know who would go in until they told me. It was somewhat surprising.

"I was a string bean by then," he continues. "I had spent the year in North Carolina in the hot, humid weather, and I was kind of worn out. I hoped I wouldn't pass out. I guess you could say I was a little anxious.

"After I had warmed up on the mound, the catcher, Joe Astroth, came out and said, 'Wanna go over the signs?' and I said, 'Just give me the posi-tion for their weaknesses. Tell me where to pitch these guys and I'll take care of the rest.' Well, he said, 'Don't be so goddamn smart, rookie. Just get the goddamn ball over the goddamn plate,' or words to that effect. He was a grouchy old guy. Billy Hitchcock, our third baseman, was standing on the mound with us, and he told me, 'Don't let him rattle you, kid. He's got the rag on,' or something like that. That helped loosen me up a little.

"Mel Parnell was the first hitter," Matarazzo says, "and he popped up. [Center fielder] Dom DiMaggio scratched out an infield hit, and the third hitter walked. [It was Boston's leading hitter that season, second baseman Billy Goodman.] Vollmer popped out. Then came Vern Stephens, and he must have hit 35 foul balls. He wore me out. But finally he popped up, too. That was it."

A Philadelphia newspaper account of the game said: "Matarazzo . . . stirred a chorus of oh's and ah's with his submarine delivery—and baffled the Bosox for an inning despite an infield hit and a base on balls."

Matarazzo returned to the bench for the top of the ninth. "I remember [A's first baseman] Ferris Fain came over and said, 'How do you feel, kid?' Dykes never said anything. Neither did any of the coaches.

"We almost won that game in the ninth," Matarazzo says, "but [center

fielder] Gus Zernial ran through a stop sign at third base and was thrown
out by twenty feet."

Here Matarazzo's memory appears to be somewhat off. According to
the newspaper story of the game, the event probably occurred in the
eighth inning when the A's, as mentioned, rallied for two runs. The story
says:

> With two out in the eighth, the A's suddenly brought victory within
> sight. [Right fielder] Allie Clark and Zernial cracked singles, and
> [center fielder] Dave Philley's one-bagger to right produced a run,
> whereupon [second baseman Cass] Michaels doubled to left-center
> for another. But despite the fact that the important run was the one
> represented by Michaels at the junction—and not his own under any
> circumstances—Philley received the green light at third base, and
> [Billy] Goodman, relaying DiMaggio's throw-in, rifled him out at
> the plate.
>
> Just how costly this rash running was to the A's cause became
> clear in the ninth; Hitchcock led off with a single which would have
> scored Philley anyway, and Astroth bounced into another twin kill, a
> mere third out if it had come an inning earlier but fatal to the A's
> coming when it did.

After the game, Matarazzo says, "I felt that wasn't too bad. I was looking
forward to the rest of the season, to tell you the truth, hoping to get more
chances. But the A's were fighting for third or fourth place, and I think
Dykes had hopes of being named Manager of the Year, so I didn't pitch
again. Besides we had a lot of pitchers on that team. Harry Byrd was
Rookie of the Year. Bobo Newsom was there—he kept everybody loose.
There was Charlie Bishop, Ed Wright, Sam Zoldak, Dick Fowler, and Carl
Scheib. They were all complaining about lack of work. Then, of course,
we had Bobby Shantz. He was the greatest competitor I've ever encoun-
tered in baseball," Matarazzo says seriously, "and the most humble person."

Matarazzo did not get another chance to pitch. In spring training the
following year, illness derailed Matarazzo's hopes of staying in the majors.
"We went to Havana, Cuba, to play a three-game exhibition set with the
Dodgers," he says, "and I came up with a case of food poisoning. At first
they thought it was the Asian flu, but when we got back to West Palm
Beach, I went in the hospital and had to stay there three days. I thought I
was gonna die."

He lost fifteen pounds during the siege and was out of action for more
than two weeks. To start the 1953 season, Philadelphia sent the weakened
Matarazzo to their Ottawa team in the International League. "I only spent
part of the year there," he says. "I was about 6 and 7, and then they sent
me back to Fayetteville." There he won 6 and lost 14.

In 1954, he started with Savannah in the Southern League, but got into only five games before being sold to Portsmouth in the Piedmont League, where he got into another eight before smashing up his knee in an automobile accident. "There were about three other ballplayers with me, and our dates," Matarazzo says, "and the car in front of me came to a sudden stop and I couldn't do anything to stop in time. The next day, when I went to the ballpark, I could hardly walk.

"The owner there, Frank Lawrence, said if I couldn't play, he'd put me on employee disability. The state compensation was something like $15 a week. This compared with my salary of $700 a month. I said, 'The hell with that,' and as soon as my car was fixed, I jumped the contract and took off for the Southern Minnesota League, which was sort of an outlaw league with guys who had jumped clubs, were running from paternity suits, or had beaten up a manager somewhere. I was in my element," he laughs.

"I played for a team in Waseca, Minnesota," Matarazzo says, "and after the season ended, the owner, a guy by the name of Roy Tyrholm, who also owned a Ford dealership, asked me if I would come back and manage the team for him the next year. I was really thrilled about that. But then, just a couple of weeks later, he goes and sells the team. So that was that.

"I couldn't get back in organized baseball 'cause I had jumped my contract with Portsmouth," Matarazzo says, "so I just hired out on the old Pennsylvania Railroad and eventually got laid off. Then I went to the New York Division, and I was furloughed during the coal strike in 1958. At that point, I joined the Long Island Railroad [a suburban commuter line outside New York City]. I started as a fireman, then an engineer, and retired in 1982 after twenty-five years as a foreman of engineers.

"Actually, I took early retirement," he says. "I was living on Long Island then and was active in Little League baseball, Pop Warner football, soccer, and basketball in the Lynbrook-Malverne area. I had a son, John, who was a good football player, and I thought he had the potential to be really good. So I retired from the railroad to take him back to New Castle, in western Pennsylvania, where he could play against some good competition and get good coaching. As it turned out, he made All-State and got a football scholarship to the University of Pittsburgh. He's graduated now and has his own business."

In 1965, Matarazzo had married Verna Moffatt, a girl from back home. "I met her through a mutual friend in New Castle," he says. Today, Matarazzo keeps himself busy doing a variety of volunteer work and taking care of his wife, who was recently diagnosed with a malignant brain tumor. "They operated to remove it," he says, "and she's recovering, but she's still scheduled for some more radiation treatments."

As for his career, Matarazzo says, "I'll tell you this. I never spent a disappointing moment on a ball field in my life. I loved every minute of it. I'd do it all again—for nothing."

Barnes Robertson "Barney" Martin

CINCINNATI REDLEGS, 1953

By the time Barney Martin reached the major leagues, he had already retired twice from professional baseball. And when he finally did arrive there as a thirty-year-old rookie pitcher, the first man he had to face was Stan Musial.

Martin, the son of a textile mill worker, was born and raised in Columbia, South Carolina, where he eventually played for much of his professional career. "I had five brothers and two sisters," he says, "and I was the baby of the family."

He went to Olympia High School in Columbia and played basketball, football, and baseball. "We had a pretty good basketball team and a very good football team," he says, "but I wasn't much. In baseball I started out as a third baseman, then I was a catcher, and finally a pitcher."

Explaining the changes in position, he says, "We just ran out of catchers one day and somebody had to catch, so I did it. Then, one day, we were getting the tar beat out of us, so I had to go and pitch. While I was in high school, I also played semipro ball for the Pacific Mills team in a textile league we had. We had a number of mill teams there, you know, Pacific Mills, Columbia Mills, and some others."

Martin graduated from high school in 1940 and, while continuing to play semipro baseball, went to work as a civilian at the post exchange at nearby Fort Jackson. In 1941, at age eighteen, he and Mary Herbert, a local girl, were married.

In the fall of 1943, during World War II, Martin was drafted into the Navy. "I went to boot camp in Great Lakes," he says, "and then was sent to gunnery school in Gulfport, Mississippi. After that, I went to New Or-

The first batter Barney Martin faced in the major leagues was Hall of Famer Stan Musial. Martin retired him twice but never got a third chance.

leans and went aboard a merchant ship as a gunner. We went all over—North Africa, Egypt, the Persian Gulf, the Mediterranean, everywhere."

Discharged in December 1945, Martin returned home. "I went out to work at the VA hospital in Columbia as a file clerk. One day, I met a friend of mine, Deke Koosa, who used to see me pitch in high school and in semipro. He was like one of those bird dogs, I reckon, and he got Bill Harris, a scout for the [New York] Giants to come down and sign me early in 1946."

According to Martin, Harris signed him to a contract to play for the Giants' Trenton farm team in the Interstate League without ever seeing him pitch. "I got $250 to sign," Martin says, "and I was to get $800 more if I stayed all year with Trenton. All together, I got about $1,000."

He went to spring training with the Trenton team in Lakeland, New Jersey, and played the year there, pitching 178 innings and 16 complete games. He won 8, lost 14, and had a 4.30 earned run average. The following season, the Giants sent him to Manchester, New Hampshire, in the New England League, where, while acquiring a 13–6 record, he struck out 116 men in 162 innings. "Hal Gruber was the manager there that year," Martin recalls.

In 1948, the Giants promoted him to Jacksonville in the Class A South

Atlantic (Sally) League. "I just couldn't win there," Martin says. "I was something like 3 and 7 or 3 and 8, so I just quit and came on home." At twenty-five, he appeared to be through with professional baseball. "I went on the 'voluntary retired' list and went to work for the railroad, "the Atlantic Coast Line Railroad," he says.

Though he continued to play semipro ball in Orangeburg, South Carolina, Martin was away from pro ball for almost two years before deciding to try again in 1950. He reported back to Jacksonville, and not only made the team but also had such an excellent year that he was named the league's most valuable player. "Hal Gruber was the manager there, too," Martin says, "but then he was replaced by Bill Alexander. I was 16 and 13 that season, with a 3.38 ERA," he recalls. He also pitched 197 innings and struck out 111 batters.

The Giants then sent him to their Triple-A team in Minneapolis to start the 1951 season. "I was 4 and 1 there," he says, "but then the railroad called me back to work, so I left and went back home again. I didn't think I was going anywhere in baseball, so I went back to the railroad. I had been working for them during the off-seasons, and I knew it was a steady job." For the second time, this time at twenty-eight, he voluntarily retired from baseball.

He was also having family problems at the time; he and his wife divorced in 1952.

"Sometime around late '51, I went to a University of South Carolina basketball game," Martin says, "and I met a guy I knew who worked in the front office of the Columbia Reds [the Sally League team based in Martin's hometown]. He asked how I was doing and I said, 'Fine,' and he asked me about pitching, and I said, 'If you can get my contract from the Giants, I'll come pitch for you.' Well, a few weeks later, he calls me and says he got my contract from the Giants. I couldn't believe it!"

After sitting out almost a full year, Martin again returned to professional baseball with a monster year in 1952. Pitching in his hometown, he hurled 258 innings, including 25 complete games, winning 23 and losing only 7 while compiling an earned run average of just 2.14.

"Columbia was in the Cincinnati Reds' farm system," Martin says, "and I enjoyed playing at home. I knew a lot of the people. It was a mill town and most of them would be in the knothole section—you know, they would sit in the bleachers for about seventy-five cents and they'd cheer for me. Then there was a separate section, 'cause the blacks and whites couldn't sit together then, and I knew a lot of the blacks, too, and they would cheer for me, too."

Because of his fine season at Columbia, Cincinnati, which officially adopted the name "Redlegs" that season (and would keep it through 1958), invited Martin to their 1953 spring training camp in Tampa, Florida. There he pitched well, made the team, and came north with the club. The team itself was not particularly good despite the presence of hitters such as Ted Kluszewski and Gus Bell. Cincinnati's pitching staff was particularly weak, and the manager, Hall of Famer Rogers Hornsby, ineffective. Hornsby was released just before the season ended and never managed again. The Redlegs would finish sixth that year, 37 games behind a dominating Brooklyn Dodgers team.

"It seems to me we started the season traveling to Milwaukee and then, from there, we were going to St. Louis and then to Chicago," Martin says. In St. Louis, about a week into the season, Martin, then just over thirty years old, got to pitch in a major-league ball game.

It was on a Wednesday evening, April 22, 1953, "the first warm night of the season," according to one newspaper account. Nearly 7,400 fans were in attendance. Starting on the mound for the Reds that night was Clarence "Bud" Podbielan, a tall, slim twenty-nine-year-old right-hander who had won only seven games with Brooklyn in three and a half years before coming to Cincinnati the previous year, where he had a 4–5 record. He would go on to win 6 and lose 16 this season.

His opponent for St. Louis was second-year man Wilmer "Vinegar Bend" Mizell, a left-hander who had already won 10 major-league games in his previous rookie season and would win another 13 this year.

It was not Podbielan's night. With one out in the bottom of the third inning, consecutive doubles by the Cardinals' shortstop Solly Hemus and second baseman Red Schoendienst, followed by a two-out single by first baseman Steve Bilko, gave the Cards a 2–0 lead. In the very next inning, a leadoff double by third baseman Ray Jablonski followed by a single from center fielder Rip Repulski extended the lead to 3–0. And in the fifth inning, the Cardinals scored three more on two walks, a triple by right fielder Enos Slaughter, and another double by Jablonski.

In the top of the seventh inning, Martin, warming up in the Reds' bullpen, found out he would be going in to pitch. Cincinnati had sent up a rookie catcher, Frank Baldwin, to bat for Podbielan. Mizell struck him out. Through seven innings, the St. Louis pitcher had allowed only two scratch hits.

"I felt nervous," Martin says. "I knew the next man coming up was 'The Man,' Stan Musial. The fans there ragged me, you know. There was a lady sitting near the bullpen, and she said, 'You know who's up next, don't you? You won't be here long.' But when I got out there, I felt real good."

Martin took the mound in the bottom of the seventh. "Hank Foiles was the catcher, and he said, 'Just relax. Just act like you did in spring training.' Musial was up, but I think he was in a real bad slump at that time, and I got him out. He grounded out to the shortstop [Roy McMillan]."

The next batter was Bilko. "I got him out, too, I think on a long fly." Then Slaughter: "I think I walked Slaughter," Martin says. The final batter of the inning was Billy Johnson, who had replaced Jablonski for defensive purposes. Martin got him out, too.

When he returned to the dugout after holding the Cardinals scoreless,

Martin recalls, "I felt real good. I got the big man out. I don't remember who came over, but a couple of the guys said, 'Way to go, Marty,' and things like that." While Martin sat on the bench, the Reds came alive against a tiring Mizell, getting three hits and two runs and making the score 6–2 going into the bottom of the eighth.

Martin returned to the mound to pitch the bottom of the eighth. Today, he does not recall exactly in what order things happened. His recollection is that "things just fell apart on me. Somehow the bases were loaded and Shoendienst hit a 3–0 pitch for a triple."

According to the box score, it didn't happen quite that way. The Cardinals only scored twice that inning on three hits. Shoendienst had two doubles that game, but no triples, so he probably doubled with the bases loaded, and two runs were scored. Martin then retired the side with no more runs scoring. Among the three outs he recorded that inning were Musial's pop-up to the shortstop and a strikeout, most likely of Mizell, but Martin isn't positive.

In the top of the ninth, the Reds made a serious threat against Mizell, who was fading rapidly. Martin was scheduled to come to the plate in that inning, but reserve infielder Rocky Bridges was sent in to pinch hit for him and flied out. "I didn't mind," Martin says about not getting a chance to hit. "I wasn't much of a hitter anyway." The Reds loaded the bases with two out, and Mizell, trying to finish, issued his sixth walk of the game to force in a third Cincinnati run. Cardinal manager Eddie Stanky then brought Alpha Brazle in from the St. Louis bullpen to get the final out and complete the 8–3 win.

"After the game, some people said, 'Tough luck,' but I felt pretty good," Martin says. "We went out and ate and it was nothing special. I had had a good spring, and I wished they'd have started me. I figured 23 wins in the Sally League ought to be good enough to get me a couple of starts. But then we went to Chicago, and that's where they told me they had too many pitchers and were gonna send me back to the minors. Hornsby and the big boss, Gabe Paul . . . told me. They wanted to send me to Indianapolis, their Triple-A team. But I said, 'If I can't play here, I'll go home to Columbia and play there.' And that's what I did."

Martin returned to Columbia early in 1953 and was immediately involved in a pennant race. Columbia, managed by former Cardinal pitcher Ernie White, battled for the Sally League championship that year against Jacksonville, which was led by a nineteen-year-old second baseman named Henry Aaron, then in his second year in organized ball. This was the year before the U.S. Supreme Court ruled segregation in public schools was unconstitutional and the first year a black man played organized baseball in the deep South.

Aaron, recounting the year in his autobiography, pointed out that Columbia that year had "the best pitching in the league." He specifically mentioned Martin and two of his Columbia teammates, Maury Fisher and Harold "Corky" Valentine, as their leaders.

Martin, again pitching in his hometown, had a 17–6 record with a 2.14 earned run average that year, while Fisher won 16 and lost 7, and posted a 3.21 earned run average. Valentine, used mainly in relief, won 13 and lost 6 and led the league with a 2.11 earned run average. A couple of years later, Valentine got into 46 games with Cincinnati, while Fisher, like Martin, played in only one major-league game (see Chapter 23).

Jacksonville eventually won the pennant that year, but Columbia won the seven-game championship playoffs, taking the last three games of the playoffs after falling behind three games to one. The winner of the last, deciding game: Barney Martin.

"Aaron was something else," Martin says. "He had no style. He just hit the ball, all arms and elbows. But he had good wrists. That's what did it. I remember one time that year I got on second base. I don't know how in heaven I got there, but he played second that year, and he came over and talked to me. 'You throw too hard,' he said, and I said, 'And you hit the ball too damn far!' But he never really hit me much. But he had a teammate, Felix Mantilla. Whew! He could hit. I remember one time when I had come back from Cincinnati, he hit a blue darter straight back at me, like to take my head off. It ended up going straight over the center field fence!" Mantilla later played in the majors for eleven years, but was never particularly known for his hitting.

Martin continued playing in Columbia in 1954 and 1955. He posted a 12–9 record with a 3.91 earned run average in 1954 and was 8 and 6 in 1955 with a 3.37 ERA. "Frank Robinson played there in '54," Martin says. "He had a real sore arm then. I remember he played first base for us, and when he threw the ball back to me, he'd toss it underhanded. But he could still hit. He hit some of the longest balls I ever saw. He was a very nice person, a good man. When he went up to the majors, I knew he wasn't coming back."

Robinson, of course, went on to play twenty-one big-league seasons and in 1975 became the first black manager in the majors. He was inducted into the Baseball Hall of Fame in 1982.

In 1956, the Columbia franchise was transferred to Savannah, and at age thirty-three, Martin started the year with the team. But when he went 0-3 in eight appearances, he decided to call it a career. "My arm was gone, then," he says, "so I told them I was going into voluntary retirement."

This time, he meant it.

Today Martin fondly recalls many of his teammates and those he played against. "I still talk with [outfielder] Jim Greengrass, who was my roommate at Cincinnati. I used to cut up with all of them. I remember [outfielder] Willard Marshall. We used to go out a lot. I remember one time in Minneapolis, one night I went out with him and [catcher] Walker

Cooper. They were both big guys and I was between them," he laughs. "In 1948, I played against Joe Adcock, and when I got to Minneapolis, he remembered me. He came right over and started talking to me like nothing happened. He could hit hard, but he used to get hit by pitches a lot 'cause he never backed up."

After leaving the game, Martin returned to full-time work on the railroad, where he became a switchman and later a foreman. "I also got motorcycle-happy around that time," he says, "and I broke my leg in 1957 and again in 1959, riding around on a motorcycle." In 1985, he underwent knee-replacement surgery as a result of those accidents.

In 1960, he remarried. He and his wife, Barbara, still live in Columbia today. Together they had one son, Nick. Martin's son Jerry, from his previous marriage, played in the major leagues as an outfielder with five different teams over a period of eleven years. Martin says, "My youngest son from that marriage, Mike, also was signed by Philadelphia [Phillies] as a pitcher, but he developed a bad arm." Martin now has three grandsons and one granddaughter.

Martin retired from the railroad in 1975 and spends a good deal of his time now in nearby Hopkintown, where he bought "a little ol' house on five acres, with a tractor and a horse. I don't ride the horse anymore," he says. "She's about thirty years old and just follows me around like a dog. I do ride around on the tractor a lot, though.

"But no more motorcycles," he laughs.

Richard Leroy Teed

BROOKLYN DODGERS, 1953

It was the year of the famous "Boys of Summer," as Roger Kahn called them. The Dodger team of 1953 was an awesome aggregation. They topped the National League both offensively and defensively. They led with a collective .285 team batting average, a .474 slugging average, 208 home runs, 955 runs scored, and they won 105 games out of 154. Four of the league's five leading base stealers that year were Dodgers. In the field, they had the best fielding average and the least number of errors of any team in the league. And the pitching staff led with 819 strikeouts.

Individually, Carl Furillo was the league's leading batter, with a .344 average, although four others in the starting lineup also hit over .300 that year. Roy Campanella, the year's Most Valuable Player, led the league in runs batted in with 142; Duke Snider had more total bases, scored more runs, and had a higher slugging average than anyone else. Jim "Junior" Gilliam led the league in triples, and Carl Erskine was a 20-game winner and had the best winning percentage in the league.

When Dick Teed was twenty-seven years old, he was also a member of that team. If it were not for a few broken hands, Teed might have stayed with them long enough to clinch the pennant and win the World Series.

Teed was born in March 1926, in Springfield, Massachusetts, the oldest of three boys. When he was young, his family moved to Windsor, Connecticut, where he played on the baseball, basketball, and soccer teams at the John Fitch High School.

"I was a pretty good athlete," he says. "I played right side forward in soccer; I was a forward for two years in basketball and then played center in my senior year, which shows you what the game was like then. I was a five-foot-eleven center. Baseball was my best sport, and I made the team as a freshman. I played shortstop, first base, catcher, and pitcher. We switched around, you know. One game you pitched, the next game you played first."

In May 1944, a month before his high school graduation, Teed attended a three-day Dodger tryout camp held in Holyoke, Massachusetts. "They were interested in me," Teed says, "but I told them I had already volunteered for the Marine Corps when I got out of school." It was the height of World War II.

After Marine boot training on Parris Island, Teed was shipped to the Pacific where he participated in a number of major battles, including Guadalcanal, Okinawa (where he was in the front wave going ashore), Guam, and Taiwan.

"When I got home in August 1946, I got a telegram inviting me to a Dodger tryout camp in Cambridge, Maryland," Teed recalls. "There were 250 kids there, and they signed seven of us. I signed as a shortstop.

"They shipped all seven of us to Thomasville [in the North Carolina State League]. Howie Hague, the manager, came over to me one day and asked if I'd ever done any catching. I said yes, and he had me catch a game. The next day, he said, 'From now on, you're a catcher.'

"I had a good arm," Teed says, "and while I was speedy, he didn't think I had a good enough first step to play shortstop. That year was my best year. I hit .300 [actually .312], made the league's All-Star team, and was catching well." By "well" he means he led the league's catchers in assists and total chances.

During the next few years, Teed progressed through the Dodger farm system. "In 1948, at Danville in the Three-I League, I led the league in hitting for about a month. Then they started curving me and curving me. But I had a good year catching. I had a real strong arm and picked a lot of guys off first base." At Danville, he led the league's catchers in putouts, total chances, and double plays.

In 1949, Teed played at Pueblo in the Western League, where he was named to the league's All-Star team and again led the catchers in putouts and set a record for assists. In 1950, he was invited to the Dodgers' spring training complex at Vero Beach, Florida.

"When I got there and went into the clubhouse and got a locker, the first guy who came over to me was Pee Wee [Reese]. He introduced himself and welcomed me and said, 'If you need anything, just let me know.' He was the captain and was just great." Other players in that camp he remembers fondly include Shuba, Hodges, Furillo, Bobby Morgan, and Steve Lembo.

For the 1950 season, the Dodgers started Teed back at Pueblo, but soon moved him up to Montreal, their Triple-A team in the International League. "There were a lot of good players on that team," Teed recalls,

Dick Teed played on one of the most famous Brooklyn Dodger teams in history but, unfortunately, he struck out in his only time up.

"Rocky Bridges, Chuck Connors, [Al] Gionfriddo, and others. I was the second-string catcher to Johnny Bucha, but I hit okay [.276]."

The following year, Teed found himself at St. Paul in the American Association. "I got off to a bad start in St. Paul," he says, "and didn't have that good a year. Timmy Thompson did most of the catching, and I didn't play that much, so I started fooling around in the cage, batting lefty. I thought about switch-hitting as a way I might pick up my [.222] batting average.

"That winter, I went home and set up a batting tee in my cellar and practiced swinging left-handed," Teed says. "When I went to Vero Beach for spring training in '52, I told [Dodger manager] Charlie Dressen that I'd like to try switch-hitting. 'Let me see you hit, kid,' Dressen said, so we went over to the cage and he watched me for a while. Then he said, 'Okay, kid, you just stay in the batting cage and keep swinging.'"

Soon Buzzy Bavasi, the Dodgers' general manager, told Teed that they were going to send him down to Mobile in the Southern Association and that they wanted him to switch-hit all year.

At Mobile, Teed had a good year. "I hit around .276 [.273] and had 14 or 15 homers [7], and I felt comfortable switch-hitting," he says. "I made the All-Star team." Among his 1952 Mobile teammates were future major-leaguers Don Zimmer and George Freese.

Teed started the 1953 season again at Mobile, but was hampered by an ankle he hurt early in the year. In June, however, the Dodgers suddenly called him up to the majors.

"Rube Walker broke a bone in his hand and, while Campanella was doing all the catching, they wanted to have another catcher, just in case," Teed recalls. "I remember I caught a game in Mobile and then flew out to Brooklyn. They picked me because their Triple-A teams were in pennant races and Mobile was in last place."

On Friday, July 24, 1953, about a month after Teed arrived in Brooklyn, the Dodgers were playing their chief rivals, the Milwaukee Braves, at Ebbets Field before a crowd of almost 28,000 fans. It was the opener of a four-game weekend series. The Braves were in their first year in Milwaukee after moving from Boston. At that point in the season, the Dodgers were hot, having won 5 games in a row and 10 of 11 on their current home stand. But today was not their day.

Right-hander Billy Loes started against the Braves' right-hander, Max Surkont. Loes was making his first start in more than two weeks because of shoulder trouble. For three innings, he pitched well, but in the fourth, he walked third baseman Eddie Mathews and left fielder Sid Gordon, and then gave up his first hit of the game, a single to Joe Adcock, the Braves' first baseman, which put the Braves ahead 1–0.

In the fifth, Loes fell apart. With one out, he walked Surkont. Center fielder Billy Bruton then doubled and shortstop Johnny Logan singled, to make the score 3–0. When Mathews hit his 30th homer of the year over the right field scoreboard (he would lead the league with 47 that year), the

Braves were up, 5–0. Ben Wade came in to relieve Loes. Wade retired Gordon, but then gave up a double to Andy Pafko, the Milwaukee right fielder, and walked Adcock. When catcher Walker Cooper hit a three-run homer, the score was 8–0.

The Dodgers got a run back in the bottom of the sixth, but the Braves scored three more off Joe Black in the top of the seventh before Jim Hughes relieved him and retired the side. Going into the bottom of the seventh, Milwaukee led 11–1, and Surkont had given up only three hits.

In the bottom of the seventh inning, Teed entered the game. "They called me in the bullpen and told me to come in and hit for Hughes," Teed says. "I was really excited. There must have been 33,000 people there. I remember running from the bullpen down the line and I came into the dugout and Furillo threw me a bat and said, 'Here, use this thing.' It was one of those big-barrel jobs.

"When I got to the plate," Teed says, "[Brave catcher] Walker Cooper made me feel relaxed by talking to me. He said, 'Oh, first time in the bigs? How long you been here?' and things like that. He really loosened me up, and I wasn't nervous. I was all set and ready. I remember Surkont threw me mostly hard sinkers and sliders, and I hit two or three foul balls before I struck out on a slider."

After he had struck out, Teed remembers, "I walked back to the bench, and guys just said, 'Hang in there,' and 'There'll be other times,' and things like that."

But there weren't any other times.

After that inning, Dodger pitchers Bob Milliken and Glenn Mickens held the Braves in check the rest of the way, and the Dodgers scored four runs in the eighth (on three walks, a Surkont error, and a three-run homer by Roy Campanella), plus one more in the ninth off reliever Lew Burdette, to make the final score a bit more respectable at 11–6. But Dick Teed's major-league career was over, mostly due to a few broken hands.

When Teed went to Brooklyn, a second-string catcher moved into Teed's role at Mobile, and the Dodgers promoted another catcher from one of their Class B teams to back him up. "Soon after I got to Brooklyn, the catcher who replaced me at Mobile broke his thumb, so the kid who came up from Class B replaced him," Teed says. "Then the kid below him broke his hand, so he had to go back to his team and I had to go back to Mobile. All of this happened within about a month. If it weren't for that, I might have been able to stay with the Dodgers for the rest of the year and gotten a championship ring."

Dressen was the one to inform him. "He just told me we ran out of catchers and he had to send me back," Teed says.

So after spending about a month with the 1953 Brooklyn Dodgers, Teed returned to Mobile and was again named to the league's All-Star team. As the league's top-fielding catcher, he also hit .275 and had 13 home runs, the most he had in any one season. For the full year, including his time with the Dodgers, Teed earned $5,000.

"You know, when I think back and stop to realize how good that Dodger team was, it's amazing to think that they were all just regular guys, just like everyone else," Teed says.

As a catcher, he knew the pitchers best, having caught most of them in the minors. "Erskine was the best one to catch," Teed says. "He had good command, and he was always around the plate. Labine had the heaviest ball I ever caught. It felt like a brick, but he had a good sinker. Preacher Roe you could catch with a finger glove. He never threw hard. Joe Black had a good fastball and slider and he had that great rookie year. I asked him later what happened. He said, 'Dick, I had the same stuff I always had, but it just seemed like every pitch I threw that year went exactly where I wanted it to go. I just had great command. It was unbelievable.'" During his rookie year in 1952, Black had won 15, lost 4, and had a 2.15 earned run average. The next five years in the majors, he was able to win only 15 more games.

Summing up some of the others, Teed says: "Campy was the quickest catcher I ever saw. He's the only one I know who could take a glove right out of the box and go out and catch with it. He liked a stiff glove and made it pop, and he was quick getting the ball out of there.

"Hodges was a great person, an outstanding leader. He took care of me. Reese also was a great guy, the captain. He took good charge of every-body. Duke [Snider] had tremendous power. Furillo was a quiet guy. One spring in Miami, I got pretty close to him. And, of course, Robinson. To me, he was one of the greatest players I'd ever seen. His running ability, his overall talent, he was a natural. He had good baseball sense and under-stood the game." As for the manager, Teed says, "I don't think Dressen knew my name. He always called me 'kid.'"

After finishing the 1953 season at Mobile, Teed played there another year and then spent the next few seasons at Montreal—with the exception of 1956, when he was inactive due to an injury. His teammates at various times included past or future major leaguers such as Don Drysdale, Tommy Lasorda, Kenny Lehman, and Bob Aspromonte. During the 1957 season, before returning to Montreal, Teed played briefly for Rochester in the International League and then for Sparky Anderson at Los Angeles in the Pacific Coast League.

During these later years, the Dodgers asked Teed if he would be inter-ested in managing somewhere in the minors, but until 1960, when he was thirty-four, Teed had always said no, feeling he could still play. That year, however, the Dodgers traded him to the Philadelphia Phillies' Buffalo farm team, still in the International League. "I caught [pitcher] Dallas Green there," Teed says, "but after I was there about three weeks, they got [catcher] Frank House from the big leagues and that was the end of my catching."

Teed accepted the Phillies' offer to finish the season as a player-coach with Williamsport in the Class A Eastern League. "Frank Lucchesi was the manager, and when I got there, we had about 18 games left to play, and I think we must have won 17 of them," Teed says. "Lucchesi took a liking to me, and when Brooklyn inquired about the possibility of getting me back as a possible manager, the Phillies said, 'No, we have plans for him.'"

Teed spent the next three years serving as a player-coach for Lucchesi at three different Philadelphia farm teams. In 1964, he began managing on his own in the Phillies' system for four years. "I was very happy doing that," Teed says. "As a manager in the minors, you do everything yourself. There aren't a lot of coaches to help you. But I really enjoyed working with the kids." In 1967, at Spartanburg in the Western Carolina League, Teed's club won the pennant, and he was named Manager of the Year.

The following year, Paul Owens of the Philadelphia organization asked Teed to become a scout. "He said, 'Dick, it'll take you three years to become a scout. I don't care what you've done before; it'll take you three years.' I didn't know if I wanted to do it," Teed says. "I talked with my wife and said, 'If I don't like doing this, I'll go back to managing or coaching.'

"Well, the first two years I hated it. I saw so many high school kids and so many high school coaches who didn't know what they were doing. It was poor. But then, after a while, I started finding some players and got to know what I was doing."

Teed scouted for the Phillies for ten years and then, in 1978, was hired back by the Dodgers, becoming their East Coast scouting supervisor. He has scouted for the Dodgers ever since. "Now that I'm getting ready to retire," he says, "they're starting to phase me out, so the past year or so, I've been the area scout for New England." Among the players he signed over the years are such major leaguers as Eric Young, Ron Diorio, and Dave Wallace.

Teed and his wife of forty-five years, Virginia, still live in Windsor. They are the parents of four daughters and ten grandchildren. "And they're all good athletes," Teed says proudly.

Guy "Moose" Morton Jr.

BOSTON RED SOX, 1954

Guy Morton is the son of a former major leaguer. His father, known as "the Alabama Blossom," was one of the top pitchers in the American League for a number of years during and after World War I.

Playing in the big leagues for eleven years between 1914 and 1924, the Alabama Blossom recorded 830 strikeouts and 19 shutouts while winning 98 games as both a starter and reliever. His record still stands as fifteenth best among all pitchers in Cleveland Indian history. For five straight years during his heyday, he held Indian opponents to less than three runs a game and ended up with a career earned run average of 3.13.

After leaving the majors, he continued to play minor-league and semi-professional baseball until he was forty, a year before dying suddenly when his son was less than five years old. His only child, Guy Jr., was born in Tuscaloosa, Alabama, on November 4, 1930.

"I still have a few remembrances of Dad," Guy Jr. says, speaking precisely in a slow Southern drawl. "I remember the day of the funeral. There was just a sea of people. Daddy was a legend in the area, having played ball in the Southern League around there for some time after he left the majors. I remember my uncle, Martin Luther Morton, having me on his shoulders, and the quartet singing.

"I remember the morning he died. He took me to the hospital because I had broken my arm and they were taking the cast off. When we got home, my mother was cleaning the debris of the cast off my arm, and Daddy laid down in the living room. A neighbor came by and came into the kitchen and said, 'Edna, Guy is dead.' My mother said, 'No, he's not.

He's just sleeping. She went inside to look at him, and I remember Mother screamed. I remember that vividly.

"I remember times he'd put a little bat in my hands and stand me by the side of the house and toss tennis balls for me to try to hit. Another time, there was a snake in the woodpile, and he shot it while he was holding me in his arms. And one time I got lost in the grandstand at a game he was playing about a year before he died. A policeman came by and I told him my name and he took me down to the dugout and Daddy kept me there on his knee.

"The country was in a depression then," he says, "and the South had been in a depression since the Civil War. So after my father died, my mother went to work at a museum at the University of Alabama while I went to live with my grandparents about two miles outside Caledonia, Mississippi, just across the border from Vernon, Alabama. I remember wearing my little baseball uniform while I went out in the fields picking cotton. I started school early, so I wouldn't be too much of a burden to my grandparents.

"That was the time that I had a chance to go through some of my father's scrapbooks. He had played in the majors since 1914, and my parents married in 1919, and my mother had put together about five huge scrapbooks. One which showed a picture of 'Shoeless' Joe Jackson on the first page. He was with the White Sox and was part of the "Black Sox" scandal in 1919, and I saw he played at the same time as my dad. That impressed me. In 1914 and 1915, Jackson had played on the same Cleveland Indians team as the senior Morton.

"When I was about twelve years old, a cousin of mine gave me a pair of baseball shoes," Morton continues, "and I don't remember ever having seen a pair before. We had a town team then—a men's team—and I played for it. Meanwhile, my mother had remarried, when I was eleven, to Vaughn Shirley, who had worked in a defense plant and then owned a grocery store in Mobile, Alabama. When I was thirteen years old, I went there to live with them.

"In Mobile, I went to Murphy High School, which was a large school—we must have had 5,000 students. Milt and Frank Bolling were there. I was a good size for my age and played basketball and baseball. In basketball I was the last man that wasn't cut. Actually, the coach kicked our best player off the team for smoking and that made room for me. In baseball, I was a pitcher and had a great curveball and played freshman ball. There was a great man, C. P. Newdome, who was the coach there. That summer [1945], I also was on a tremendous American Legion team that won the state championship. As a sophomore, I had a tremendous year and was named the most outstanding player. That was when the big-league scouts recognized my name and began following me.

"My stepfather bought a grocery store in Tuscaloosa then, and I moved back there and finished up at Tuscaloosa High School.

*Guy Morton Jr., who became a preacher, thinks baseball is the greatest game of all,
but serving God is the real big leagues.*

"Back then, there was tremendous interest in baseball in that area. In addition to the high schools, all the big steel mills had teams. I remember pitching against Frank Lary in high school, and I remember Frank House and Willie Mays playing with Bessemer. It wasn't unusual for us to draw two to three thousand people to a high school game then. Our high school team played an exhibition game against the University of Alabama. We lost 4–3, but I hit one off the scoreboard. I also think I remember seeing Jimmy Davenport as a batboy for a semipro team, Buck Creek, in Siluria, Alabama.

"I graduated in 1948 and got a scholarship to the University of Alabama. I made the team as a freshman along with Alan Worthington and Frank Lary. Butch Hobson's dad, Clell Hobson, was on the team, too. But right after the season started, they made the ruling that no freshmen could play varsity ball. This was after the season had already started. So we played freshman ball. And that summer, in June 1949, I signed with the Red Sox. Johnny Murphy, who was then the farm director, signed me. I got a $6,000 bonus, which was the most they could give me, and I think I was paid $500 a month.

"They flew me to Boston in a hurry. They had a great team then," Morton recalls. In 1949, the Red Sox lost the pennant to the Yankees by only one game after finishing second to the Indians the previous year, losing a one-game playoff. "I met Joe McCarthy, who was the manager," Morton continues. "There was [Ted] Williams, [Bobby] Doerr, Vern Stephens, Birdie Tebbetts, [Dom] DiMaggio, Tex Hughson, Mel Parnell, Pinkie Higgins, and Al Zarilla.

"I had jammed my shoulder playing football in my last year of high school and wasn't able to pitch with the same sort of stuff I had before then, so they asked me what I wanted to be, a catcher or an outfielder, and I said a catcher. There was a shortage of catchers then. I was nineteen years old and a power hitter, and I remember that the first time I took batting practice at Fenway Park, with that short, high left field wall, I hit nine out of ten out of the park."

Boston sent the six-foot-two Morton to Marion, Ohio, to play that year in the Ohio-Indiana League under the direction of manager Walter "Wally" Millies, a former Brooklyn, Washington, and Philadelphia Phillies catcher who was given the job of turning Morton into a receiver. "Walt was a tremendous teacher," Morton says, "and there was no foolishness about him. He worked me hard and really helped me. Another catcher on that team was Bernie Schmidt, who played a lot of minor-league ball, and he really helped me, too. As I think back, I think almost everybody else on that team was Italian," Morton laughs. "That's when they started calling me 'Moose,' a nickname that stuck with me throughout my career. I also remember that in the playoffs that year, I hit two home runs."

Off the field that year, Morton met Jean Carroll, the daughter of a local minister, who was to become his wife a year later. "She lived across from where we were staying," Morton recalls, "and Vinnie Fufaro, another player on the team, and I used to see her outside all the time doing her gardening. One thing led to another, and we got married on Thanksgiving a year later. She always insisted I go back to school between seasons, which I did 'cause I wanted to be a coach. I majored in physical education. Today we've got three fine children, two girls and a boy, and eight grandchildren."

In 1950 the Red Sox moved Morton—and Millies, his manager—to Kinston, North Carolina, in the Coastal Plain League, where his education as a catcher continued. "I had a good first half," he says, "and I hit that year's first inside-the-park homer in organized baseball. But it was so hot there it just drained you. I started at 213 pounds but lost a lot as the season wore on. We had a good team and won the playoffs that year. Ken Aspromonte was our shortstop, and Jim Davenport's brother played second base. He was only there a couple of weeks. I remember he came in and hit two home runs and then they just let him go," he says incredulously. That year, Morton played in 120 games and batted .270 with six home runs and 63 runs batted in.

In November, after the season ended, Morton also joined the National Guard. "I thought I could beat it," he says of the military draft brought on by the Korean War, "but my unit was activated the next month, right after I got married."

After going through basic training at Fort Jackson, South Carolina, Morton was transferred to Camp Atterbury, Indiana, where he helped train new draftees and recruits. He also played on the camp's baseball team. "It was a great baseball team," he says. "We had Art Dittmar; Tom Brewer of the Red Sox; Ray Herbert of the Tigers; Jay Sauer, a good left-handed hitter; and Wade Blasingame. Our manager was Billy Rigden, a good semipro player. Only one team beat us. It was Bobby Brown's team, you know, the one who was president of the American League. He played first base. I think it was the Brooks Medical Center out of Fort Hood, Texas.

"They had the fastest pitcher I ever faced—Arnold Portercarerro." Portercarerro struck out 132 men in his rookie season of 1954, but then had an undistinguished six-year major-league career, winning 38 and losing 57.

Morton was discharged in August 1952, in time to start the September term at the University of Alabama. The following spring, he was assigned to Roanoke in the Piedmont League, which was then managed by Elmer Yoder, and hit .302 in 87 games. "I had a good year; I led the All-Star balloting," he says. "That year Bobby Richardson was a rookie at Roanoke. The team folded in August, though, and I was sent to Albany in the Eastern League. That was a good league. I played with people such as Frank Sullivan and Dave Sisler, and I remember hitting against Herb Score. Rocky Colavito was in that league, too, and he had a great arm in right field." Morton finished up the season at Albany, batting .224 in 35 games.

In 1954, the twenty-three-year-old had an outstanding year at Greensboro in the Carolina League, hitting .348, with 120 runs batted in and 32 home runs, more than double his total in his three previous years of professional ball.

"It was my best year ever," he agrees. "I always had power. I told you about hitting them out of the park when I first took batting practice at Fenway Park, and even at Kinston I hit a 450-foot homer, so I always had traces of power. In fact, Ted Williams and I are the only ones ever to hit one over the flagpole in center field in Birmingham. But I always played in huge ballparks before. And while I was a power hitter, I wasn't a pull hitter, so I used to hit a lot of deep outs to center and right center. The park in Greensboro was more to my liking."

His year at Greensboro was acknowledged some forty years later when Morton was named the catcher on the All-Time, All-Carolina League team, beating out Hall of Famer Johnny Bench. "The pitchers on that first team were Doc Gooden and Harvey Haddix," he reads from his notes, "and the infielders were Muscle Shoals at first, Carl Yastrzemski at second, Ray Jablonski at third, and Gregg Jefferies at shortstop. The outfielders were Curt Flood, Leon Wagner, and Brad Kominski. The designated hitter was Woody Fair, and Bill Slack was the manager."

In early September 1954, the Red Sox called him up from Greensboro. "I remember I went to Baltimore and had to wait two days for them to arrive. That was kind of a new experience for me, sitting around in a strange town with nothing to do, just waiting. When they got there, I roomed with Jimmy Piersall. One thing I'll never forget. I was only there a couple of days, but I was in the dugout with Piersall, Ted Williams, and Jackie Jensen, and they were talking about hitting. Jensen said that Casey Stengel once told him never to swing at a change-up until you had two strikes on you. Williams said, 'Say, that's a good idea. I never thought of that.' Now, here's Williams, a guy who hit over .400, one of the greatest hitters in the game, saying 'I never thought of that.' It goes to show how he was always willing to observe new things.

"I guess I was with Boston about three and a half weeks before the season ended," Morton continues. "Lou Boudreau was the manager, and they were fighting for fourth place. Every day was crucial. Boudreau was having problems with his stomach and was taking pills to help him. I have a number of memories of that time. I was a kid, all ears and eyes.

"I remember that when we got to Boston, Grady Hatton was my roommate. At the park, I had the locker next to Williams, and the photographers were all over the place every day. They thought he might retire at the end of the year, and they were all over him. I know he had a tough reputation about not talking with the press and all, but he was one of the nicest people I ever met. He thought I was gonna be good." Morton chuckles, "I guess he had bad judgement."

Morton says, "I remember catching batting practice when he was

hitting, and at the end, I went out to field the last one, which was supposed to be a bunt. 'Guy, get back in here,' he said. 'That's what all the
newspapermen want me to do. I don't bunt.' Let me tell you, he was the
greatest I ever saw. Nobody could hit like him, not Mantle or anybody.
But that wasn't all. Whenever he went out on the field, everyone watched
him. All eyes were on him. Never has a player had such an effect on the
people in the stands."

Morton also remembers a conversation in the bullpen with Mel Parnell, Sid Hudson, and Billy Goodman. "They were talking about who in
the league could put their hands on $20,000 cash. There weren't a lot of
big salaries then, and I've often thought of those guys and that conversation when I hear about how much some mediocre player is making today.

"The first time I saw Goodman, I thought he was the batboy. In Sarasota one time, he was sitting on a trunk when I walked in, and he looked
so young. He was an excellent hitter, and I think he even led the league in
hitting one year [in 1950], but he would walk away when anyone was
talking about hitting. 'Don't talk to me about hitting,' he would say. He
didn't want anyone to confuse him or make him change what he was
doing."

Morton's recollections of the pitching staff include Frank Sullivan, his
former Roanoke teammate ("I remember his stories of how rough and
cold it was when he was in Korea"); Tom Brewer, who played on the same
army team as Morton ("The best change of pace I ever saw"); Mel Parnell
("A tremendous guy. You could catch him in a rocking chair"); Willard
Nixon ("A fine Christian. He never cussed. He threw a knuckle-curve
and taught it to others later when he coached"); and Ellis Kinder. "He
threw a spitter," Morton says. "He'd signal you he was gonna throw it by
spitting at you, but first he'd knock the guy down before he threw it.
Then, when everybody's attention was on the batter, he'd spit in his glove.
He always treated me as a front-line catcher."

As for Hudson: "He was tough for a righty, even in batting practice. I
once faced him and fouled one off that broke my nose. I figure he cost me
some playing time because of that."

Memories of others include Piersall ("He saw me catching one time
down on my knees and said, 'What's the matter? Didn't you go to church
this morning?'"); Jackie Jensen ("He wouldn't go on an airplane"); Billy
Consolo ("He was a jewel, a real hustler"); and Harry Agganis. "He was so
great," Morton says. "I don't remember the exact circumstances, but one
time me and him and Piersall were walking in a street in Chicago, and we
met up with these three guys in zoot suits, tough guys. Well, we got into
an argument about who should move aside as we passed on the sidewalk,
and one of these guys pulled a gun and put it in Harry's stomach. Harry
just stood there. He wouldn't move out of the way even with a gun in his
stomach. He was tough and stubborn. The next year he had a bad cold,

and the doctor didn't want him to play, but he did and he died right in the middle of the season."

Fenway Park also inspires memories. "I remember seeing a woman with a beard selling newspapers outside Fenway Park. I had never seen a woman with a beard before, but she was there selling newspapers. And I remember there was a group of men, about 300 of them, who all sat together, all with business suits and always together. They stirred around at the strangest times, and I finally found out what they were doing. They would bet on foul balls. Each time someone came to bat, they would bet on whether or not he would hit a foul ball. It was the strangest thing."

On September 17, 1954, when the Red Sox were playing the Nationals in Washington's Griffith Stadium, Morton finally got into a major-league game. The two teams were in a tight three-way fight with Detroit for fourth place. The game started with Boston's right-handed Sullivan, going for his 14th win of the year against Washington's left-handed Dean Stone, who was seeking his 12th. Stone, who had celebrated his twenty-fourth birthday four days earlier, had shut out the Orioles in his previous start two days before that. On this day he retired the Red Sox without much trouble in the first two innings, and in the bottom of the second, he came to the plate and hit a three-run homer off Sullivan—the only home run he ever hit in the majors—as Washington took a 4–0 lead.

Sullivan was scheduled to bat in the bottom of the third. Boudreau, fighting to stay in every game, sent Guy Morton Jr. in to pinch hit for Sullivan. "I remember going up," he says. "I had a lot of confidence; I wasn't scared. It was just another time at bat. I was well schooled and had done this before. I just didn't do it. I don't think there was anyone on. I remember he [Stone] pitched from a full windup. I saw the ball well, and I had good cuts. I swung at them all—one, two, three. I think the last one was a slider above the belt. I was a high-ball hitter, and I swung over it.

"I didn't feel anything particularly about it. It was just another day's work. I had struck out before. I had the philosophy of Mickey Owen about it. He's the old Dodgers catcher, whom I met when he was managing Norfolk. He said, 'I'd rather have a good swing and miss it than a half-swing and bounce it back to the pitcher.' That's the way I felt."

Morton doesn't recall anyone saying anything to him afterward, nor does he remember any feelings he had about his major-league appearance. "I guess I was too busy," he says. "I remember I had to go back down to the bullpen to warm up pitchers after that. It was dark down in that bullpen and these guys are throwing ninety to ninety-five miles an hour and it was scary. In those days, you didn't wear masks or shin guards to warm up pitchers, or they'd think you were a sissy." The game ended later with Stone pitching his second consecutive shutout, and Washington beat Boston, 8–0.

Why was it Morton's only major-league appearance? "I mentioned they were fighting for fourth place and every game was crucial," he says.

"Boudreau thought my swing was too long, and he was probably right, and I guess he was reluctant to use me again." When the season ended a few weeks later, Morton returned to the University of Alabama to resume his off-season studies. Boudreau left Boston to manage the Kansas City A's.

The next year, the Red Sox assigned Morton to their Triple-A farm team in Louisville, which, in turn, sent him to play at Montgomery, Alabama, in the Sally League, near his home. "I hit around .265 and had about 12 home runs," he recalls, "and made the All-Star team along with Albie Pearson. That was the year they had the Martin Luther King bus strike in Montgomery, and I remember Frank Robinson playing in the league then, along with Wes Covington. I still have a scar on my leg where he slid into me one time."

At year end, Boston traded Morton to Washington, and he went to spring training with the Nats. When spring training ended, Morton was assigned to Chattanooga, back in the Sally League, where he spent the next few years. In 1956, he hit .268 in 90 games, but caught in only 32. "My playing time was limited that year," he says. "I started off good, but that must have been the biggest park in the history of baseball, and it just wasn't made for me. I pinch hit a lot. Cal Ermer was the manager, and Bob Oldis, who had caught there the year before, came back and had an outstanding year. It was tough to play behind Oldis and not play. I didn't think I had a fair shot that year, but Ermer had confidence in Oldis."

In 1957, Morton did make the league's All-Star team, despite spending most of the year on the disabled list. "I tore my Achilles tendon in my left foot in Little Rock during infield practice one day. I went out to field a bunt and was about to throw to second when I slipped on the wet field and that did it.

"I do remember that year, though. We had [Harmon] Killebrew, [Bob] Allison, and Jimmy Hall on that team. I remember Killebrew hitting a home run out of the park in Chattanooga, but he also struck out a lot on high pitches. I remember telling him to lay off the high ones. Then there was a time that year when they wanted to let Allison go. He was hitting around .240, and they were talking about letting him go. I remember I spoke up for him with Joe Engel, whom I could talk with, and they eventually kept him."

In 1958, John "Red" Marion took over as Chattanooga's manager and Morton's production declined. In 1958, he hit only .249, and in 1959, after only 14 games, he was traded to Atlanta, his third team in the Sally League. "I had a little run-in with Red Marion," he admits. "I don't know what happened. It was nothing personal. We just disagreed about something."

At Atlanta, Morton hit .263 in what would prove to be his last season in professional baseball. "I liked the ballpark in Atlanta," he says, "and I hit three grand-slam home runs there that year. I think I led all the catchers in the league in runs batted in, too. Bob Uecker was one of the other catchers on the Atlanta team that year, and he was a good guy. He really tried hard. [Bob] 'Hawk' Taylor was the other catcher there. He later was a catcher and outfielder for the Mets [and for the Milwaukee Braves].

"I guess it was during that year that my wife and I decided it was time to retire after the season," Morton says. "Ever since I hurt my foot, I had to catch on one knee or sit down when I was catching, and we felt it was time. She had insisted I continue going to school every winter, and I had gone to the University of Chattanooga at night when I played there. It's just tragic to keep playing too long and then see the friends you had when you were going to school well established in their careers while you're not sure about what you can do.

"Sacramento had my contract for the next year, but at the end of the season, I just walked away and never looked back. Milwaukee was interested in me, but I felt it was time to go."

He was almost twenty-nine years old and a relatively recent college graduate. He spent the next year completing courses that earned him a master's degree in education, and was hired as a baseball and basketball coach at the high school in Gordo, Alabama.

"I was there in 1961 and 1962, and left in June of 1962, after the teams won county championships in both sports," he says. "I also was chosen as the coach of the All-Star baseball team.

"But God was directing me to be something else—a preacher," Morton says. "I had become a Christian back in June of 1951, while I was in the army at Fort Jackson. Back then, I was picking up a little extra money on weekends pitching for some of the local town teams around there. Well, one day I was hitchhiking from one place to another, and some farmer stopped and picked me up. He asked me, 'Are you a Christian? Would you like Jesus Christ to save your soul?' I didn't know what to answer, but I said yes."

Morton did not go to a seminary. "You can become a Southern Baptist minister in two ways," he explains. "You can go to a seminary, or you can decide for yourself that it's what God wants you to do with your life. I'm one of those who did not go to a seminary. I did speak with people at a large Southern Baptist seminary in Mississippi and one in Louisville around then, and they told me that if I were to go back to school, I would be in classes with people ten or twelve years younger than me, and they felt I might be too old for that."

He and his wife moved to Marion, Ohio, and started a little church in their home, while Morton taught at Whittier Junior High School. "At the time," Morton says, "I was doing a little street-corner preaching. Our pastor there was George Wilson and some Sundays he was invited to preach over in Wooster, Ohio. One Sunday he couldn't make it and asked me to go in his place. So I went over and," Reverend Morton laughs, "stayed for twenty-eight years. Actually, it was twenty years, and then I went to

Lorraine, Ohio, where I spent three years as a pastor there before return-ing to Wooster.

"Then, a couple of years ago, I kept getting calls from a church in Ver-milion, Ohio, right by Lake Erie, that had been without a pastor for twenty months. They wanted me to join them. Well, I never thought much about doing it, but they kept calling. Finally I just had to realize that I was just a pilgrim passing through. The church in Wooster was in good shape, and this one was struggling. So we moved here, and now I'm the senior pastor of the Lakeview Baptist Church, and it's growing very nicely. Today we get 350 or 400 people at our worship service every Sunday."

Reverend Morton still follows baseball and has his own opinions about it. "Two things: Americans are choked for time. If you go to the game, it's not so important, but if you're watching on TV, you may be sitting there for three hours. There's no telling how long the game is gonna be and the TV audience won't wait around for that. Baseball is the only game with-out a time limit.

"Then, I think the pitching is diluted today, and it's gonna become even more so when they add the two more expansion teams they've got scheduled. So I look for some phenomenal batting averages coming in the future and a lot more home runs."

When he's asked about retirement, Morton says, "I never think of it. This takes a lot out of you, though, going into hospitals and visiting peo-ple you know are dying, but I'm happy to be able to do it. This is my thirty-third year as a Christian pastor, and it has been a real joy to me.

"Baseball is the greatest game of all, in my opinion, but serving God is the real major leagues."

Maurice Wayne "Maury" Fisher

CINCINNATI REDLEGS, 1955

B ert Shepard (see Chapter 15) pitched in the major leagues with only one leg. Maury Fisher did it with only one eye. Although both pitched decently, neither ever appeared in another major-league game.

Fisher, the middle of three sons, was born, with normal sight, in Uniondale, Indiana, on February 16, 1931, and his family moved to Green Hills, Ohio, when he was six years old. He played basketball, football, and baseball at Green Hills High School. In basketball he was an All-State center, and in football he played both offensive and defensive end. But because he was such a standout on the diamond, and since he wanted to play professional baseball, he deliberately did not play football in his senior year in order to reduce his chances of injury.

A hard-throwing right-hander, Fisher pitched 10 no-hitters in high school, including one perfect game. He also played American Legion baseball and in 1946 pitched in an All-Star game for Cincinnati against Cleveland. "Babe Ruth threw out the first ball that game," he remembers, "and I shut them out in the three innings I pitched."

"I graduated on a Friday night in 1949," he says, "and the next day I had ten major-league scouts at my house, and we saw them at one-hour intervals." He signed a contract with Cincinnati, which called for a bonus of $10,000 and a $300 a month salary. "I guess I chose Cincinnati mainly because I was a fan," he says, "although I found out later I could have got a lot more if I signed elsewhere. The [Philadelphia] Phillies' scout never made a specific offer, but he said he would top anyone else. My high school coach told me later that the Phillies' scout told him he was authorized to go as high as $30,000 for my contract."

After signing with Warren Giles, the Cincinnati owner, Fisher stayed with the Reds for a short time during a home stand before being farmed out. "The Cincinnati team was not very good back then," Fisher recalls. They had [Ted] Kluszewski, and I guess [pitcher Ewell] Blackwell was good, too, but that's about all. When I signed, I actually signed a contract with Tulsa, one of their farm teams, and after a couple of weeks, they sent me to Muncie in the old Ohio-Indiana League for the rest of the season."

At Muncie, Fisher won 5 and lost 7, but posted a credible 3.19 earned run average. "I pitched a no-hitter there," he remembers, "a perfect game—and Giles was there to see it."

In 1950, just before spring training, a freak accident interrupted his career. "My brother and I were just fooling around with a rubber band, and he snapped it and it went into my eye. It started hemorrhaging behind the eye, and they took me in and operated on it, but I lost my sight in that eye."

It was June before Fisher recovered enough to play again. After various transfers of his contract between Tulsa and Ogden, Utah, he eventually was sent to play in Lockport in the Pony League. At Lockport, his record was 2 wins and 10 losses, with a 6.82 earned run average. He also walked 60 men in 66 innings. "I just couldn't see well," explains Fisher.

In 1951, he went to spring training with Tulsa, but his contract was again shifted to other franchises, including Charleston, West Virginia, and Columbia, South Carolina. He ended up playing that season at Ogden, Utah, in the Pioneer League, where he won seven and lost six, but brought his earned run average down to 4.02. His eyesight continued to trouble him, and he gave up 124 walks in 150 innings.

In 1952, when he was twenty-one years old, the Korean War was going strong, but Fisher was not called into the military because of his eye. That year, after more contract dealings among Tulsa, Columbia, and Salisbury, Maryland, Fisher ended up playing at Salisbury in the Interstate League. "I was the opening-day pitcher," he says, "and I won. Then we had three days of rain, and I started again and won. So I pitched and won their first two games of the season. Overall that year I won 14 and lost 10 for a last-place team."

For the next three years, Cincinnati brought Fisher to their major-league spring training camp. "In all those three years in spring training, I never gave up an earned run," he says, somewhat defiantly. Despite that record, Rogers Hornsby, managing in 1953, and Birdie Tebbetts, in 1954, farmed him out.

In 1953 he played at Columbia, South Carolina, in the Class A Sally League and had his best year ever. He won 16, lost 7, and posted a 3.21 earned run average. While he continued to walk batters, he also was the league's fourth best strikeout artist. "Ernie White, the old Cardinal pitcher, was the manager there, and he was responsible for my turnaround," Fisher says. "He provided me with a great deal of help."

*Maury Fisher had sight in only one eye when he pitched—and batted—
in the major leagues. On orders, he deliberately decked the opposing pitcher.*

That was the year Columbia fought a tight race for the Sally League championship against Jacksonville, the team on which nineteen-year-old Henry Aaron played second base. As noted earlier, Aaron wrote that Columbia had "the best pitching in the league" that year and specifically mentioned Fisher, Barney Martin (see Chapter 20), and Harold "Corky" Valentine. While Jacksonville won the pennant, Columbia won the championship playoffs.

In 1954 after spring training, Fisher started the season with Havana, where he won three of his first four decisions. "But I got into it with my manager there," he says. "I had gone eight innings this one time, and I was ahead by about three runs. I gave up my first walk of the game in the ninth to Joe Black, the opposing pitcher. My manager, Reggie Otaro, [a Havana native who had played for the Chicago Cubs briefly during World War II] came out to take me out of the game, and I threw the ball at him. He sent me back to Tulsa.

"At Tulsa, I was 8 and 12, but the team didn't score much," he says. "In the four games I pitched, Tulsa never scored a run. One time I pitched 14 innings and lost 1–0, and the next time out, I pitched eight innings and lost 1–0 again."

In 1955, he again went to spring training with Cincinnati, and this time Tebbetts kept him on the opening-day roster. "That was my third year there, and I knew most of the guys," Fisher says, "but I wasn't really close to any of them. I was a loner. I roomed with [catcher] Andy Seminick, and I have to say he helped me more than anyone I ever met in baseball.

"As an example, in one of the spring training exhibition games, we were playing the [Pittsburgh] Pirates, and they really didn't have anybody beside [Ralph] Kiner. Well, I pitched the last three innings of the game, and they didn't get a loud foul off me, including Kiner. But after the game, Seminick said, 'Fish, you didn't have shit out there today. We got to develop another pitch.' Well, I always had a good fastball, but he took me out the next day, and we started working on a sinker. And day after day, we kept working on it, and I kept getting better and better."

In the first week of the 1955 season, the Milwaukee Braves, managed by "Jolly" Charlie Grimm, came into Cincinnati to play the Redlegs (the official name of the team from 1953 through 1958), and on Saturday, April 16, Maury Fisher got his chance to pitch in a major-league ball game.

Tebbetts selected Jim Pearce to start the game against Lou Burdette of Milwaukee. Both right-handers would face heavy-hitting lineups. The Braves' sluggers included right fielder Hank Aaron, first baseman Joe Adcock, third baseman Eddie Matthews, catcher Del Crandall, and left fielder Bobby Thomson, while the Redlegs had such bangers as Ted Kluszewski at first, Gus Bell in center, Wally Post in right, and Ray Jablonski at third.

In the top of the second inning, the Braves scored once, and in the top of the third, they scored three more times off Pearce to lead 4–0. Tebbetts had seen enough. With one out and two runners still on base, he called to the bullpen and waved in Fisher.

"I was excited. I was nervous," he admits. "After all, I knew a lot of people there. It was my hometown." The attendance for the game was 5,131.

Fisher, with his roommate, Seminick, behind the plate, got the final two outs of the inning without giving up any additional runs, although today he cannot remember exactly whom he faced at that point or if he gave up any hits or walks in that inning before retiring the side. "When I went back to the bench," he recalls, "nobody said anything, but I felt pretty good.

"And, hey, don't forget, I got up to bat in the bottom of the third," he chuckles.

If it is difficult to pitch while blind in one eye, just imagine trying to *hit* a big-league pitcher under those circumstances, without any depth perception. "I was nervous," Fisher says. "I hit a knuckleball right down in the dirt in front of home plate, and Crandall threw me out. But, hey, I didn't strike out, and that made me feel good, too."

Fisher then went out to pitch the top of the fourth, and among the batters he faced that inning was Crandall. "Andy called for a curveball inside," Fisher says, "and it was right there, exactly where he wanted it. But Crandall chopped at it and pulled it down the left field line, just inside the foul pole for a home run, into that short porch they had out there in Cincinnati."

The next batter was Burdette. "I knocked him down twice," Fisher says. But it wasn't because he was angry about Crandall's homer. "Birdie Tebbetts had told me he wanted to see Burdette on the ground. I don't know why, but you did what your manager told you back then."

Later that inning, Fisher gave up a walk and two singles, which resulted in another Milwaukee run, putting the Braves ahead 6–0. "I'm pretty sure the walk was to [center fielder Billy] Bruton," Fisher says, "and I think one of the hits was by Bobby Thomson. He hit a ball that must have hopped six times before it went by Jablonski, but Jablonski wasn't much of a fielder. They gave him a hit on it, but it should never have been called a hit."

Cincinnati failed to score in the bottom of the fourth, and Fisher shut out the Braves in the top of the fifth. In the bottom half of the inning, Jablonski led off with a home run, and after left fielder Jim Greengrass was retired, Seminick also homered, making the score 6–2. Post made the second out of the inning, and it was Fisher's turn to bat again. But this time, he never left the bench. Tebbetts sent up Bob Thurman, a rookie outfielder. Thurman, pinch hitting for Fisher, hit the third home run of the inning, cutting the Braves' original lead in half.

That was the end of Maury Fisher's major-league career. In the two and two-thirds innings he pitched, Fisher struck out one, walked two, and gave up five hits and two runs. Today he does not recall whom he struck out or whom else he walked besides Bruton, and he's not sure who else besides Crandall and Thomson got hits. Milwaukee shortstop Johnny Logan, however, went 5 for 5 that day and likely was one of them. But Fisher is fairly sure that Aaron didn't get a hit off him. "I don't think Aaron *ever* got a hit off of me," he says with proud defiance.

Cincinnati scored two more runs that day, on homers by Post and Jablonski, the latter's second of the game. But the Braves went on to score three additional runs off three more Redleg relief pitchers, and they eventually won the game, 9–5. All together, the game produced eight solo home runs.

"I thought I did pretty well," says Fisher, recalling his thoughts after the game. But not well enough evidently. A few days later, between games of a doubleheader, he was called in to see general manager Gabe Paul, who told him he had been optioned to the San Francisco Seals in the Pacific Coast League. "I was *really* disappointed," Fisher recalls, "especially because I had had a really great spring. I remember, shortly before opening day, I came in to relieve in exhibition games against the [Washington] Senators two days in a row, and I was terrific. I shut them out both times. So I was really disappointed.

"I remember, after I spoke to Gabe Paul, Birdie Tebbetts called me up to find out what happened. He hadn't been told about it, and he raised some hell about it," Fisher says.

"In San Francisco, I pitched until July 26, when I got hurt. It was in the second game of a doubleheader, and I had pitched eight and two-thirds innings. By then it had gotten to be around midnight and I was sweaty, but it had gotten very cold, around 39 degrees. That's when I tore a muscle in my arm. The funny thing was that when I went out, we were behind in the ball game, but we scored three runs in the bottom of the ninth to win it, and the pitcher who relieved me got credit for the win after throwing only one pitch."

San Francisco returned Fisher to Cincinnati, but he didn't pitch again until the next year. Before the start of the 1956 season, however, Cincinnati sold him to Seattle which, in turn, sent him to Sacramento. "I didn't stay in Sacramento long," he says. "I got spiked one day when I got credit for double on a bunt. The first guy up had tripled, and I bunted to try to sacrifice him home. They made a play for him at the plate, but he scored as I was running to first. I saw nobody was covering second base so I just kept on running and made it into second. The second baseman came over to cover and spiked me as I was sliding in. But they gave me credit for a double." It also ended his tenure at Sacramento. "I got shifted to Vancouver and then back to Sacramento and finally to Amarillo that year," he says. At Amarillo, he got into 11 games, winning one and losing four.

"At the end of the year, I got a check for $25," he says, "and that got me mad. See, in some of the contracts, I negotiated that I would get 25 per cent of my sale price if I was sold from one club to another. And then I found out they'd been shifting my contract around for only $100."

In 1957, the twenty-six-year-old Fisher was still angry and refused to sign a new contract with anyone, despite being optioned to Monterrey and Savannah. He was placed on baseball's restricted list.

"I felt I had gotten a rotten deal in 1956," he says. Instead of playing baseball, he stayed in his off-season job as a die maker with General Motors in Mansfield, Ohio. "For the next couple of years, I played semipro ball, and I led Mansfield to the Ohio State title," he says.

In 1960, he became a tool-and-die designer at General Motors. In 1961, Fisher was reinstated, but not because he wanted to return to professional baseball. "I wasn't interested in coming back," he says. "I just wanted to be free. I didn't want any complications, so I went through the commissioner's office to get my release."

In early 1956, Fisher had married Shirley Rawlings from his boyhood town of Green Hills. He retired from General Motors in 1988. Today, two sons and two granddaughters later, Fisher and his wife live on a 100-acre farm about forty-five miles north of Columbus, where he runs his own small tool-and-die design business and gives little thought to baseball.

Gordon Vincent Sundin Jr.

BALTIMORE ORIOLES, 1956

Gordie Sundin has to figure out how to explain to his five grandchildren that his major-league earned run average in the record books for all time is infinity. Sundin, of course, is not the only player to have a one-game major-league earned run average of infinity, but he is the only one who consented to be interviewed for this book.

Earned run averages are based on every nine innings pitched, the length of a full game. The exact formula used is the number of earned runs a pitcher allows multiplied by nine, then divided by the actual number of innings pitched. For example, if a pitcher allows one earned run in three innings, his earned run average would be 3.00 ($1 \times 9 \div 3$). Two earned runs in four innings would mean a 4.50 earned run average ($2 \times 9 \div 4$). The lower the number, the better the pitcher—and vice versa.

Mathematical complications arise when the pitcher pitches only a fraction of an inning, but the system of measurement is the same. Technically, an earned run average of infinity means a pitcher allowed at least one earned run without having retired a single batter. In theory, it means that no matter how long he pitched, he would continue at that pace, allowing runs and never getting anyone out.

It's not good.

Those who knew Sundin back at Washburn High School in Minneapolis in the early 1950s would be hard pressed to believe this could have happened to their schoolmate. At Washburn, Sundin was All-City, All-State, and All-Region both in basketball and baseball. As a running back on the football team, the handsome young man was named the most

Gordie Sundin has a major-league career earned run average of infinity.

valuable back in a five-state region. Standing six-foot-four and weighing 215 pounds, he was the athlete personified.

In addition to his exploits in high school, Sundin also played American Legion baseball. "I did everything," he says. "I pitched, I even caught, played shortstop and left field. We never made it out of the state tournament, although I think we did get to the finals. But all the teams I was on in high school were good, and I got a lot of recognition."

One of those who recognized his talents was Phil Galivan, a scout based in Minneapolis for the Baltimore Orioles. When the seventeen-year-old Sundin graduated from high school in 1955, he was undecided about his future. "I thought I would go to college," he says. "I had a number of scholarship offers to play football. Among others, I heard from the University of Minnesota, Wisconsin, and even Notre Dame.

"But Phil Galivan invited me to go to Baltimore to work out for the Orioles. I got to Baltimore and stayed at the Southern Hotel, downtown. I think I had about 20 bucks with me. The first day, I took a cab and went out to the ballpark to work out.

"I didn't know it at the time, but I was told later that I didn't impress them when I first got there. They didn't think I could throw hard enough. I forgot that a couple of days before I left, I had pitched 11 innings in a semipro game back in Minneapolis, and I didn't tell them about that. I guess it affected my velocity when I first got to Baltimore.

"Anyway, after that, I began to throw hard and that impressed them. I remember some of the guys—[shortstop] Willie Miranda especially— didn't want to get in there against me. They had a lot of their bonus baby players there then— Wayne Causey, Bob Nelson, and others—and I was doing well. I started to figure that I belonged.

"But there was one problem," Sundin says. "I was running out of money. I only came with a few dollars, and I would go to eat in these chili places to save money. A kid my size could eat a lot. I called home and told my mom, and she said I should talk to Mr. [Paul] Richards [the Orioles' manager]. When I told him, he laughed like hell, but only for a minute. 'Son, you go in to that hotel dining room and order whatever you like,' he said. I didn't know you could charge the meals to the hotel room. So from then on, I went into the dining room of the Southern Hotel and had shrimp and steak and everything I wanted," Sundin laughs. "Let's face it," he says, "you *are* just a kid. I was seventeen years old, and I stayed there by myself.

"I was there about three weeks, and nothing formal was said about signing me," Sundin continues. "It was getting close to my mom's birthday on July 4, so I just decided to go home and I did. I figured I'd decide on a college. But a couple of weeks later, Paul Richards called and invited my folks and me to come to Chicago and meet him there.

"We stayed at the Chicago Hilton, and we went up to his suite. It was an overwhelming experience for us. My father was a steel engraver and we didn't have a lot of money and here I was—I had my own room in the Chicago Hilton! Mr. Richards took us to lunch and to dinner at the Stock Yards, and then to the game. It was really something.

"And then he lays a big number on us," Sundin says. "I guess I was one of about five bonus kids they had at the time, and we were given money under the table. I'm not telling you anything secret. The IRS found out about this later, and they got us all. It was a darn good handful of money, but for a seventeen-year-old, it was a hell of a decision to make."

A player at that time had to be kept on the team's roster if his bonus exceeded $4,000. "The $4,000-bonus rule kind of hampered them," Sundin continues, "so what they said was that they would give me $50,000 to sign, and pay it out over three or four years. It was a verbal agreement, but that's what they did. They kept their word. Every year they would mail me the money, and that was my 'salary' for the year. Later on in the minors, because of that deal, I would be making $6,000 or $8,500 a year, while most of my teammates were making much less.

"Brooks Robinson and I signed a couple of weeks apart in July 1955," Sundin says. "Brooks was eighteen and I was seventeen. They sent us both to York, Pennsylvania, in the [Class B] Piedmont League. George Staller [an outfielder for the Philadelphia Athletics during World War II] was the manager."

Robinson and Sundin played at York for two months and then were re-called together to the parent Oriole club for the last month of the 1955 season. In the time he spent at York, Sundin appeared in only five games, winning one and losing two. "The Class B ballplayers didn't impress me," he says. "I was throwing a lot of strikeouts, and when I got back to the Orioles, I felt I really did belong. I mean this sincerely. I really felt part of the team."

That last month of the season, Robinson, now in the Hall of Fame, played in six games at third base for Baltimore. He batted only .091, with just two singles in 22 times at bat. In the field, he made two errors in 12 chances, which would turn out to be—by far—his worst fielding average in his twenty-three-year major-league career. Sundin, however, did not get to play in any of the late-season games with the Orioles. "My arm was acting up," he says, "and it hurt when I threw. So they told me to just go home and rest it."

In the off-season, Sundin enrolled at the University of Minnesota. "I didn't know what I wanted to major in," he says. "I was interested in the arts, but I just started taking required freshman courses."

In early 1956 Sundin reported to the Orioles' training camp in Scottsdale, Arizona, but realized his arm was still not right. "I found my arm would hurt and my hand would go numb after a while," he said, "but I tried to throw through it." It didn't work. The Orioles sent him back to Baltimore to have the arm examined at the Johns Hopkins University Hospital.

"They told me it was a damaged nerve in the elbow, which may have come from playing football," Sundin says. "But they needed to operate on it. The doctor who did it was a Dr. Bennett, who, I believe, was a well-known surgeon who had operated on a number of ballplayers."

The surgery was performed in late March, and Sundin's arm was placed in a cast. "My girlfriend, Mary Ann Dorsey, was a figure skater who was on the U.S. Olympic team," Sundin says, "and she had just come back from Germany then and was going to be skating in the Nationals [Championships] in Boston. I went up there to see her and it was kind of funny. There I was in Boston with my Arizona tan, no coat, and my arm in a cast, bent out from my body.

"Then, just before spring training ended, I went back and joined the ball club with the cast still on my arm," Sundin says. "I didn't think about the fact that I couldn't pitch or anything. I just went back.

"In early April, before the season started, I was on the road with the Orioles in New Orleans," Sundin continues. "I remember calling Mary Ann from there. She was gonna join the Ice Follies and was going out to Denver to train. I told her if she went, we might never see each other again. We had gone to school together and had known each other since we were in ninth grade. I proposed to her over the phone and talked her out of going. We were married right after the 1956 season."

By then, Sundin had become a one-time major leaguer.

Baltimore carried Sundin on the disabled list when the 1956 season started, and his recovery was slow and painful. "But I really had a good time," he says, "even though I worked hard on my therapy. I traveled with the team all year and was a part of it. Tito Francona was my roommate, and he was a few years older, but we had some things in common. We were both getting married at the end of the season, for example. He was a quiet guy, a nice guy. But I didn't really have any close friends on the team. I was pretty much of a loner.

"During the games, sometimes I'd sit in the dugout and sometimes I went upstairs and sat with Ernie Harwell and the other announcers. As time went on and my arm got better, I pitched batting practice."

The Orioles, formerly the St. Louis Browns, were in their third year in Baltimore. In the first year, 1954, under Jimmy Dykes, the team lost 100 games. The following year, with Richards at the helm, they lost 97. This year, they were still far from being contenders. Their lineup mainly was composed of older players trying to hang on, along with a few youngsters who were either not quite ready to take over or who never would.

First baseman Bob Boyd, second baseman Billy Gardner, and left fielder Bob Nieman were twenty-nine years old, and center fielder Dick Williams was twenty-eight. All had seen their best days. The same could be said of shortstop Willie Miranda, thirty, and third baseman George Kell, thirty-four, who was ahead of the nineteen-year-old Brooks Robinson. Gus Triandos, twenty-six, shared the catching duties with Hal Smith, twenty-five, until Smith was traded away in midseason for Joe Ginsburg, age twenty-nine.

"Willie [Miranda] was a fun sort of guy," Sundin says, recalling some of his teammates. "One time he and [pitcher] Mike Fornieles took me to some Cuban joint in New York, and we had a lot of fun. Bob Boyd was really a nice guy. He hit ropes. Nieman was an aristocrat. I thought he was hot stuff. He was major-league all the way—or so he thought. Dick Williams always seemed angry. I remember he had a fight with Triandos in the clubhouse early in the year over nothing. He was the same way later when he was managing."

The pitching staff was plain old. It included Morrie Martin, Connie Johnson, and Bill Wight, all thirty-four years old; Hal "Skinny" Brown and George Zuvernick, both thirty-two; and Ray Moore, thirty. Other hurlers included Erv Palica, twenty-eight, in his last year in the majors; Billy Loes, twenty-seven; and Don Ferrarese, a twenty-seven-year-old rookie. Moore, who won 12 games that year, was the only one on the staff who won in double figures.

"I liked Moore," Sundin says. "He threw real hard, and I sort of fashioned myself after him. He also had a kind of swagger. But he could be somewhat childish. One time he hit me in the head with a ball in the dugout. Morrie Martin was my 'godfather,' and I'd go out to eat with him a lot. I remember Skinny Brown and Jim Wilson [who was traded early that year] had their lockers together. They were older and both were really nice. I thought of them as dads. Palica was trying to hang on. So was Wight. Loes could throw hard when he felt like it. He was a Brooklyn guy. I don't mean that he just came from the Dodgers. He was a Brooklyn *guy*. I thought he was neat. He was like a 'hood.' I remember him drinking his rye whiskey."

Among the regulars, the only younger player was the left fielder, Tito Francona, Sundin's roommate, who was twenty-three. Other players included two young pitchers, Fornieles, twenty-four, and Billy O'Dell, twenty-three; a catcher, Tommy Gastall, twenty-four; two utility men, Jim Pyburn and Bob Hale, both twenty-three; and four bonus babies, Brooks Robinson, Wayne Causey, and Bob Nelson, all nineteen, and, of course, Sundin, the sore-armed pitcher, who was eighteen.

"Pyburn also was a bonus baby," Sundin says. "He had been a halfback at Auburn, and he was a flake. I used to compete with him a lot, especially in athletic things like foot races, and I would beat him. He used to get so frigging mad. He and Triandos had a fight one time, and why anybody would want to pick a fight with Gus is beyond me. Nelson was supposed to be the next Babe Ruth, but wasn't."

The team eventually won 69 games that year and lost 85, finishing sixth, 28 games behind the first place New York Yankees.

On September 1, when the rosters were allowed to expand, Sundin was activated. But it wasn't until Wednesday, September 19, 1956, that he got to pitch in a major-league game.

That day, the Orioles were playing the Tigers in Detroit's Briggs Stadium, and it had turned cold. The game was played in 50-degree weather before only 1,435 fans, the smallest crowd of the season in Detroit but enough to edge the Tigers' home attendance for the year over the one-million mark for the eleventh time in twelve years.

Detroit's ace, Frank Lary, would lead the league with 21 wins that year. He was going for his nineteenth that day, against Hal "Skinny" Brown (9–5) of the Orioles. The win, which he had little trouble getting, also gave him at least one victory over every team in the league that year. Lary walked three, scattered eight hits and, aided by a couple of double plays, limited the visiting Orioles to just one run, which scored when Triandos knocked in Francona in the top of the sixth.

Meanwhile, the Tigers scored five runs off Brown and three more off of relievers Zuvernick, Palica, and Martin. They led 8–1 as they came up to bat in the bottom of the eighth inning.

In the cold and the gloom, the eighteen-year-old Gordie Sundin was called in from the bullpen to mop up. It was a getaway day, with the Orioles scheduled to return to Baltimore following the game, so Richards also replaced some of his older regulars with his youngsters. The outfield at that point in the game consisted of Pyburn, Nelson, and Francona. Robinson had come in to play third, relieving Kell, and Tommy Gastall was catching in place of Triandos.

"I knew all the guys," Sundin says. "I'd been throwing to Gastall for five months. Being a glorified batting-practice pitcher all year, I was anxious to get into a game—maybe too anxious. It was a bit overwhelming. If somebody just said, 'Throw strikes,' maybe it would have helped me.

"Frank Lary, the Detroit pitcher, was leading off the eighth inning," Sundin says. "I was so nervous. I walked him. I don't remember what I threw him, but I know it wasn't all fastballs. I had a good slider and a curve. And I got some strikes. I felt so awful to walk Lary, who was up there just to make an appearance."

The next hitter was Harvey Kuenn, Detroit's shortstop and leading hitter that year. "I was really trying to get Kuenn," he continues. "I felt good, and he was easy to pitch to. He stood up there at the plate. I didn't feel nervous anymore. I felt aggressive. But I walked him, too.

"I don't remember who the next batter was," Sundin says. "I've been told it was Jack Phillips [Tiger first baseman]. I don't remember whether or not it was the first pitch, but I almost hit the guy. I threw one high and tight, knocking him down. I think it was Lum Harris, one of our coaches, who came out of the dugout to the mound, not Richards. Harris was sort of a go-between between Richards and the players. I was afraid they were gonna take me out, and I said, 'Lemme take care of this guy.' He took the ball from me and said, 'That's what we're afraid of, son.' I felt like a dumb shit."

Sundin went to the bench and was told to go in to take a shower. "I went in the clubhouse, and I was really crushed," Sundin says. "I was hurting. I thought how good I felt being with the team and how comfortable I was sitting on the bench all year and now that I finally got my chance, I blew it! I was down and feeling bad for a long time.

"I remember George Kell was in the clubhouse, and he saw how low I was. He came over and put his arm over my shoulder and said, 'Don't let it get you down. You got a long career ahead.' I'll never forget that."

While Sundin was in the clubhouse, Billy O'Dell went in to relieve him. Years later, Sundin found out that O'Dell also walked a batter in that inning and that Lary eventually scored on a sacrifice fly by Tiger right fielder Al Kaline. That run, which gave the Tigers a 9–1 win, also gave Sundin his eternal major-league earned run average of infinity.

The following day, back in Baltimore, Sundin's catcher, Tommy Gastall, was killed in a private plane crash.

There was no game scheduled that day. "I remember Tito Francona and I were sitting in a diner we used to go to when somebody came in and said, 'Did you hear what happened to Tommy?' His plane had crashed in Chesapeake Bay," Sundin says. "We didn't even know he was taking flying lessons."

The season ended shortly thereafter, and in October, Sundin and Mary Ann Dorsey were married. "I had planned to play winter ball that year because I hadn't thrown in a while," Sundin says, "so we left almost on our wedding night for Puebla, Mexico, where I played that winter."

In 1957, Sundin again went to spring training with the Orioles in Arizona, but "my arm didn't come back," he says. The Orioles sent him to Vancouver in the Triple-A Pacific Coast League, where he made eight appearances before again going on the disabled list. After resting his arm for a month, Sundin was optioned to Phoenix and got into 11 games there before the season ended. "It was a kind of wasted year," he admits.

The following year, at Baltimore's spring training facility in Scottsdale, Sundin says, "I was throwing well. My arm was getting better." Nevertheless, Baltimore sent him back to Vancouver to start the 1958 season. "That was probably my most active year," Sundin says. "I started out winning six and losing two, and I was leading the league in earned run average early in the year. I lost a couple by one run. Then my arm went bad again." He lost his next six decisions.

"Charlie Metro was the manager, and I hated his guts," Sundin says. "We got into it one day. It was in Seattle, and Seattle hit the shit out of me. He wouldn't take me out. He just let me stay in and take the punishment." Sundin and his wife "had just had a baby a few weeks earlier, and I didn't think it was right for him to do that. After the game, we had a physical fight."

On August 11, in a game against Phoenix, George Bamberger, Sundin's thirty-three-year-old teammate, set a Pacific Coast League record, having pitched 68⅔ consecutive innings without giving up a walk.

"Yes, I remember something about that," Sundin says. It was the same day Sundin was demoted to Knoxville.

"George Staller, who was my first manager in York, Pennsylvania, was the manager at Knoxville, and he welcomed me there," Sundin says. "I guess he was the only one who wanted me then." Before the season ended, Sundin pitched in three games at Knoxville. "I was disappointed," he said. "That year was the closest I came to doing something."

Back for another spring training camp with the Orioles in 1959 (the last year he would be paid out of his initial bonus), the twenty-one-year-old continued to feel frustrated. His arm was still not right. After five games with Vancouver and another 11 with Amarillo, where he had been sent that season, Sundin returned to Johns Hopkins to have bone chips and a spur removed from his elbow. "The therapy following that operation was even longer than the first one," he says.

He was out for most of the 1960 season. "Baltimore sold me," Sundin says, "and I went to Quad Cities that year to try to get myself back in shape." But it took until early 1961 before he was able to pitch professionally again. "I went to Tri-Cities in the Northwest League," he says, "but I was done in the middle of the season." He managed to win three while losing five, but the two operations on his arm had taken their toll. He decided to leave professional baseball at the age of twenty-three.

"When I was with the Orioles," he says, "we had bought a home in Phoenix, near where they trained. When I retired, we sold it and moved back to Minneapolis. I didn't know what I wanted to do."

For a few years, he worked as a salesman for the Campbell Soup Company, for a liquor distributor, and then for an insurance company. In 1968, he became sales manager of Midwest Trucks, leaving in 1976 to become a broker in the steel business. In 1985, he entered the real estate sales and development industry and has been there ever since. Today, he is the development director of a 1,200-unit development in Estero, Florida, where he has lived for the past ten years.

Sundin and his wife have three daughters and those five young grandchildren, all of whom are under six years old. "I don't know what I'll tell them if they ask about my earned run average," he says, explaining that he learned about this record only a few years ago. "I haven't thought about it. I guess I'll treat it as lightly as it is," he says. "I mean I didn't really accomplish anything in baseball. I wasn't a major leaguer, so it doesn't really mean anything to me."

Rodney Carter Miller

BROOKLYN DODGERS, 1957

Rod Miller had a difficult childhood. After his older brother—only eleven months older—drowned when he was eight, Miller's parents separated and divorced. He lived in Portland, Oregon, with his financially strapped mother and his younger sister, but then their house burned down.

"I was in about the seventh grade," he says, "and I was a batboy for a semipro team and an American Legion team coached by a cop named Ted Marletto. He took me in, and although he didn't formally adopt me, I lived with him and his family, and we moved to North Long Beach, California, where I grew up.

"When I was thirteen, I played in a North-South American Legion All-Star game," Miller says, "and had a great day. I hit a huge home run over a light tower and also beat out a drag bunt. A scout for the Chicago Cubs came up to me after the game and handed me his card. His name was Gene Hanley. He asked me how old I was, and I said, 'Thirteen.' He said, 'Say, what?' He couldn't believe it. He says, 'Well, son, hold on to that card. I want you to remember me when you get a little older.'"

As a teenager in North Long Beach, Miller attended Hamilton Junior High School for one year and then moved over to Jordan High School. "I played freshman baseball at Hamilton and varsity ball at Jordan," he says. "But in the middle of my sophomore year, I transferred to Lynwood High School. They didn't know me, so they put me on the junior varsity team that year. I only played varsity ball there my last two years."

Standing five-foot-ten and weighing 160 pounds, Miller was a second baseman who hit left-handed despite throwing right-handed. "I just

Miller now lives in Reno, Nevada, a city he fell in love with when he played there.
He works for a company which makes baseball pitching machines.

started left-handed and kept on going," he says. "I remember my dad telling me he thought I was a natural-looking lefty hitter. Oh, I used to fool around hitting righty once in a while, but it wasn't until my last year in pro ball that I began to hit both ways. I probably should have done it earlier."

While in high school, Miller attracted the attention of a number of major-league teams, and after his graduation in 1957, the seventeen-year-old Miller signed with the Dodgers. "Cincinnati, Philadelphia, the Red Sox, and the Dodgers all were interested in me," he recalls, "along with the Cubs. But it finally came down to either the Reds or the Dodgers. They both offered me about the same, but I chose the Dodgers because they seemed to have a larger farm system and I thought there would be more opportunity for me. I also thought they were a classy organization."

"The people who signed me were Lefty Phillips and Dick Walsh. Phillips was the chief scout for the West Coast, and Walsh was a vice president of the Dodgers," Miller says. "I got a bonus of $4,000, which meant they had to keep me on the roster for a year and couldn't send me down below Class B. I also got a major-league salary of $6,000."

The Dodgers had already announced plans to move to Los Angeles for the 1958 season. The team was at the tail end of a glorious decade. In 1946 they had tied for the National League pennant before losing a play-off to St. Louis (see Chapter 16). Then, with the addition of Jackie Robinson in 1947, they won the pennant in six of the next ten years—in 1947, 1949, 1952, 1953, 1955, and 1956. They also tied for first in 1951, only to lose another playoff series on Bobby Thomson's historic home run. In addition, they finished second in 1950 and third—by only one game—in 1948. The span encompassed Robinson's entire major-league career (he retired at the end of 1956).

While keeping Miller on their roster, the Dodgers sent him to play that year at Cedar Rapids in the Three-I League. In 77 games there, he made 36 errors as a second baseman and batted only .183. "I was never that good a fielder," he says, "but that year I was a butcher."

But there was a reason. "I tried to keep it quiet," Miller says "and didn't tell anyone, but an eye doctor told me I had no depth perception. My eyes didn't operate together. One eye went blind, but I could never tell which one it was going to be at any particular time. You may have heard of 'lazy eye.' Well, mine were so lazy they never functioned together. I didn't find all this out till later when I was in the [military] service. I got beaned seriously twice."

Despite his shaky statistics at Cedar Rapids, the Dodgers recalled Miller in September to finish out the season. "Danny Ozark was the player-manager at Cedar Rapids," Miller says, "and he called me in and gave me some money and said, 'Here's train fare to Chicago.' That's where I was supposed to meet the Dodgers. But he didn't tell me anything else.

"So I got to Chicago, and I didn't know where to go. So I asked a cab driver, 'What hotel do the big-league teams stay at?' He says, 'The Edge-water Beach Hotel.' So he drives me there, and I think the fare was about fifteen dollars. But when I got there, the desk clerk told me that's only where the *American* League teams stay. He said the National League teams stayed at the Hilton. So I went outside and got another cab to take me to the Hilton. I figured it was only a few blocks away, and I had about fifty bucks in my pocket.

"Well, this cab driver gave me one of those joy rides you hear about," Miller continues. "He went all over Chicago, and when we finally got to the Hilton, the meter said $56. I had to go in the hotel and find Lee Scott, the traveling secretary, and he loaned me $6 to pay off the cab driver. I was only seventeen years old, and this cabbie just took advantage of me. And since I had no more money and payday was still a week or so away, Scott had to loan me some more money just so I could get through the week.

"The biggest thrill of my career," Miller says, "was going into the Dodger clubhouse the next day, seeing all these legends, and putting the major-league uniform on."

Miller spent the month of September with Brooklyn, but it wasn't until the next-to-the-last day of the season before Miller got to play. On Saturday night, September 28, 1957, at the age of seventeen, he became a major-league baseball player.

The Dodgers were visiting the Philadelphia Phillies that night, and both teams were playing out the schedule. Brooklyn had already clinched third place, their worst finish since third in 1948, and Philadelphia was solidly entrenched in fifth. Only about 5,800 people showed up to watch.

It was a game most observers—but not Rod Miller—might call forgettable. The Dodgers, helped by a three-run homer by third baseman Randy Jackson, scored five runs in the third inning off Phillie starter Don Cardwell. Later, they scored three more runs and led 8–1 going into the bottom of the fifth.

The Dodger starter was rookie Rene "Latigo" Valdez in his first and only major-league start. He had given up a run in the bottom of the second on a wild pitch. Now, in the bottom of the fifth, he was able to get two men out. He needed only one more out to be credited with the win, but he couldn't quite make it. He gave up two more Philadelphia runs, including a pinch-hit homer by Marv Blaylock, and was relieved by Ed Roebuck, the eventual winner.

The game dragged on into the top of the ninth with the Dodgers still ahead, 8–3. "[Dodger manager] Walt Alston asked me to pinch hit," Miller says. "I didn't believe him at first. I thought he was kidding me. I had to be coaxed by [Pee Wee] Reese and [Duke] Snider that Alston wasn't kidding me. Then I couldn't find a bat. My bats weren't shipped when I came back to the club, so I always borrowed bats that belonged to the nonregulars, and even then, I made sure it wasn't a *good* bat. But this time, I couldn't find a bat under 34 ounces. I just grabbed the first bat I could. It was

Duke Snider's bat, and it must have weighed about 42 ounces. I knew it was Snider's bat. He was my idol. But I figured if I choked up on it a lot, I could handle it.

"I particularly remember being in the on-deck circle," Miller says, "knowing I was going to go to bat my first time in the big leagues. I was holding this heavy bat and just hoping I wouldn't embarrass myself. I thought about the compassion Walter Alston had for me, letting me get to bat. He was the classiest human being I've ever known. I loved that man. He could be a role model for anyone."

Miller knows that Alston also played in only one major-league game, striking out in his only time at bat. "I think he set it up that way, so I could have an at-bat," Miller says. "That's part of what I mean when I say he was compassionate, a good human being. You can't imagine the residual benefits I've had in my life from that one time at bat. It's opened more doors than I could ever have imagined."

Miller went up to bat for Jackson, who had hit the three-run homer earlier in the game. "The pitcher I faced was [right-hander] Jack Meyer," he says. "I got up there and the catcher [Joe Lonnett] said, 'Fastball, kid, fastball.' Well, I didn't know whether to believe him or not, so I took the pitch. It *was* a fastball and it was a strike. He said, 'Fastball again, kid.' This time I swung, and I hit a line drive down the line and over the fence in right field, but foul. Well, I worked the count to 2–2, and he kept telling me every pitch. On the next pitch, though, I struck out. I struck out swinging. There was no way I was gonna *take* a third strike," Miller chuckles.

Why would Lonnett tip off the pitches? "Because he was a nice guy, because he was a big-league person," Miller responds. "In those days, people who reached the majors were big-league *persons*, not just big-league players. Remember, back then the average big leaguer had already spent about five years in the minors. Lonnett was probably ten or twelve years older than me and he knew I was just a kid starting out.

"I was disappointed not making contact," Miller says, "but I was thrilled to have gotten up. I went back to the bench, and [outfielder] Sandy Amoros said, 'Good swing,' or something like that, and Jackson said the same thing. [Pitcher] Danny McDevitt said, 'Good rips.'"

In the bottom of the ninth, Reese, not Miller, went in to play third base in place of Jackson. "I think that's the way Alston planned it," he says. He just designed it for me to get an at-bat." As an afterthought, Miller adds with a laugh: "Besides, if he looked at my fielding record, he wouldn't want to put me in."

In that final inning, Roebuck ran into some trouble. With two out and the bases loaded, he walked the Phillies' first baseman Ed Bouchee to make the score 8–4 and bring the potential tying run to the plate, in the person of cleanup hitter Harry Anderson. But Johnny Podres came in and struck out the rookie left fielder to end the game.

Today, Miller can name just about every player on that Dodger team. "I roomed with Billy Harris, a rookie pitcher, on the road," he says. "The people I liked the most on that team were [Carl] Furillo and [Jim] Gilliam. And John Roseboro treated me great. I remember Elmer Valo was there and Bob Kennedy. Both of them were old and at the end of their careers, and I was surprised to see them there. Gino Cimoli was there. He had just been voted the best-looking guy in baseball, but he was a great outfielder.

"The catchers were [Roy] Campanella, [Joe] Pignatano, Rube Walker, and Roseboro. [Gil] Hodges was at first along with [Jim] Gentile and Tim Harkness. Gilliam and I were at second. Reese was at third with Jackson. Charlie Neal and [Don] Zimmer were the shortstops. In the outfield, Amoros was in left, Snider and Cimoli were in center, and Furillo and Valo were in right." The pitchers? "[Don] Newcombe (who had been named the league's most valuable player the previous year) and [Don] Drysdale were there. [Sandy] Koufax was there, and he was a nonstarter! I remember Latigo Valdez," Miller says. "He had worse legs than anyone I ever saw, including me. He had no calves, just skinny little legs. Then there was Don Bessent, Roebuck, Danny McDevitt, Billy Harris . . . who am I forgetting?" Podres, Clem Labine, and Roger Craig.

How did the team feel about moving to California in the following year? "Most of them were sad to be moving," Miller says. "The Brooklyn fans were great. The town was great. Maybe Snider, who came from California, looked forward to moving, but that's about all. Even I came from California, but I would rather have stayed there. The fans were so great. The only fans I've seen in recent years who approach them are in San Francisco. But I think most of them [the players] would rather have stayed."

After the season, Miller returned home and enrolled at Compton Junior College, taking general education courses. That winter, the Dodger catcher, Roy Campanella, was left paralyzed in an automobile accident that stunned the sports world. "I heard about it when I was in college," Miller says, "and I got sick to my stomach. I threw up."

Shortly thereafter, spring training began, and Miller attended the camp of the newly minted Los Angeles Dodgers in Vero Beach, Florida. "I remember a couple of things," he says. "First, I remember being measured for a uniform that fit. That made me feel good. Also, I set a record for being in spring training. I started out in February with the pitchers and catchers and lasted until April, right up through the end of spring training. I was there because of my contract. They didn't sell my contract to Montreal [the Dodger farm team in the Triple-A International League] until late in April.

"Frank Howard and Don Miles were in that camp, and they could hit farther than anyone else I've ever seen," Miller recalls. "I also found I wasn't as intimidated by the other players as I had been before, now that I knew they were nice people. But, most of all, I started to learn how to become a better ballplayer. The Dodgers had teachers—coaches or older players—showing us things, how to throw, how to slide, how to steal. We'd sit in the stands and hear lectures about these things, and then we'd go out on the field, or into the sliding pits, and *do* them.

"I remember Reese telling me once the difference between a major-league player and a minor-league player. He said they both run the same and throw the same, but the difference was a few percentage points. What he meant was that the major-leaguer fielded .980 and the minor-leaguer fielded .975. The major-leaguer hit .300 and the minor-leaguer .270. In other words, the major-leaguer did it consistently. They both could make the difficult plays, but the major-leaguer would make them all the time, while the minor-leaguer wouldn't. Consistency was the key.

"You can't say that about the ballplayers today," Miller says. "Today, they learn the game in the big leagues. It's on-the-job training."

Miller blames expansion for the reduction in quality he believes has taken place since 1962. "There are probably the same number of players with major-league abilities," he says, "and probably more because of the black ballplayers coming in, but the talent pool has been diluted because of expansion."

After spring training in early 1958, Montreal assigned Miller to the Reno Silver Fox team in the California League. "Ray Perry was the manager there," Miller recalls, "and we called him the Little Buffalo. I fell in love with the city of Reno when I was there, and I decided then that some day I was gonna come back and live there."

But Miller didn't stay in Reno long at that time. He appeared in just 26 games, playing both second base and third, and hit .260. Then he was sent to Thomasville, Georgia, in the Georgia-Florida League. "It was cut-down day in the big leagues," he says, "and that had a ripple effect on all the minor-league teams."

At Thomasville, Miller again played second and third, and appeared in 52 games. While there, he averaged more than one walk per game while hitting .258. But one day he got into trouble with his manager.

"Rudy Rufer [a former infielder who had spent parts of two seasons with the New York Giants] was the manager," he says, "and one day we were having a morning workout before playing against Marietta, practicing the cutoff play with runners on first and third. Well, we kept practicing and practicing and I'm going out to be the relay man all the time and my arm is getting tired and starting to hurt. So I asked him if someone else could take the throws, because I couldn't lift my arm. And he said, 'No. You keep taking them.' Well, I got mad and I swore at him and he fined me for insubordination. I went to the president of the team and said I didn't want to play for him anymore. They got me transferred to Columbus in the Alabama-Georgia League. About two weeks later, Rufer had some sort of mental or psychological breakdown."

At Columbus, Miller's season ended after only 18 games when he suffered a broken elbow after being hit by a pitch.

He did not return to college during the off-season. "I did what most eighteen-year-olds do," Miller chuckles. "I hung around and chased skirts. I did it the following year, too."

In 1959, Miller was assigned to Kokomo, Indiana, in the Midwest League. "The highlight of that year," he says, "was that Brent Musberger got run out of baseball. He was an umpire in that league that year and was a real horseshit umpire, if you'll excuse my language.

"There were a number of players in that league who went on to play in the majors," Miller says. "I remember Jose Tartabull, Galen Cisco, and some others. I played center field that year, and I remember our team had a lot of home runs. I think we either tied or set a league record for homers that year. We had a pitcher named John Bozich who hit nine home runs [actually six]. Another guy, Don Reichert, hit 42 and led the league."

Although Miller batted only .251 that year, he had 14 homers himself, a career record, along with 25 doubles and six triples. In addition, he picked up 115 walks in 120 games, second in the league. Another teammate, Jorge Gomez, walked 112 times in 106 games (and hit 23 home runs). "Jorge carried a .32 caliber pistol in his belt," Miller says, "and nobody fooled around with him. Everybody knew Jorge was 'carrying.' He also had huge forearms, and nobody could beat him in arm wrestling."

In 1960, the twenty-year-old Miller played at Great Falls in the Pioneer League, where Spider Jorgenson, a former utility player with the Dodgers and the New York Giants, was manager. "That was my worst year," Miller says. "I don't know if Jorgenson didn't like me or what. But I didn't play regular. I pinch hit a lot. I seemed to become a better hitter as I got older. Maybe I was just getting smarter. [This also was the year he began to hit from both sides of the plate.] My fielding was still poor," he admits.

Toward the end of the season, Miller received a draft notice. "The draft was still on at that time, and the situation in 'Nam was getting started," he says. Rather than wait for induction, Miller enlisted for a three-year hitch in the Marine Corps. "It was extended twice, and I was actually in," he recites, "for four years, three months, and two days."

After boot camp, he was stationed at San Diego in the shore patrol. "Somehow the general there found out I was a professional ballplayer," Miller says, "and a major came around to get me to join the base team. He asked me what position I played, and I told him I was a pitcher. I always wanted to be a pitcher," Miller chuckles. "So that year I pitched and went 14 and 3!"

That year he also met and married a local San Diego girl, Marian Campbell. (They were divorced in 1965.)

"After that year, I got sent to Pearl Harbor and pitched there for a couple of years. I had three pitches, a fastball, a change-up, and a knockdown pitch. I never told them I wasn't a pitcher. I was having too much fun."

The fun ended one day, however, when Miller was badly beaned. "My eyes weren't working together, as usual, and I lost sight of the ball," he says. "I remember the catcher yelling, 'Look out!,' but I ended up with a multiple concussion.

"When I went into the Marines, they gave me an eye exam and told me they suspected something was wrong, but it was a cursory exam and they let it go. They didn't care. After I got beaned, they gave me all kinds of tests, and they found out what was wrong, that my eyes didn't operate together. But they wouldn't discharge me then. They would have had to pay me for all that time I had spent in the service."

When he was finally discharged in November 1964, Miller went to work in the order department of the Allen Fry Steel Company in Los Angeles. He remained there for nine years before joining the Shultz Steel Company, also in Los Angeles, and becoming their chief estimator. While there, he met Robin Joy Jividen, the secretary of his best friend, and they were married in 1979. Their daughter was born in 1985. (Miller also has two older children from his first marriage.)

In 1988 the Millers moved to Reno, Nevada, where Miller once promised himself he'd return. After working at Viking Metallurgical Company, in 1992 he joined the Athletic Training Equipment Company, known as ATEC. The firm manufactures baseball-pitching machines, among other products. "Jack Shepard, a former big-league catcher, is the owner," Miller says. "He was part of the Pirates 'Gold Coast' kids—you know, Dick Groat and the O'Brien twins [Eddie and Johnny]. Well, he was the catcher. He hired me because I just kept pestering him until he gave me a job."

During the past few years, Miller also has returned to college at nights and is working towards a degree in business. "I may not get it until I'm a hundred," he laughs, "but I'm improving myself. When I was younger, I never thought about improving myself. I didn't play winter ball. I didn't try to improve my fielding, which I should have done.

"But if there's one thing I'd like to say, it's how fine a man Walter Alston was. That one at-bat has continually opened doors for me in many areas, and I'll never forget him for that."

Nicholas Testa

SAN FRANCISCO GIANTS, 1958

Nick Testa is a New Yorker through and through. He was born and raised in New York City. He went to high school and college there; he taught school there. He spent most of his professional baseball life with a team in New York. He lives there today and pitches batting practice for both the New York Yankees and the New York Mets. And he still speaks with an accent that sounds as if he never left the Big Apple.

But the baseball career of this native New Yorker reads like a world travelogue.

The youngest of four children (two girls and two boys), Testa is the son of an Italian immigrant who came to the United States in 1917, in the middle of World War I. "They put him in the army and sent him right back to Europe," Testa laughs. "That's how he got his citizenship." Nick was born June 29, 1928.

At Christopher Columbus High School in the Bronx, Testa was a catcher on the baseball team. "Because I was short and stocky, five-foot-eight and 180 pounds," he explains, "they put me back there and I got beat up for a while." In 1943, when he was fifteen years old, Testa went to a New York Giants tryout at the Polo Grounds. "It rained that day, so they wouldn't let us go on the field, so we had the tryout outside, under where the elevated trains ran. They had us run and throw on the sidewalk."

Testa was signed by the Giants to play on their "Eddie Grant Team," which was composed of top high school prospects from around the city. The team played exhibition games at the Polo Grounds against other traveling teams when the Giants were away. "When the Giants were home, I caught batting practice," he says. He was still just fifteen or sixteen years old.

Nick Testa is pictured here in 1958 with the bat he almost got to swing in his one major-league game.

As a direct result of a play he made at the plate in one of the exhibition games, Testa was offered a college football scholarship.

"One time, a guy who was a football player tried to score from second on a hit to the outfield and came barreling into me at home plate. I was fine, but they had to revive him. After the game, a scout named Bob Trocolar, who used to punt for the New York Giants football team, asked me if I played football, and I said no, just sandlot stuff. My high school didn't have a football team. But he got me a football scholarship to the University of Florida."

After graduating from high school in 1945, Testa went to school in Florida for a little over a year and played blocking back. During that time, he was extremely active in the classroom. "I doubled up on courses and finished two years' worth of credits in one and received an associate of arts degree."

Back in the New York area in 1946, he took advantage of another football scholarship and enrolled at Bergen Junior College across the Hudson River in New Jersey. "That summer, I also played professional baseball in Walden, New York, in the Northern League, under another name. I used another name so I wouldn't lose my college eligibility," he says. The name he chose was Nick Warren. "When I was catching batting practice for the Giants, there was a catcher there named Ben Warren who was very nice to me and helped me a lot," Testa says. "Since he was the first big leaguer I ever knew and who was nice, I chose his name."

The Giants scout, Bob Trocolar, kept tabs on Testa, and in 1947 signed him for the Giants organization. "I got a bonus of $500 and $200 a month to play for Seaford, Delaware, in the Eastern Shore League," Testa says. "It was Class D. I hit around .400 'til July Fourth and then tailed off to .292. But I played every day."

His travels had begun.

Over the next ten years, Testa was shifted almost annually from one Giants farm team to another. "In those days, most teams had around twenty farm teams," he says, "and they kept switching players around from one team to another each year." During the winter, Testa went to school at the University of Delaware, where he majored in physical education, eventually earning a bachelor of science degree in 1952.

For the Giants, he played in Trenton, New Jersey, in 1948. "I had a horrible year. I batted .190 [.184], but caught well," he says. In 1949 and 1950, he was in Erie, Pennsylvania. "I did well. I was the most popular player and hit around .260 to .265," he recalls. The following year, he played in Idaho Falls, Idaho, and in 1952, at Jacksonville, Florida. Then, near the end of the Korean War, he was drafted and spent two years at Fort Belvoir, Virginia, where he was in Special Services, which meant he played on the fort's baseball team.

After his discharge in 1954, Testa finished the year at Sioux City, Iowa, and then played in Wilkes-Barre, Pennsylvania, and Dallas, Texas, in 1955.

"I had a very good year, batting over .300," he says. In 1956, he went to Johnstown, Pennsylvania. "They have the craziest ballpark in America," he says, "260 feet down the left field line, with a fence about 80 feet high." In 1957, he returned to Dallas. "Willie McCovey was on that team in Dallas," he remembers.

Generally, Testa was not that good a hitter. "One year [1955] I hit over .300, but mostly I was a .260 hitter. But my job was to be a defensive catcher and handle the pitchers, so I never concentrated too much on hitting," he says.

He also seemed to handle his finances well. Although never making much money in his minor-league travels, the young bachelor followed his father's advice. "My father told me to save every other paycheck, and that's what I did," he says.

In 1958, the year the Giants moved from New York to San Francisco, Testa, approaching thirty years of age ("I told them I was twenty-eight"), went to spring training with the big-league team for the first time. "It was in Phoenix, Arizona, and I was a little in awe of some of the players, Willie Mays, Hank Sauer, and others," he says. "But I did fairly well and made the team as the third-string catcher." His salary for the year was to be $5,600.

The Giants' primary catcher that year was another rookie, Bob Schmidt. Schmidt was backed up by Valme Thomas who, in the previous year, when he was a rookie himself, had shared the position with Ray Katt. (Katt had since been traded.) In fact, the Giants had a number of topflight rookies on the team that year. In addition to Schmidt, there were first baseman Orlando Cepeda, who would become the league's rookie of the year; third baseman Jim Davenport; and outfielders Leon Wagner, Willie Kirkland, and Felipe Alou.

"We played that first year in Seals Stadium [built in 1931]," Testa says. "The team was doing well, and the fans were packing the place. It only held about 22,000, but they filled it all the time."

Major-league baseball's arrival on the West Coast that year swelled attendance. The Giants played before a home crowd that topped the one-million mark that season.

"Cepeda was doing well and even overshadowed Mays," Testa says. "The fans there loved him." Mays, for one, had difficulty understanding that. That year Willie batted .347, second highest in the league, below only Richie Ashburn (and they both had three hits on the final day of the season). Cepeda hit .312. While Mays and Cepeda both had 96 runs batted in, Mays hit 29 homers to Cepeda's 25. And while Cepeda led the league in doubles that year, Mays led it in runs scored and in stolen bases. Mays also had more than 200 hits that year. "While Cepeda was phenomenal as a rookie and a favorite of the fans," Testa says, "Mays could beat you every day in every way. He really came to play."

The team, under manager Bill Rigney, started strong and were in first place at the end of July before slumping and finishing third, 12 games behind the Milwaukee Braves (spearheaded that year by Hank Aaron, Eddie Mathews, Warren Spahn, and Lew Burdette), and four games behind the Pittsburgh Pirates, who were led by Frank Thomas, Roberto Clemente, Bob Skinner, and Bob Friend.

On the Giants, Testa became closest to teammates Rueben Gomez and Don Taussig, with whom he had roomed in the minors. "Johnny Antonelli [who led the Giants' pitching staff that year] also sort of took me under his wing," Testa recalls, "a fellow *paisano*."

Testa was not just a catcher who warmed up pitchers, however. He did many other things to make himself useful to the club. He particularly remembers throwing "a lot of extra batting practice to Sauer. He used to take a lot of batting practice," Testa says, "and I was his favorite pitcher."

Early in the year, on April 23, 1958, the St. Louis Cardinals played the Giants in Seals Stadium and jumped out to a 5–0 lead in their very first time up, knocking Gomez out before he could retire more than two batters. The Giants, over the course of the next seven innings, managed to scratch out a couple of runs. In the fourth inning, when they scored their first run, Whitey Lockman batted for Thomas, the starting catcher, who was then replaced by Schmidt. But the Giants still trailed 6–2 going into the bottom of the eighth.

In that inning, however, San Francisco rallied for two more runs, and in the course of the uprising, Ray Jablonski pinch hit for Schmidt and singled. Rigney, who would use twenty-four players in the game, brought Testa in to run for Jablonski. Testa doesn't remember that today, but according to the box score, he remained on first as the Giants were finally retired.

What Testa remembers is going in to catch the top of the ninth.

"I was ready. Oh, I was ready to go," Testa says. "I ran down the right field line from the bullpen, got my stuff on, and was all ready. Nobody said anything. It was 'just do it.'"

Marv Grissom was the Giants pitcher when Testa went in. "He kept shaking me off a lot and moving me around from one side of the plate to the other. I just kept putting down fingers 'til he got what he wanted."

In his first outing in the major leagues, Testa made an error on a windblown pop foul that looked as if it would land in the grandstand between home and first base. He followed it over to the stands and then the infamous freezing, swirling San Francisco winds blew it back and it landed near the first base coaching box. "It just sort of drifted. Neither I nor Cepeda touched it, but I was the nearest to it, so I got the error," he says. "I looked at him and he looked at me and I just put on my mask and sort of hid behind home plate."

In that top of the ninth, the Cardinals scored again. "On that occasion, Grissom threw his sinker—he referred to it as a screwball—to Stan Musial," Testa says. "It was just where he wanted it—low and outside. I thought it was a perfect pitch, and 'The Man' obliged by hitting a line-drive double down the left field line. It knocked in a run and put them ahead by 7–4."

In the bottom of the ninth, however, the Giants came back to load the bases. "There was either one out or no outs [there were two outs]," Testa says, "and I was on deck. [Giants shortstop] Daryl Spencer was up. I was sure I was going to get an at-bat, and I was ready to swing at anything because I knew I would not get many chances to hit after that. I'm thinking, 'First thing that's over.' I was ready to take my hack. I figured I'd try to go up the middle with it, not pull it. That's the way I hit mostly. So I had a sort of game plan about how I'd hit.

"So what does Spencer do but hit a grand slam in that wind and the game was over. He hit a shot. Into the wind and over the left field fence. Boy, he had a lot of power. I think he led the Japanese league in home runs a few years later. Anyway, I'm on deck and I'm hoping it *wouldn't* go out. As I shook his hand when he crossed home plate, I didn't exactly compliment him. I cussed him out. I said, 'You son of a so-and-so.' Later, in the clubhouse, I congratulated him, but I still let him have it for not giving me a chance to hit."

About his own play that day, Testa says, "Afterward, I was relieved that I got into a game, but it was bittersweet. I was happy I had it under my belt, but I had mixed emotions about my performance, the error, and not getting to hit."

A few days after Testa's one-time appearance against the Cardinals, manager Bill Rigney called him into his office. "He told me that with the team doing well, he only needed to carry two catchers and would be sending me out. But he said, 'I'd really like to keep you, though. You're well-liked and you do so much to help. Would you be interested in staying as a coach?' I told him I'd fight [Rocky] Graziano if he wanted, if it meant I could stay with the team. So they made me a coach, and I stayed with the team for the whole year."

The Giants that year had a surplus of talented hitters. In addition to Davenport, Mays, Cepeda, Lockman, Jablonski, Spencer, Sauer, Wagner, and Kirkland, they also had Bill White and Jackie Brandt on their roster. Lockman, Jablonski, and White were traded away after the season, but another slugger was added—Testa's old teammate at Dallas, Willie McCovey.

Testa does not recall whom the Giants brought up to take his spot on the roster, but thinks it was a pitcher named Dom Zanni. This right-hander, who was born in the same part of New York City as Testa, picked up a win in relief for the Giants in the only game in which he appeared that year. Zanni then went on to play a total of seven years in the majors.

Another New York City–born pitcher, John Fitzgerald, started a game for the Giants that year but was not involved in the decision. Testa remembers Fitzgerald as being "a happy-go-lucky left-hander with a great arm." Fitzgerald struck out three men in the three innings he pitched, but the appearance was the only one he ever made in the major leagues. This made Testa and Fitzgerald one-timer teammates. (Fitzgerald could not be reached for this book.)

Following the 1958 season, Testa began taking graduate courses at New York University, which would lead to his master's degree in administration and physical education. At the same time, he says, "I just kept on playing ball."

In 1959, he was a player-coach for Omaha, Nebraska, in the Triple-A American Association. "I caught Bob Gibson there," Testa says, "and he was terrific. He was great. You could tell he was gonna be big. He had great stuff, was always around the plate, a great competitor, everything you've ever heard about him—and more."

In 1960, Testa played in Little Rock, Arkansas, and then, in the next year, in Macon, Georgia. In 1962, he went to Japan to play and coach with the Tokyo Orions in Japan's Pacific League. "I liked the country," he says, "but not the baseball. I saw little action. [Larry] Doby and [Don] Newcombe were there that year."

Back in the United States in 1963, Testa was a player-coach for Pittsburgh's Reno, Nevada, affiliate, and then, in 1964, he played at Yakima, Washington, in the Atlanta Braves' system. While in the Braves' spring training camp in 1965, Testa hurt his knee badly and had to take most of that year off. He applied for a teaching position at Lehman College in New York City, part of the City University of New York system, and began teaching physical education and health courses there in 1966.

But Testa's baseball career was far from over. "As a college instructor, coach, and professor, I had long summer vacations," he points out, "so I was able to keep playing professional ball." He played five more years in Canada's Provincial League, with teams in Granby, Sherbrooke, and Trois Rivers, and then played periodically for many more years. "I played actively till I was sixty years old," he says, "which was something I always wanted to do."

Testa retired from teaching, and finally from playing baseball, in 1987. But he still throws batting practice for the Yankees in the Bronx, near where he lives, and when the Yankees are out of town, he travels to Shea Stadium in Queens to do the same thing for the Mets. "I still enjoy it," Testa says. "For a 7:30 game, I'm dressed by 3:30 in the afternoon, pitch batting practice, then spend some time in the gym and go home. All in all, I'm still in uniform about four hours a day.

"The teams both call me a traitor," he says, "and once in a while, not often, they're both home on the same day. That's when I'm really in trouble. That's what I call 'the moment of truth.'"

And how did being a one-time major leaguer affect him? "It was a big thing for me personally," Testa says. "Just being on the Giants as a player, and later during the season as a coach, was a lifetime ambition. People still seem to respect me for it, and even though I never did much then, I *am* a little proud of it all."

Charles William "Chuck" Lindstrom

CHICAGO WHITE SOX, 1958

A couple of things make Chuck Lindstrom and his one-game major-league career different from most others. To begin with, he is the son of a baseball Hall of Famer, the former New York Giants third baseman, Freddie Lindstrom. Then, in the one game he played, he was the battery-mate of the son of another well-known major leaguer, probably the first time in major-league history that ever happened. And finally, like Curly Onis (see Chapter 4), he is among the handful of players with a major-league "career" batting average of 1.000.

Lindstrom, the third of three boys in his family, was born in 1936, the last year of his father's 13-year major-league career. "Being the youngest helped me," he says. "My oldest brother, Fred Jr., was six-foot-three, and in the early 1940s, he was the best athlete in Chicago. But he was always being compared with Dad. He was always known as the son of Freddie Lindstrom, and that made it very difficult for him. It wasn't that easy for my other brother, Andrew, either, although he wasn't the athlete that John was. But by the time I started playing, I was never really burdened with comparisons to Dad."

The youngest Lindstrom attended New Trier High School in Winnetka, Illinois, a suburb north of Chicago. In addition to baseball, he played some basketball and a little football. "In my sophomore year, I compressed three vertebrae, and that ended my football career," he says. He describes his ability as a starting guard on the basketball team as "decent," but reports his team lost the game that would have gotten it into the "Sweet 16" of the state tournament.

In baseball, however, Lindstrom excelled as a high school catcher and was named first-string All-State at that position in his senior year. "I became a catcher because, at the time, it was the position that seemed to offer the most potential," he says. "I had talks with my dad along those lines, and there seemed to be a need for catchers. There were not a lot of people then who wanted to catch."

While in high school, Lindstrom also played American Legion ball in Chicago. In 1953, he was on the team that finished second in the Legion's national tournament, held that year in Miami. "We only lost to one team that year," Lindstrom says "and we lost to them twice. We went 30 and 2 that year. Early in the tournament, Yakima, Washington, beat us. We ended up playing them in the final, and they beat us again.

"That was a unique team," he recalls. "We only had eleven guys and three of us used to rotate. One day Mike Layden would pitch and Tom Lorch would play third while I caught. Then, I would pitch, Tom would catch, and Mike would play third. In those days, there was no limit on how many innings a week you could pitch, and I remember one time that year I pitched seven complete games in sixteen days." For his pitching, catching, and hitting abilities, Lindstrom was named the 1953 American Legion Player of the Year.

After he graduated from high school in 1954, Lindstrom looked forward to following his dad's footsteps into professional baseball. Instead, he followed him to Northwestern University.

"When I played ball, my father never stuck his nose in. He never told a coach he was wrong, was never in conflict with anyone about my playing. But my father, who was coaching baseball at Northwestern then, insisted I go to college, although I was not overly thrilled about it," Lindstrom says.

"Dad was an associate professor at Northwestern, but it was honorary. He didn't have a degree, or at least I never saw a diploma. But he felt he could have been the athletic director at Northwestern if only he had a degree, and so he wanted me to go to college."

Lindstrom didn't get his degree from Northwestern until six years later, however, because he took time away from his studies to embark on his four-year professional baseball career.

"At Northwestern, I started in the School of Radio and TV," Lindstrom says, "and then the School of Speech, to become an announcer, because I figured I could do sports announcing. Later I transferred to the School of Business." He also played on the freshman baseball team.

"In those days, we used to have summer baseball leagues for college players, and in 1955 and '56, I played for Watertown, South Dakota, in what was called the Basin League. It was mostly good college players, and some of the guys that played there included Dick Howser, Norm Stewart, Ron Perranoski, Howie Bedell, Bill Horning, and many others."

During his high school and college days, Lindstrom also got the chance to work out often with both Chicago teams, but especially with the Cubs at Wrigley Field. "I was around big leaguers as a kid, so they didn't mean anything special to me. I was never in awe of them," he says.

In the early summer of 1957, his junior year at Northwestern, he was working out with the White Sox and was offered the chance to go on a road trip with the team. "But I was not overly thrilled with the American League," he reports. When they then offered him a contract and a signing bonus, he still hesitated.

"This was probably the most interesting part of my whole career," Lindstrom says. "About two or three days later, my dad got a call from the New York Yankees. They said, 'We hear your son worked out for the White Sox and they want to offer him a contract. Whatever offer you get, please do not sign until we talk to you.' Now this was on a Tuesday or a Wednesday. The Yanks were scheduled to come into Comiskey Park to play the White Sox that weekend, and I was supposed to go over there to work out for them on Saturday or Sunday.

"This was the time when catcher's masks were changing from wire masks to those magnesium, single-bar masks. Well, it just so happened that [Yogi] Berra had just had a foul tip break his nose and was out of the lineup for a couple of weeks. At that time, there was a 25–man roster limit. There was also the $4,000 bonus rule, which said that anyone getting a bonus of that amount had to be kept on the major-league roster.

"Well, I went over to work out for the Yankees, and there was a lot of hoopla and excitement, and the media was there to watch. [Yankee manager Casey] Stengel sat in the dugout with my dad for about a half an hour. They were old friends. And Stengel said, 'Freddie, we would really like to sign your son. But here's my situation. We're one and a half games in front. With Berra out two or three weeks, [Elston] Howard is my catcher and [John] Blanchard is my backup. If we sign your son, I got to drop Blanchard. If Howard goes out tonight and splits his finger in the first inning, who's my catcher? Your son. And I'm not comfortable with that yet. If you can hold off a while . . . that's the predicament.' And I accepted that."

The summer college-league season was starting. "In that summer of 1957, I was playing in a better college league, the Southern Minny [Minnesota] League, where they had some minor leaguers as well as college players. I played for Winona, but I only played there two or three weeks. My heart wasn't in it. In mid-July I called my dad and said, 'Let's do it, let's go ahead with the White Sox.'"

Today he ruminates, "It did not turn out that well, for whatever the reason, but that's the way it is."

Lindstrom signed a major-league contract with the White Sox on July 17, 1957, for the minimum salary of $6,500 a year and a $4,000 signing bonus. "That December, the bonus rule was changed," Lindstrom says, somewhat ruefully, "and they started giving out big money bonuses."

*Chuck Lindstrom thinks a spring training card game was a major factor in his
not getting another chance to play in the big leagues.*

Although on the White Sox 25–man roster, he was sent to play for Colorado Springs in the Class A Western League.

"When I went there, I found a bunch of old ballplayers, old minor leaguers or former major leaguers on the way down. None of them were prospects," Lindstrom says. "I was twenty years old and this was the first group of guys I was around and I found it difficult to acclimate. Fortunately, they had a lousy catcher, and I was able to step right in and play."

He describes his season at Colorado Springs, starting in late July, as "hot and cold." One day, against the league-leading Topeka team, he drove in nine runs, but against the last-place Sioux City club, he couldn't hit at all. "I did learn in a hurry, though," he says. "In the third game of the series, after I knocked in those nine runs against Topeka, I had a fastball thrown at me. I put up my arm to protect myself, and it broke my arm and then bounced off and broke my nose.

"I didn't play for ten days. Then the manager asked me if I could play and I said, 'I can't hit, but I can catch.' So he put me in the starting lineup. In those days, if you were starting, you took infield practice and then went back to the dugout to put on your shin guards and chest protector and then went out carrying your mask. Meanwhile, the second-string catcher warms up the pitcher in the bullpen. This day," he continues, "we had a knuckleball pitcher, and I went out to take his warm-ups from the mound, not having seen what he had in the bullpen. The second pitch he threw jumped, and because I had broken my left arm, I couldn't get it up fast enough and the ball hit me in the left eye and sent me to the hospital. That was just about the end of my season."

In 1958, he went to spring training with the White Sox in Tampa. "At that time, I think the Sox shared the training facilities with another team, and there was not a lot of time to do much," Lindstrom says. "I was introduced to a term then that I had never heard before. Walt Dropo, our first baseman, told me that I was hitting 'frozen ropes' all spring, which meant line drives. That was the kind of hitter I was. Mainly I hit up the middle and to right center. I didn't pull the ball."

One time that spring, Lindstrom hit a "frozen rope" back through the box into center field against teammate Early Wynn. "The players started laughing a bit, and I didn't know why. I learned later that Wynn didn't like it for you to hit the ball back at him. The other players knew what was coming. He didn't knock me down, but he did brush me back enough to teach me a lesson.

"I warmed up pitchers 90 percent of the time, then took my eight or ten swings and that was it. Then they'd have exhibition games, with split squads. I found it disillusioning. I didn't learn anything," Lindstrom says. "I remember one spring training exhibition against the Yankees on a rainy, overcast day, being on deck to face Ryne Duren. On that occasion, fortunately, I didn't get to bat."

Lindstrom was assigned to play in 1958 at Davenport Iowa, in the

Three-I League. "That was okay," he says. "The White Sox had a lot of catchers. Sherman Lollar [who led the team in RBIs that year] was first-string, and Earl Battey, a good catcher with a good arm, was behind him. John Romano had been a first-string Double-A catcher for them, and then there was Les Moss and me."

At Davenport, Lindstrom was with a good team in a good league, with some "real good ballplayers," he says. His teammates included Joe Hoerner, Gary Peters, and Don Mincher. Other standouts in the league that year were Dean Chance, Boog Powell, and Frank Howard.

But Lindstrom was an All-Star, too. "I caught every game that year but two," Lindstrom says, "and played second base in the other two. It was a big ballpark, and I hit 17 [14] home runs. I hit well over .300 most of the year, but I got so tired at year end, I had to go to the doctor to get [vitamin] shots, and my batting average dropped to about .290 [.276]."

"As a defensive catcher, there was nobody better," Lindstrom says. "I know a scout out here, Ellswsorth Brown, who signed Kirby Puckett, who told me that mine was the best arm he had ever seen. I enjoyed throwing, and in '58, I must have picked 15 people off third.

"There were two guys who were unanimous choices for the league's All-Star team that year and I was one of them," he says. "I think Dean Chance was the other one."

When the 1958 season ended at Davenport, Lindstrom was called up to the White Sox for the last month of their season. Chicago, managed by Al Lopez and led by a pitching staff featuring Dick Donovan, Billy Pierce, and Wynn, would finish second that year for the second straight time, ten games behind the Stengel-led Yankees. Only second baseman Nellie Fox would hit as high as .300. But with the pennant race still not mathematically over during the early part of September, there was not much opportunity for rookies to play.

On September 28, however, the very last day of the season, with the White Sox at home in Comiskey Park against the Kansas City Athletics, Lindstrom became a one-time major-league ballplayer. Only three weeks earlier he had celebrated his twenty-second birthday.

"It wasn't anything special," he says of his one-time experience. "I never got overly excited. I was told the day before that I would play," he says, although he can't remember who told him. "I thought I was supposed to start the game, but John Romano was given the assignment. I came in in the middle of the game."

In that last game of the 1958 season, the pennant was out of reach, so the White Sox started young Stover McIlwain, who had just turned nineteen a week earlier. It was the only game McIlwain would ever start in the majors, although he had relieved once the year before. These two games were his only two major-league appearances. (He died seven years later at the age of twenty-six.) On this day, however, he pitched four innings, giving up two earned runs on four hits while striking out four. "One of the reasons I thought I was going to start was because I had caught Stover that year in Davenport," Lindstrom says.

"Stover also almost beat my record in that game," he recalls. "In his one time at bat, he really hit a ball. It went up against the outfield wall, and the outfielder jumped up and robbed him of a home run. Otherwise, he would have had a homer in his only time at bat."

McIlwain was scheduled to bat again in the bottom of the fourth inning, but Earl Batty pinch hit for him. Batty hit a sacrifice fly to bring in one of the two runs the White Sox scored that inning. They went ahead 3–1.

In the top of the fifth inning, the White Sox came out with a new battery. Lindstrom replaced Romano behind the plate, and Hal Trosky Jr., on the eve of his twenty-second birthday, came in to pitch. "He threw a heavy ball, a sinker, and was tough to catch," Lindstrom says of Trosky, "and in that first inning, I had a passed ball."

In the bottom of the fifth, the White Sox scored three more runs to extend their lead to 6–1, but Trosky gave back all three in the top of the sixth, although one of them was unearned. In the bottom of that inning, when Chicago scored another run to go up 7–4, Trosky was removed for a pinch-hitter, "Jungle Jim" Rivera, who struck out.

Although he pitched only two innings and gave up three of the four runs the Athletics scored that day, Trosky, who led 3–1 when he entered the game, led 7–4 when he left and was credited with the win, his only major-league decision. In comparison, McIlwain, the starter, pitched four innings and gave up one run, and Bob Shaw, who finished, pitched three scoreless innings.

Lindstrom today does not recall whether it was Trosky or Shaw—or both—who gave him trouble behind the plate. About one of them, he says, "He was hard to catch. He threw sidearm and submarine, like Ewell Blackwell. He had a hard screwball and was all over the place."

Defensively, Lindstrom is credited with making two putouts in that game, which came on strikeouts by Shaw. He remembers being walked his first time at bat. "Coming to the plate was no big deal to me," he says. "I was not overly thrilled or anything. I knew I was having difficulty catching that day."

His second time at bat, however, is another story. "Frank House [who had been traded to Kansas City from Detroit the previous winter in a blockbuster trade involving a dozen players] was the catcher. It was a 3 and 1 count, and he sort of tipped me off. He said, 'If I were you, I'd be looking for a fastball.' House knew the circumstances," Lindstrom says. "He knew it was my first game, that it was the last day of the year, and that the game wasn't going to affect the standings, or anything. I said, 'Don't worry, I am.' It was 3 and 1, and I'd be looking for a fastball anyway.

"I hit it a foot from the fence in right center, and while I wasn't a fast runner, I ended up sliding into third with a triple. I remember saying to myself, 'That figures. Me hitting a triple. Why not?'"

With the triple, he batted in a run and then later scored himself, but he doesn't recall any specifics. Most likely, Lindstrom knocked in the White Sox outfielder, John "Bubba" Phillips, who batted ahead of Esposito. Phillips had two singles and a double that day and did score a run.

Scoring four more times in the seventh and eighth innings, the White Sox won the game, 11–4. The record book shows Lindstrom walked and tripled in his only two plate appearances in the major leagues, which has to be one of the most productive 1.000 batting averages ever. It doesn't say, however, that when the White Sox made their last out in the bottom of the eighth, the on-deck batter was Chuck Lindstrom. He never batted in the major leagues again.

"My mom was thrilled by the hit," he says. "She gave me a big hug after the game and was all excited. But I thought it was no big deal. It was all well and good, but it didn't knock me off my feet. I remember we went out to dinner after the game to George Diamond, a steakhouse in Chicago, Mom and Dad and myself, and I had absolutely no reservations or doubts that after the season I had, after a year and a half in the minor leagues, I really felt it was going to happen in the future," he says.

But something went wrong in spring training in 1959. Again, Lindstrom spent most of his time there warming up White Sox pitchers. "In the times I had an opportunity to play, I thought I did well," he says.

But a trip to St. Petersburg to play an exhibition game against the Cardinals, Lindstrom feels, could have started him down the road toward the end of his professional baseball career. "It was about a twenty-minute bus ride from our camp in Tampa to St. Petersburg," he says, "and I was sitting with Tito Francona [a former roommate of Gordie Sundin—see Chapter 24], whom I didn't know very well. Tito asked me if I wanted to play some cards while we rode over, Crazy Eights or Hearts or some game that only took two to play. So I said okay, and we played a few hands before we reached the ballpark.

"Well, we got there and the ballgame started. In one inning, our leadoff batter doubled. I was up next and got the sign to bunt him over to third. I bunted the ball down the third base line, and it was a pretty good bunt, but I got under it just a little and it stayed up in the air. The Cardinals' pitcher ran over, dived for it, and snared it backhanded for the out. The runner couldn't advance. The next batter, [Earl] Torgeson, flied out. It was deep enough so the runner could have scored if he had been at third. The next guy went out, and we didn't score that inning. The game ended later, and the Cardinals won by one run, 5–4.

"We got back on the bus to go back to Tampa, and Tito Francona asked me if I wanted to finish the card game we had started on the way over. I didn't know what to say or anything, so I said, 'Sure.' Well, when we got back to Tampa and got off the bus, [coach Tony] Cuccinello and [coach] Don Gutteridge started tearing into me, saying I cost them the game, that I didn't care enough about it 'cause I was playing cards on the way back, and stuff like that. They were real hard-nosed about it. That was the way things were. I was kind of shocked," Lindstrom says.

"I remember my dad telling me that if you were going to succeed in sports, you had to have skin like an alligator, you had to overcome things, which he did all his life, but I guess I didn't have that mental toughness."

Lindstrom was soon assigned to Chicago's Triple-A Indianapolis affiliate and completed spring training with that club in Hollywood, Florida. "Spring training ended, and we were supposed to go back to Indianapolis to start the season, but we had a side trip for a last exhibition game in Havana, Cuba," he recalls. "They were still playing ball down there at that time. Well, in the typical way the White Sox did things, they hung a roster on the door for the team going to Havana, and I saw my name had been crossed off in pencil and the name [Camilo] 'Carreon' written in. I was really taken aback. I knew Carreon couldn't throw. I heard he could swing the bat pretty well, but he was not very smart and not as good a catcher as me.

"I went back to the motel where we were staying and over to the office of player personnel, a guy named Miller. We used to call him Elmer Fudd because he was five-foot-two and looked like Elmer Fudd. I said, 'Would it be possible to get an explanation for sending me back to [Class] A ball and keeping Carreon? I had a great year last year. I was All-League. I had a great spring. There's no explanation.' He said, 'We don't think you hustle enough. You *jog* out to catch. Carreon *runs*.' 'Listen,' I said, 'this spring I caught every session I was supposed to catch and half of his. I always hustle. I know how to catch, to call pitches, and play the game of baseball better than him.' He says, 'Well, we don't seem to think so.'

"So I said, 'Well, I think we got a problem here. I'm not going to go back to Class A ball. The heck with it.' So I got in my car and drove from Florida back to Chicago. When I got back, my dad asked, 'Do you know what you're doing?' I said I hated the life. I never did anything wrong, but I wasn't going to live my life that way.

"I stayed home a couple of weeks," Lindstrom says. "They kept calling my dad, and he asked me, 'Are you sure? Do you want to give it another shot?' So I went back."

Lindstrom reported to Charleston, South Carolina, in the South Atlantic (Sally) League for his third year of professional baseball. "It was a pitcher's league," Lindstrom says. "There was one player, a forty-five-year-old black catcher named 'Senator' Sam Hairston, who hit .300 or .305, and I think there was only one other player in the league who hit over .270. I ended up hitting about .225 [.219]. I caught most of the time, but I also played every other position on the team except shortstop. I even pitched."

In the winter following that season, Lindstrom, who had become fairly disenchanted with professional baseball by then, interviewed to become the baseball coach and a teacher at Lincoln College, a small, private junior college with about 500 students, near Chicago.

Also around that time, the White Sox, having used up their third and final option on him, sold Lindstrom's contract to San Diego of the Pacific Coast League. "Ralph Kiner was the general manager there, and he sent me a contract for 1960, offering me $700 a month, or about $4,200 or $4,500 for the season," Lindstrom says. "I had been making $5,800 the year before. I sent it back. He returned it and said this was all he was going to give me. I sent it back again with a letter that said something like 'Dear Mr. Kiner: I know you have some concern about my hitting, but I want more money, and if I don't make it back to Triple-A by the end of the season, then we can split the difference,' or something. I don't recall exactly what I said.

"I don't know what the postage was in those days, maybe about seven cents, but he sent the contract back to me unchanged with a letter that said, 'This is the last stamp I'm wasting on you. Either sign it or forget it.'

"So I signed it. I went out to Palm Desert and pitched wildly. I said to myself, 'I don't want to do this.' When they sent me for reassignment—they wanted me to go to Hawaii—I went home again. That was the second time. I called the White Sox and asked them if they needed a catcher anywhere. They said, 'As a matter of fact, we do.' They sent me to Lincoln, Nebraska, in the Three-I League," Lindstrom says.

"Just about then, I heard from Lincoln College that I had gotten the job and was supposed to start on August 18. I notified the White Sox and the Lincoln, Nebraska, team that I would have to leave on August 17, about ten days before the season ended. When I finally did leave, George Noga, the manager of the team, told me, 'I really appreciate the fact that you gave me 100 percent while you were here,' and that made me feel good." It was a pleasant ending to what was, generally, an unhappy period in Lindstrom's life.

Looking back, Lindstrom recalls talking often with his father about the game. "My father had some very definite opinions on fundamentals. He was not just a great player; he was very intelligent. He analyzed. A lot of times I'd disagree with him when we discussed fundamentals, but I told him why I thought as I did, and he told me why he thought as he did. We would talk about such things as the difference between technique and natural instinct. We'd have discussions about such things as how you should go after a fly ball. It was like listening to Ted Williams talking about hitting. To him, it's a science. To somebody else, like a Pete Ward, you go up, see the ball, and just hit it hard. I know when I was playing, I worked very hard at being a good catcher."

Lindstrom's father certainly hasn't been forgotten. In 1988, as the baseball trading-card business began to flourish, a 1932 card picturing his father was valued at $1 million by a seller claiming it was the only known copy in existence.

The younger Lindstrom has some strong opinions about players today, especially catchers. "There have been changes in baseball," he points out. "The philosophy has changed. There used to be a saying that a ball club had to be strong defensively up the middle, meaning the catcher, short-stop, second baseman, and center fielder were supposed to be good defensively, while your hitting came from the sides—first, third, left field, and right. That changed with people like [Johnny] Bench. Today, they concede defense.

"Most catchers today don't know how to catch or throw" he says. "It's a different world. We used to throw out about 70 percent of the base stealers. Now they feel good if they can get 30 percent." Lindstrom does not believe this trend has anything to do with expansion, speedier runners, or the ability of pitchers to hold runners on. "There isn't one catcher today who knows about sliding his foot outside to catch a breaking ball," he says. "They reach over across their bodies. Their footwork and mechanics are bad. When I talk to people about 'patterning' the ball, they don't know what I'm talking about.

"One of the best defensive catchers I ever saw," Lindstrom says, "was the old Cubs catcher, Clyde McCulloch, who used to catch [knuckleballer] Dutch Leonard with his small stiff mitt, not one of those big pillows. McCulloch had a small pocket in that mitt—it was actually a hole in the middle—and he used to catch the ball with the mitt before it ever got into the pocket, and he'd have it out of the mitt in a flash. That was the secret—getting the ball out of the mitt fast and being ready to throw. That changed when catchers started putting their hands behind their backs—I think it was Randy Hundley who started that—and when they turned the catcher's mitt more into a first baseman's glove. They can't get the ball out of there fast enough."

In 1960, Lindstrom began a 23-year college coaching and teaching career at Lincoln College. "The first year, we didn't have enough kids to field a team, and we won only the last game of the year for a 1 and 16 record. The second year, we were 18 and 6." The third year, after he had been named the school's athletic director, he scrounged up enough money to buy his players new double-knit uniforms. "I remember the manufacturer telling me it was like putting a $150 saddle on a $50 horse," he laughs. Lindstrom helped form a Central Collegiate League and, during the summer, attracted a number of excellent college players, including Art Howe and Del Unser.

While at Lincoln College, Lindstrom also commuted to the University of Illinois, where he took courses leading to the master's degree in education that he received in 1967.

As a baseball teacher and coach, Lindstrom was familiar with various items and products used in sports facilities, and these eventually turned his life in a new direction. In 1976, he came across a product used to dry wet playing fields and began marketing it the next year while he was still teaching and coaching. At Lincoln, he illuminated his own field and thus became introduced to the sports lighting business. "One thing led to another," Lindstrom says, "and I went to work for a lighting company for a year or two, but then they changed their direction, and I started my own business."

He now has owned and operated his sports lighting business, Universal Sports Lighting Company, for about ten years. The company designs, engineers, and produces lighting systems for a variety of high school, college, and professional sports facilities, including those now used at Chicago's Wrigley Field and Comiskey Park, Baltimore's Camden Yards, the Kentucky Little League State Tournament site, and the new Sam Houston Racetrack in Houston, Texas.

Lindstrom was married in 1958 and divorced in 1972. He and his current wife, Elaine, whom he met while at Lincoln College, have five children, four from his first marriage, and five grandchildren.

Lindstrom sums up his career this way: "As time went on it became clear my baseball was not going to develop into much," he says, "so the uniqueness of a 1.000 batting average became something of a conversation piece, but baseball people know 1 for 1 means nothing except luck. Nice, but no big deal. I just didn't have the mental toughness for pro ball."

Harold Rudolph "Rudy" Stowe

NEW YORK YANKEES, 1960

In 1954, the year after Chuck Lindstrom was named the American Legion's Player of the Year (see Chapter 27), seventeen-year-old "Rudy" Stowe was named its outstanding pitcher.

Not only did Stowe pitch in the American Legion's championship game that year, but in 1958 and 1959, he also pitched in two consecutive college World Series for Clemson College.

And, as a major leaguer in 1960, he pitched in a game for the New York Yankees, the American League's championship team that featured Mickey Mantle, Roger Maris, Yogi Berra, and Whitey Ford. And he almost won that game.

"But when it comes to making it in the major leagues," Stowe says, "I believe 90 percent of it comes down to 'somebody likes you.' The talent is so equal when you reach that level, and everybody is pretty much the same. I think most of the people who only played one game [in the majors] didn't get a chance simply because somebody didn't like them."

In his case, he knows who it was.

Stowe was born in Gastonia, North Carolina, on August 29, 1937, the second of two boys, the first of whom is now a physician. "Actually, we lived on a farm between Gastonia and Belmont," Stowe says, "a few miles closer to Belmont. But I call Gastonia my home and list my mailing address there 'cause that's where I made my name playing American Legion baseball."

At Belmont High School, Stowe played basketball ("I was average, and we never won anything") as well as baseball. "I was good," he recalls. "I was the only pitcher and I did good, but we never won a championship or anything," he says in a deep, slow North Carolina drawl.

Though his high school team didn't do well, the left-handed Stowe also pitched for Gastonia's American Legion Post 23 team. He led it into the 1953 state finals, which they lost. The next year, however, Stowe pitched his Legion team all the way to the national finals held in Yakima, Washington, where the team finished second. "San Diego beat us, 3–2, in 11 innings," he says, adding that he pitched the complete game. "I was about 14 or 15 and 3 that year and was named the outstanding American Legion pitcher for 1954."

After graduating from high school in 1955, Stowe enrolled at Clemson College where he later earned a bachelor's degree in education.

"At that time, they had a rule that freshman could not play, and in my sophomore year, we had a mediocre team," he says. "In my junior year, we got a new coach, Bill Whilhelm, who was an outstanding coach and who turned out to be one of the best college coaches over the years. He really brought us around," Stowe reports. "I think I was 14 and 4 the first year and 10 and 2 the last year." In both 1958 and 1959, Stowe pitched in the College World Series held in Omaha, Nebraska. "Both years we won one and lost two," he says.

In December 1956, while a sophomore at Clemson, Stowe married his high school sweetheart, Betty Taylor. "She had gone away to college, and I heard she was going out on me, so I went and got her, straightened her out, and brought her back to marry me," he laughs. Their first child, Laura, was born in May 1958.

"Right after the College World Series in 1959, right in Omaha, the Yankees signed me," Stowe says. "I was signed by a famous Yankees scout, Tom Greenwade [who had signed Mickey Mantle], and he was helped by a fellow named Bill Skiff [who worked for the Yankees in various capacities after a brief tenure in the majors in the 1920s]." Stowe received a bonus of $30,000, to be paid in three equal annual installments, and a big-league contract. "I guess I was what you'd call one of those bonus babies," he says.

The Yankees immediately assigned Stowe to Greensboro in the Carolina League where Vern Hoscheit was the manager. "We used to call him 'Horseshit,'" Stowe says. "I don't know if I should say this, but Vern didn't like college graduates. He thought they were hot dogs. I'm not sure, but I think I pitched four or five times at Greensboro and then got sent to Fargo, North Dakota, where [Damon] Dee Phillips was the manager."

Completing the 1959 season at Fargo, Stowe pitched well. "I did real well there," he says, "although we had a mediocre team. I got there in July and pitched regular." Although he won only five and lost four, the tall, slim (six feet, 170 pounds) Stowe struck out 90 men in 95 innings, while walking only 33, and compiled a 2.75 earned run average. He describes himself as a "finesse-and-control" pitcher.

Although Hal Stowe was almost the winning pitcher in his one game in the majors, he evidently didn't throw hard enough to please a new manager.

That winter, Stowe played with the Yankees' Instructional League team at St. Petersburg, Florida, under the tutelage of manager Johnny Neun and pitching coach Cloyd Boyer. When spring training began in 1960, Stowe was part of the major-league Yankee team.

"That first spring, it was unreal how well I was accepted and treated by big-league ballplayers," he remembers. "I remember Roger Maris, whom I respected a lot, came over and introduced himself to me. He knew I had played in Fargo, and that's where he was from, and he asked how everything was there.

"Casey [Stengel, the Yankee manager] and Mr. [Roy] Hamey [the general manager] ran a fine Yankee organization. And they did not have an abundance of players in that camp. A lot of teams bring a lot of players to spring training, but the Yankees didn't. They were all very close. Everybody stayed together. We played at Miller Huggins Field, and I even pitched some that spring."

Evidently, Stowe pitched well enough to be brought north with the team when it moved up to New York to begin the season. "I'll never forget the feeling I had the first time I was in Yankee Stadium," he says. "I remember walking through the tunnel and coming out to the ball field. The first thing I did, I walked to the monuments in center field. I wanted to see the monuments. In those days, if you remember, they had them in front of the fence. Everybody laughed at my doing that. Bobby Richardson, who sort of took me under his arm that whole spring, said, 'Don't feel bad. Everybody goes to the monuments.' I was just dumbfounded. The country boy going to the big time.

"I think I stayed with them about three weeks," Stowe recalls. "I pitched batting practice, I sat on the bench, and I threw in the bullpen." And, he reports, "Stengel liked me."

But with Whitey Ford and Bobby Shantz as established left-handed starters, and with Luis Arroyo as their left-handed reliever, the Yankees assigned the twenty-two-year-old Stowe to Amarillo in the Texas League, where he could pitch regularly.

"They were in last place," Stowe says. "It was a lousy damn team, and they had a lousy damn bus to ride on. It was a terrible year." However, he got a chance to throw regularly there, pitching more than 200 innings, and ended with a 12–12 record.

The Yankees recalled him at the end of Amarillo's season in late August. On the night of September 30, 1960, Rudy Stowe pitched in his only major-league game. It was against the Boston Red Sox at Yankee Stadium.

At that point, the Yankees had a 12-game winning streak and had already clinched the American League pennant—the first of five in a row they would win. They were an emerging dynasty.

That night, Stengel used the game mainly to tune up some of the pitchers he would be using in the World Series against Pittsburgh. The game against the Red Sox that night was not going particularly well, even though Ted Williams was not in the Boston lineup.

Boston led 4–2 at the end of seven innings. Shortstop Tony Kubek and pinch hitter Jesse Gonder, both hitting solo home runs off Boston's ace pitcher, Bill Monbouquette, accounted for the Yankees' score. The homers were the team's 191st and 192nd of the year, establishing a new American League season record.

Art Ditmar had started for the Yanks and was followed by Bobby Shantz and Ryne Duren. When Gonder homered, batting for Duren in the bottom of the seventh, Stowe, warming up in the bullpen, first realized he would be going in to pitch in a major-league game.

"I was scared," Stowe admits, "very nervous, like a cat on a hot tin roof." The first batter he faced was the number-three hitter in the Red Sox lineup, veteran first baseman Vic Wertz, who had more than 100 runs batted in that year.

Wertz walked.

"I had a couple close ones," Stowe says of his pitches to the left-handed batter, "but I couldn't get the calls." With Wertz on first and nobody out, catcher Russ Nixon came to the plate. "On the first pitch, I picked Wertz off at first base," Stowe says. But first base umpire Frank Umont disagreed. He called a balk on Stowe and sent Wertz to second base. "It was not a balk. The ump missed it," Stowe insists.

"Dale Long was playing first then, I think, and he said it wasn't a balk. Casey came out and calmed me down. He said I picked the umpire off, too. He asked me if I was nervous. I told him, 'Yes.' He said, 'Well, just throw the goddamn ball over and the other people will make the outs.' I don't use words like that, but it sure helped me then."

Nixon, also a left-handed hitter, sacrificed Wertz to third with a bunt down the third baseline, and Frank Malzone, the Red Sox third baseman, came to the plate. He was the first right-handed batter Stowe faced. "I think it was [John] Blanchard who was catching then," Stowe says, "and he came out and told me to keep the ball away from him, not to pitch him in tight." Despite Stowe's efforts, though, Malzone hit a sacrifice fly to Hector Lopez in left field, allowing Wertz to score after the catch and increasing the Boston lead to 5–2.

Stowe retired the final batter of the inning, rookie second baseman Marlan Coughtry, on a pop-up to Kubek at shortstop and returned to the dugout to watch the rest of the game from the bench.

"I thought I had done a pretty good job," he remembers. "Several players told me I did well. [Pitching coach] Eddie Lopat told me I threw the ball good."

In the bottom of the eighth, the Yankees scored once more on back-to-back doubles by Maris and pinch-hitter Bob Cerv to make the score 5–3. In the top of the ninth, the new Yankee pitcher, Duke Maas, allowed the first two men he faced to reach base, but then retired the next three without a run scoring. If Stowe, and not Maas, had pitched that ninth inning, Stowe would have been the winning pitcher, for the Yanks erupted for three runs in the bottom of the ninth to win the game, their thirteenth victory in a row.

The game actually had a startling and somewhat funny conclusion. Down by two runs, Richardson led off the bottom of the ninth with a single, and manager Pinky Higgins brought in right-hander Tom Brewer to replace Monbouquette. Gil McDougald, hitting for Maas, also singled. After Kubek flied out, Lopez lined still another single into right field, which scored Richardson and sent McDougald to third with the potential tying run. With the Red Sox infield drawn in for a play at the plate, Maris singled through the middle to tie the game. On the play, Lopez hustled into third.

Higgins then brought in a rookie right-hander, Tracy Stallard, to face Cerv, who had stayed in the game after pinch hitting in the previous inning. Cerv hit what looked to be an inning-ending double-play grounder to the rookie Coughtry, who had replaced Pete Runnels (the league's leading hitter) at second base earlier in the game. But instead of starting the double play by throwing to shortstop Pumpsie Green, who was covering second, Coughtry held on to the ball so he could tag Maris on his way to second and then throw to first himself.

But Maris simply stopped running.

Lopez didn't. The Yankee left fielder streaked home with the winning run before Coughtry could run over to tag the retreating Maris. The first base umpire, Umont, waved that the game was over, leaving the red-faced Coughtry still holding the ball and the fans howling in glee.

"When the game was over, I thought I didn't hurt them too bad," Stowe chuckles. "I thought it was an honor just to be part of the Yankees. I thought there were gonna be more games I'd be in. It's just a shame I didn't get another chance."

For the year, Stowe received his $7,500 salary; a bonus of $8,000 (what was left of his signing bonus after taxes); and a $1,000 World Series cut. He is, perhaps, the only one-game major leaguer ever to receive a World Series check.

To prepare himself for another chance, Stowe again played winter ball with the Yankee rookie squad, this time managed by Steve Souchock, a former American Leaguer. In 1961, Stowe reported to the Yankees' spring training camp, this time at Fort Lauderdale, where he found that Ralph Houk had replaced Stengel as manager. "I have no doubt that if Casey would have managed in 1961, I would have made the team," Stowe says. "Casey really liked me. I was his type of pitcher. I threw strikes. But that's life. Houk wanted these dart throwers, guys who threw 100 miles an hour through a brick wall. I wasn't like that. I was a finesse pitcher. I threw strikes, and the other guys made the plays. Look at the kind of pitchers Casey had and the kind that Houk had and you'll see what I mean."

Stowe started the season with the Yanks, but didn't get to pitch. He was soon farmed out to Amarillo, where he had a spectacular year. He won 14 games and lost only 1 and was named the Texas League's pitcher of the year. But instead of recalling him to the major-league squad, the Yanks moved him up only as far as Richmond in the Triple-A International League to finish out the season. During that year, Stowe's son, Harold Jr., was born, and the new father chose to return to Clemson to complete his degree instead of playing winter ball that year.

But in 1962, Stowe again was on the Yanks' opening-day roster. "I thought for sure I was gonna be in the big leagues then," he says. "That spring I had pitched 17 innings and had given up only three runs. But no. I just sat on the damn bench in '61 and '62. I stayed 'til around the first of June, or whenever it was they had to cut down to 25 players, and all I did was sit on my ass. Houk was the one who gave me the axe. He said he thought what he had was better than me. I said I thought I already proved myself in the minors. But he didn't like me. Casey had gone to the Mets and Lopat also had gone, and Johnny Sain was the pitching coach, and he liked the kind of pitchers Houk liked. It was a crusher."

Stowe returned to Richmond, where manager Preston Gomez tried unsuccessfully to turn him into a relief pitcher. "It was a bad ball club," Stowe recalls. "It was in last place when I got there, and it was in last place at the end of the year." The only bright part of the year for Stowe came with the birth of his child, Jeffrey.

Stowe remained with Richmond in 1963 as a reliever, winning one and losing five but garnering a credible 3.23 earned run average, which was better than that of his teammate, Mel Stottlemyre. But the spark was gone. The Yankees released him after spring training in 1964. "I came home and got a call from Phil Howser, who is a really great guy and an outstanding baseball man," Stowe says, "and I signed on with his Charlotte Hornets [in the Southern League]. I went 10 and 4 that year."

For one of his wins, he never had to throw a pitch. In a game against Asheville, Stowe was called in to relieve with two out in the top of the ninth inning, the game tied 5–5, and an Asheville runner, Roberto Herrera, on first. Immediately after his warm-up tosses, Howe picked Herrera off base for the final out of the inning. In the bottom of the ninth, when Charlotte scored to win the game 6–5, Stowe was credited with the victory.

At the end of that 1964 season, however, the twenty-seven-year-old Stowe decided to retire from professional baseball. "I had been in discussions about a job earlier with Burlington Industries, and I decided to take it," he says. He became the personnel director of the company, which produces textiles, and remained with them for nine years.

In 1972 he bought out his father's restaurant, Stowe's Fish Camp. The father ran the place for forty years; the son still runs it today.

When he played with the Yankees, Stowe remembers being closest to

Bobby Richardson, Jim Coates, "Moose" Bill Skowron, and Ralph Terry. "I still see Bobby Richardson and just talked to him last week. He's doing religious work around Sumter now. He really took good care of me when I first came up, and he meant more to me, personally, than anyone.

"Moose was always good to me. In spring training, he'd go out of his way to help me. I roomed with Ralph Terry on the road. He was a super guy, and I lived with him at a Manhattan hotel when we were at home. I remember I played golf with him several times.

"I really admired Bobby Shantz. I just loved the way he pitched. Whitey Ford, though, was my idol. I think he was just the cleverest lefty of all time. Mantle certainly was one of the top five players of all time. If his health and his legs were better, maybe one of the top two. I told you about Maris. I really respected him, and he was nice to me. Berra was great to me. He would encourage me and teach me. Lopat was the same way. He loved to teach young players.

"I'd rather pitch to [Elston] Howard than anyone else. He could motivate people, and he encouraged me. Crow [coach Frank Crosetti] was unforgettable. He liked me."

Reflecting on his career in professional baseball, Stowe remarks, "As I said, when you get in a situation like that, either somebody likes you or they don't. People sometimes tell me that I didn't stand up for myself strong enough. I rolled with the punches. But I don't have any regrets. Baseball got me almost everything I have in life. I've been very successful financially. I've been lucky. My health is good. What more can you ask?"

Larry Lynn Foster

DETROIT TIGERS, 1963

There was never much doubt that Larry Foster was going to be a ballplayer. "The day I was born, my dad bought a baseball and bat," he says. "He had a dream for me. I was his only son."

During the 1920s and early 1930s, Foster's father, John, a manual laborer, had played ball for a number of small Pennsylvania towns that competed heatedly through their teams. Often state troopers would be called in to stop fistfights. "His second wife, my mother, met up with him in eastern Pennsylvania in a little Susquehanna River town named Liverpool," Foster says. By the time his son was born on Christmas Eve in 1937, John Foster had moved near Lansing, Michigan, where he worked on the assembly line at Fisher/Body.

"Dad, along with Mother and my two half-sisters from dad's first marriage, worked a small, two-cow farm, growing some grain and raising some hogs. He rose at 5 A.M. to milk the cows before driving to the factory in Lansing," Foster says. "Later my parents moved into the mom-and-pop grocery business. First they rented a small grocery, and then borrowed to build a new one."

Soon the family moved to Lansing where John Foster operated a Phillips 66 gas station. Larry recalls that his father's limited time at home in those days was often spent playing catch and swinging a bat.

The young Foster took part in pre–Little League ball games. "They were less formal and regimented then," he says. "Neighborhood kids also could walk to local parks and play 'scrub.' When I was about age ten, I tried to pitch, and I could throw the ball hard and fast. Batting left-handed

Larry Foster (center) says his biggest disappointment in baseball was not getting a chance to bat in the one game he pitched for the Detroit Tigers.

and throwing right seemed to be the best advantage," he says. "It just turned out that way."

As a youngster, Foster set out to strengthen his throwing arm. "I went to a local junkyard to find pieces of pipe, the diameter being the same as of a baseball," he says. "For two winters, I threw sawed-off pieces of pipe against a mattress in our old Michigan cellar. The pipe sections were heavier than a ball. My intention came from hearing my dad talk about the importance of being strong, giving that extra, staying in shape, and other bits of coaching wisdom."

At Lansing Sexton High School, Foster made the varsity ball team as a freshman. In 1955, his junior year, the team won the league championship as Foster recorded nine wins and no losses. "Scouts began to show up, and some introduced themselves," he remembers.

"That year, they were holding tournaments around the country for high school ballplayers," Foster says. "One of them was at Michigan State University [in Lansing], and I pitched one game and played outfield in another. The next weekend I was asked to pitch in Ann Arbor, but on the day of the game, it rained. We didn't know whether to drive over there or just assume it would be too wet to play. A friend of mine said, 'Those are just light showers.' So we went.

"I pitched on a muddy field after the clouds cleared, and won 1–0. A week later, a call came to our grocery store in Lansing, where my parents had started another mom-and-pop business. I was chosen, along with Tom Orton from Detroit, to represent Michigan in the National All-Stars baseball game at the Polo Grounds in New York. It was one of the few times I saw my father cry," he says.

The All-Star game was an opportunity for players to meet scouts, former major leaguers, and celebrities. "Sitting in the dugout," Foster recalls, "and walking around the on-deck circle, we shook hands with Whitey Ford, Rocky Marciano, Phil Silvers, Frank Sinatra, and others.

"The New York All-Stars were the home team," he continues. "Our team batted first and then began to fall behind as the game went further into the mid-innings. I came in to pitch two innings. I struck out one and retired the next five hitters. I also got the first hit for the National All-Stars. I heard later that I was on the way to winning a trophy as most valuable player. But following me in pitching was Mike McCormick, a left-hander from California. He struck out six in a row. He won the trophy, and we ended up losing that night. A number of players on both teams went on to careers in the major leagues."

As a result of Foster's performance, the scouts were keenly interested in signing him after graduation. "Almost every club made contact or had someone come to the house or the store," he says. "A Dodger bird dog who lived in Arizona, a millionaire, came to the store, and invited us to his home where grapefruit grew in his yard.

"Cleveland offered to fly me down for a tryout. I took them up on it just to see what would happen. See, I also had a college education in the back of my mind. I had heard about the importance of a college education from my father. He often talked about not getting beyond the sixth grade himself. So an education, as well as playing baseball, were held up as dreams and goals for his children," Foster says.

"While trying out at Cleveland," he recalls, "I was asked to warm up on the sidelines so the Indians coaches could observe me. Mel Harder stood next to me. Mel was the pitching coach behind the heydays of Bob Feller and Bob Lemon."

Harder's coaching proved momentous for the young Foster. "In three minutes, he showed me how to throw a curve that broke sharply. I never forgot the subtle adjustments he indicated which allowed a hard spin and a quick break in the ball. All the coaching up to this point emphasized aspects that Harder went beyond. Then he had me grip a fastball differently. The first toss hopped, and the catcher dropped it. The Indians were interested."

At this point, Tom Petroff, a friend and former pro ballplayer, advised Foster to go to school first. "This made sense at the time," Foster says. "The highest offer a club could make in those days was $4,000 without having to put a new player on the major-league roster. I took this advice and completed two years of college before signing."

Foster entered Michigan State University in 1956, intending to study electrical engineering. "I made varsity freshman year," he says. "In six outings as a sophomore, I was 3 and 3, beating Notre Dame, Iowa, and the University of Michigan. During that year, I played with Ron Perranoski, later a Dodger [pitcher and] pitching coach, and Dick Radatz, later called the 'Monster' for the Red Sox. The three of us were pictured in *Sports Illustrated* when someone wrote an article on college teams.

"We ended the season going into Minnesota for a doubleheader, and we needed to win one game for the Big Ten championship," Foster says. "Perranoski started and lost the first game. Radatz started the second and got into trouble, and manager John Kobs put me in. I had a 3–2 count on a hitter with the bases loaded. The pitch cut the outside half of the plate above the knees for an obvious strike, but the umpire called it a ball. A run came in and one huge argument ensued. We lost the game by one run, and the championship."

In the summer of 1958, the Dodgers and Tigers strongly urged Foster to turn professional. "The Dodgers said they'd fly me to Los Angeles where I could work with their coaches and stay as long as I wanted," he says. "The Tigers wanted me in Detroit to work out. My father advised me to go with the Tigers, the local home team."

It's no surprise Foster preferred the Tigers, since he could recall listening to their games on the radio when he was a child.

"On the way to Detroit," he recalls, "the car radiator blew and stained my only available shirt. So I finally arrived, worked out, threw well, and was called before the Tigers' brass, stained shirt and all. Offers and counteroffers were made. I settled for a $35,000 bonus and a start in Class A, after a period of travel with the Tigers to get acquainted. The rules had changed about having to be on the major-league roster if one signed for over $4,000. This was also the time when bonuses were beginning to appear on the scene for ballplayers. My bonus was a huge sum for the time, but small for the present day.

"I joined the Tigers in the midsummer of 1958 for a week of travel," Foster says. "The first player to offer a handshake and welcome was Billy Martin. He held out his hand and said, 'Hi. I'm Billy.'" Martin, the Tiger shortstop/third baseman, was in his first season with Detroit that year.

Foster was then sent to the Lancaster Red Roses in the Eastern League, where Johnny Pesky, the former Red Sox shortstop—and boyhood friend of John Leovich (see Chapter 6)—was the manager. Foster appeared in eight games there, winning one and losing two. "I was also used as a pinch-hitter and hit safely 9 times out of 13 at-bats," he boasts.

Following the season, he returned to Michigan State University to continue his education. "They were on a quarterly system, so I was able to complete a whole quarter that winter," Foster says. (He would return to school every winter except for those years when he was in military service.)

When he recalls his first spring training camp in Lakeland, Florida, in 1959, two scenes stick in his memory. "One day, three of us stood behind a batting cage. It struck me later that the three of us were Tigers bonus babies. I was a 'can't-miss' right-hander. Doug Gallagher, a left-hander, was also a 'can't-miss' player. The third person was known to be questionable. As it turned out, Mickey Lolich eventually won three games in the World Series [in 1968] after almost quitting the game.

"I roomed with Lolich three years in the minors," Foster recalls. "He was his own person and not everybody wanted to room with him, but I got along with him fine. One time, he really was ready to quit the game. Another roommate of mine in the minors was Purnell Goldy. He was very intelligent. I remember we'd play word games and read a lot of books. He later married the daughter of the owner of the Denver Bears.

"Another time that spring, the Yankees came to play on the main field," Foster says. "That day someone shot a six-foot rattlesnake, the largest I've ever seen. Shot it next to the barracks. Another person had the idea of coiling it up and putting it in the Yankee dugout. The reaction," he laughs, "was clear and dramatic."

Foster adds, "That spring, I pitched against the Yankees myself and got them out except for Yogi Berra. He hit a single through the middle. Twice I faced Stan Musial and got him to hit two ground balls for outs."

Detroit sent the twenty-one-year-old Foster to Knoxville in the Southern League to begin the 1959 season. He started three games, winning one and losing none, before being promoted to the Durham Bulls in the

Carolina League. "Pesky was the manager at Knoxville, too," Foster says, "and he was sorry to see me go. I remember in that one game, I pitched six hitless innings for him.

"My first outing with Durham, playing in Greensboro, was a no-hitter," Foster says. "I remember [shortstop Dick] 'Muggsy' McAuliffe fielded the last out of that game. But the rest of the season was mediocre. Control of the fastball seemed to be my nemesis. It would often hop or take off." While striking out 118 in 129 innings there, Foster won eight and lost seven. "I remember the road trips were always very short at Durham, and this was handy for me because I was able to take a course at Duke [University] while I was there.

"I don't remember whether it was that year or the next, but Tommy Bridges, a former Tigers pitcher with a great curveball, was sort of a roving coach for the Tigers then, and he seemed to take a personal interest in me," Foster says. "He worked with me a lot and even came to my house in the off-season. Anyway, one day, a friend of his, a former teammate, came over to the ballpark and caught me a while. It was Mickey Cochrane [the Hall of Fame catcher]. That was a real treat.

"The next year," Foster says, "I went to Knoxville again and finished 13 and 11 with a high strikeout record [147, third best in the league]. That year, the bus trips through the mountains were *long*. It seemed everybody smoked cigars and the air conditioning on the bus was poor and it was always smoky. Sometimes you'd be up all night. I remember buying a hammock and stringing it up in the back of the bus so I could get some sleep. There was also a black-and-white situation that year, whereby the players had to stay in separate places. I remember one time, I think it might have been in Jacksonville, when a few of us went into a restaurant and sat down. A couple of minutes later, Sandy Amoros and some of the black players came along, and they closed the door on them. They said they didn't have any more room, but that wasn't true."

That winter, Foster did not return to college but instead enlisted in an Army reserve program which called for six months of active duty, but which would then allow him to remain free of future military obligations unless a national emergency was declared. "In the case of a national emergency, you would be the first called," Foster says.

In 1961, Foster pitched at Denver in the Triple-A International League where, for the first time, he relieved as well as started. "I was a flame thrower," he says, "and Charlie Metro, the manager, thought I might be effective as a reliever." But his performance that year was erratic. He won 6 and lost 14, with a 4.19 earned run average. Though he recorded 113 strikeouts in 144 innings, he also walked 92 and led the league in wild pitches with 16.

"After that season," he says, "I planned to play winter baseball in order to work on control and a change of pace pitch. With these plans in mind, I purchased a new car with some of my bonus money, traveled to Tampa, and unpacked. The next day my mother called. She said a registered piece of mail from Selective Service came to their house in Michigan and was being forwarded to me in Tampa. When I opened the mail, I read that I was called to active duty at the opposite end of the country, Fort Lewis, Washington. Khruschev had put up the Berlin Wall, and President Kennedy was activating two National Guard divisions, which needed reservists to complete the divisions. My name came up on the computer.

"That winter and most of the next summer, I trained with a division of infantry soldiers," Foster says. "When summer began, tension in Germany grew to a stalemate. I was allowed to meet with other reservists who played ball, and we became the Fort Lewis Rangers. This team had mostly pro players on it, Tony Kubek [of the New York Yankees] at short, George Thomas [who had recently been traded from the Tigers to the Los Angeles Angels] in the outfield, and others. We easily beat everyone we played. But a senator heard about the team and placed limits on the range of travel."

While at Fort Lewis, Foster met Virginia Lee, who became his bride the following year. "I had Christmas leave in 1961," he reports, "and went back home to get my new car. On the way back, I stopped off to see a friend in Rock Island, Illinois. His nephew was there, and the nephew had just graduated from Pacific Lutheran University in Tacoma, Washington, right near Fort Lewis. He gave me a list of people to look up when I got back, and the first name on the list was Ginny Lee, who was still going to school there. I never got to the second name," he laughs.

Foster was released from the Army in time to finish the 1962 season with the Denver Bears. "Bill Freehan was catching, McCauliffe was at short, [Don] Wert was at third, Lolich was pitching, and there were others who were on the World Series Championship Team in 1968," he says. "When I was able to throw to Freehan, I seldom lost. He caught and worked me well." In fact, Foster never lost at the end of that year. His record at Denver was 3–0.

In spring training camp in 1963, Tigers manager Bob Scheffing told the press: "Foster has a good fastball and a lot of poise. He's definitely a big-league prospect." Though Foster thought he'd kept in shape with his Army team, after a full year in the service, he wasn't quite ready for the majors. "I'd like to see him pitch every four days, get in a full season's work, and then I think he'll be ready to help us," Scheffing said.

Foster was sent to start the season at Syracuse, the Tigers' top farm club, where he had a 3–4 record in 11 games. "Then, he says, "the Tigers loaned me to the Red Sox team in Seattle, a Triple-A club managed by Mel Parnell [a former Red Sox pitcher]. Here again, I threw well, yet lost close games or had control trouble. One night, I remember they had a huge promotion and got a large crowd, and I threw a one-hit shutout at Portland. The only hit came from a former teammate, Jim Hughes." At Seattle, he won three but lost seven.

As the season drew to a close, the Tigers called Foster up to the major-league club. "That gave me a nice warm glow," he says. "I felt it was a real privilege, the culmination of something I wanted to achieve. I called my dad, and he was thrilled. I flew to Detroit to join the club. Others who were brought up included Lolich, [Willie] Horton, Wert, and [Jim] Northrup. My first roommate in the big leagues was Denny McLain, who was also joining the club. He would become a 30-game winner [31 in 1968]."

On September 18, 1963, Larry Foster played in a major-league game for the first and only time. "It was in Metropolitan Stadium in Minneapolis, against the Twins," he says. "It was a wet, damp night game, and we were at least six runs behind, as I recall. Charlie Dressen had me warm up and then brought me in to relieve."

That night, before nearly 11,000 fans, the Twins had ambushed Tigers starter Phil Regan in the very first inning, scoring three runs before he could retire a batter. In the next four innings, they picked up three more off reliever Willie Smith and led 6–0. After Smith went out for a pinch-hitter in the top of the sixth, Dressen called on Foster to pitch the bottom half of the inning.

"I rode to the mound on an electric cart," he says, "and warmed up. My ball was really moving. It was a hot, humid night, almost misty. I recall my fastball and curve being sharp and quick. Freehan had said to me that I had the most stuff on the club. He told me to throw it over. I felt good, and I was just trying to concentrate. The first batter I faced was Rich Rollins. The first pitch was a ball outside. I proceeded to strike him out with a curve that dropped over the plate.

"I remember thinking about control and throwing strikes, which meant I may have taken a little off the fastball at first," he says. Foster also pitched against rookie center fielder Jimmy Hall, who batted. Left fielder Harmon Killebrew batted soon thereafter. "I jammed him with a fastball. He popped into short right field where Rocky Colavito lumbered toward it. It dropped just in front of him." Then, after first baseman Don Mincher and right fielder Bob Allison batted, "catcher Earl Battey hit a low outside fastball for a single." Three runs scored before the side was retired.

In the two innings Foster pitched, he struck out one, and gave up four hits and one walk.

Foster returned to the dugout. "I didn't feel too bad," he says. "I was relieved about getting over the hump. I was there. I did it! Oh, I felt bad about the runs, but I really didn't mind it at all when I was pitching. It was fun. I know I took a little off the fastball. But the next inning, I got them out. I had reached a goal. I made it there. That was something."

In the top of the eighth, Foster was scheduled to come to bat, but Goldy, one of his former roommates, pinch hit for him and struck out against the Twins' Camilo Pascual. Pascual would go on to shut out the

Tigers that night, allowing only two hits (both by Colavito) for his nineteenth victory of the season.

"That was my biggest disappointment in baseball," Foster says, "not hitting. But when it was all over, I felt glad to have made it, but I was wishing I had done better.

"After we returned to Detroit," he continues, "the White Sox came to town. Dressen mentioned possibly starting me or McLain. He went with McLain, and Denny won 3–2. He also hit a home run [McLain's only hit in five times up that year]. From then on, I only warmed up on the side, coming close to relieving on a couple of occasions. My curve and fastball were at full tilt. Mike Roarke, the bullpen catcher, dropped a sharp curve and Dressen saw it. Later he called me in for a talk about next spring and plans he had for me."

The next spring, however, one morning early in the conditioning process, a mishap occurred. "I ran toward the first base line in order to field a bunt," Foster recalls. "I felt something in my shoulder pull. It was a sharp kind of pain. It turned out to be a tendon problem that didn't respond to cortisone or heat very well. I tried to go easy and take longer to warm up before going into games. Soon thereafter, we played the Cardinals and Stubby Overmire, the pitching coach, hurried me in the warm-up. I gave up six runs and ended up back at Syracuse. Eventually I was sent to Knoxville. Bobby Mavis was the manager there." It was Foster's poorest season.

The following year, Detroit released him in spring training. "It was kind of matter-of-fact," Foster says. "I asked them if they knew of anyone who could use me. They said they'd give Cleveland a call and I spoke to Hoot Evers there and he signed me. I remember him telling me, 'We do a lot of rehabilitating of Tigers ballplayers.'"

In 1965, Cleveland sent Foster to play in Salinas, California, and then to Reading, Pennsylvania, in the Eastern League. "Phil Cavaretta was the manager at Salinas," Foster says, "and he was an excellent manager. I did well there [5–3] and developed an underhand pitch." At Reading, Foster's record was 4–7, but he ended his season early after hurting his foot in a game at Williamsport. It was his last season in professional baseball.

Today, Foster recalls a few of his former Tigers teammates. "[Pitcher] Frank Lary, the Yankee killer, was a very interesting guy," he says. "I remember him telling us once about clearing forty acres in Alabama with a hatchet. Another time, he had a cricket someone killed, in a matchbox. He would have it on a seat in the dugout and talk to it. One day someone decided we ought to have a funeral for the dead cricket, so we had a funeral procession in the locker room, which was draped in towels. Then we had a trial for the 'murderer' of the cricket. There was a defendant, a prosecutor, and [pitcher] Fred Gladding was the judge. That was the kind of thing they used to do.

"Al Kaline used to pitch batting practice, and I liked to hit off him. I remember hitting one off the face of the right field deck," Foster recalls. "I also remember one spring Willie Horton had to lose forty pounds and Dressen told him he'd give him a ham weighing as much for each pound he lost. Dressen was a short, quiet guy who was friendly. He used to send me Christmas cards even after I left the Tigers. [Pitcher] Bill Faul was the one who would always beat me out. He was a little different. He would *hypnotize* himself when he pitched. He was a bonus baby, too, and always seemed to end up as the eleventh man on the staff while I was the twelfth."

After the 1965 season, nine years after he had graduated from high school, Foster was awarded a bachelor's degree in social science at Michigan State. "I had just about made up my mind then not to go back to baseball," he says. "I was getting near thirty, and I couldn't see myself coming back and going anywhere. I went on to graduate school, then to the seminary, to be ordained into the Lutheran Church in America. I became a parish pastor in 1969 and served at Grace Lutheran Church, an inner-city parish in Lansing, for six years. During this time, I also finished a master's degree at MSU in 1974."

For twenty-four years Foster served as a pastor, including eighteen years at a parish in Whitehall, Michigan, where he resides today. In 1989, he completed a doctorate in ministry, then joined the American Association of Pastoral Counselors and became a clinical member of the American Association for Marriage and Family Therapy. He is now a licensed therapist and teacher of family theory, with a private practice in individual and family therapy. He also serves as a resource-consultant for clergy who face conflict and leadership issues in their parishes.

His wife, the former Virginia Lee, is now arts consultant for the Muskegon Intermediate School District. One of their sons is a professional musician, and the other is a graduate student at Michigan State.

"I still get requests for autographs from kids all over the country," Foster says. "And the spot in Minnesota where I pitched years ago is now located in Camp Snoopy, inside the Mall of America, the largest mall in the world, some say. Home plate is still there. You can see it."

John Francis Paciorek Jr.

HOUSTON COLT .45'S, 1963

John Paciorek's performance in his one game in the major leagues almost makes you shake your head in disbelief.

As an eighteen-year-old, Paciorek came to the plate five times that day and reached base each time, with three hits and two walks. He drove in three runs, scored four times, made two sparkling catches in the outfield without an error, and was named the Associated Press Player of the Day.

Of all the players who batted 1.000 in their major-league games, he has more hits than anyone. And yet, he never appeared in another major-league game.

The oldest of eight children, Paciorek was born on February 11, 1945, in Detroit, where his father worked on an assembly line at a nearby Chrysler-Plymouth plant. The five boys and three girls were all athletic; four of the boys eventually played professional baseball. Tom had an 18-year major-league career and appeared in the 1974 World Series; Jim appeared in 48 games with the Milwaukee Brewers in 1987; and Mike played for a while in the Dodger organization.

As a youngster, John was one of Michigan's best all-around athletes. At St. Ladislaus High School in nearby Hamtramck, he played baseball, football, and basketball, and made All-State in all three. "I was also named honorable mention to some of the All-American teams," he adds.

"In football, I played both quarterback and tailback, and I was a guard/forward in basketball," Paciorek says. "In baseball, I made varsity in my freshman year and played third base. But then I switched to shortstop for the next three years." In 1962, his senior year at St. Ladislaus, he hit 13 home runs and batted .500.

To build himself up physically, John Paciorek, shown here in his Houston Colt .45s uniform, did handstands, headstands, and neckstands, and even used his brothers as weights.

"When I was a kid, I used to fantasize about being a baseball player during baseball season and a football player during football season," he says. "I played American Legion ball and Federation ball. In between, I thought I'd box. I was big and strong and brash and everything. I was real arrogant. I remember when I was in high school, I just wanted to be the best I could be. If anyone was better than me, if I played in a basketball game or anything against them and they were better, then I'd go out and practice hours and hours until I played against them again and proved I was better. I just kept doing that in everything I did, and I was expecting to do the same in baseball."

While young, Paciorek became an exercise freak. "My dad was a powerful man, and I guess he started me in that. I think he did it initially to get us to work around the house. He used to tell us we needed to strengthen our hands and our wrists and that washing the dishes and scrubbing the floors would be good exercises," Paciorek chuckles. "But I used to do a lot of stupid things. I would lift heavy chairs, and sometimes I'd even use my brothers as weights. I wanted to be the best that ever was. I wanted to be like Mickey Mantle. So I was always doing exercises, doing some crazy things. I didn't really understand what I was doing. I was just doing exercises.

"I wanted to have a nineteen-and-a-half-inch neck. I used to do neck exercises. You know how you do handstands? Instead of using my hands, I used my head. And all my weight would be on my neck. Every once in a while, I'd slip and I'd be out of action for two weeks. It was stupid, the stuff I used to do," Paciorek admits. "But the only thing I could think about was being the best there was."

Paciorek had thoughts of going to college and playing all three sports, but especially football and basketball because of the national press attention those two sports received. "I thought about the University of Michigan," he says, "but I was really more inclined to go the University of Houston. I thought I wanted to live farther away from home at that time, and Bill Yoemans had just gone there to coach football."

These plans, however, were thwarted by Paul Richards, who recently had become general manager of the Houston Colt .45s, one of the new expansion teams which came into existence in 1962. "Paul Richards had come to see me play earlier in high school, and he came to the house," Paciorek recalls. "I told him about college, and he said he was gonna offer me enough money to forget about going to college. I was about six-foot-two and 210 pounds and had a lot of speed and I was good. I was thinking he was gonna offer something like a million dollars," Paciorek laughs.

When it came time to sign, however, it turned out to be a bit different. "I don't remember if it was Richards or Eddie Robinson who actually signed me," Paciorek says. "I think I signed on August 17, and I would have been in a better bargaining position if I hadn't sprained my ankle that summer playing summer basketball. Richards kept sending scouts to see me play, but I wasn't at my best playing on that ankle, so they didn't want to spend the money.

"At that time, it was a vanity thing, you know. I wanted what everyone else was getting when they got a bonus. I thought I wanted $100,000."

What did he get? "The paper said it was $90,000," Paciorek says, "but it wasn't anything like that. It was more like $45,000. They gave me $15,000, and they gave my parents $15,000. Then, the first year I played, they gave me another $15,000 along with my regular pay, which was $500 a month, I think. And because of my ankle, I had to bicker to get *that!*"

After the contract was signed, Richards was quoted as saying that Paciorek "could become one of the really great power hitters and all-around players in baseball." Paciorek thought so, too. That winter he played in an instructional league, and in early 1963, shortly after his eighteenth birthday, he reported eagerly to Apache Junction, Arizona, where Houston held its spring training camp.

"I did really good," he says. "Al Kaline had played in the majors at seventeen, and I thought sure I could do it at eighteen. I hit really well. I was not nervous. I felt I really belonged there."

Paciorek was so sure he was going to make the major-league roster right out of high school that he was truly shocked when told he was being sent to Houston's minor-league camp.

"It was because I did so well that they sent me down," he says today. "They kept a couple of guys who weren't as good. Richards told me he wanted me to go where I could play every day and develop my talent. He said I had too much promise to sit on the bench in Houston." But Paciorek felt he belonged in the big leagues and took the move as a demotion.

Reluctantly, he reported to the Colts' minor-league training camp in Moultrie, Georgia. "When I went down to the minors, I felt like I had to protect myself so I wouldn't get hurt," Paciorek says. "I used to hear things when I was a kid about somebody who was a good ballplayer but got beaned. That was in the back of my head, and here I was going down to the minor leagues with a bunch of young, wild rookies.

"In Moultrie, Georgia, it was like a cow pasture. If you were standing out in deep left field, sometimes you couldn't even *see* home plate 'cause you were down in a gully. When you were batting, there was no green background—you were up against white. You're facing all these fireballing sidearmers, you know. And here I was. All I wanted to do is preserve myself. I was bailing out and everything.

"So I was kind of like a prima donna at that point. Houston thought highly of me. They wanted me to go out there and really rip it up. I didn't do anything. I just didn't feel motivated. I should have really capitalized on the opportunities instead of acting like I did," he says.

That spring he was most impressed by Jimmy Wynn, a young infielder who would move to the outfield and later be dubbed "the Toy Cannon." "He was the third baseman then and he was just a tiny little thing," Paciorek recalls. "He was five-foot-six at the most. I was playing center field in a intrasquad game, and when he came up, I moved way in. Next pitch, he rifled a shot off the 450-foot sign, and I said, 'Wait a minute.' It was ricocheting off the wall, and I finally held him to a triple.

"I picked up some grass and threw it up in the air. I wanted to see if there was a wind or something. But there was nothing. I thought, 'That's probably the best hit he ever got in his life.' So the next time he came to the plate, I didn't back up. I just stayed in the same place, and I'll be darned if he didn't hit another one off the wall, 450 feet.

"As a kid," Paciorek says, "my life was so *matter*-based. The bigger you are, the farther you can hit the ball. At that point, it was such a contradiction. Wynn was so small. He was wiry, streamlined, but he wasn't bulky. I realized, after watching him, that it was speed that was converted into power."

The Colts assigned Paciorek to Modesto of the Class C California League, where his teammates included future major-leaguers such as Walt Williams, Sonny Jackson, Carroll Sembera, Danny Coombs, Leon McFadden, and Joe Morgan.

"Our double-play combination was Jackson to Morgan to the bleachers," Paciorek chuckles. "Jackson is the one who threw it into the bleachers. Morgan's throw was always in the dirt. He couldn't even throw the ball from second base to first on the fly, that's how ridiculous it was. I mean, he wasn't a bad fielder, but he wasn't real good, and he couldn't throw the ball.

"But he just worked and worked and worked," Paciorek says. "He just couldn't get enough work, and he was so smart about how to figure out things. He was probably the gutsiest and smartest guy you'd ever want to meet. They gave us old hand-me-down uniforms. He was so small that when he was wearing a short-sleeved shirt, it covered his wrists. It was a sight to behold.

"You could hardly see him from the outfield," Paciorek continues. "He was a little left-hander, but it didn't matter to him if it was a left-handed pitcher, he just stayed right in there. He just had determination. He looked like he was five-foot-five or whatever it was, but when he stood up there at the plate, he looked ten feet tall. He just dug in."

Paciorek started strongly in his first professional season, batting .326 with two home runs and a team-leading 12 RBI in the first 13 games. Modesto, under Dave Philley, who was in his first managerial job after completing an 18-year major-league career, was 9–4 at that point and had five players hitting better than .300.

Paciorek also attracted attention because of his hustle. He ran everywhere, even in the summer heat of 110 degrees. He would race from his position in the outfield at the end of each inning, attempting to beat the rest of his teammates to the dugout. "I'd be hustling all over," he says. "If I was in right field and our dugout was on the third base side, I'd sprint in and out, and I'd try to beat the third baseman to the dugout. I'd also back up *any* position. Lots of times I'd even make putouts at third base. It was impressed upon me early in life to hustle. I heard that from one of the dads in the Pony League when I was a kid, before I ever heard about Pete Rose. It probably gave everybody a good impression of me because I was always diving and running through people."

Meanwhile, he continued with his unusual exercises, constantly doing handstands, headstands, and neckstands. "I didn't understand what I was doing. I was just doing exercises," he says. "There was no scientific logic in what I was doing. I was just doing all kinds of sit-ups and push-ups and all that. I wore lead weights around my ankles. I'd do all these exercises, and then I'd go out and throw."

Soon Paciorek began experiencing problems with his upper back, which were aggravated by his throwing, but he didn't want to come out of the lineup. "I kept playing about a month after I became hurt," he remembers, "and my back became so severely strained that I couldn't lift up my arm. Everybody got mad at me as my average went down, but they didn't know I was hurt. Dave Philly was one of those blood-and-guts guys, who used to tell us how he would play with injuries and all, how he wouldn't let anyone take his place, and I think I kept playing to impress him."

But Paciorek finally had to confess his pain and come out of the lineup. As he sat on the bench, resting the injury, he began to notice his lower back stiffening. He responded by launching into a new set of stretching exercises—a major miscalculation.

In and out of the lineup for the remainder of the season, his productivity fell off dramatically. His final batting average was only .219. But despite his health problems, Paciorek showed definite signs of power. Almost half of his 60 hits that year went for extra bases.

In September, following the California League playoffs, the parent team recalled Paciorek to Houston so his back could be examined by specialists. While there, the Colts asked him if he was well enough to play in Houston's final game of the season.

"My back was hurting like anything, but I said, 'Yeah!' God, no matter what, I was gonna play."

It was the final two days of the 1963 National League season, and the Colt .45s were completing the schedule against the New York Mets, the league's other second-year expansion team. Both teams were basically inept—Houston finished ninth and the Mets finished tenth in both 1962 and 1963. Their expansion strategies, however, had been different, and the result of those differences was becoming apparent. Houston, under the guidance of Richards, had put together a group of promising young players on their way up, while the Mets had remained with veterans on their way out. In their last 22 games of 1963, Houston won 16.

To show off its youth movement, Houston decided to put all-rookie lineups on the field for the last two games of the year. So on September 29, the final day of the season, the starting right fielder for the Colt .45s was eighteen-year-old John Paciorek, an injured Class C minor leaguer who was in Houston only by chance.

The Colt lineup that day also included the core of what would be the Houston team through the remainder of the decade. In the infield, there were nineteen-year-old Rusty Staub; Joe Morgan, who had just turned twenty years old; Bob Aspromonte, twenty-five; and Glenn "Sparky" Vaughan, nineteen. The outfield, in addition to Paciorek, included Wynn and eighteen-year-old Ivan Murrell. The rookie battery had nineteen-year-old Chris Zachary on the mound and twenty-one-year-old John Bateman behind the plate.

Starting against Zachary, according to the box score, was the Mets' rookie relief pitcher, Larry Bearnarth, twenty-two, who was being given his second start of the year. The line score shows that Houston went ahead 2–0 in the bottom of the second, but that the Mets came back with four runs in the top of the third to lead 4–2. These would be the last runs the New Yorkers would score that year.

In the bottom of the fourth, the first five Houston batters reached base and eventually scored, giving the Colts a 7–4 lead. During the uprising, both Umbricht and the Colt leadoff hitter, Vaughan, were removed for pinch-hitters. The Mets' Bearnarth was replaced by Ed Bauta.

In the very next inning, the Colts clobbered Bauta and his successor, Tracy Stallard, for four more runs to go ahead 11–4 at the end of five innings. Finally, in the sixth and seventh, they also scored single runs against Mets rookie Grover Powell and won the game 13–4. While it was the last game of the season, it was the first game of the year in which Houston scored in double digits, according to Paciorek.

Few details of the day stick in Paciorek's mind now, but he says, "I remember it was a hot, humid day at the old Colt .45 stadium, and I liked hot weather. I remember all the cheering fans [the attendance was given as 3,899] and the excitement of being on a big-league field." And, most important, he says, "I had the feeling that I belonged there."

Batting seventh and playing right field, Paciorek reached base safely in all five of his at-bats. He had three singles and two walks, scored four runs, and batted in three.

According to the box score, the men who hit directly in front of him were Wynn, Staub, Aspromonte, and Murrell. They had five hits and four walks among them that day and scored a total of five runs. The two men who batted right behind Paciorek were Bateman and Bob Lillis, who came in to replace Vaughan at shortstop, but batted ninth, in Umbricht's spot. Bateman and Lillis both had two hits and, between them, batted in five runs that day.

As for Paciorek's feelings that day, he says, "It felt great to go out to right field at the start of the game. I felt it was where I belonged. I really don't remember much else. I do remember on the bench between innings, I couldn't wait to get up to bat or to go back in the outfield. Also, when I came up toward the end of the game, it seemed like most of the fans gave me an ovation. I don't know if it was a standing ovation, but it was an ovation. That was great.

"I was hurting the whole time," he says, "but I just didn't let it bother me that game. It was really exciting. I felt great. I was looking forward to more of it.

"After the game," Paciorek says, "I wasn't even expecting it, but on the TV back at my hotel, I saw Guy Savage [a Houston sports announcer] talking about me and saying I was gonna be on the Houston team for years. That was a thrill." The *Houston Press* also called him "a cinch to make it as big leaguer."

As one of Houston's "faces of the future," Paciorek couldn't wait for the next season to begin.

At spring training in 1964, Houston gave him every opportunity to make the major-league roster. "They played me everywhere," he says. "It was like I was going to be their starting center fielder." Paciorek remembers he played nearly every day that spring, but also remembers not playing well. His back problem from the year before had become even worse.

At first, he did not tell the team of his physical problems, afraid it might kill his chance of making the team. "There was always pain," he says, "and I tried to relieve it by exercise, but it didn't help. I was nineteen years old and I was worried about getting *released*. They knew I had a great arm at one time, but I just couldn't throw or hit. Sometimes, all of a sudden, out of nowhere, I'd be reaching for a ball without thinking and *jeez*, it'd be like a *knife* going through me," he recalls. "So finally, I just couldn't take it anymore. I either wanted to be completely healed or an invalid.

"I just had to tell the team. I mean, they knew *something* was wrong, but unless you tell them specifically, they'll just go by what you tell them. I was always known for being strong," he says, "so they just thought I was looking lame, that's all."

A further physical examination revealed a congenital spine problem, a birth abnormality which might never have bothered him unless triggered by something, in this case probably the combination of his upper-back problem the year before and his exercise routine.

Houston hoped Paciorek would be able to avoid an operation and that the injury would somehow heal itself or that he could make adaptations in his playing style that would allow him to stay in the lineup.

To start the 1964 season, Paciorek was sent to Durham in the Carolina League under manager Billy Gardner, but could hit only .155 in 39 games as his back problems continued. Shipped to Statesville in the Western Carolina League and reunited with his manager from the previous season, Dave Philley, he could manage only one single and a double in 32 at-bats, an average of .063. Half of his at-bats that season resulted in strikeouts. "I couldn't adjust and turn at the plate," he says. "I just told Dave I couldn't play anymore. It was like I had a knife in my back all the time."

Convinced now that rest and adaptation would not solve the problem, the club sent Paciorek to Houston Methodist Hospital to undergo spinal-fusion surgery. The operation involved fusing Paciorek's vertebrae back together to stop the abnormal movement which was the root of his discomfort. There was a risk that the fusion could place greater strain on the rest of his spine—causing even more back pain.

"I was in bed for three-and-a-half weeks," he says, "and had to wear a back brace, which was like a cast, for nearly a year after that. I had to follow a ritual of lying down to get the cast on and off. In all that time, I couldn't even take a bath or a shower. I could only take a sponge bath. But I was real patient with it 'cause I knew that I just had to let it set and everything and get well. And then I thought it was gonna be as good as ever."

Although regaining his mobility, Paciorek had to stay out for the game for the rest of 1964 and all of 1965. "One thing funny happened around this time," he says. "I was always a big powerful guy, 210 pounds with lots of muscles. Well, I remember wearing the back brace one day and my clothes draped over a bit, but I didn't think much about it. But when you're in the hospital, you don't realize how much weight you're losing. Well, that day I went to a game that Houston won, and I went into the clubhouse afterward to see the guys. It was a really happy clubhouse 'cause they didn't win that much that year, and they were all yelling and laughing and having a good time. When I walked in, suddenly a huge hush came over the room. They thought it was Death walking in. I had lost about 50 pounds and was down to about 160, but I never realized how bad I looked 'til then. I thought that was funny."

During his enforced absence from baseball, Paciorek started going to college. "When I signed originally, one of the things they did was set up a scholarship for me," he says. "Thank God they did. That was the best thing in the contract." He enrolled at the University of Houston, the school he once thought of attending to play football, and completed two years of study on his way to a degree in physical education.

As he recuperated, Paciorek was determined to continue his baseball career. "When I was out of the back brace and I could start exercising and stuff—I was real gung-ho on that—I thought I was gonna come back faster than anybody had ever. And I got myself in good shape."

Paciorek started his comeback in 1966, playing winter ball in Sarasota, Florida, on a combined team with players from both Houston and the Boston Red Sox. "I remember Tony Conigliaro and George Scott were there," he says.

To start the season, Paciorek was assigned back to the Western Carolina League, this time to Salisbury, and he seemed to make some progress early in the year, batting .247. But problems soon developed. "I didn't realize how much the lower back comes into play when you run," he says. "With the spine being fused, I thought I'd be as strong as ever. I thought that when the pain was gone, I'd be better. But I began pulling muscles. I never pulled muscles before, especially in my legs. I was always pulling my hamstrings. Then, when I tried to throw as hard as I could, I just really screwed up my shoulder because I couldn't follow through right."

Later that year, he moved up to Batavia in the New York–Penn League, but his physical problems continually caused him to miss games. At Batavia, he hit only .158 in 46 games and struck out 61 times in 133 at-bats.

Again he tried to rehabilitate his sore back and weak shoulder through continued exercise in the off-season. But it didn't work. He began the 1967 season at Asheville in the Carolina League, lasting there for 25 games, hitting .128, and striking out 23 times in 47 at-bats. He was then sent to Cocoa in the Florida State League, where he got just one hit in 20 times up, for a .050 average, while striking out 10 of those 20 times.

"That year, I hurt so much that I was never able to play two days in a row," Paciorek recalls. "At Cocoa, I could not throw at all. It was my overall hustle that kept me going. If I was playing left field, I was very good running in quickly on a ball, and was able to hold runners because I looked so close to them. But then they finally started running on me and that was it. I was feeling so bad that I went on my own to a doctor."

Houston released him.

Paciorek was then twenty-two years old and had just recently married. He returned home and tried to rest his aches and pains. "One day the next spring, I went to a college game at the University of Houston, where my brother Tom was playing," he recalls. "I bumped into a guy I knew who was a scout for the Cleveland Indians, and he asked me how I was feeling. Since I was rested and hadn't aggravated anything by playing for a while, I felt good again and told him so. He knew I was always hurt but that I played well. He asked me if I'd be interested in doing anything in the way of playing again, and I said I would."

So Paciorek signed with Cleveland, and in 1968 was sent to the club's Rock Hill franchise in the same Western Carolina League where he had played immediately before and after his spinal surgery. At Rock Hill, he banged out three home runs in 13 games, while hitting .225. The Indians shipped him up to Reno in the California League.

At Reno, Paciorek had the best season of his career, batting .275 with 17 home runs and 65 RBI in only 82 games. Half of his hits went for extra bases, and his slugging average was an impressive .553. However, he was still plagued by injuries such as pulled muscles, and his playing time was limited.

Still, his work that year offered the Indians hope that his potential might yet be realized, so the following year they promoted the twenty-three-year-old to their Waterbury, Connecticut, affiliate in the Double-A Eastern League. "I looked like a big leaguer there," Paciorek says. "I had a reputation as an unbelievable outfielder and had demonstrated power."

But he was again plagued by injuries. "I was out a month because of a pulled Achilles tendon," he says, "and because of my back, I had to come out hours before the game to stretch. For example, if we were going to play at seven in the evening, I used to have to come out at three in the afternoon just to limber up and get rid of the stiffness. It would take me that long."

Paciorek got into only 29 games with Waterbury in 1968 and batted just .213. The Indians had seen enough.

"When they released me, I was almost relieved," Paciorek says. "It wasn't real bad because I realized at that point that I didn't really want to go through that anymore. It was just too grueling. I always thought I could adapt and I tried to make adaptations along the way, but I *had* to play at full speed. If I couldn't, I didn't want to play at all."

Paciorek returned to school and obtained his bachelor's degree at the University of Houston in the early 1970s, and then became a physical education instructor at the Jewish Community Center in Houston, where he worked for seven years before deciding to move to California. "We came here because I had changed my religious beliefs and was looking to work with an institution in that religion. I joined the Christian Science movement after having been a Catholic," he says. Along with his wife, Linda, and their five children, he moved to San Gabriel, California, where he joined the teaching staff at the Clairborne School, an institution whose faculty is composed of Christian Scientists.

Linda died of cancer in the late 1980s, and Paciorek later married Karen Purdy, a divorced mother of two. They recently celebrated the birth of their new daughter.

"I coach all the sports here at the school—flag football and soccer, basketball, track, and baseball," Paciorek says. "I guess the competitive fire is still there because when I coach, sometimes I can be real calm before a game. Then I get into it when I see my kids and everything. It makes me feel like I'm in there.

"I miss competition from that standpoint, but I don't miss some of the aspects of it. I coach four basketball teams and I have to referee these practice games, and I hate it when people act unsportsmanlike instead of just concentrating on the skill of the game. I just liked the idea of playing and keeping my mouth shut. I tell my kids to do the best they can and not worry about the extra stuff—all the badmouthing and stuff that you see on TV. I always hated yelling at umpires. I thought it just took away from the game. Managers kick dirt on umpires and people consider it a show. It disgusts me. They're just trying to make excuses for themselves."

Reflecting on his baseball career and what might have been, Paciorek says, "I definitely have regrets. I kind of like what I'm doing, but I always relished the idea of playing. I don't know what I would have done had my back been better. I'd like to think I would have been a star. I wouldn't have settled for anything else. Baseball is my favorite sport, and the idea of being in the big leagues remains with me as I see my own kids play. One of my sons has been drafted by the San Diego Padres, and he hustles, too. And it's always coming back to me. After so many years, kids still come up to me to ask about it. I'm like the answer to a trivia question.

"Today I'm more family-oriented and spiritually based. When I used to think about bulk, I thought about things in a material way. It's the metaphysical that really runs your life, rather than what seems obvious. My life is probably more peaceful now. It's kind of fun."

That performance in his one game in the major leagues was kind of fun, too.

John Paul Braun

MILWAUKEE BRAVES, 1964

John Braun pitched two scoreless innings and struck out the National League's leading hitter, Hall of Famer Roberto Clemente in his one major-league game.

In a way, his experience was similar to that of John Paciorek (see Chapter 30). He turned in a fine performance at the age of twenty-four and, with the prospect of a fine career ahead of him, Braun then injured himself so badly that he never got into a second game.

Born in 1939, the day after Christmas, in Madison, Wisconsin, Braun grew to be a tall, strapping youngster (standing six-foot-five and weighing 218 pounds) and a fine athlete.

"At Madison West High, I played baseball, basketball, and football," he remembers. "In football, I was second-string quarterback to an All-Stater, Jim Bakken, who went on to play in the NFL and, I believe, was the league's top kicker one year. We were also shirttail relatives," Braun says, explaining: "His mother and my mother were cousins once removed, or something like that.

"In basketball, I was a first-string forward, and one year we went to the state tournament and lost in the finals. Jim was on the team and was All-State in basketball, too," Braun says.

"I was always a pitcher in baseball and played three years on the varsity. In my senior year, I had a very good record, something like 10 and 1, or 9 and 1." Asked if Bakken was an All-State baseball player as well, Braun answers, "No, but he was an All-Conference third baseman."

During his last two years in high school, Braun also pitched in a summer league in Madison, where a coach from Florida State University was

250

serving as one of the city's recreation officials at the time. This eventually led to Braun's enrolling at Chipola Junior College in Miriana, Florida, after his high school graduation in 1957. "Chipola was a sister school of Florida State," he says, "and I played basketball there for a year."

But in the fall of 1958, he was granted an athletic scholarship to his hometown college, the University of Wisconsin, and transferred back there. "I never did play for Wisconsin, though," he laughs. "I was only there for a year and a semester. When I first got there, I had to go through a one-year residency before I could play, because of the transfer, which I did. But then, in the summer of 1959, I had one of those really super summers playing semipro ball, and a lot of interest developed." His right-handed pitching attracted scouts from both Chicago teams, the White Sox and the Cubs, as well as from the Cincinnati Reds, the Los Angeles Dodgers, and the Milwaukee Braves.

"I decided to turn professional because the offers finally got to be so good," Braun says. "I was helped a lot by Gene Calhoun, who was an assistant coach and catcher of mine at the time. He's now a lawyer in Madison, and I think he became the head of Big-Ten football officials. Over the years, I know he's helped a lot of guys, a lot of players, and gratis."

In 1960, Braun signed a contract with John Mullen, then the farm team director at Milwaukee. The Braves had moved their franchise there from Boston seven years earlier and would stay in Milwaukee through the 1965 season before moving to Atlanta. "They gave me a bonus of $25,000," Braun says, "and my salary was $800 a month." The bonus, he says, went for taxes, a car, and living expenses.

Braun began his professional career that year at Davenport, Iowa, in the Quad City League, where Hall of Famer Travis Jackson, a former New York Giants shortstop, was his manager. "I'm not sure if he had been elected to the Hall of Fame yet or not," Braun confesses. "I think I was something like 10–8 there that year [with a 2.90 earned run average], although I was out for a while with an elbow problem.

"In 1961, I was put on the Vancouver roster, but I got called by Milwaukee to come down to spring training with the big club. That was pretty awesome," Braun says of the experience. "I guess I was just a star-struck kid seeing all those name players, but you knew you weren't gonna stay. [Manager Charlie] Dressen sent me over to the minor-league camp in Waycross [Georgia], and I ended up starting the season at Cedar Rapids."

At Cedar Rapids, Jimmy Brown, a former Cardinal and Pirates infielder, was the manager. "I was going good," Braun says, "but early in the season, I pulled a rib cage and was sent down to Eau Claire. It was a disaster. It was a bad season. It was not a good team, and I had an attitude problem." Under manager Jim Fanning, who had spent some time as a catcher with the Cubs, the right-hander won only two and lost seven.

Braun did not play professionally in 1962, but he played baseball nevertheless. In April 1962, his army reserve unit was assigned to Fort Leonard

In his one big-league game, John Braun threw two scoreless innings and struck out Hall of Famer Roberto Clemente. After that, Braun never played again.

Wood, Missouri, for six months of active duty. "I mostly played on the baseball team there," he laughs. He also took off a dozen pounds.

During the winters, after each baseball season ended, Braun had worked a part-time reporter for his hometown newspaper, the Madison *Capitol Times*. "I worked in the sports department and covered high school sports," he recalls. He returned there in October 1962, following his discharge from active duty.

When spring training began in 1963, Braun again reported to the Braves' minor-league complex in Georgia and was eventually assigned to Greenville, South Carolina, where Jim Fanning, his manager at Eau Claire in 1961, now was piloting the team. "For some reason," Braun recalls, "he was replaced about halfway through the season by Paul Snyder, who was then a major-league scout and who I think is now head of scouting for the Atlanta Braves.

"That was just a breakthrough year for me," Braun says. "Everything came together. I pitched short relief and I think I was 5 and 1 [6–2] and had a 1.32 earned run average. They sent me up to Boise, and I was about 7 and 2 with a 1.30-something earned run average, and I had a ton of strikeouts. It was just a great year for me."

One day, after returning home to Madison that fall, Braun struck up a conversation with an attractive girl named Julaine Onsager, whom he met in a local restaurant. "I saw her and just started to talk to her. We had a nice conversation, and that was the start of it," he says. They were married in February 1965, a year and a half later. By that time, Braun had already finished his major-league career.

In 1964, however, the twenty-four-year-old played most of the year at the Triple-A level with the Denver Bears. "I was something like 6 and 5 with a 4.95 earned run average," he says, "which, for Denver, wasn't bad. In August, though, they sent me down to Austin, Texas. John Mullen told me that they needed help and said that if I went there, I'd be called up to the Braves at the end of the season.

True to their word, the Braves brought Braun to the big leagues on September 9, 1964, after his minor-league season ended. "Milwaukee was on the road then," he says, "and I had to wait at home for a couple of days for them to get back.

"That first day I joined the team was pretty special," he recalls. "I specifically remember pulling into the parking lot at the stadium and thinking that this was where I was working. I wasn't as star-struck seeing the players 'cause I knew most of them from prior springs or from playing with them in earlier years."

Braun joined a Milwaukee team that was extremely offensive-minded. The Braves had the highest aggregate batting average in the 10-team league that year and scored almost 100 more runs than anyone else. They were led by outfielders Rico Carty (.330), Hank Aaron (.328), and Lee Maye (.304), as well as catcher Joe Torre (.321). Also on the roster were such solid major-league hitters as Eddie Mathews, Felipe Alou, Dennis Menke, Ed Bailey, and Frank Bolling. The pitching staff was led by Tony Cloninger (19–14), Dennis Lemaster (17–11), and the veteran left-hander, Warren Spahn.

When Braun joined the Braves, only three weeks remained in the season. "Most of that time, I worked with Whitlow Wyatt, the pitching coach, and got a good opportunity to work on things. He was trying to get me another pitch. I was mostly a fastball-slider pitcher, and he was trying to teach me to throw a change-up. A lot of the guys had come up from Triple-A then, and it was a good time to learn. And he had the time to spend with us teaching, time he wouldn't have had in the spring. So I felt good about it.

"One singular thing I remember about those three weeks was a trip we made to Philadelphia," Braun says. "That was the year Philly folded like a tent at the end of the season. I think they had a four- or five-game lead when we got there. I think we came in on a Thursday and had a five-game series through Sunday, and we swept them. When we left, they were tied for first. It was one of the all-time choke jobs."

As Braun indicates, the Phils suffered one of the most famous collapses in baseball history that year and eventually lost the pennant by one game to the St. Louis Cardinals. The team seemed invincible, maintaining their lead from July 16 until September 26—just a few days before the season ended. Then they relinquished it by losing ten consecutive games, half of those to Braun's teammates on the Braves.

"It was in that series with them that Hank Aaron hit the hardest ball I've ever seen in my life," Braun says. "It was a line drive off [Jim] Bunning. Bobby Wine, the shortstop, jumped up to try to catch it, and it landed two rows in. It just kept going like a bullet."

On the night of October 2, 1964, in Milwaukee, John Braun got a chance to pitch in a major-league game. The fifth-place Braves were playing the visiting seventh-place Pittsburgh Pirates in a twi-night doubleheader to make up for a rainout earlier in the season.

The first game turned out to be a pitching duel between the Braves' Cloninger, who was going for his 19th win of the year, and the knuckleballer Wilbur Wood, whom the Pirates had acquired from the Boston Red Sox earlier that season.

After six scoreless innings, both teams scored twice in the seventh. At the end of nine, the game was tied, 2–2. Then in the bottom of the tenth, Milwaukee pushed across the winning run to give them their eighth consecutive win.

With the season winding down and neither team going anywhere, two relief pitchers were given the starting assignments in the second game. For Pittsburgh, Tom Butters, who boasted an excellent 2.38 earned run average, took the mound against a tall, slim Braves lefty, Dan Schneider.

The Pirates started quickly against Schneider, getting three runs in the first two innings, then adding two more in the top of the third before he could get anyone out. Among the Pirates' hits were home runs by shortstop Gene Alley and right fielder Clemente. With the score 5–0, Bobby Bragan, the Braves' manager, brought in a twenty-three-year-old rookie right-hander, Clay Carroll, who finished the inning without further trouble.

But Carroll went out for a pinch-hitter in the bottom of the inning, and John Braun, warming up in the bullpen with catcher Joe Torre, learned he would be going in to pitch the top of the fourth. "I didn't think much about it at that time," he says. "It was very cold that night, and I concentrated on getting warmed up. Oh, I was nervous, I guess, but I was trained well enough, so I wasn't *overly* nervous. When the time came, someone said 'Hey, you're in there,' and I went out. I remember the crowd [7,800] was not overwhelming."

The record indicates that Braun pitched two innings against the Pirates, giving up two hits and a walk, and striking out one. The Pittsburgh lineup in that second game had left fielder Manny Mota leading off, followed by Clemente in right, and then infielders Donn Clendenon at first, Bob Bailey at third, Bill Mazeroski at second, and Alley at shortstop. Center fielder Bill Virdon batted between Bailey and Mazeroski. The catcher, Jerry May, and the pitcher, Butters, completed the batting order.

"I don't remember exactly whom I faced that first inning," Braun confesses, "but it seems to me I gave up back-to-back hits." Based on Braun's recollection today that he got out of the inning when his own center fielder, Ty Cline, "charged a sinking liner and caught a ball hit by Mota to retire the side," the hits against him most likely were made by Mazeroski, Alley, or May. The box score of the game shows Mazeroski and Alley each had two hits that night, and May had one. Virdon and Butters were hitless.

"I was relieved to get out of that mess," Braun says when asked about his thoughts after the first inning he pitched. "I settled down between innings, sitting on the bench, and the second inning was a normal inning for me."

After the Braves failed to score, the first batter Braun faced in the top of the fifth was Clemente, who, at that point in the season, already had 211 hits and led the league with a .339 batting average. This confrontation is the only part of the game Braun can remember clearly today.

"He took a strike the first pitch, and on the second pitch, I threw him a high-in fastball. Now, he was a good hitter, but he was a notorious bad-ball hitter. He hit a rope past Mathews at third base that went foul. I think it was Mathews, but it might have been [Lou] Klimchock. Anyway, whoever it was yelled over to me, 'Hey, I'm a married man!' I was told later that you should throw nothing up and in to Clemente, but I didn't know it then. The next pitch I wasted outside. Then I threw a slider, a bit outside I thought, but the ump called him out.

"Clemente was not happy about the call, and their dugout really got on the umpire after that," Braun recalls. "You know, I think that was the last game Clemente played that year. If I remember right, that game was on a Friday night, and on Sunday the season wrapped up. Clemente was in a fight for the batting title, and I think he sat out the last two days while the guy chasing him had to have a 3-for-4 day on the final day to beat him." Clemente won the title with his .339 average, which was comfortably above his nearest challengers, Aaron and Torre at .328 and .321, respectively.

After retiring the Pirates in the fifth, again without any runs being scored, Braun returned to the Braves' dugout. "I felt pretty good about that," he says. "I felt I was throwing well after that first inning, and some of the guys said, 'Hey, good job,' and 'Good game, rook,' and things like that."

When it was Braun's turn to bat in the bottom of the fifth, the Braves sent up a pinch-hitter. "I don't remember who it was," he says, but I stayed in the dugout and watched. It seems to me we got a rally going then and scored a couple of runs, and I got a little excited." The Braves scored two runs in the next inning, the bottom of the sixth.

Three other Milwaukee pitchers followed Braun to the mound that night—Dick Kelley, Dave Eilers, and Chi Chi Olivo—and they, too, held Pittsburgh scoreless. Meanwhile, the Braves scored two more in the eighth to bring the score to 5–4. But that was as close as they could get, and their winning streak ended at eight. Two days later, the season and John Braun's major-league career both ended.

Braun would never again pitch meaningfully.

Shortly after the start of spring training with the Braves in 1965, Braun, at that time a newlywed, injured his pitching arm. "Outside of striking out Roberto Clemente for my only major-league 'K,' I guess hurting my arm that next spring training was what I remember most about my time in the majors," Braun says today.

The diagnosis was nerve damage, and at first, rest was prescribed, but it didn't help. "Then they sent me to pitch in Austin, Texas, because they thought that hot weather would help. But it didn't. Then they gave me cortisone shots in the elbow, but that didn't work, either. Finally, they sent me back to Milwaukee for an operation. I had a nerve transplanted, and they cut so much muscle that my arm was out at a right angle for about a year after that time. There was no question I'd never pitch again. They told me they just wanted to make my arm comfortable and usable."

At the age of twenty-five, Braun was out of baseball. "I decided I'd go into sales," he says, "and I worked for a wholesale liquor distributor in Wisconsin for twenty-nine years." He and his wife raised a son, Todd, and a daughter, Lisa. "My son is a deejay, and he got a job in San Diego. We went out to visit one time, and we just decided to move to the West Coast ourselves to be near him and my sister, Phyllis, who also lives near there." In January 1994, the Brauns moved to La Costa, California, where Braun is presently employed at a business consulting firm.

Asked to reflect on his days in baseball, Braun says, "Playing with three

Hall of Famers—Spahn, Aaron, and Mathews—was really special. I remember Spahn was near the end of his career around then, but he felt he could still pitch effectively. I remember one time he came back from a meeting with [general manager John] McHale and was grousing. I think the story going around the clubhouse was that he was offered either a coaching job or a minor-league manager [job] or going in the radio booth, but he didn't want to be told he couldn't pitch. I think that next year he went to the Mets."

As for today's ballplayers, Braun says: "I think the very good ballplayers, people like Tony Gwynn, [Barry] Bonds, [Ken] Griffey [Jr.], and so forth, could play at any time. But overall, the major-league talent has been diluted because of expansion. Don't forget, back then we had three Triple-A leagues, the International, the Pacific Coast, and the American Association, and they were all eight-team leagues. All that talent has been absorbed into the majors today. It's given a lot of people jobs, though, and that's good."

Braun's one-game major-league career, he finds, "has had a very positive effect" on his life. Over the years, he has often heard people say they'd give up their right arm for the chance to play in the major leagues. He just smiles and shrugs. That's just about what he did.

Ralph Michael Gagliano Jr.

CLEVELAND INDIANS, 1965

Born and raised in Memphis, Tennessee, Ralph Gagliano started to play with the "big boys" when he was thirteen years old, tagging along after his eighteen-year-old brother, Phil, who preceded him to the big leagues. (The older Gagliano brother, while primarily used as a utility man, was able to last in the majors for a dozen years, including appearances in two World Series.)

In high school, the younger brother played basketball and football as well as four years of baseball. "I was a three-sport athlete at Christian Brothers High School in Memphis, and I was probably better in the other sports than in baseball," he says. But he made All-City teams in both basketball and baseball, and was an honorable mention in football.

On the baseball team, he was a shortstop who threw right-handed and hit left-handed. In his senior year, he batted .390. "I don't know why I hit left-handed," he says. "I guess my dad or my uncle just put the bat in my hands that way when I was a kid. I never thought about it.

"I played varsity baseball as a freshman and was the only player to ever make All-Memphis as a freshman and all four years of high school," Gagliano says. His team won state championships in both his freshman and his senior years. In 1964, when he was a senior, the team lost the first game in a double-elimination tournament, then won four straight, including a doubleheader, for the title. Gagliano was named not only the outstanding athlete, but also the outstanding student in his graduating class.

Gagliano also played four years of American Legion ball for Memphis Post 1, and in 1963 the team finished second to Long Beach, California, in the national tournament held that year in Keene, New Hampshire. "I came from a baseball family," he says. "My uncle, Tony Gagliano, was a coach who was a legend around Memphis. He won 19 straight State American Legion Championships, one Little World Series, and was runner-up twice. They named a field for him. I was a batboy for my brother Phil's team, which also included Tim McCarver. My uncle would make me hit against the older guys, and so I never learned fear. I never got to feel afraid of the ball. I started playing American Legion at age thirteen, as soon as I was eligible, and one year I led the league in hitting with a .500 average. I must have broken thirty bats, if you know what I mean. It was a weak .500.

"I was scouted very heavily—and we won, which helped," he says. "Scouts began following me as a freshman, and it culminated my senior year with the state championships," he says. When he graduated from high school, Gagliano was signed by Cleveland Indians scouts Walter Shannon and Joe Morlan. "I was a $40,000 bonus baby," Gagliano says. "Hoot Evers was the vice president of personnel then, and he came down for the actual signing."

And the money? "I don't know. Seventeen-year-old kids don't think about money."

Gagliano had pulled a hamstring in his last high school game, so the Indians brought him to Cleveland for a few days to meet the local media before sending him to Dubuque, Iowa, in the Midwest League. In 75 games there, he batted only .226, but the young shortstop managed to get an average of almost one walk every game. "I was a very disciplined hitter," he says, believing a walk is as good as a hit. His on-base percentage at Dubuque was .396.

Following that first season as a professional, Gagliano started taking courses at Memphis State University. That winter, he suffered an injury which eventually affected his major-league career. "I was playing some one-on-one basketball in the off-season with a friend of mine, and I just tore ligaments in my knee," he says. As result, he was not able to go to spring training in 1965.

"They had to protect me by putting me on the big team, however, and I was kept on the [Cleveland] roster," Gagliano says. "I was put on the disabled list and spent the season working myself into shape. It was about June or July by the time I got through rehab. I used to work out with the team when they were home. I'd take batting and fielding practice before the games, go take a shower, and then go up and sit in the press box with Bob Nieman, a Cleveland scout. When the team was on the road, I'd stay back in Cleveland at the Auditorium Hotel and go out to the park every day with a batting-practice pitcher to work out.

"I wasn't really close to anyone on the team," Gagliano says, "because I was much younger than most of them. I do remember guys at the hotel, such as Stan Williams, Lu Clinton, and Ralph Terry. They were always playing gin.

"They activated me in September when they brought a lot of guys up,"

Gagliano says of the Indians. "I remember talking to Nieman about money 'cause I hadn't gotten any, and he said, 'Well, I'll talk about that with [Cleveland general manager] Gabe Paul.' Well, I got called in by Gabe Paul, who was sitting in his big old office, behind his big old desk, and he said, 'I'll give you $500 a month for every month you been out and then prorate you on the minimum for the rest of the season.' I think they paid me around $4,000 for the year. They were supposed to give me $7,500, which was the minimum, but I had no agent, and in those days you take what they give you. Besides, what does an eighteen-year-old kid say to a legend in those circumstances? 'Thank you, sir. I appreciate it.' I tell you, Curt Flood [who sued to obtain free agency in 1972] saved the day for everybody.

"I remember [manager] Birdie Tebbetts getting mad as hell with Hoot Evers about me," Gagliano says. "I must have been with the team three or four days, and I wasn't sure Birdie knew who I was. He may have thought I was a batting-practice pitcher or something. Anyway, he raised hell when he found out I was activated. 'Nobody tells me *anything*,' he was yelling at Evers. He didn't know."

On Monday, September 20, 1965, Cleveland hosted Detroit in a twi-night game before leaving for New York to begin a road trip. The game, between fourth- and fifth-place teams who were no longer in the pennant race, had a paid attendance of only 1,831. By the time it was over, some five hours and 14 innings later, only a handful remained. The Indians, using 21 players, finally won it thanks to a pinch-hit by Chico Salmon, and five and two-thirds innings of scoreless relief pitching by Sam McDowell. It was a weary Indians team that traveled to New York.

The next night at Yankee Stadium, eighteen-year-old Ralph Gagliano got his chance to play in the major leagues.

At the end of the first four innings that night, the Yanks held a commanding 9–1 lead and had already knocked out their former teammate Ralph Terry, the Indians' starter, as well as reliever Floyd Weaver. Cleveland was able to come back and scratch out three more runs over the next couple of innings, but the Yankee starter, Mel Stottlemyre, going for the 19th of his 20 wins that year, then shut them down.

Trailing 9–4 in the ninth, Cleveland shortstop Larry Brown, who had previously doubled off Stottlemyre, singled for his second hit, which was only the Indians' fifth hit of the game. Gagliano entered the game as a pinch-runner for Brown. "It was funny," he says, "because Birdie said, 'Gags, go run.' I had been there a month, and as I said, I didn't think he knew my name. I like to fell out when he said that.

"Joe Pepitone was holding me on, Bobby Richardson was playing second, and I think Bobby Murcer, who came up as a shortstop, was playing short. Our first base coach was George Strickland, and third base was Solly Hemus.

"I was petrified—eighteen years old in Yankee Stadium, where all the great players had played. I took about a two-foot lead because I didn't want to draw a throw. I was almost frozen. It was hard to get my legs to move. If he [Stottlemyre] would have thrown, he would have got me, because I couldn't move. I was scared to death.

"I know Richie Scheinblum pinch hit [for catcher Joe Azcue]. I was rooming with him. I think Shiner hit the first pitch, a high chopper to Richardson, and they forced me at second. I tore my pants and got a strawberry on my butt. It was great. Now I could walk around the locker room and show off my battle scar. From then on I walked around naked a lot," he laughs. Thus ended his one-game major-league career.

But Gagliano has a number of recollections of his teammates and his experiences with the team. "I remember being on the bench when, I think it was [Bill] Monbouquette, pitched a no-hitter against us [it was Dave Morehead]. I remember waiting for Birdie to say, 'Okay, Gags, bust this thing up.' That was my dream. I really felt I could get a hit off him.

"I remember [second baseman] Pedro Gonzalez charging Larry Sherry, who was with Detroit, with a bat. Suddenly I'm on the bench by myself. I stayed close to [outfielder] Leon Wagner," he laughs.

"I remember 'Daddy Wags' [Wagner] saying one day that only in Cleveland can you get 'a spook, an injun, and a dago in the outfield.' He was referring to himself, Vic Davalillo, and Rocky Colavito. He was a character.

"I remember seeing a young kid in Boston taking early batting practice. He became one of the greats, Carl Yastrzemski.

"In Detroit, Scheinblum and I walked in a restaurant and Rocky Colavito was eating by himself. He motioned us over, and we joined him. I said I wanted to pick up the check so I could tell my dad I bought Rocky Colavito dinner. He picked up the tab and said, 'Tell your dad that Rocky Colavito bought you dinner.' A gentleman's gentleman. He was class all the way. And he had a great arm, you know. I'd warm up with him before a game, and Rocky would tell me to get a catcher's mitt 'cause he didn't want to hurt me.

"Louie Tiant was old then, but he said he was twenty-three. Vic Davalillo had great talent, but if there was something he didn't like, he gave you that 'no-speak-English' stuff. Other times he spoke fine.

"Sam McDowell would always try to drag bunt when he hit. He never did beat one out. He was unbelievable. Nobody could hit his fastball. He had the best fastball in baseball, but he loved to throw his curve. That was the only pitch they could hit. He struck out Willie Horton five times in one game.

"I remember what a great guy Dick Howser was and how they [all] treated me. They would include me in golf outings and the Peppermint Lounge in New York—they treated me like a teammate. I'll never forget the class with which I was treated. Lu Clinton and Ralph Terry took me to play golf at a private club in Detroit. Terry was a good golfer and played there when he was with the Yankees. Everything was free—

clothes, shoes, clubs, sweater, and so forth. I asked him what I should do, and he said, 'Tip the clubhouse guy $10.' I remember Duke Sims prodding Terry. If you know anything about Terry, you'll know what I mean."

In 1966, Gagliano was sent to Portland for spring training and then assigned to Reno in the California League. "Phil Cavaretta was the manager, and he was mean as a snake," Gagliano says. "He was a good manager, though, but if you loafed, he really got in your face.

"Cleveland was a weak team financially and in its management, and that was a strange year," Gagliano says. "All my life, I played shortstop. All through spring training that year, I played shortstop. All of a sudden, on opening day, I was playing second base. I had never played second base in my life, but that season I played the entire year at second. The guy who played shortstop was Don Gadbury, and we could hardly make a double play all year long. We were always missing by a step. We didn't make many friends on the pitching staff that year," he chuckles.

Remaining a "disciplined" hitter, Gagliano had a batting average of only .243 that year, but again garnered an average of almost one walk a game, thus bringing his on-base percentage to .403.

"That was during the Vietnam conflict," Gagliano says, "and they were drafting something like 60,000 men a month. Ray Fosse, my roommate, and I were both ordered to report for army physicals at the same time. I had had a school deferment up 'til then 'cause I had been going to Memphis State in the off-season. Another guy on the team, Phil Hennigan, who was a pretty dadgum good pitcher, also got drafted then. [Both Fosse and Hennigan later had successful careers in the majors.]

"I notified the ball club, and they said they couldn't help. So about two weeks before the season was over, I went home to Memphis to sign up in the reserves, figuring I might be able to stay out of the draft that way. I signed the papers and they were sent through and I waited to hear. We took off around then to go to St. Louis to see my brother, Phil, and McCarver play with the Cards. When we got back, my draft notice was waiting for me. I called up the reserve guy and told him I got my draft notice and asked him if I should tear it up, since I already signed up for the reserves. He said, 'Did you open it?' and I said, 'Yes,' and he said, 'Well, then, I can't touch you.' That was the most depressing time of my life."

Gagliano was drafted into the army in August 1966 and sent to Fort Campbell, Kentucky. "I was training to be an infantry grunt," he says. "But I decided to apply for artillery OCS [Officer Candidate School]. It involved ten months of school and then a two-year commitment. I discussed it with my folks, and we agreed that since I really didn't have any real schooling, another ten months wouldn't make a lot of difference in my life. So I went to OCS and became a lieutenant and served in the Third Armored Division in Germany."

Discharged in 1969, Gagliano reported to the Indians' training camp in Tucson to start 1970. "When I returned, there were all new people—Al

Cleveland Indians News Release

Write, Phone or Wire for Further Information • Cleveland Indians • Cleveland 14, Ohio • TOwer 1-1200

Monday, June 8

FOR IMMEDIATE RELEASE

The Cleveland Indians today announced the signing of Ralph Michael Gagliano of Memphis, Tenn. to a contract. In making the announcement, General Manager Gabe Paul indicated that the Indians had given the 17 year old infielder a large bonus. Seventeen of the 20 major league clubs had sought the youngster.

A graduate of C B C High School in Memphis, Gagliano was one of the finest student athletes in Memphis scholastic history. He was All-City in baseball, basketball and football in 1963-1964 and captained the baseball and basketball teams.

He won the Julius Lewis trophy for the best student athlete at his high school and was the winner of the Memphis Civitan Award for the best contribution of any student to his school. He had a .390 batting average in high school. Gagliano is five feet, 11 inches tall, weighs 170 pounds, bats left, throws right.

His older brother, Phil, is an infielder with the St. Louis Cardinals.

The news release sent out by the Cleveland Indians when they announced the signing of seventeen-year-old Gagliano for what he says was a $40,000 bonus.

Dark, Ken Aspromonte, Joe Lutz—who didn't have any idea who I was," he says. "Evers was gone, and I went from an eighteen-year-old phenom to a twenty-two-year-old who hadn't played in three years and had no political connections. I think they gave me number 122 in spring training. I had a good spring, but they had their own agenda."

Gagliano was assigned back to Reno, where he played the 1970 season, batting .275. Counting the bases on balls he received, his on-base average reached .417. But again, the Indians passed him over at the next year's training camp. "I had another good spring," he says, "but they still had their own agenda. They wanted to go with young kids and wanted me to go to Jacksonville. My career was over. At that time, there was no free agency, and they would not give me a release. I went home and went back to college on the GI Bill."

About a week later, he got a call from Hank Peters, Cleveland's director of player personnel. "He asked if I'd be interested in playing in Memphis, right in my own hometown. He said he was working on a deal with the Mets which would bring me to Memphis," Gagliano says. "I told him I *definitely* would be interested. But the deal was nixed.

"I didn't find out about it 'til later, but it was Johnny Antonelli, who was managing Memphis, who quashed the deal," Gagliano says. "See, Johnny is from Memphis, too, and he didn't want the pressure of managing me here in our hometown. You know, if he had me on the team and didn't play me, he could get a lot of local heat."

After another month passed, Cleveland asked Gagliano to return to play at Jacksonville and he agreed. "They had a kid named Clark at shortstop who couldn't hit lefties," Gagliano says, "so we alternated. I played against lefties and he played against righties. It was a bad situation, and after about a month, I quit and came home."

At twenty-five, the one-time major leaguer was out of professional baseball. "I had some tough years adapting," Gagliano admits. "They wanted me to go to Reno as a player-coach, but I was just not interested. I operated a hamburger place for a while—my dad had been in the wholesale food business most of his life—and I played a lot of golf."

In 1978, fourteen years after he first enrolled at Memphis State, Gagliano graduated with a bachelor's degree in business administration. "It wasn't easy," he says. He was married in 1980 and joined his father working at D. Casale Foodservice in Memphis the same year. The marriage ended five years later, but Gagliano is still with the 128-year-old food service company, currently as its general manager. "Today, my dad works for me," he laughs. He remarried about two years ago.

Summing up his major-league experience, Gagliano says, "It has given me a thrill that can't be replaced. I do not like to look back because sometimes it is depressing, since I had a great chance to have a good career. Fate was not with me. However," he adds, "it is great to still get requests for autographs in the mail and sign cards people send."

Lavern George "Woody" Holtgrave

DETROIT TIGERS, 1965

Though he played a little basketball in high school, baseball was clearly Vern Holtgrave's sport. He was a tall, skinny kid who threw really hard. At the time, he stood six-foot-one and weighed only 140 pounds, but nobody could touch him.

"When I was three years old, I had a hernia, and they wouldn't let me pitch when I was growing up," he recalls, "so I was a catcher first. I really didn't pitch until high school." But when he pitched in high school, he *pitched*.

"In my three years there, I had 12 no-hitters and an earned run average of 0.026," he says. "They were only seven-inning games, but still no-hitters. My high school coach said he wrote his college thesis on me. Because I threw hard, one time he took me down to a coaching clinic in Carbondale [Illinois], along with a football player and a wrestler, and they put us through some tests to test arm strength. Well, it turned out that I could push as much as they could and could pull as much as they could. I never did see the thesis, but I'm told it's still down there in Carbondale."

His high school was in the small town of Aviston, Illinois, where he was born in 1942, the fourth of five children. Probably because of the lack of high-quality competition, the school was never invited to a state tournament despite Holtgrave's impressive statistics. "But as a fifteen-year-old, I played on the county team with grown men," he says.

After graduation in 1960, Al Thomas, a bird dog for Detroit, approached the youngster. "He had five of us," Holtgrave says, "Pat Jarvis, Tom Timmerman, Floyd Logger, Dave Richter, and me. He brought Joe Mathis, the head scout, around to sign us.

"But I didn't want to sign with the Tigers," Holtgrave says. "You see, just before then I had gone to a tryout camp with Pittsburgh, and I could tell they liked me. I told them that the Tigers were coming to talk with me, and the people from Pittsburgh told me, 'Whatever you do, don't sign.'

"So that night, Al Thomas and Joe Mathis from Detroit came to my house, and they sat around the table with me and my mother, talking. My dad was very stubborn and sat in the other room. He wouldn't take part in the discussion. They offered me a salary of $400 a month and a $500 bonus that night. Well, I wanted to wait for Pittsburgh, but my dad walked into the room and said, 'Goddamn it, if you want to be a ballplayer, sign it or forget it!' So I signed with the Tigers.

"The next day," Holtgrave continues, "the guy from Pittsburgh came around—I think his name was Paul Trediak—and he offered me $600 a month and an $8,000 bonus! I had to tell him I already signed with Detroit. When my dad came home from work that night—he was a trackman on the B & O Railroad—I told him what happened, and he cried."

In early 1961, the eighteen-year-old Holtgrave reported to the Tigers' training camp in Lakeland, Florida. "I was nervous," he admits. "I remember it was my first plane ride and the camp was a small version of army camp. We stayed at a former air base barracks, I think, with cots, and everybody ate together at the same time—very regimented."

For his first season in professional ball, Detroit assigned Holtgrave to Decatur in the Class-D Midwest League, under the tutelage of Johnny Groth, a former Tigers outfielder and veteran of fifteen seasons in the big leagues. "I was 7 and 13 there," he says, "but my earned run average was in the low threes, like 3.20 [3.81]."

In 1962, the following year, he moved up to Duluth in the Class-C Northern League, where he won 13 and lost 8. His earned run average remained at 2.83, not quite as low as his high school record, but still impressive.

"That year I played winter ball in Dunedin, Florida," he says, "where Phil Cavaretta was managing. We understood that if the team wanted you to play winter ball, they were interested in you; they thought you were a prospect. So I was pleased to go and work on my curve. I felt they thought well of me." By then, he had added about forty pounds to his formerly skinny frame.

When spring camp began in February of 1963, Holtgrave had been pitching all year long and had not had much rest. The Tigers sent him to their Class-A farm team in Knoxville in the Southern League that year. He pitched well, mainly as a reliever and spot starter, and had an excellent 2.48 earned run average. "My roommate in Knoxville was Denny McLain. Denny and I and Tom Matchick and Tom Timmerman would always ride horses together almost every day we were at home off the road trips," he remembers. "I also heard that year that a team in Japan was

*Warming up on the mound. Vern Holtgrave was so wild, he says, the
first batter he faced "never stepped in solid and I struck him out."*

interested in buying my contract from Detroit, and I was approached
about it, but I just didn't want to go."

After the 1963 season, for the second straight year, Holtgrave returned
to Dunedin, where Tiger coach Bob Swift was then managing, and again
pitched winter ball.

Returning home before training camp was to start in 1964, he went
out one February evening to what he calls "a local dance hall," where he
saw his friend, Timmerman, sitting with some other people. "I went over
to say hi," Holtgrave says, "and Tom introduced me to one of the girls at

the table. I had seen her before, but I never had met her. Then they played a slow song, so I asked her to dance."

The girl was Peggy Brassel, and they were married just three months later. "I knew her ninety days before we were married," Holtgrave laughs, "and sixty of those days I was away in training camp. I came home in April to get married, and the next day we flew to Knoxville [where he played again for most of that year], and I left immediately on a 12-day road trip."

While the courtship was short, the marriage lasted more than twenty-seven years until Peggy's untimely death in 1991, after a three-year illness.

As a newlywed, Holtgrave won 8 and lost 10 for Knoxville in 1964, again primarily as a reliever. He was then promoted to Syracuse, Detroit's Triple-A franchise in the International League, and finished the year there, winning two and losing one.

After that season, for the first time in three years, Holtgrave did not play winter ball, choosing instead to work with his father as a switchman and foreman for the B & O Railroad in East St. Louis. He was able to go to training camp in 1965 without being "played out" from another winter. As it turned out, it was some year for him.

"First, my appendix busted," Holtgrave says. "We had just gotten to spring training, and I wasn't feeling well. My stomach was bothering me, so I went to the doctor and he treated me for the 24-hour flu. But, evidently, the poison was already in my system. One morning about 6 A.M., I woke up in such pain I couldn't move. The appendix had burst. My wife and my sister, Marilyn, bodily carried me into the Plant City, Florida, hospital.

"After I recovered, they sent me back to [Class] A ball, down to Rocky Mount, North Carolina, for a month to get myself back in shape. I was 3 and 3 there [as a reliever] and had a real low earned run average [2.25]. Then they sent me to Montgomery, Alabama, in Double-A, and I had a 1.91 earned run average. Late in the year, for about three weeks, I went back to Syracuse, but I had no record there although my ERA was fine."

After suffering a ruptured appendix, playing with three different teams in three different leagues, and becoming a father (his daughter, Cori Ann, was born in August), Holtgrave's one-time major-league appearance in 1965 was almost anticlimactic.

Detroit called him up from Syracuse for the last month of the parent team's season. "They finished fourth that year," Holtgrave says, "and were still fighting for playoff money that month, so they didn't use the rookies much." He recalls traveling with the team to Cleveland, Baltimore, Chicago, and New York before returning to Detroit. "I remember being in New York for Mickey Mantle Day," he says.

Among his closest friends on the team then were McLain, Matchick, and the rookie left-handed pitcher John Hiller. "I knew most all the players on the team fairly well from either the minors or spring training," he says.

"Al Kaline was very nice to me. I used to pitch batting practice, and he always made you feel at home, made you feel part of the team, even if you were a rookie. And Mickey Lolich was the club nut. He was a very funny guy, and he was always the guy you watched to see what he'd do next. Gates Brown was another nice guy, and so was Mickey Stanley, who is still a good friend."

On Saturday, September 25, Tigers manager Charlie Dressen told Holtgrave he would start the second game of the next day's doubleheader at Tiger Stadium against Detroit's chief rival, the Cleveland Indians. The Indians finished fifth that year, just two games behind Detroit.

"Oh, I was excited, nervous, anxious, you name the word," Holtgrave says. "I called home and told my folks. I didn't sleep much. You know."

In the first game the next day, left fielder Gates Brown hit a home run, and Lolich shut out the Indians, 2–0, on three hits. But when the second game began, Phil Regan, not Vern Holtgrave, was the Tigers' starting pitcher. "I guess the race was still too close with the playoff money at stake," Holtgrave says, "so Dressen wanted to use someone with more experience. But when Cleveland scored four or five [five] runs off of Regan in the first few innings, Dressen told me to warm up.

"I was warming up in the bullpen, and you know how catchers can sometimes make it sound like you're really throwing hard by letting it make a big popping sound? Well, the fact was I was throwing it harder then than I had ever thrown it before," he continues. "I don't remember who the catcher was. It was either Jackie Moore or John Sullivan [it was Moore], and I remember some fan leaned over from the stands and asked him, 'Who *is* that?'"

After Bill Roman pinch hit for Regan in the bottom of the third, Holtgrave was called into the game to start the top of the fourth inning. "I'll never forget the walk from the bullpen to the mound," Holtgrave says. "My stomach was nervous, and it just kept getting smaller and smaller. Man, was I nervous! I started warming up and I threw my first pitch over Bill Freehan's head and it got stuck in the back screen." (The Tigers' catcher in this second game was actually Sullivan; Freehan had caught the first game.)

Cleveland center fielder Vic Davalillo, a .301 hitter that year, was the first batter Holtgrave faced. "After seeing me throw the warm-up pitch over the catcher's head," Holtgrave says, "he never stepped in solid, and I struck him out. I was throwing blind. I didn't know what I was doing."

After striking out Davalillo, however, Holtgrave gave up two runs. He doesn't recall exactly what happened, but remembers two walks and an error and then Indians shortstop Dick Howser "hit a rope, a line drive rope" that scored the two runs and made it 7–0, Indians.

After that inning, Holtgrave went on to pitch two more innings against the Indians, holding them scoreless. "I was feeling a lot better as the game went on," he says. "I was more relaxed." He remembers striking out

Cleveland outfielder Leon Wagner. "And Rocky Colavito popped up on a change-up." In addition to the hit by Howser, Holtgrave gave up three others during his three innings on the mound. "The others weren't hit hard, though," he says. "Texas Leaguers."

By the time Holtgrave's turn to bat came around in the bottom of the sixth, Detroit was still down 7–0, and Indians rookie Tom Kelley was on his way to a two-hit victory. "I really wanted to bat," Holtgrave says, "but Ray Oyler, of all people, pinch hit for me. I think he popped out."

The pinch-hitter was actually rookie Wayne Redmond, although Oyler did play shortstop that day. Oyler, a good defensive infielder and a close friend and roommate of Holtgrave's, was a notoriously poor hitter. Redmond's batting record was not impressive, either. In seven official times up in the major leagues, he never got a hit.

"I was still nervous and excited after the game," Holtgrave remembers. "People kept telling me I did okay, you know, and all that crap, but I felt bad that I gave up those two runs." (A seventh inning home run by Detroit's first baseman Norm Cash had made the final score 7–1.)

With the season coming to an end, Holtgrave was called in to see Dressen and the Tigers' general manager, Jim Campbell. Holtgrave had earned the major-league minumum of $14,000 that year. "They wanted me to go down to Dunedin and play winter ball again, but I didn't want to go. My wife and I had just had our first baby that August, and I didn't want to go. I told them I had a railroad job lined up for that winter. They had told me on the railroad that I had a job whenever I wanted it.

"'I don't care,' Dressen said. 'I want you to go down and pitch once a week and throw your fastball and your curve.' He promised that if I played ball that winter, he'd bring me up to the Tigers the next year."

Dressen's managing career with Detroit—and Detroit's own field leadership—was somewhat strange in the early 1960s. After managing four other teams in the big leagues during the course of a dozen years, the sixty-five-year-old Dressen replaced Bob Scheffing as Tigers manager in mid-1963. Dressen managed the team through the 1964 season, but in 1965 the Tigers started the year with Bob Swift as their manager. Dressen, however, came back to replace Swift after only 42 games and, consequently, was the manager when Holtgrave first arrived.

"So I went down to Dunedin," Holtgrave says, "and even before I got to play in a game, we were all sitting around outside one day—Mickey Stanley, Ray Oyler, and me—and the phone rang and it was for me. Instead of playing at Dunedin, the Tigers wanted me to go and play in Puerto Rico. I asked my wife, 'What do *you* want to do?' She said, 'I don't know. What do you want to do?' I said, 'What the heck, we'll probably never get another chance to go to Puerto Rico. Why not?' So we went to Puerto Rico, and that's when I hurt my arm."

Something happened to Holtgrave's shoulder in Puerto Rico that caused him pain when he threw. It proved to be the end of his major-league career. "It was too bad because I knew I had a major-league fastball, but when I went to spring training in 1966, I just didn't have it anymore."

The Tigers sent him back to Syracuse. "But my arm still hurt. I couldn't control it," Holtgrave says. "I started favoring the shoulder and that hurt my elbow and finally my arm became crooked. Detroit sent me to a doctor for some tests, and he gave me cortisone and put my arm in a cast. I went home for the rest of the year and sold cars."

In 1967, Holtgrave returned to the Tigers for spring training in Mayo Smith's first year. "But it wasn't there anymore," he says. "Every night, I would get a five-gallon tub of ice and a five-gallon bucket of water as hot as I could stand it, and put my arm first in one and then in the other. Finally, one night, I just said to myself, 'What do I need this for? I've got a wife and child to support.' So I called it quits."

Holtgrave returned home to Illinois and spent the next six years working for the B & O. But, for a fleeting moment, there was almost a comeback.

"In 1968," Holtgrave says, "I began pitching for the Clinton County team, where I had played when I was a kid. It was amateur ball, but I pitched six shutouts in a row. The arm was feeling good again. In my first three games, I gave up only seven hits and seven walks, but I struck out 54 men in those three games. I called Detroit and told them about it and said I'd like to try again if I could get my old salary. They said no, that I'd have to start all over. But I didn't want to do that. So I thought I'd try Montreal because I heard when I was at Knoxville that they were interested in me. I thought about being a player-coach. But Detroit refused to release me, and to this day, I've never seen any release papers."

In 1970, Holtgrave's second daughter, Staci, was born, and in 1973, he left the railroad to move to a warehouse job with Sears and Roebuck. He currently is employed in the sales department of the Haag Food and Poultry Company. In addition to his two children, he has three grandchildren. "And one on the way," he laughs.

Holtgrave still misses baseball and, in recent years, has travelled to Florida for Tigers alumni get-togethers. "I really enjoy those," he says and admits he'd be receptive to a baseball-related job offer.

"I just wish I had a chance to redo the opportunities I had later—like being a player-coach for Montreal and taking the chance to play in Japan," he says. "I was young, scared, and stupid. But my seven years in baseball were the most fun years of my life."

Harvey Tillman Shank Jr.

CALIFORNIA ANGELS, 1970

Harvey Shank was an outstanding athlete as a youngster, he was a mainstay of his high school and college teams, and in his one major-league appearance, he pitched three scoreless innings.

Yet he was never given the chance to play in the major leagues again.

The oldest of three sons and a daughter of a design engineer, Shank was born on July 29, 1946, in Toronto, Canada, but grew up in Woodside, California, where his parents moved in 1949.

"I played all three sports in high school—baseball, basketball, and football—" Shank says, "and I was good at all of them. I was a tight end in football, a forward on the basketball team, and pitched in baseball. We had some good teams. We were always competitive in basketball and football, and in my senior year, we were the district champs in baseball."

After his graduation from Woodside High School in 1964, Shank enrolled at Wheaton College in Illinois. "My mother had been involved and associated with that school for a long time," he says, "and they offered me a full ride. I was only there a year, but I had a great time. I played both varsity baseball and basketball and had a great time. I didn't have anything special in mind as far as studies went.

"After a year, I switched to Stanford," he continues, "for the opportunity to play in a top baseball program. I had to sit out a year because of the transfer, because that was the rule, so I only played there as a junior and senior."

(In 1967, Shank's junior year, his coach at Stanford was a man who had played in one major-league game with the Chicago White Sox back in 1934, William "Dutch" Fehring: see Chapter 3.)

In his junior year, Shank compiled a 2.70 earned run average as a relief pitcher, winning two and losing one. In 20 innings, he struck out 24 batters and helped lead the team to the Pacific 8 Conference title. In the district playoff, he pitched three shutout innings in relief against Fresno State and was awarded a save when Stanford won the rubber game of the three-game series to advance to the College World Series.

"Dutch retired the next year, and Ray Young was the coach in my senior year," Shank says. As a senior, Shank completed 12 of his 13 starts, pitched 5 shutouts, struck out 83, and walked only 19 in 98 innings, while winning 10 and losing 3. His earned run average was 1.10, which still stands as a conference record.

"I graduated in 1968 with a degree in political science," Shank says, "and right after that, I went to play semipro ball for the Boulder, Colorado, Collegians. The [California] Angels drafted me that summer, in the tenth round, I think."

Two weeks before his twenty-second birthday, the six-foot-four, 220-pound right-hander was signed by Ross Gilhousen of the Angels and immediately assigned to San Jose in the California League. "Del Rice was the manager," Shank says, "and I'll never forget this. The day before I was supposed to pitch my first game in professional ball, Del got real upset at the pitchers on the staff and decided he was going to run the pitchers 'til they dropped. He had us all running and wore us out. Well, the next day, I started my first game as a professional and I won the game. I thought I'd be too tired out, but in fact, it was one of the better games I ever pitched." Shank laughs, "I thought maybe he ought to run us like that before every game.

"Del was a wonderful man, an excellent teacher, and he really cared for his players," Shank says. "He was my manager later at El Paso and Salt Lake City. I remember he loved to play golf, and he would sometimes come out to the ballpark with a bunch of golf balls and put them down around the third base line and then hit seven-irons over the left field fence."

At San Jose, Shank won four and lost six, but had a fine 2.22 earned run average. In 73 innings, he struck out 53 and walked just 18.

"Right after that season, I went traveling with my dad to Chicago and Detroit, where he had some business," Shank says, "and I remember we went to one of the 1968 World Series games in Detroit that [Mickey] Lolich pitched. I don't remember which game it was, but I know Lolich pitched."

It would have been game five, played on October 7. That year, Lolich led Detroit to victory over the St. Louis Cardinals by winning three games of the exciting Series—two in St. Louis. On this particular day, with the Cardinals leading the series three games to one, Lolich, who had started and won game two, went all the way again for Detroit's second win.

"After the Series, I just went home that winter and worked out to get ready for the next year," Shank says.

Shank began the 1969 season at El Paso in the Texas League, where Rice again was his manager. "That year, they turned me back into a relief pitcher," he says. He won eight, lost three, had an earned run average of 3.09, and was chosen to play in the league's All-Star game. "It was a thrill to be selected," he says, "but I didn't play. I was in the [Army] reserves, and by the time the game was played, I had been called up for six months of active duty." He missed the last eight weeks of the season, spending the time in service at Fort Leonard Wood, Missouri.

In December of that year, shortly after being released from active duty, Shank was married to Mary Jo Thiessen. The marriage ended in divorce in 1985, but today their son is pitching at Stanford University.

In 1970, Shank attended his first big-league training camp. "It was my *only* big-league training camp," he laughs. "It was in Palm Springs, and the players I remember most were [rookie pitcher] Dave LaRoche, who was my roommate, and [shortstop Jim] Fregosi.

"Johnny Sain was the [Angels'] minor-league pitching coach there, and he had his own philosophy about training," Shank says. "Sain's approach was 'Run if you want to.' Norm Sherry was the major-league pitching coach, and he was responsible for the major-league pitchers and those who had a shot at making the team. Sain handled the fringe players or those who were going to end up in the minors, which was the group I was in, and he just didn't think that running a lot had that much to do with getting ready to pitch. So, by the second or third day, our group was all showered and dressed by the time the first stringers came in collapsing with their tongues hanging out. I remember Rudy May coming in, and he was sweating bullets. He saw us and said, 'I'm gonna have a talk with someone. This stuff has got to stop!' So, the next day, they had someone else in charge of our running.

"Sain was good, though, a tremendous teacher, and I found it [training camp] enjoyable," Shank says.

The Angels assigned Shank to their Triple-A affiliate in Hawaii in the Pacific Coast League to start the year. "Chuck Tanner was the manager there. He was a very intense guy, but he really looked out for his players," Shank says.

"I was only in Hawaii a short time when I suddenly got called up to the Angels for a weekend," Shank continues. "I was going up to replace Steve Kealey, who was one of the Angels' pitchers. He had been called up for a weekend military commitment, so I knew I was only going up for the weekend.

"Why me? I don't know. I guess they just called Tanner and asked, 'Who do you have available you can spare?'" Shank laughs. "I flew from Hawaii to Oakland on a Thursday and met the team there. The day after I got there, I was interviewed by the Angels' play-by-play announcer, Dick Enberg, on the radio. That was a big thrill. I played that Saturday and then went back to Hawaii.

"I had a very heavy tan when I arrived," Shank says. "When you play at night in Hawaii, you spend most of the daytime on the beach, so I had a very deep tan when I got to Oakland. I remember getting a lot of grief about it from all the players, everybody from Fregosi on down. 'It looks like you're sure working *haaard*,' they'd say, and things like that."

The game in which Shank appeared was played on May 16, 1970, at the Oakland Coliseum, two days after his arrival. The A's, under the ownership of Charley Finley, had moved to Oakland from Kansas City two years earlier. The stadium, which could seat more than 47,000 fans, held only 5,553 that Saturday afternoon. "It was interesting," Shank says, "but, you know, there were more people at the minor-league game in Hawaii than there were at the big-league game I was in. In Hawaii that year, we set a minor-league attendance record. I remember Al Michaels was the play-by-play announcer there, and now I watch him doing *Monday Night Football*."

The game started with right-hander Tom Murphy on the mound for California, against another right-hander, Chuck Dobson of Oakland. Home runs by Felipe Alou, Dave Duncan, and Dick Green helped Oakland jump off to a 7–0 lead in the first four innings, including a five-run outburst in the bottom of the fourth, at which point Paul Doyle was called in to relieve Murphy and get the final out. "I was in the bullpen," Shank recalls, "and Lefty Phillips, the manager, called down and said, 'Warm up. You're going in.'"

In the top of the fifth, the Angels came back to score twice on a single by left fielder Alex Johnson and a home run by third baseman Ken McMullen. With the score 7–2, the twenty-three-year-old Harvey Shank came in to pitch the bottom of the fifth for California. The Oakland lineup he faced had Bert Campaneris at shortstop, Rick Monday in center field, Alou in left, Reggie Jackson in right, Sal Bando at third, Don Mincher at first, Duncan behind the plate, Green at second, and Dobson pitching. (It was the core of the team that went on to win a divisional championship the following year in 1971, and three consecutive World Series in 1972, 1973, and 1974.)

"I felt nervous going in," Shank admits. "I was excited to be out there. Tom Egan was the catcher, and he was giving me the signs. He must have thought I lost it 'cause I shook him off on everything. I was calling my own game."

Shank held Oakland scoreless for the three innings, giving up two hits and two walks, and striking out one. "I don't remember the exact order, but Campaneris got a bunt single in that first inning I pitched," he says. "I just knew he was gonna bunt, but I couldn't do anything about it. The other hit was by Alou in the next inning. He hit one through the middle that Fregosi knocked down but couldn't do anything with.

"One of the walks went to Reggie [Jackson]. I walked him on a 3–2 slider. I'll never forget that. The two strikes I got on him were swinging strikes on sliders. He missed them, but the wind blast from his bat would part your hair. If he ever hit one, it would still be going," Shank says with awe. "I don't remember who got the other walk. I struck out Dick Green.

"I remember I threw a slider to Bando that was up in his eyes. His eyes got so big when he saw it; he couldn't wait to hit it. He swung so hard that he just popped it up to the catcher. If you ask him today, I'll bet he'll say he should have hit that one out of the park."

In the top of the sixth, between Shank's first and second innings on the mound, California scored another run against Dobson, this one unearned, to bring the score to 7–3.

"The first inning I pitched, I don't remember very much. I was operating on adrenaline," Shank says. "But by the second inning, I had settled down, and I remember thinking, 'I'm actually *here*.' It was a thrill."

Shank remembers the bottom of the sixth most about his appearance. "I loaded the bases in that second inning I pitched," he says. "Now I've played ball ever since I could remember—high school, college, everything. But in all that time, I had never ever tried to pick a runner off second with the bases loaded. And here I am, in my first game in the major leagues, and Fregosi is giving the signal for the pickoff play at second!

"According to the way the play is supposed to work, as soon as the catcher drops his glove, I'm supposed to whirl around and throw to second, where Fregosi is coming in behind the runner. But when the catcher dropped his glove, I hesitated just a second before throwing. Had I not hesitated just that little bit, I would have picked the guy off second.

"I never, ever tried that play before or since," Shank says, "but it happened in the only game I played in the major leagues."

Today, Shank does not recall any between-innings conversation. "I think Egan told me, 'Just keep throwing strikes.'"

After retiring the A's again in the bottom of the seventh, Shank was scheduled to bat in the top of the eighth. "There was no way they were gonna let me hit," he laughs. Chico Ruiz pinch hit for him unsuccessfully against Dobson, who allowed only three hits in the whole game. Shank's roommate, LaRoche, then came in to pitch the bottom of the eighth and was greeted by a leadoff home run by Campaneris. The A's went on to score four runs in that inning and eventually won the game, 11–3.

"I felt bad for David," Shank says, "but for myself, I was elated that I had gone three scoreless innings. It was a great thrill."

Recalling some of his major-league teammates, Shank says Fregosi is the one he remembers most. "He went to Serra High School, which is near Woodside, and I had known of him as a tremendous athlete for some time. He was the one I was in awe of. He was definitely the leader of that team.

"I remember seeing Alex Johnson do something in spring training that I had never seen before," Shank says. "He was a massive man, with huge arms, and he would crank up the pitching machine so that it was throwing about 105 miles an hour. Then, instead of getting into the batting cage sixty feet away, he would stand only about forty-five feet away and just fight the ball off, trying to speed up his swing. It was awesome.

"[Pitcher] Andy Messersmith was a [University of] Cal product and I was from Stanford, and we'd get into it once in a while, teasing each other about our schools. Paul Doyle had the best pickoff move in all of baseball," Shank continues. "He'd go through all kinds of crazy motions and looked like an octopus, coming from all over. You never knew where the ball was coming from. He used to pick off the umpires!"

After his weekend in the big leagues, Shank returned to Hawaii and finished the year there with a 7–3 record, mostly in relief, and a 4.28 earned run average. He spent the off-season working part-time in customer relations in Chicago for Servicemaster, a major industrial cleaning company.

In 1971, Shank again played in the Pacific Coast League, this time at Salt Lake City, where he was reunited with manager Del Rice. He got into 53 games that year, all in relief, and pitched a career-high 103 innings. He had a 4–3 record and his earned run average was 4.28, exactly the same as it was in Hawaii. "One day that year, I gave Greg Luzinski one of the longest home runs he ever had in his life," Shank says. "Every June 12, the people in Salt Lake City look up in the sky and see it coming around again," he jokes. "But we had a good team and won the championship, even though we didn't finish first in the regular season.

"After that, I wanted to give it one more year," he says. "I had no real illusions that I was going to be the world's best relief pitcher. I had turned twenty-five, and I had my degree from Stanford, and I talked it over with my wife and decided to get on with my life.

"I took an off-season job with the Phoenix Suns in the front office, primarily marketing and selling tickets," Shank says. "It was only their third season, and Jerry Colangelo was the general manager then. He helped advise me in my contract negotiations with the Angels. The amount of raise they were offering me was small, and I wanted something more substantial. After we went back and forth for a while, the Angels suggested I might be better off if I kept working for Mr. Colangelo instead of playing baseball. That's what I did, and I've been here ever since."

In 1987, Colangelo bought the Suns and became the president of the National Basketball Association team, and Shank was named vice president of marketing. He is currently in charge of corporate and group sales, radio and broadcast relations, among other things.

"I really enjoy it," Shank says of his job. "I guess I should tell you about Charles Barkley," he says. "I remember when we got him in 1992, Jerry and [Suns' coach] Cotton Fitzsimmons were showing him around America West Arena. They specifically pointed out that the building had been built before he got here. Then they pointed to the seats and told him, 'All these seats were sold before you got here.' Finally, they pointed to the rafters and said, 'But there are no NBA championship banners up there. That's why we got you.'

"In all my years in pro sports, Barkley is one of the best people I know in handling interviews," Shank says. "He's mentally the quickest on his feet, and his intelligence belies his demeanor. He's got a tremendous depth of knowledge.

"Right after we got him, we had a press conference, and the second question out of the box was 'How do you feel about playing in the only state that hasn't approved the Martin Luther King holiday?' Now, there must have been fifty to a hundred reporters there from all over, and that's the second question asked. Everybody was waiting for him to say something that would create a headline saying, 'Barkley blasts Arizonians,' or something like that. Instead, he starts out by saying that if he lived in a state where some people were threatening to cancel the Super Bowl there or not play the Fiesta bowl or cancel conventions, he would be concerned, but would say, 'Nobody threatens me.' Then he went on and said, 'Martin Luther King is one of my heroes, but right now, I think we got more than enough holidays to go around.' Now, he did that on the spur of the moment, right off the top of his head. That's what I mean about his ability to handle interviews."

In 1988 Shank was married to Maryse Vindez, whom he met in Phoenix, where they live today. "She wasn't a basketball fan," he says.

And, as for Shank, although it was a thrill for him to play in the major leagues one time, he confesses he's no longer much of a baseball fan, either.

35

Larry King Yount

HOUSTON ASTROS, 1971

Few players had a shorter appearance in the major leagues than Larry Yount. In 1971, he came into a game as a relief pitcher, hurt his arm warming up on the mound, and was removed without ever actually throwing a pitch. But since he was officially announced into the game, today he is considered a one-time major-league baseball player.

In 1963, when he was thirteen years old, Yount pitched for a Pony League team that included future major leaguers Pete LaCock, Rick Auerbach, and Rick Dempsey. The team was good enough to go to the Pony League World Series in Washington.

"When we came back from Washington," Yount says, "I was picked on a team that was going to throw out the first ball in one of the World Series games that year [between the Los Angeles Dodgers and the New York Yankees]. We were scheduled to do it before the fifth game, but it turned out there was no fifth game that year. [The Dodgers swept the Yankees in four straight.] So, instead, I got to throw out the first ball on opening day of the 1964 season in Dodger Stadium," Yount says.

Back then, nobody knew it would be his only real throw in the major leagues.

At Taft High School in Woodland Hills, the right-handed Yount continued to pitch superbly and was named to All-Valley, All-City, and All-Los Angeles teams during his high school years. He received encouragement from his older brother, Jim, who played on the football team, as well as from his kid brother, Robin, who "hung around all the ball teams I was on."

When he graduated from high school, Yount, at six-foot-two and 185

Larry Yount, shown here pitching in the minor leagues, had what was probably the shortest "appearance" in a game in major-league history.

pounds, was selected by the Houston Astros in the fifth round of the 1968 draft. "I got a bonus of $20,000 plus college expenses," he says.

But college was put off for a while. The Astros sent him to play at their Oklahoma City affiliate, then in the Triple-A Pacific Coast League. "My first game there," Yount says, "I started against the Phoenix Giants in Phoenix and pitched a three-hitter. But I lost the game because we didn't score any runs. I don't remember too much about that team, though. I remember Cot Deal was the manager and I was eighteen years old and there were a lot of older guys there. That's about it."

In seven games at Oklahoma City, Yount lost three and won none. "The Astros felt I should go down to a league where I could win, so I wouldn't lose my confidence," he says, "so they sent me to Greensboro in the [Class-A] Carolina League." He finished his first year as a professional there, winning one and losing four. In 47 innings pitched, however, he struck out 49 batters.

"That winter, I went into the Army, the reserves, or the National Guard, I don't remember which," Yount says, "for six months. I got out in time for the start of the next season, but I still had to go to monthly meetings and two weeks of summer camp."

In 1969, Yount again played in the Carolina League, this time with the Peninsula team. "That year, we had a lot of young guys on the team," he recalls. "We were all about the same age and just had too much time on our hands." But Yount pitched well that year, limiting the opposition to just 2.25 earned runs a game. He won 6, lost 4, and struck out 56 men in 60 innings.

"That winter, I went to the Instructional League in Florida," Yount says, "and there were a lot of big-leaguers there, and big-league management. I learned a lot, and it was pretty helpful."

In 1970, Yount was invited to spring training with the Astros. "That was my first big-league training camp," he says, "and I was impressed with all the good players there. Joe Pepitone I remember distinctly. But there were so many more, Jimmy Wynn, [Joe] Morgan, Don Wilson, [Larry] Dierker. They had nothing but good ballplayers." Yount wasn't intimidated by their talent. "I thought I could compete," he says.

But Houston had a solid, veteran pitching staff that year, led by Dierker and Wilson, both of whom were twenty-five, and Jack Billingham, twenty-seven. They were backed up by the experienced Fred Gladding, thirty-three, and Denny Lemaster and Jim Bouton, both of whom were thirty-one. Other pitchers on the roster included five-year veteran Jimmy Ray, twenty-five; second-year-man Tom Griffin, twenty-two; and rookie Ron Cook, also twenty-two.

Yount, who had just turned twenty, was sent out again for additional seasoning, this time to the Double-A Columbus team in the Southern League. Teammates there included two other future major-league pitchers, Bill Greif (a close friend of Yount's) and Ken Forsch. He had an excellent year. He won 12, lost 8, and posted a 2.84 earned run average while striking out 149 batters. That year he was named to the league's All-Star team.

"Following that season," he says, "I went to the Arizona Instructional League, and while I was there, I started taking college courses at Arizona State University, mainly in business." In later off-seasons, Yount would take additional courses at other colleges, eventually ending up, he says, "about halfway toward a degree."

In 1971, Yount went back to spring training with the Astros. "I got to pitch some that spring," he says, "but I think it was a foregone conclusion that I was going to end up that year at Oklahoma City" [which had become part of the American Association].

He did. "I pitched okay at Oklahoma City," he says about his season there, "and learned what Triple-A was all about." Yount says he believes he pitched better than his record of five wins and eight losses would indicate. "When the season ended, in early September I think, the Astros called me up," he says.

How did he feel at that time? "I thought I should be called up. I always thought I'd be called up," Yount says. "But I didn't report right away. I went to Bill Greif's wedding, and then I had a reserve meeting or something, so I was a week or so late reporting. I was just sitting around and hadn't thrown a ball in a while.

"I was only there a day or two when I was told to warm up," he says. It was on September 15, 1971, during a game between two Western Conference foes, the fifth-place Astros and the visiting Atlanta Braves, then in third place. Some 6,500 fans were in attendance.

The game started auspiciously for Houston as they scored a run in the bottom of the first inning off Atlanta pitcher Phil Niekro. But Billingham, the Astro starter, could not hold the lead, and the Braves, aided by Hank Aaron's forty-fourth home run of the season, soon took a 4–1 lead.

After five innings, Billingham was replaced on the mound for Houston by another recently recalled pitcher, left-hander Skip Guinn, who held the Braves scoreless through the eighth. In the bottom of the eighth, however, still trailing 4–1, Astros manager Harry Walker sent up a pinch-hitter for Guinn.

"I was warming up in the bullpen," Yount says, "and I usually had some stiffness when I had come back from other layoffs, but I knew in the bullpen my arm was hurting. My elbow hurt. But I was twenty-one years old, and I wasn't going to turn down a chance to show them what I could do. Then they told me, 'You're in.' So I said to myself, 'Let's go out there and maybe the adrenaline pumping will make the pain go away.' But it didn't. It was something I had known or should have known.

"Maybe facing [Ralph] Garr, Aaron, and [Earl] Williams [the first three batters up in the ninth] had something to do with it," Yount says, "but after I threw a few warm-ups, something in the elbow popped. I called the manager [Walker] out and told him I hurt my elbow. I said, 'Look, I can *do* this, but if I do, I may not be able to pitch again.' They took me out and into the clubhouse and had a doctor look at me. The team didn't want to fool around. They wanted me to just go home and rest my arm and make no attempt to pitch until next year. The doctor said I had popped a tendon and gave me some cortisone. It hurt a lot, but it was just a two-week injury.

"You know, looking back, I still think it was one of the smarter things I did. I could have seriously hurt my arm," Yount says. "Right after this happened, in October, I was right back pitching, and very successfully. I fully expected to be back on the team the next year. Never in my wildest dreams did I figure it was the last time I'd be in the majors.

"In 1972, I had a *great* spring," Yount says. "I struck out the first six guys I faced, and I was pitching very, very well. Then, in around my third game against the Dodgers, I gave up a three-run homer to Willie Davis. After that, I didn't start again. I did pitch in relief against Cincinnati, and I did very well.

"But because two other guys [Tom Griffin and Scipio Spinks] had run out of options and I hadn't, they sent me back to Oklahoma City," Yount says. "I won my first four games there that year, and then I just came unglued and ended up with a 5–14 record. I can't give you any reason for it. I wish I knew."

In 1973, Yount pitched at Denver, winning only 3 and losing 12. "I was clearly heading down," he said, "and at the end of spring training in 1974, Houston traded me to Milwaukee for [outfielder] Wilbur Howard. According to the scouts, they felt a change would do us all good."

With the American League Milwaukee Brewers, Yount was reunited with his eighteen-year-old brother, Robin, who was about to start his first season in the major leagues after being the club's top draft pick in 1973. (Robin went on to play for twenty years with Milwaukee and is currently expected to be elected to the Baseball Hall of Fame.)

"But I was just terrible," the older brother says, "and I ended up sitting out the 1974 season. I tried a comeback in 1975. I went with Burlington, Iowa, for a few weeks and then was with Thedford Mines in Canada for the rest of the year." He won one, lost five.

"That's when, for the first time in his life, my father told me what to do," Yount says. "He told me, 'It's over.' But I went back to spring training with Milwaukee in 1976 anyway, and they released me. Then it was over."

Yount returned home that year and married Gail Radenbaugh. They had known each other since their high school days but had dated for only the last year or so. The couple then moved to Arizona where Yount entered the real estate business. Eight years later, he formed his own company in Phoenix, LKY Development, which has been involved in the development of office buildings and shopping centers, and which currently specializes in the sale of commercial land. He and Gail have four children, two daughters and two sons.

In more recent years, Yount also served as president of the Triple-A Phoenix Firebirds, but when a major-league franchise was awarded to the Arizona Diamondbacks in that city, the Firebirds moved to Fresno, California, and Yount is no longer involved. "It was a lot of fun," he says, "and I enjoyed the business side of it, but the money issues in baseball today have taken a lot of the joy and the fun out of baseball." Currently, however, he is building a brewery which will be part of the new major-league team's ballpark, in partnership with his brother and the Diamondbacks.

Over the years, Yount also has handled contract negotiations and other business matters for Robin. "I have some background and knowledge in this area," Larry Yount says, "and I think that's helped him, and allowed him to concentrate on playing the game. Of course, it's a joy for me to watch him play and remember him hanging around as a kid and becoming a major-leaguer at age eighteen. I guess it's also helped my situation for him to come along."

Looking back at his extremely unusual one-time appearance in the majors, Yount says, "While it created some of these questions, basically it was a non-event, a glitch that had no factor in what followed. Sure, I regret not having made it. I'd much rather have been a ballplayer than have had to go to work. I've probably made more money than I ever could have in baseball, but I would still love to have had a chance to play longer. It just didn't work out."

Donald Lee Leshnock

DETROIT TIGERS, 1972

While injuries sometimes were responsible for limiting a player's major-league career to one game, in Don Leshnock's case, it was an injury to another player which gave him the chance to play that one time.

Leshnock was born in Youngstown, Ohio, on November 25, 1946, the second of two sons. He attended Youngstown-Ursline High School, which did not have a baseball team, but he played amateur ball outside of school. "It wasn't American Legion, but it was like it," Leshnock says. "They had a Pony League for younger players and then another one for fifteen- and sixteen-year-olds." He says he did "very well."

Leshnock was a left-handed pitcher, but batted righty. "There was no reason. I guess I just picked up a bat that way when I started out," he says.

Leshnock graduated from high school in 1964 and, following in his brother's footsteps, entered Youngstown State College. He pitched one year of junior varsity ball and three years on the varsity. Again, he says he did "very well," at least well enough to be selected by the Detroit Tigers in the twenty-seventh round of the 1968 draft.

Detroit scout Cy Williams, a former National League outfielder, signed Leshnock to a Tigers contract.

"I got a small bonus," Leshnock says. How small? "Very small. About $7,500." With it, he and his hometown sweetheart, Cheryl Kopko, got married that year.

Detroit sent Leshnock to Sarasota in the rookie league, where, he says again, "I did well." In 1969, he was assigned to Detroit's Lakeland club in Class-A ball. He recalls that Jim Leyland was the assistant manager there. At Lakeland, Leshnock had a 4–4 record, but his earned run average was a

*In the one inning he pitched, Don Leshnock gave up no runs and
struck out Vada Pinson and Nolan Ryan.*

fine 2.85. "I started the year as a reliever," he says, "but as the season progressed, I became a starter. It seems that was the pattern I followed over
the next few years." Leshnock also completed his studies and graduated
from Youngstown State that year with a bachelor of science degree in
business administration.

In 1970, the young left-hander pitched for Rocky Mount, and in 1971,
for Montgomery. Rocky Mount was managed by former Cardinals
pitcher Max Lanier, and Dick Tracewski, a former Dodger and Tiger infielder, managed at Montgomery.

But Leshnock's performance in those years was not particularly encouraging to the Tigers. Over the next two years, he won 13 and lost 11, and in both years, his earned run average went above 4.00.

Despite that, Detroit invited him to spring training camp in 1972. "That was my first big-league camp," Leshnock says, "and I threw the ball well. I remember in my second intrasquad game, I gave up a homer to Willie Horton, but then I struck out Al Kaline. I thought that impressed them, you know, to see me come back and strike out a guy right after a homer." However, the twenty-five-year-old Leshnock was sent to start the year at Toledo, the Tiger's Triple-A team managed by Johnny Lipon. "My record was not good that year," Leshnock says, "but I was throwing well."

On an off-day in late May, Leshnock and some Toledo teammates were exercising and playing racquetball at Bowling Green University when he was informed he had been called up by Detroit. An opening had developed on the Tigers' pitching staff because a starter, Les Cain, had suffered an arm injury. The fact that Leshnock had been "throwing well" at Toledo, despite an unimpressive won-lost record, evidently influenced Detroit's decision.

The Tigers that year were an aging, veteran club that was being driven to the pennant by manager Billy Martin, then in his second year at the helm. For most of that season, Detroit was engaged in a four-team, seesaw race with the Red Sox, the Yankees, and the defending champion, the Baltimore Orioles. When Leshnock joined them, the Tigers were ahead by a game or so.

Martin pulled out all stops to eventually win the divisional championship by platooning most of his aging veterans and using only two regulars, third baseman Aurelio Rodriguez and the slick-fielding but weak-hitting shortstop, Eddie Brinkman. In the outfield were Willie Horton, Al Kaline, Jim Northrup, Mickey Stanley, and Gates Brown, none of whom enjoyed their reduced playing time.

The other position players on the team that year included first baseman Norm Cash; second baseman Dick McAuliffe; utility man Tony Taylor; and catchers Bill Freehan, Tom Haller, and, later, Duke Sims. (Eight of these thirteen team members had already played with the Tigers for between nine and twenty years.)

Although Leshnock was unaware of it, there was friction and dissension under the team's surface, but it was kept under wraps so long as the team was winning. Northrup and Kaline (among others) were particularly upset and outspoken concerning their manager.

That year, the team scratched out victories primarily on pitching and defense. Only Kaline, in his 20th season, and Taylor, in his 15th, were able to hit over .300.

The club's leading pitchers were Mickey Lolich, with 20 wins, and Joe Coleman, who had 19. Those two, along with Chuck Seelbach and Tom Timmerman, all posted earned run averages below 3.00 that year, keeping the team in contention. While it was a good staff, it was not a particularly happy one. A number of the pitchers reportedly resented the way Martin "pampered" Lolich, who had been with the team ten years, and this added to the turmoil on the team.

But it was the addition of Woody Fryman that really made the difference. Fryman was acquired from the Phillies on August 2 for cash "and a player to be named later." Down the stretch, Fryman, who had been 4–10 with Philadelphia earlier that season, pitched masterfully, winning 10 and losing 3 for Detroit, while posting a 2.05 earned run average.

When Leshnock reported to the Tigers, however, Fryman was still with the Phillies, and Detroit was scratching for every win. "I was with the Tigers about three weeks and all the games were close and Billy didn't have a chance to put me in to get my feet wet," Leshnock says. "The team was fighting for the pennant, and Billy preferred to use veterans. In the one time I got in, I just mopped up in a game that Nolan Ryan was dominating."

That game was on the night of June 7, 1972, when Detroit faced the visiting California Angels in front of slightly more than 14,000 fans. In the fifth inning, the Angels had erupted against Tigers starter Joe Niekro for four runs on three successive singles, a double by shortstop Leo Cardenas, and a later single by second baseman Sandy Alomar. At the end of eight innings, they led 5–1, while Ryan limited Detroit to just three hits all game.

Leshnock became Detroit's fifth hurler that night, and as he said, he came in to "mop up" in the top of the ninth. "I wasn't nervous," he said. "I had a belief that if I had my fastball, I could get anyone out. I didn't feel nervous. I thought it was about time. Tom Haller was the catcher and he wished me luck. He was a pretty nice guy. Otherwise, it was kind of quiet. I was just concentrating on the batters."

The first batter Leshnock faced was Cardenas, who had doubled earlier. This time he grounded to McCauliffe at second. The next batter was Ryan, the California pitcher, and Leshnock gave him "nothing but fastballs." He struck out Ryan. Understandably, it is the one moment of the game that sticks out most in Leshnock's memory today.

At the time, he did not get a chance to savor the moment for very long. Alomar, the next batter, singled. Center fielder Mickey Rivers followed immediately with a second single, putting runners on first and third, and the dangerous Vada Pinson, the Angels' left fielder, came to the plate. Pinson had twice led the National League in hits. In his first three official times up in this game, he had a single, plus a walk and a run scored.

But Leshnock got Pinson as his second strikeout victim and ended the inning with a flourish.

"I felt pretty good after the game was over," Leshnock says. "I was upset about giving up a couple of hits after two were out, you know. I knew I wasn't gonna get too many chances, but I thought I would get another chance. But, as I told you, we were in a pennant race, and Billy usually stayed with the veterans."

As for the team, Leshnock says, "The veterans kept to themselves." The only players he really got to know on the Tigers were his roommate, utility outfielder Wayne Comer, and those with whom he had played in the minor leagues, such as pitchers Fred Scherman and Bill Slayback and outfielder Ike Blessitt. "The experience of playing in Detroit's minor-league system was enjoyable," Leshnock says. "I'm still best friends with a catcher I played with for four years. That's Dave Bike, and he coaches basketball at Sacred Heart University in Lakeland, Florida."

After the game in which he struck out Ryan and Pinson, Leshnock remained on the bench for another two weeks. Finally, Leshnock was told he was going back to Toledo. "Billy told me that John Hiller was coming back and he didn't have room for me," Leshnock says.

Hiller, who had been one of Vern Holtgrave's close friends on the Tigers in 1965 (see Chapter 33), was a veteran reliever who had pitched for Detroit in the World Series in 1968, but had unexpectedly suffered a heart attack that had kept him out the entire 1971 season as well as the first half of 1972. But now, in a remarkable comeback, he was ready to rejoin the Tigers for the stretch run, and Martin wanted him.

Meanwhile, Leshnock returned to Toledo and finished out the season as a one-time major-league ballplayer.

In an ironic move at year end, Detroit sent him to the Philadelphia Phillies as the "player to be named later" in the trade that had brought them Woody Fryman.

The Phils gave Leshnock a chance to make their team in spring training in 1973. "But I didn't make it," he says. Philadelphia assigned him to Eugene, Oregon, where a former Tigers and Philly pitcher, Jim Bunning, was the manager. "I was a spot starter and reliever," Leshnock says, "but I never did get into a groove that year." His record was 4–7, and his earned run average rose to 4.75. He was traded again and ended up in Charleston, a Pittsburgh affiliate, pitching mainly short relief during 1974 and 1975.

"After 1975, I just retired," Leshnock says. "I knew I wasn't going anywhere. I remember when the Pirates were looking for left-handed help, they got Juan Pizzaro from the Mexican League or somewhere."

In 1976, the twenty-nine-year-old Leshnock joined the sales staff of the Family Life Insurance Company and remained with that organization for thirteen years. In 1990, he became a customer service representative for the Copeland Company, which develops and supervises municipal pension plans. He is employed there today.

"Being a major-league baseball player didn't affect my life," Leshnock says, "but it is nice just to say I was in that small percentage of players who start in the minor leagues and who got to the big leagues."

Today, he and Cheryl reside in Columbus, Ohio, and take pride in their son, Donnie, who played baseball at the University of North Carolina and is now in the minor leagues, hoping to reach the majors like his dad.

Albert Autry Jr.

ATLANTA BRAVES, 1976

Only twice since the end of World War I has a player started and won the only game he ever played in the major leagues. One of them was Al Autry, playing for the Atlanta Braves in September 1976. The other was Earl Huckelberry, a pitcher for the Philadelphia Athletics, who won his game in 1935.

Autry and Huckelberry had something else in common. They both played for last-place teams, yet both were denied the opportunity to pitch again in the majors. Autry says he cannot really understand why he was never given a second chance.

Born in Modesto, California, on Leap Year Day in 1952, the third in a family of five children, Autry was a big kid even in high school. Standing six-foot-five and weighing 225, he was an imposing figure on both the pitching mound and on the basketball court at Modesto's Grace Davis High School. He was named to all-conference and all-district teams in both sports.

"Scouts started to come around to watch me in both baseball and basketball," he says, "and I started getting scholarship letters in my junior year. By the time I was a senior, I was getting a lot of recruitment letters from places like Stanford, Arizona State, San Francisco State, UCLA, Fresno State, and others. I had good grades. I carried a 3.2 average, and had good S.A.T. scores, so I could have gone where I wanted, but I kind of narrowed it down to Stanford and Arizona State. But college was a conflict with baseball, because I was sure I'd be drafted fairly high when I graduated from high school in 1969 and that I'd play professional ball."

As it turned out, Autry was drafted in the fifth round by the Kansas

Al Autry started and won his only major league game, and believes this 1977 picture is the only one ever taken of him in his full uniform.

City Royals in 1969. "They set up a college scholarship fund of $8,000 as part of my contract," Autry says, "and it's funny, but that first year, I played winter ball in Tempe, Arizona, and I was able to attend school at Arizona State after all, even though I couldn't play for them.

"Rosy Gilhousen, an old left-handed pitcher, was the one who signed me," Autry remembers, "although he wasn't the one who scouted me. Gilhousen was a short, fat, jolly sort of guy then, and I remember him telling me about how they used to travel around when he was playing." In addition to the scholarship fund, Autry received a cash bonus of $17,000 and a rookie contract to play the 1969 season at Winnipeg in the Class-D Northern League for $500 a month.

"I was awesome," Autry says of his initial season. "My velocity was intimidating. I threw hard, in the mid- to upper nineties. Unfortunately, I couldn't get the ball over the plate." While he struck out 40 men in just 30 innings that season, the seventeen-year-old pitcher also gave up 43 hits and 28 walks, winning no games while losing five.

The following year, 1970, was not much different. At Waterloo in the Midwest League and at Billings in the Pioneer League, he pitched a total of 54 innings and struck out 64 batters. But he also walked 52 and allowed 54 hits. He won three, lost five, and made $550 a month.

"I was one of those guys who threw real, real, *real* hard," he says, "and they didn't care if I won or lost. They just kept saying, 'Well, hell, he's only seventeen.' 'Well, hell, he's only eighteen.' 'Jeez, he's only nineteen.' Just thinking it was gonna come. I didn't really know how to pitch, and it was a lot *my* fault because I liked to throw hard, and it was a lot *their* fault because nobody was telling me, 'Hey, let's learn how to pitch.' They kept thinking, 'He's young, he's young.'"

Autry played winter ball again after the 1970 season, this time in a Sarasota, Florida, instructional league under the direction of Jack McKeon. McKeon told a reporter then that Autry had talent, showed promise, threw hard, and that there was a real possibility of his joining the Royals' starting rotation in the future. Autry recalls McKeon saying his success was "just a matter of maturity, getting his control and learning how to pitch." Later, however, when McKeon managed the Royals from 1973 through 1975, he didn't keep Autry on the team.

But Autry felt good about McKeon's early assessment and reported for spring training in early 1971. "They had put me on the [Class A] San Jose roster and that was real close to home and I was looking forward to it." He and his high school sweetheart, Paula Warda, were thinking about marriage, and his playing in San Jose, just seventy-five miles away, would allow them to see each other often.

"But then, with eight days of camp left, they assigned me to go back to Waterloo. Well, I was so disappointed I just packed up and flew home to California. I told my roommate to let them know I was totally disappointed, and I just left. I went home and got married then. Paula arranged everything in eight or ten days, and meanwhile the team kept calling me to find out what was happening. They were real pissed off. We were married on April 16, 1971, and the next day we drove to Waterloo. Well, I only pitched three games for Waterloo, and don't you know, they sent me right back to San Jose for the rest of the year."

In his three games at Waterloo, Autry struck out 28 in just 20 innings and cut the number of hits and walks he allowed to 11 and 12, respectively. He compiled an earned run average of just 0.90, yet still won only one of his three decisions.

When he got to San Jose in the California League, however, the nineteen-year-old Autry began to win. In one game, he pitched a two-hit shutout, and in another, he struck out 14 in six innings. For the year overall, he struck out 177 batters in 164 innings and was paid $625 a month.

At the year's end, Autry was pleased when the Royals added him to their 40-man roster. In early 1972, he reported to the team's training camp in Fort Myers, Florida, looking forward to the year ahead. He recalls manager Bob Lemon as "a nice guy, but a little bit of a hard-ass."

One of his sharpest memories of his first major-league training camp, however, involves George Brett, a former roommate of his in Sarasota and by then a good friend. Brett is often remembered for the wild rage he showed when his two-run homer against the Yankees was disallowed because he supposedly had too much pine tar on his bat. But his explosive temperament is not limited to the ballpark. Once, when he phoned home, his father asked, "Get any hits?" When Brett said no, his father said, "George, your brother [Ken] is only a pitcher and he's outhitting you." According to Brett, Ken happened to get two hits that day during a doubleheader, including a pinch-hit triple. Brett's response to his father's criticism: he hung up the phone, threw it against the wall, ripped it out of its mounting, and then slammed and shattered a full-length mirror. "Buck Martinez was my roommate then," Brett said, "and poor Buck didn't know what to say."

Brett, however, also had a calm side, and he showed that to Autry back in 1972 when the two of them were driving Autry's new sports convertible to the beach. While wading in the surf, Autry was bitten by a stingray, and his foot began to swell quickly. Autry panicked and thought he was about to die. Brett got him back in the car to rush him to a hospital. According to Autry, however, Brett took his own sweet time getting to the hospital, taking the long way around, just so he could test-drive the new convertible, while calmly assuring the stricken Autry that, yes, he'd take care of Paula. Eventually he soaked his foot in warm water and everything returned to normal, but the story was the talk of the 1972 training camp.

After training camp, the Royals assigned Autry to Jacksonville in the Double-A Southern League, where he struck out 173 batters while winning 11, losing 13, and compiling a respectable 3.33 earned run average. "I also led the league in starts with Jacksonville that year," he points out. But even though he was on the major-league roster, he earned only $640 a month for the six-month minor-league season. A bit perturbed, Autry did not play winter ball that year, but enrolled at Cal State-Stanislaus instead, where he began to major in physical education. He would return there every winter for the next five years instead of playing baseball in the off-season.

In 1973, the Royals sent him to Omaha, their Triple-A team in the American Association, where he pitched regularly, starting 28 games, but without distinction. Although he was still part of the Royals' 40-man major-league roster, Autry was assigned to the Double-A Jacksonville team in 1974, where he again would receive a minor-league salary. When he returned the contract, Autry sarcastically included a note asking where the food stamps were.

In Jacksonville, Autry pitched credibly, winning 10 and losing 5 while compiling a 2.89 earned run average. In one game that year, he pitched a complete game against Denny McLain, the two-time Cy Young Award winner. Autry lost the game, 4–3, after giving up three home runs. He finished that season back at Omaha.

During these years, Autry's minor-league teammates included the core of the Kansas City Royals team that would win the American League divisional championships in 1976, 1977, and 1978. At various times, he played on teams with Al Cowens, U. L. Washington, Frank White, John Wathan, Mark Littell, Steve Busby, Lou Piniella, Hal McRae, and, of course, George Brett.

"George was one of the purest hitters I've ever played with," Autry says. "Although he never really hit as well in the minors for average, you could tell that one day he would become a great hitter. You know, line drives off the left center field wall, inside-out smashes down third base. And Hal McRae was one of the best hitters I ever saw. Kansas City had just acquired Hal [in 1973], and he was in Sarasota, Florida, for winter ball. I can remember him intentionally fouling off five or six pitches to avoid walking, and then lining a double when he got the pitch he wanted.

"Lou Piniella was one of the *last* guys I would've ever thought would become a manager," Autry says. "One day in spring training, he struck out, and when he came back, he took his bat and smashed every light fixture in the dugout. And this was an exhibition game."

In 1975, at the age of only twenty-three, Autry entered his seventh season of professional ball, still at Omaha in the American Association. He was becoming frustrated and discouraged. Playing in a talent-laden farm system limited his opportunities to move up to the big leagues with the Royals. On the other hand, he could not be drafted by any other team while still on the team's 40-man major-league roster. There was no such thing as free agency then. "I wasn't playing in the big leagues," he says, "and I wasn't making any money, either. Yet I was good enough to be protected on the big-league roster. I found I was subsidizing my career with the bonus money I got for signing."

But after he pitched solidly again for Omaha in 1975, everything changed.

At the end of Omaha's season, the Royals traded Autry along with his friend, pitcher Norm Angelini, to the Atlanta Braves to complete a deal, made earlier that year, which bought pitcher Ray Sadecki to the Royals and sent pitcher Bruce del Canton to the Braves.

Autry learned of the trade when he arrived home in Modesto that August after returning from Omaha. He immediately telephoned the Braves, and they invited him to travel with the team on their West Coast trip in September. "It was total exhilaration," he says. "It was about ten days in San Diego, Los Angeles, and San Francisco, the grand tour. It was tremendous fun, and I felt tremendous acceptance. I got to meet a number of men from my area of the country, like Dusty Baker, and some others, like Ralph Garr. I once went duck hunting with Dusty Baker, but it was a fiasco. Anyway, they made me feel like I was something special. We had a chartered flight, not a packed commercial flight, and our pilot used to imitate John Wayne. The whole atmosphere was a huge jump from what it was like even in Triple-A."

Autry felt he had been given a new start. He went home, went back to school, ran to keep in shape during the off-season, and looked forward to 1976.

His memory of the Braves' spring training camp that year was "most enjoyable. I'm an avid fisherman," he says, "a bass fisherman. We trained at West Palm Beach, and we were able to fish at Lake Okeechobee. Phil Niekro also was a fisherman, and we used to spend a lot of time fishing. We had fish fries at the ballpark with the fish we caught, with all the wives and girlfriends.

"I also met a lot of guys there that I had played against in the minors, or had read about as I was growing up." Autry says. In particular, he remembers Andy Messersmith, who had just joined the Braves that year. From Messersmith, Autry learned to throw a change-up. "They had a good team," he says, "and I really didn't expect to make the team." (The Braves finished last in their conference.)

As expected, Autry didn't make the team. The Braves assigned him to Richmond, Atlanta's Triple-A team in the International League. The manager at Richmond in 1976 turned out to be Jack McKeon. Autry had mixed emotions about McKeon then, because he felt the manager did not do enough to help him move ahead while they were both with the Royals. But Autry does not totally blame McKeon for that. "I think in some ways I let Jack down," he says, "and when I went to the Royals' training camp, I thought Jack gave up on me.

"When I got to Richmond, he was pretty friendly to me, and he decided I was gonna be a reliever," Autry says. "He thought I would be another Goose Gossage. So the first two or three games he brought me in, I threw hard, but I was wild. Soon, I found my ass on the bench. It was the first time in my life I hadn't started every fifth day. Johnny Sain was the pitching coach that year, and he just kept saying, 'Be ready, be ready.'

"So I threw every day. Norm Angelini, who is a great, great friend, caught me in the bullpen every day, and I owe him a lot for that. But I still wasn't playing. Finally they let me pitch some middle or long relief, and I didn't give up any runs. But it wasn't until late May or early June that I got a start, and I never had a bad game from then on."

By the end of the 1976 season, Autry had become the best pitcher on the staff. He pitched 8 complete games in his 18 starts after moving into the starting rotation. His earned run average for those games was only 2.11. For the whole year, it was 2.85. A major weapon in his arsenal was the change-up he picked up from Messersmith in spring training. "I was beating people like [future Cy Young Award winner Ron] Guidry and [Dennis] Martinez, and I really felt I had become a pitcher," he says. His growth also was noticed by Sain. "When I'd come in and pitch a shutout," Autry recalls, "and had only three strikeouts, Sain would always make sure

KANSAS CITY ROYALS BASEBALL CLUB
P. O. BOX 1969, KANSAS CITY, MISSOURI 64141

Dear Player:

    You have been scouted by the Kansas City Royals
scouting staff and recommended as a player with possible
major league abilities. In order that we might get to
know a little more about you, would you be so kind as
to fill out the enclosed questionnaire and drop it in
the mail.

    By filling out this questionnaire in no way do
you become obligated to us or do you break any rules
of your high school, junior college, college or amateur
standing. This is just a simple way for us to get
some information about you without having to bother
you when you are on the field playing.

    Just a short note about our organization. We
are new to baseball, 1969 is our first year in the
American League. Our owner is Mr. Ewing Kauffman who
owns the Marion Laboratories (manufacturer of pharma-
ceutical products). Our General Manager is Cedris'
Tallis who has a twenty-five year background in baseball and our field manager is the ever popular Joe
"Flash" Gordon in his playing days the best second-
baseman in baseball. We will have a new domed stadium
shortly in Kansas City and we hope that you will be
there to play in it.

                        Sincerely,

                        "Rosey"

                        Ross "Rosey" Gilhousen
                        Western Director of Scouting

encl

P.S. Please fill out and return the enclosed questionnaire
      by May 20, 1969.

*While still in high school, Autry received this letter from the Kansas City Royals,
the team which eventually drafted him.*

to say, 'Hey, I told you that you could throw eighty-five and beat them.' That helped me 'cause it made me think about it."

Autry's final record at Richmond that year was only 9–6, but it could easily have been 12–3. He lost three games that year to Scott McGregor, twice by the score of 1–0, and once by 2–1 in ten innings. "It was the best year of my life," Autry says. "And I felt that only *one* person got me there and that was *me*. Even before the season was over, the Richmond papers were calling on [last-place] Atlanta to bring me up, and when we got into the [International League] playoffs, [Atlanta owner] Ted Turner came flying down to see our playoff instead of staying in Atlanta."

Autry won the two games he pitched in the playoffs against Syracuse, but Richmond lost the series. "I'll never forget what happened after that last game in Syracuse," Autry said. "I was told that Atlanta had recalled me for the rest of their season, and McKeon came over and said, 'I told you I'd get you to the big leagues.' I thought, 'You goddamn front-runner!'"

Autry and pitching teammate Rick Camp, who had lost the last playoff game in Syracuse, were recalled together from Richmond. At the time, the Braves were away on a road trip, so they were told to report when the team returned about ten days later. The two pitchers decided to spend the time hunting doves at Camp's farm outside Atlanta. They both went more than a week without picking up a baseball, and both ended up with arms bruised from the recoil of their shotguns.

On September 15, when the Braves finally returned home, Autry met with Bill Lucas, the Braves' director of player personnel, to sign his contract. Afterward, Lucas mentioned casually, "By the way, you're pitching the second game against Houston tonight."

"I felt a certain amount of butterflies," Autry admits, "but I really wasn't nervous. I thought to myself, 'You've earned this; you worked hard for this.' I felt confident. I wasn't scared. I had had a great season, and I felt that I'd be starting every five days from now 'til the end of the season."

The twi-night doubleheader started in misty, chilly weather, and only 970 paying customers bothered to show up. In the first game, Mark Lemongello made his major-league pitching debut for the Astros and won by a score of 4–3, thanks to a home run by Enos Cabell off pitcher Dick Ruthven.

Autry went to the bullpen to warm up for the second game. "I was a little concerned 'cause I hadn't thrown in a while and I normally needed a long time to get loose. I usually had to throw twenty minutes to get ready. Well, I started to warm up, and I found I didn't have my stuff. My rhythm wasn't there, *nothing* was there. But I told myself, 'You've learned to win without your good stuff, so let's go and see what happens.'"

In the first five innings of the game, Autry walked three, struck out three, and gave up three runs on four hits, two of them home runs. "I don't remember whom I walked or struck out," Autry says, "but Jose Cruz and Cesar Cedeno hit the homers. I had a 3–1 count on Cedeno and threw him a fastball up and away that he hit. When I went into the dugout after that inning, somebody on the bench told me, 'Cedeno *likes* them up and away.' I thought, 'Now you tell me?'"

But thanks to a three-run homer by Braves first baseman Willie Montanez in the third inning, which broke a 1–1 tie, Atlanta and Autry were leading at the end of five innings, 4–3. There would be no more scoring that night.

"I was pretty relaxed, didn't feel too bad," Autry says, "and when I came in after the fifth inning, [Atlanta Manager Dave] Bristol said, 'Hey, good performance, rookie. That's all we need you for. Take a shower.'"

The six-foot-five, 225-pound Autry was relieved by the five-foot-ten, 145-pound Mexican right-hander, Max Leon, who walked only one batter in two innings, and then by Adrian Devine, who gave up a single in his two innings and got the save.

"I sat around in the dugout 'til about the seventh," Autry says. "Then I moseyed back in the clubhouse. They had a TV in there, and it wasn't until maybe about an out or two in the eighth when I started thinking, 'Hey, I could *win* this game!' I hadn't really thought about the win. I just thought, 'Hey, I'd had a decent performance,' and I was figuring I'd get about three or four more starts before the season ended."

After the game, it appeared Bristol thought the same way, too. "I'm gonna play them," he told the press about his rookies. "Autry was impressive tonight. He got his breaking stuff over when he had to." Bristol also announced that Camp would start within the next day or two.

"Camp had a bad game," Autry says. "I'll never forget it. Rick was gonna pick a man off first base, and when he turned and threw, he absolutely launched it. I mean like two hundred feet, into the bleachers. It wasn't like a bad throw to first; it wasn't even *close*. So they take him out and we're walking off to the clubhouse and we got talking about it and we got tickled. We were chuckling and laughing, and when we got to the top of the runway, just about to go into the clubhouse, Bristol was standing there and he looked at us and he said, 'It wasn't that fucking funny.' I was a rookie, and I could understand Bristol being mad, but not hold a grudge."

After that incident, Autry never appeared in a big-league game again. "I warmed up once or twice after that, but I never got in," he says. "I couldn't figure it out. I had thrown so well." He watched from the bench as San Francisco's John Montefusco pitched a no-hitter against the Braves on September 29. The season ended four days later.

"I was contacted to go to Venezuela to play winter ball and they were offering me a lot of money and I told the Braves about it. Bill Lucas told me, 'Don't go to winter ball.' I said, 'I really don't understand anything that's happened this year. I had a good year at Richmond, I come up to the big leagues, I pitch my first game, and I win. I don't get the ball for three weeks. Now you don't want me to go to winter ball. What's going on?'"

Autry was assured by Lucas, who had been promoted to general manager, that changes were going to be made and that he should go home and rest up for next year. "I felt better," Autry says. "I thought, 'Well, what the hell. Big leagues. Won my first game. I'm on my way. Things are gonna happen for me.'

"I got my contract earlier than usual that year," Autry recalls, "around Christmas, and I was elated. The minimum was $19,500, and my contract called for around $22,500. And the important thing was that it was a 'one-way' contract, meaning I'd get paid that amount even if they sent me to the minors. Up to then, I'd been getting 'two-way' contracts. I was on a cloud."

The contract made him certain the Braves had plans for him in 1977. Autry thought he had an excellent chance to make the starting rotation and also was encouraged to hear that Johnny Sain had been made pitching coach for the Braves that year. Autry went to spring training with an extremely optimistic outlook.

That changed quickly, however. He pitched some batting practice and intrasquad games, but when the exhibition games began, the team went through the rotation twice without him. "I think I had four outings all spring," he recalls, "two excellent, one good, and one poor.

"I sat down in the locker room one day and both Messersmith and Niekro were there and I talked to them and I told them what happened. Both of them pretty much said, 'You should go talk to Bristol and tell him just what you told us. How you feel, that you want to pitch, you want to make this club. And you think you deserve the chance to make it and you don't think you're getting a fair shot.'

"So I did. And it was a big mistake.

"I went in and said, 'Dave, can I speak to you a minute?' and he said, 'Sure, come on in.' I said, and I think these are my exact words, 'Dave, I want to be a part of this team. I think for me to be a part of this team, I have to prove to you that I can pitch. But I don't feel I'm being given a chance to prove it.'

"He blew up. He really did. He said, 'Listen, I make the fucking decisions around here and you'll pitch when I decide to pitch you.'

"Four days later, we split into A and B squads, and I went with the B squad to play against St. Louis. Chris Cannizzaro was in charge, and he told me Bristol wanted me to pitch. He said, 'He wants you to throw as long as you can.' Well, that day, I got nine guys in a row."

Shortly thereafter, however, Autry was optioned to Richmond.

"I can understand it was Sain's first year as pitching coach and maybe he was afraid for his job, but I won't forgive him for not confronting Bristol and saying, 'He should be on the team,'" Autry says today.

Because of his one-way contract, Autry could not be recalled from Richmond without first passing through waivers, which made it difficult for Atlanta to bring him back. In addition, Bill Lucas was gone from Atlanta's front office, the victim of a fatal heart attack.

Returning to Richmond with Autry was Dale Murphy, who had caught there the year before, as well as in Autry's one major-league game. Murphy was sent back to regain his confidence.

"When we went to spring training," Autry says, "Murph was the biggest thing since Johnny Bench. He had the size, the power, the arm, the youth, the good looks. He was a churchgoer, the All-American guy. He was one of those guys that hit your mistake pitch out to right field. So you could just tell he was gonna be good. Same way when I played with Brett, you could just tell. Murph had it all going for him. All the press was there, and they were on him like flies, bad. All around his locker and Murph this and Murph that, and the phenom that's gonna bail Atlanta out. I think he just absolutely got so much pressure put on him that he cracked. And the way he cracked was in his throwing. He couldn't throw the ball. If he was trying to throw to second, he might throw it five feet in front of the mound or he might throw it in the air to the center fielder."

On opening day in Richmond, Autry was the starting pitcher and Murphy was behind the plate. "First guy on base, first situation, I'm in the stretch, throw it, turn and duck like a pitcher does," Autry says. "The guy takes off. Murph drills me in the back. After a couple of months, they got him out of there to the outfield."

Autry lost his first six decisions for Richmond in 1977, but then won six straight to even his record. At that point in 1977, the "politics of the big leagues," as Autry calls it, came into play. The Braves sold him to the St. Louis Cardinals for $20,000, which was the same as the waiver price. "If they [the Cardinals] had acquired me *on waivers* for $20,000, they would have had to bring me up to the majors," Autry says, "but because they *bought* me for $20,000, they didn't have to."

St. Louis assigned Autry to New Orleans in the American Association, where he finished the season. "I had a couple of good games there," he says. But by then, he had lost his appetite for the game. He stayed in the American Association the following year, this time with Springfield, but in midseason he tore some cartilage in his knee while on the mound. His knee required surgery, and that ended his ten-year playing career at age twenty-six.

"I did go back to spring training in 1979," Autry says, "but only at the coaxing of some friends. I really didn't want to play anymore. I went late and was out of shape and I had no desire. They released me but, in reality, I had already quit."

For about ten months, Autry joined a beer distributor and then went to work selling retail advertising for the *Modesto Bee*, his hometown daily newspaper. He has been there ever since, including a year at the paper's Sacramento office. Today he is its advertising manager, supervising a staff of eighteen. He and Paula have a daughter and two sons.

"Timing is important," he says of his athletic career, "and baseball is a business. It's a great game, but it's a business. When I think back, I have no big regrets, but I probably think of it more today, as my kids are growing up and playing ball, than I did a few years ago. I think if I had only given it a little more effort, a little more intensity, I could have made it. But I can't change that. I never was a baseball fan; I'm not a very good baseball fan now. I don't follow it closely, and I didn't follow it when I played. I didn't work at it very hard. I only went to winter ball the first three or four years and then said, 'To hell with it, I'd rather not.' It just wasn't my dream. The majority of the fault lies with me, and I've accepted that.

"But I've *learned* from my experience in baseball," Autry says. "I approach my job now with a fun-loving attitude, but more aggressive than I did in baseball. I've got a good company and a good job, and I figure I won't let this one get away quite as easily as I did the other one."

John Henry LaRose

BOSTON RED SOX, 1978

John LaRose faced a bases-loaded, no-outs situation as a relief pitcher in the major leagues, and got his team out of the jam by retiring the side without a run scoring. That was his job and he did it.

And the one game John LaRose pitched in the major leagues could have decided a pennant race and, perhaps, a World Series championship.

Unfortunately, it didn't work out the way he would have liked. When he came to the major leagues, LaRose was known as a "closer"—a relief pitcher who would be called in often at the very end of a game or any time his team needed help getting out of a tight spot. Usually, a closer expects to pitch no more than an inning and, as a result, does not pace himself to last a full nine innings. He gives his full effort on every pitch.

In fact, a closer often is called a *short* reliever, to distinguish him from a *long* reliever, who might be called into a game in the early or middle innings of a game. The long reliever tries to keep his team in contention over a longer period of time until it is time for the closer to come in. Consequently, a long reliever is not under quite as much immediate pressure and can pace himself a bit more.

When LaRose came in to pitch in the major leagues, his manager used him as a closer—which he did in excellent fashion—but then made the mistake of continuing to use him as a long reliever, which didn't work.

Born in Pawtucket, Rhode Island, in the fall of 1951, LaRose was the older of two sons of a tinsmith who soon moved his family to nearby Cumberland, where the boys grew up. "I went through the Cumberland school system and went to Cumberland High School," LaRose says, "and I

*John LaRose, in a Pawtucket cap and Boston Red Sox shirt,
pitched out of a bases-loaded, no-out situation in the majors.*

pitched there all four years and also played first base and the outfield." He
was a tall, slim left-hander, standing six-foot-one and weighing 185.

"I also played basketball there a couple of years," he says, "but I was always the sixth man. I didn't have anywhere near the ability in basketball
that I did in baseball. In baseball, I was All-State in both my junior and senior years and we won the state championship in my junior year. As a
matter of fact, in the state championships that year, I pitched and won all
three games—because of rainouts—which was unusual. In the last game, I
had an 18-strikeout, no-hitter against Central High School. The one guy
who got on base against me walked, and I picked him off.

"During my senior year, the [New York] Yankees were following me,
and we knew they were interested in me. In 1969, the year I graduated,
they drafted me in the third round, which was pretty high. They offered
me something like thirty or thirty-five thousand dollars, but I was a minor
and my dad was looking for something more like fifty or sixty thousand
dollars. Well, right about then, I pulled a muscle in my arm, and the Yankees took back their offer. So that winter, the [Los Angeles] Dodgers
drafted me in the second phase of the draft, but they only offered $5,000,
and we just refused it. So then, the Red Sox drafted me. One of their
scouts, [Bill] Lefty LeFebvre, asked me how my arm was, and I said, 'Fine,'
so he asked me to throw for him. I got a catcher to come out and we
went out to the field at Cumberland High and I threw and he signed me.
I ended up getting $12,500, a far cry from what I could have got from the
Yankees if I signed right away," LaRose recalls.

To start the 1970 season, Boston sent the eighteen-year-old lefty to
Jamestown in the New York-Pennsylvania League, where their former
outfielder, Jackie Jensen, a three-time All Star and three-time American
League RBI leader, was managing. "One time a number of years later, in
1977 I think, I was on an airplane flying somewhere when someone taps
me on the shoulder and says, 'Hey LaRose, how's your career going?' It
was Jackie Jensen. I think he owned a Christmas tree farm down in Richmond then." (This story is interesting especially because Jensen was famous for his fear of flying, even trying hypnosis to get over it.)

At Jamestown, LaRose made 14 starts, winning four and losing four,
with a 3.36 earned run average. But he struck out 87 men in 83 innings
while walking only 39. "When I was young," he says, "I was a hard
thrower. I was throwing ninety-plus [miles per hour] when I was in high
school. But then, I didn't really know how to pitch."

Late in the season, the Red Sox promoted LaRose to their Pawtucket
team in the Double-A Eastern League. The hometown atmosphere
seemed to agree with him. In his only two starts there, he threw two
straight shutouts, allowing only seven hits in the 18 innings. In both
games, his catcher was another Boston prospect, Carlton Fisk, who later
caught LaRose in his one major-league appearance.

In 1971, LaRose went to spring training with Pawtucket but failed to make the team. "I was getting roped," he says. "Batters were just teeing off on me that spring. They sent me to Winston-Salem [in the Single-A Carolina League]. But things didn't get much better." When the season began, LaRose started six games but lasted just 24 innings. He won only once and lost three times and had an earned run average of 7.50. "I know I had some arm trouble that year," he says, "but the real reason I didn't pitch much is because I went into the service in May or June."

He had joined the National Guard, and his unit was called up to Fort Campbell, Kentucky, for a six-month tour of active duty during the Vietnam War. "They sent us to Fort Sill, Oklahoma, for basic training and I didn't get out until fall. I didn't play any winter ball at that time," he says. "Usually, after every season, I'd take a month off to relax, and then I'd just try to keep in shape between seasons. Then, about a month before spring training, I'd start tossing the ball around, just to get ready."

LaRose recalls he pitched relatively little, but he had good numbers. Just twenty years old, he played the season at Winter Haven in the Class-A Florida State League. In the 33 innings he pitched, he struck out 29 men and walked only 7. While his record was only two wins and two losses, his earned run average was an outstanding 0.82.

In 1973, he was back at Winston-Salem, where he relieved as well as started but had only mediocre success. He also started the 1974 season there but was not showing any improvement. Both years, his ratio of strikeouts to innings pitched declined substantially, his earned run average climbed to 4.55 and 5.14, respectively, and he lost more than he won. "I was just not pitching well," he admits. The Red Sox sent him back to Winter Haven.

"Rac Slider was the manager there," LaRose says, "and he told me, 'You know why you're down here, don't you? To learn how to pitch!'"

At Winter Haven that season, LaRose started 10 games and relieved in 19—and learned how to pitch. He also met a local girl, Janet Smith, whom he married the following February.

"Somehow that year I started putting it together," he says. "Bo Diaz was catching there, and I was learning to go inside-outside, and I guess I also was losing some off my fastball." He won six and saved five and was credited with an earned run average of only 1.82. In 104 innings pitched, he struck out 56, well below his average in prior years. "I wasn't just trying to throw it by everyone," he explains.

But Boston failed to protect LaRose after the season, and he was picked up by the Minnesota Twins and assigned to Tacoma, their Triple-A affiliate in the Pacific Coast League. Even before the 1975 season started, however, he was returned to the Red Sox. "I was sort of in limbo," LaRose says. "Boston didn't know what to do with me. They had kind of given up on me, I guess, and they sent me to Bristol, Connecticut, [in the Double-A Eastern League] 'til they figured out what to do with me. At the start of the season, I was with Bristol, but I wasn't allowed to do anything but throw on the sidelines and try to stay ready.

"One day, after quite a while had gone by," he continues, "we were in a game, and after a few innings, our starting pitcher gave up about eight runs. Dick McAuliffe was the manager, and he put me in. I just wasn't very sharp at all. Throwing in warm-ups is nothing like throwing in a game. I gave up eight runs in one inning, and I'm waiting for McAuliffe to take me out. I look over at the dugout, and he's just standing there laughing at me. He just let me take a pounding. It really made me mad.

"A few days later, he puts me in again, and this time I pitch six scoreless innings. After the game, I got called into the general manager's office, and he tells me that the pitcher who started the game had been sent out and that I was being kept. He said if I hadn't pitched good in that game, it would have been *me* who would have been sent out. Well, you know something? If I had been sent out then, I would *never* have reported. I would have quit baseball. That was a real turning point for me," he says.

At Bristol that year, the twenty-three-year-old LaRose started and relieved, and had his second strong season in a row, again pitching 104 innings. In addition, he won eight, lost only one, and had an earned run average of only 2.42—and Bristol won the league championship. "It was a funny year," he says. "At the end of the year, Boston called Dick McAuliffe back up to the majors, and he played a few games for them that season."

After the 1975 season, LaRose played winter baseball for the first time in his career. "I went down to play in Mexico that winter, but I didn't do much," he says. "It seemed to me the Mexicans expected, because you were an American, that you'd pitch no-hitters all the time. They expected a lot. I got sick drinking the water and was weak most of the time, and then the team I was with sent me to another Mexican team. I just came home and forgot about it.

"I started off with Bristol again in 1976," he continues, "but someone got hurt—Lance Clemens, I think—and I got promoted to Pawtucket [which had then moved to the Triple-A International League] for a while, but then I went back to Bristol and finished up there again." Outside of getting a chance to play back home for a time that season, it was not a particularly memorable year.

But 1977 was entirely different. He went to spring training with Pawtucket, the Triple-A club. "I did really well in spring training," he says, "and made the team. Joe Morgan was the manager, and I got off to a strong early start, going 7 and 2, and I made the All-Star team."

At Pawtucket, LaRose pitched 151 innings, more than he had ever thrown in any previous season. Used primarily as a starter, he had an 11–7 record and a 3.04 earned run average and made an impression, not only on his hometown fans, but also on his manager. "Morgan told me that it was in those years, '75, '76, and '77, that the Red Sox really thought of me as a prospect, and I know he was pulling for me.

"That season, they had a John LaRose Night for me in Pawtucket during the season. They had the ballpark packed with about six or seven thousand people. My high school coach was there, the mayor was there, and my wife. It just so happened that I was scheduled to start that night, and Joe Morgan thought that maybe it'd be easier if I *didn't* pitch. He said, 'Why don't I just scratch you tonight and you can just relax?' He thought I'd be putting too much pressure on myself because the ceremonies would be taking place before the game, and then I'd have to go out and pitch after getting all the gifts and all. But I told him I didn't want to miss my start, so I pitched. It just so happened I had a 2–1 lead over Richmond after seven innings, and Rick Kreuger came in to relieve me. He got the save and I got the win. It was a big night for me."

If the 1977 season was exciting for LaRose at Pawtucket, it paled in comparison to 1978. "At the end of spring training," he says, "Joe Morgan asked me if I'd be willing to pitch relief that year. He said he needed someone who could come in and relieve, and I said, 'Sure, let's give it a try.' Gary Allenson was the main catcher there that year, and I had an *awesome* year."

That was the year he became a closer. Though he had one start, LaRose got into 50 other games that year as the short reliever. In his 51 appearances, the most of any pitcher in the league, he pitched only 73 innings, but got credit for 10 wins and also led the league with 15 saves. His earned run average was only 1.60. "That year, we were the International League champions, and I was on the All-Star team," he says. "Not only that, but I was also named to the All-Triple-A All-Star team. They used to pick an All-Star team from the three Triple-A leagues, the Pacific Coast League, the International League, and the American Association."

"I think the highlight of my whole career took place that year," LaRose says. "That year the International League All-Star team played the Red Sox in an exhibition game right in Pawtucket. We were all excited. Don Zimmer [the Red Sox manager] was going to be there, and it would be a chance to show what we could do. The pitchers on the team were gonna pitch one inning each, and we each picked an inning out of a hat. I picked the ninth inning. I said, 'Oh, shit! What a shitty inning!' But when I went in, we were leading by just one run. The first batter was Rick Miller, and I struck him out. The next batter was Bernie Carbo, and I struck him out. The last batter was Bob Bailey, and I got him on a grounder to [third baseman Butch] Hobson. I never felt so high as I did that night, even higher than playing in the major leagues.

"I remember the Pawtucket papers kept talking about me being called up to the Red Sox. They kept writing, 'Will LaRose get a shot?' But Boston wouldn't make a move. We were in the playoffs, and they wouldn't do anything 'til they were over. Finally, around mid-September, they called three of us up, me, Gary Allenson and [outfielder] Sam Bowen.

"We met the team in New York," he continues. "We got there early on a Sunday morning and got into a cab and told the driver, 'Yankee Stadium.'

He turns around and looks at us and says, 'Yeah, sure,' like he didn't believe us. But we told him we meant it, that we were with the Red Sox. He drove us there, and we went inside and walked into the clubhouse and saw how big it was, real big-league. Then I went up the ramp out to the field. It must have been nine or ten in the morning and I'm still in my street clothes and nobody else is around. It was really something to see. I walked out to the mound, still wearing my suit jacket, and I threw a fictitious pitch. I was thinking back to the fact that the Yankees almost drafted me.

"I didn't play in New York," LaRose goes on, "but then we flew to Detroit, and I don't remember if it was the first or second game of the Detroit series that I pitched."

The date was September 20, 1978. The Red Sox were then in a final stretch drive to overtake the Yankees in the American League's Eastern Division. The race was nip and tuck and every game was crucial.

At Detroit that evening, the Red Sox started their thirty-two-year-old ace, Mike Torrez, who had been one of the leading Yankee pitchers only the year before. This season, the six-foot-five Torrez had won 15 games against 11 losses, but was tiring down the stretch. He had lost his last five decisions. His mound opponent for the game was Detroit's six-foot-four Dave Rozema, who, although 8–10, had just pitched two consecutive complete-game wins.

Torrez started off shakily. In the bottom of the first, the Tigers scored quickly thanks to an RBI single by designated hitter Rusty Staub. Over the next few innings, Torrez did not show much improvement and was continually in trouble. In the fourth, the Tigers scored two more runs, aided by a wild pitch and an error. Meanwhile, Rozema was holding Boston at bay.

"I had warmed up in the bullpen about three times in the first few innings," LaRose said. "Every time Torrez got in trouble, they called down to the bullpen, and Bob Montgomery, the bullpen coach, would say, 'LaRose, warm up.' That bullpen in Detroit was so small. It was like being in jail. But he kept saying, 'LaRose, warm up. LaRose, warm up.'"

In the bottom of the fifth, after Torrez had put the first two men on, Red Sox manager Don Zimmer called LaRose into the game. "After warming up so many times, I felt I left my best stuff in the pen," he says. "When I got out on the mound, my curveball was flat, and about the only thing I had was my sinking fastball. But I'd been in that position before. It was a hot night, and I was more exhausted than anything else. I knew I was supposed to be nervous in my first game in the majors, but I really didn't have the jitters. I figured whatever will happen will happen.

"Fisk was the catcher and I had pitched to him before, so I was familiar with his game plan. The situation was runners on first and second, no outs. The first batter was a right-handed hitter, I don't remember who it was. I went to a 3–2 count, and then I threw one right over the outside corner. It was close, but we had him struck out. But the umpire [Russ

Goetz] squeezed us, so he ended up on first with a walk. Fisk came out and said it should have been called a strikeout."

The bases were now loaded with no outs, and Detroit was already ahead by a 3–0 score.

"The next hitter, another right-hander, grounded to third," LaRose continues. "Hobson threw home for the force, but Fisk couldn't get the second end of the double play at first. Now we had bases loaded, one out. The next hitter grounded to short, and Rick Burleson turned over a 6-4-3 double play to get out of the jam."

Based on the box score of the game, the three batters LaRose probably faced that inning were the Tigers' catcher, Milt May; pinch hitter John Wackenfuss batting for right fielder Tim Corcoran; and another pinch-hitter, Aurelio Rodriguez, batting for third baseman Phil Mankowski.

"How did I feel?" LaRose asks. "I felt I did the job. I said, 'Here I am! See what I've done!' I felt *great*.

"When I got to the dugout, the first guy to say anything to me was Carl Yastrzemski. 'Hell of a job, John,' he said, 'hell of a job.' That was ironic in a way because back in '71 or '72, I had some arm problems and I was in Boston and was being worked on by [trainer] Buddy LaRue, and along comes Yaz, who didn't know me, but of course I knew who he was. He said, 'What's wrong with you, kid?' and I said I had some arm problems. 'You'll never make it to the big leagues with arm problems, kid,' he said, sort of sarcastic. I'm sure he doesn't remember that, but I did."

At that point in the game, the Red Sox trailed only 3–0, but still had four more innings in which to catch up. LaRose, the closer, had come in and gotten the team out a jam. He had done his job.

But after Boston again failed to score against Rozema in the top of the sixth, LaRose was sent out to pitch the bottom of the inning. "A lot of guys have told me, 'Zimmer never should have sent you back out there,'" he says.

Today, LaRose remembers only two of the batters he faced in the sixth. "I gave up two hits," he recalls. They were probably to shortstop Alan Tramell and center fielder Ron LeFlore. "And then [second baseman] Lou Whitaker hit a home run on a hanging breaker. I dropped down on him, and the curve broke in. They have that short porch in Detroit, and that's where he hit it." LaRose eventually went on to retire the side in the sixth inning although the only other batter he specifically recalls facing was Staub. "I threw him a backup curveball, and he stepped in and kind of jammed himself, and I got him on a pop-up."

The Tigers then led 6–0, with only three innings to go. When Boston failed to score in the top of the seventh, Zimmer again sent LaRose out to pitch the bottom of the inning. After walking the first two men he faced in the seventh, he was replaced on the mound by his roommate, rookie Jim Wright.

"A few minutes later," LaRose says, "I was sitting in the locker room, disgusted and exhausted, having a beer, when here comes Wright. I said, 'What are you doing here?' and he says he got roped, too. They clobbered him right after me. We just sort of sat there then and kind of laughed it off."

Detroit scored six runs in that inning, including the two men whom LaRose had put on, two whom Wright had put on, and two more whom another reliever, Tom Burgmeier, had allowed. Included in the onslaught was a three-run homer by Staub. While the Red Sox scored twice in the ninth, the Tigers won 12–2, giving Rozema his third straight complete game victory.

"After that game," LaRose reports, "I never even warmed up."

At the time, nobody knew that if the Red Sox had won that game, they would have won the Eastern Division pennant. As it was, they won 10 of their last 12 games that year and tied the Yankees on the final day of the season.

A one-game playoff was set for Fenway Park on October 2, 1978. It proved to be one of the most exciting games of the decade. "I wasn't eligible for the World Series," LaRose says, "but I was in the bullpen that day and I almost got in the game."

Almost 33,000 crowded into the old Boston ballpark that afternoon. Torrez was again on the mound for the Red Sox, facing the Yankee ace, Ron Guidry, who was pitching on three days' rest and finishing the kind of year that would make him the 1978 winner of the Cy Young Award.

In the second inning, Yazstremski homered down the right field line, and in the sixth, Boston scored again when Burleson doubled, was sacrificed to third by Remy, and came home on a single by Jim Rice, a .315 hitter that year.

With the Red Sox ahead 2–0, Chris Chambliss and Roy White singled in the top of the seventh. "We got a call in the bullpen," LaRose says. "I was told, 'LaRose, warm up.' Reggie Jackson was due up soon, and I think they were thinking of having me come in to pitch to him if it got to that point. Bob Stanley also was told to warm up."

Torrez got Jim Spenser to fly out, and Bucky Dent came to the plate. According to various accounts of what happened then, Mickey Rivers, who was on deck, noted Dent's bat was cracked. Dent then borrowed Rivers's bat and hit his now historic home run into the netting over the Green Monster wall.

After Rivers walked, Torrez was replaced by Stanley. "I was told, 'LaRose, sit down,'" LaRose recalls today. Stanley was a reasonable selection since he, then in his second season, led the league's relievers that year with 13 wins. He was on his way to a 15–2 record overall and also had 10 saves. But when Thurman Munson doubled Rivers home, the score was 4–2, Yankees.

In the top of the eighth, Jackson, facing Stanley, homered to center field, making the score 5–2. At the time, it seemed like a meaningless and superfluous run. But in the bottom of the eighth, Remy doubled, and Yastrzemski, Fisk, and Fred Lynn singled to bring Boston within a run of a tie. The rally was squelched when Goose Gossage struck out Scott.

In the bottom of the ninth, Burleson walked with one out. Remy then singled to right, but despite third base coach Eddie Yost waving him on, Burleson held at second instead of trying for third. Rice then hit a long fly to right field that allowed Burleson to tag up and go to third after the catch, but would have scored him easily if he had already been there.

Gossage, ever the closer, ended the game, the Red Sox season, and John LaRose's major-league career by then getting Yastrzemski to foul out. The Yankees went on to beat the Kansas City Royals for the American League pennant and the Los Angeles Dodgers in the World Series.

To this day, LaRose wonders what might have happened if he and not Stanley had faced Reggie Jackson that afternoon in Boston.

"In the Red Sox spring training camp in 1979, I only pitched two innings," he reports. "Tom Burgmeier was there, and it seems they always put him ahead of me. Anyway, I wasn't even scheduled to pitch, and then one day before a game with Atlanta, Allen Ripley and I were called into Zimmer's office. 'Each of you is pitching two innings today,' he tells us. Well, that was pretty short notice, but that's what happened. Each of us went out and pitched our two innings. That was my two innings for the whole spring.

"The next day, Johnny Podres, our pitching coach, comes up to us and says there's a rumor going around that the [San Francisco] Giants are interested in us. That's why Zimmer pitched us. We were in a showcase. Anyway, Ripley went to the Giants. I wished I had gone," LaRose says.

He stayed a while longer with the Red Sox. "I know Joe Morgan was trying to sell me to Zimmer. He told him, 'He pitched well for me last year' and things like that, but they said they needed a right-hander."

Boston optioned LaRose back to Pawtucket. "The major-league minimum then was $21,500, I think, and they sent me a contract for $19,500," he says. "I had an agent at that time, I don't remember his name, and he advised me not to report. I held out for a while but finally reported because I felt if I didn't play, I'd get way out of shape. That holdout left a bad taste in the Red Sox's eyes, and I'm sure they held it against me. I was dejected at not being given a chance, and in my mind, I've always questioned it."

He played at Pawtucket that year and again in 1980, appearing almost always in relief and normally as the closer. In the first year, he relieved 47 times but pitched just 53 innings. He won two, saved four, and had a 4.92 earned run average. "In 1980," he says, "I told myself, 'This is gonna be it.' Then, in spring training, I pulled a muscle warming up. After a while, they started putting pressure on me to pitch, but it still didn't feel right. I guess I came back too soon and reinjured it. So I really had no spring training at all. On the last day of spring training, they kept me on the team by putting me on the disabled list."

He returned later in the year, pitching 39 innings in 34 relief appearances, winning one and saving one, but posting a fine 2.77 earned run average. At the end of the season, he turned twenty-nine.

"My arm was not right that whole year, and I just left," he says.

For a few years after that, LaRose bounced from job to job, and he and his wife were divorced. "I was in factory-type work, shipping and receiving, and then I went to bartender school and became a bartender," he says. "I was lost and alone for a while and had no niche."

LaRose relocated to Atlantic City, New Jersey. "I always liked to play blackjack," he says, "and I inquired there about becoming a dealer. I went to a dealer school, and I dealt blackjack at the Showboat Casino in Atlantic City in 1986 and 1987. But I didn't like the city. I was alone and my parents were ill, so I moved back to Rhode Island."

In 1989, he joined the Senior Professional Baseball League. "I went down to play at Winter Haven, Florida, where I had played in the minors. I had that feeling that it was 'deja vu all over again,'" he laughs. "I played there in 1989 and '90. Bill Lee, who was on the Red Sox the year I was there, was my manager, and I really enjoyed those couple of years and the camaraderie. I remember Cecil Cooper, whom I had played with at Winston-Salem, coming over and saying, 'Hiya, John,' just like it was back then. And I'll tell you, when I played against those former major-league players, I *knew* I could have played at that level if I had gotten the chance."

When the senior league folded, he returned home and joined the postal service for a short time. Then, when the Foxwood Casino, a new gambling resort, opened on an Indian reservation in Ledyard, Connecticut, LaRose was hired as a blackjack dealer "on the spot." He has been there since March of 1992. "My parents are gone now," he says, "but I'm back living in the house I grew up in Cumberland, and it's a nice feeling."

LaRose still has the itch. "When the teams were looking for possible replacement players [in early 1995], I called the Florida Marlins and told them about myself over the phone," he reports. He was forty-three years old at the time.

"They sent me a package of material and gave me the date of an open tryout. They said to bring your own glove, be ready to play, and that there were no lockers available. I decided not to go. If they had offered to pay transportation or gave some sort of contract, I might have considered it.

"I met a lot of nice people in baseball, and I got a chance to travel. I wish some things could have been different. I think the quality of baseball is down these days. It was very hard then to make the majors. Today, they're giving the younger kids more of a chance. They don't keep them hanging around, and they don't spend a lot of time in the minors. I spent more than seven years in the minors before I got even a small chance. And I'm convinced I could have made it."

Perhaps more than once, anyway.

Roger Lee Slagle

NEW YORK YANKEES, 1979

When Roger Slagle entered the eighth grade in the mid–1960s, in Larned, Kansas, he stood only five-foot, three inches tall. Six months later, he was five-foot-ten.

"I had a disease which caused me to grow too fast," he says, "and my bones would chip. But the surgeons didn't want to remove them 'til they were sure I stopped growing, so I had to wait until I was eighteen."

When he finally stopped growing, Slagle was six-foot-three and 190 pounds. "I had surgery on both knees to remove the bone chips when I was eighteen, and I also had an operation on my right foot to remove some calcium deposits," he says. Despite his affliction, Slagle went on to play basketball, football, and golf in high school, as well as run on the track and cross-country teams.

"We had no baseball team in high school," Slagle says, "so I didn't play any baseball at all between fifteen and eighteen. But I did play for an American Legion team that finished third in the state. In football, I played quarterback and defensive back. In my senior year, we switched to the 'Wishbone,' and I played running back. I could throw better than most of the others, and harder, but if you know the game, you got to have 'touch.' You can't just burn it in there.

"The football coach was also the track coach, so you had to run track. I ran the sprints, the 100, the 220, and the quarter-mile. In golf, I shot in the eighties one year with a broken hand." How did he break his hand? Slagle explains: "In boxing class, I put my hand in the glove, and it had a hole in it so that my pinky was crossed over my ring finger, and when I hit the kid, I broke it. But it was my top hand, so it didn't affect my play-ing golf too much.

"In basketball I was all-league and the coach had us run cross-country for the conditioning," he says, recapping his high school athletic career. "But it was easy to be on teams there in the Midwest," Slagle says. "We didn't have that many kids going out for sports."

In 1972, after graduating from high school, Slagle enrolled in Hutchin-son County Community Junior College in Hutchinson, Kansas, about seventy miles from his home, to study medical technology. "I had an uncle in NASA in that capacity," he says, "and I thought that might be a field I'd be interested in. But I really went there because I thought they had a good basketball program. The coach was from my hometown, although I didn't know him then. His name was Gene Keady, who later became head coach at Purdue."

In his two years there, however, Slagle excelled more at baseball than he did at basketball. "I did real well," the right-hander says. "I had two no-hitters. I averaged something like two strikeouts an inning, and I hit .400. The fields were real rough and there were a lot of errors behind me, so we weren't that good, but I felt I could really pitch then. We went to the state tournament in Garden City, and that's where scouts first came around to look at me—college scouts mostly, but some pro scouts."

After completing his two-year course at the junior college, Slagle en-tered the University of Kansas in Lawrence in 1974 and made the varsity in his first season. "They gave me a medical-hardship season the first year," he says, "because I hurt my shoulder and they operated on it. Then I got mono."

His pitching attracted the pros, who were not deterred by his medical problems. On June 4, 1975, in the twenty-ninth round of the free-agent draft, Slagle was selected by the Philadelphia Phillies. "But I wasn't inter-ested," he says. "They made me a very low offer, something like $500 a month if I could make one of their farm teams."

Seven months later, on January 7, 1976, the San Diego Padres picked Slagle in the secondary phase of the free-agent draft. "They were willing to let me pitch through the school year," Slagle says, "and then play after I graduated." (With credits transferred from junior college, Slagle would graduate from the University of Kansas that summer with a bachelor of science degree in psychology.)

"But I got some bad advice," he says. "I held out for more money, and I guess I've regretted it ever since. They needed pitching. The Yankees didn't."

The New York Yankees, unbeknownst to Slagle, also were interested in him and, on June 8, 1976, chose him in the secondary phase of that year's draft. "I had no idea the Yankees were interested in me," he says, "but when they came along, I felt I had no choice, that I didn't have anymore options. They offered me a $5,000 incentive bonus. That meant I'd get so

*Roger Slagle pitched two perfect innings for the New York Yankees
but was never given another chance to pitch for them again.*

much if I stayed ninety days with their Class-D team, so much if I stayed ninety days at Class B, and so on. I was twenty-two, and they told me to take it or leave it. I don't remember who it was, but I think his name was Morgan. I signed, but I felt I could have done better. I ended up only getting $2,500 of the incentive bonus."

That summer, the Yankees sent him to their Fort Lauderdale farm team in the Florida State League. The manager was Mike Ferraro, a former Yankee infielder who later had brief managing flings at Cleveland and Kansas City. "I flew down to meet them in St. Petersburg, and when I got there, I hadn't slept in two days," Slagle remembers. "The first night I got there, I checked into the hotel and then went down to the ballpark just to say hello and meet the team. It turned out they were short of pitchers, and I ended up pitching five innings and won. I think I was the only one on the team who spoke English. They were all Dominican. The catcher came out and asked me, 'Tired?' Then he just stayed there for a while, never said another word, and finally went back behind the plate. I looked around and shook my head, and I said to myself, 'You know, the team I left is better than the team I'm on.'"

As the season continued, however, Slagle changed his mind. "We had a number of players on that team who eventually made the majors," he says, "including catcher Juan Espino; Damaso Garcia, our second baseman; and Domingo Ramos, our shortstop."

Slagle finished the year at Fort Lauderdale, doubling the number of his wins over losses (six wins, three losses) and strikeouts to walks (70 to 35) and compiling a 2.25 earned run average. All six of his wins were complete games, and two were shutouts. That winter, he played with the Yankees in the Instructional League in Sarasota, where he again was managed by Ferraro.

Although he was not originally invited to the Yankees' 1977 spring training camp, Slagle received a phone call to come down shortly after camp opened. "A lot of guys wanted to take extra batting practice, and they called to ask if I'd be interested in pitching to them, and of course, I said yes. It was a big thrill," he says of the experience. "I was awestruck at first, being around players like [Jim] Catfish Hunter, Reggie Jackson, [Chris] Chambliss, and Sparky [Lyle]. It was a real treat. But it was funny, in a way, to see how really normal these people were. After about a week, I really felt good about being there."

For the 1977 season, Slagle was assigned to West Haven in the Class A Eastern League, along with his manager, Ferraro. "We were becoming a team," Slagle laughs.

"The parks were small and the bus rides long, especially up to Canada," Slagle recalls, "but we had a good team, a top lineup. We had a good mix of good, young Yankee prospects and older veterans, and everybody enjoyed playing. There was no back stabbing there. We all pulled for each other. I think with the Yankees going out and getting all the free agents at that time, we all thought we'd end up with some other team and we all just felt free to go out and just play ball."

Slagle's record that year was 10–9, but he pitched 12 complete games and his earned run average, for over 170 innings, was only 2.81. He chalked up 100 strikeouts compared to just 47 walks.

After playing winter ball again and participating in the Yankees' spring training camp, Slagle was sent back to West Haven to start the 1978 season. He threw a six-hit shutout in his first start, striking out eight and walking one, and was immediately promoted to the Triple-A Tacoma club in the Pacific Coast League. "I think that was the year that everybody in the Yankee organization threw shutouts on opening day. I think it was [Ron] Guidry for the Yankees, [Jim] Beattie at the Triple-A team, Chris Welsh for the B team, and me."

At Tacoma, Slagle had another good summer, pitching 179 innings, winning 13, and losing 8. He struck out 96, walked 36, and his earned run average was 3.07. "I really enjoyed the season at Tacoma," Slagle says, "but I couldn't believe how far the ball traveled in the lighter air out west. [He gave up 13 homers that year compared to only 6 in the previous two years combined.] Then we got a chance to travel to Hawaii and play there, and that was a big blast."

But then came winter. "The Yankees wouldn't let us play winter ball that year because one of their super prospects, Gil Patterson, was injured playing winter ball and they didn't want anyone else to get hurt that way," Slagle says.

The decision backfired.

"I went to live with a friend of mine in California that winter and took a $5-an-hour job in a factory," Slagle says. "One day, another guy and I were carrying a piece of heavy machinery and it slipped out of his hands so all the weight came down on me and I tore a tendon in my elbow. I also dislocated my shoulder." His hopes of moving up to the Yankees in 1979 were quashed.

"For me, spring training in 1979 was for rehabilitation," Slagle says, "but there was one day I thought I'd get canned. I was feeling pretty good and was pitching batting practice. Thurmon Munson was at bat, and he and the catcher, a friend of mine named Dennis Irwin, who was a catcher of mine in the minors, were fooling around. Munson was deliberately trying to foul off the pitches into the dirt so they'd hit the catcher right in the nuts. He was doing a pretty good job of it, too, and they both were laughing about it. But then the catcher gives me the sign to flip him, you know, knock him down. So, to protect my catcher, I tossed one in close to Munson, and all of a sudden it tailed in. Munson couldn't get out of the way of it, and I thought it was gonna hit him right in the head. But luckily he stuck his hand up, and it hit him in the hand.

"[Yankee owner George] Steinbrenner was sitting in the stands, and I thought, 'Oh, God. I'm gone. I just hit the Yankees' meal ticket and

Steinbrenner saw it." The Yankee owner was known to have ordered the immediate demotion or sale of players he felt made poor plays while he was present. Fortunately, Munson was not hurt seriously.

"I went to Munson afterwards and apologized. I told him I didn't mean to hit him," Slagle recalls. "He said, 'Forget it. You were only trying to protect your catcher, and I know you'd do the same for me. I like you more for that. And, besides, it gives me a few days off.'"

Still rehabilitating his arm, Slagle started the 1979 season back at Fort Lauderdale, where he showed signs of recovery. In 15 innings there, he struck out 12, walked 6, and had an earned run average of 2.40. The Yankees sent him to the Columbus Clippers in the Triple-A International League, managed then by Gene Michael.

"I didn't throw well that year," Slagle says. "I was inconsistent. We played on Astroturf, and it was the first time on that for me. I just had no consistency. I was the fifth starter, and I felt it was a struggle the whole year." Slagle's record at Columbus that year was 8–11, with an earned run average of 4.64. His ratio of strikeouts to walks, however, remained excellent, 96 to 31.

On September 1, 1979, the Yankees recalled him. "The main reason I was called up," Slagle says, "is because I was on their 40-man roster and I wouldn't get to pitch in the playoffs [at Columbus]."

When Slagle arrived, the Yankees were in turmoil. First, Munson had been killed in a plane accident a month earlier. Second, Steinbrenner and manager Billy Martin were feuding again.

It would get worse. The volatile Martin, who had taken over for manager Bill Virdon with about two months to go in the 1975 season, had led the team to a pennant in 1976 and a World Series championship in 1977. Despite that, he was fired on July 24, 1978, and was succeeded by Bob Lemon, who had been elected to the Hall of Fame just two years earlier. Lemon went on to guide the team to a third straight American League flag and a second straight World Series victory over the Los Angeles Dodgers.

But when the team failed to get off to a fast start under Lemon in early 1979, Steinbrenner became impatient. After 65 games, he sacked Lemon and brought Martin back.

In any event, Slagle joined the Yankees, who were then mired in fourth place, on September 1, 1979. "[Infielder] Brian Doyle and I got called up together, and we got there on a Sunday," Slagle recalls. "Right after we got there, I thought I might get in a game. I was warming up a long time as the game was going on. Finally it went into extra innings, and I was getting exhausted. I was afraid if I went in, I'd get killed. I threw a whole game in the bullpen. Finally [Yankee outfielder] Oscar Gamble hit a home run to win the game, and I was relieved I didn't have to go in."

But Friday evening, September 7, 1979, he did get to pitch in a major-league game in Detroit, against the fifth-place Tigers, a team previously managed by Martin (see Chapter 36). At 8:05 P.M., when the game was scheduled to start, however, the temperature was a cool 58 degrees, and it was raining hard enough to delay the opening pitch for twenty-eight minutes. Despite the weather, nearly 30,000 people were in the stands. The game finally began with Ken Clay on the mound for the Yankees, against rookie left-hander Bruce Robbins of the Tigers.

In his previous start, Clay had lasted only two and a third innings, giving up four runs on five hits and prompting Steinbrenner to call the dugout to scream at Martin and call Clay a few names.

Tonight was almost a repeat. Clay gave up three runs on four hits in the first two innings, and when the first batter in the third singled on the first pitch, he was through. The phone rang in the Yankee dugout. "[Graig] Nettles answered the phone and said it sounded like George," Martin recalled. But the caller turned out to be a prankster. "I got on there and this guy says, 'What's going on there?' It was pretty good imitation, though. I can't believe they let the call through."

Jim Kaat came in to relieve Clay and pitched four innings, giving up three more runs on four hits.

Meanwhile, Robbins, the Tigers rookie hurler, also had to leave the game in the third inning after being hit on the knee by a line drive off the bat of center fielder Bobby Murcer. He was relieved by the 12-year veteran, Jack Billingham, who continued to stifle the Yankeee bats. At the end of six, the Tigers were ahead 6–0.

In the sixth inning, when the Tigers scored their last two runs off Kaat, Slagle learned he would be going in to pitch the bottom of the seventh. "I remember how nice the people were by the bullpen and how calm I was. The fans were real close to us, and they were very friendly, even though we were in Detroit," Slagle recalls. "We had a pleasant conversation throughout the game. They seemed genuinely excited about me pitching in my first game.

"I wasn't nervous at all," he says. "I was ready. I remember thinking to myself, 'I can't believe I'm not nervous.' I felt good warming up. Goose Gossage stood next to me and offered advice. As I was going in, he asked me if I wanted to know how to pitch to any of the hitters. I jokingly said 'Billingham' because I knew he wouldn't bat. I was surprised that I was calm and not nervous at all."

After the Yankees failed to score in the top of the seventh, Slagle went to the mound. The temperature by then had dropped to the low forties. "Steve Kemp [Tigers left fielder] was the first hitter," Slagle says. "I knew he was aggressive, so I pitched him careful and fell behind, 3–1. I threw him a batting-practice fastball, and he reached out and pulled it to first. Chris Chambliss [Yankee first baseman] fielded it and tossed it to me covering first. That little run over to first helped me settle down and concentrate on the batter.

"Champ Summers [Detroit's designated hitter, batting cleanup] was next, and I got him struck out on screwballs in the dirt," Slagle says. "Next was [first baseman] Jason Thompson. On the first or second pitch, he fouled it in the dirt, and it came up and hit my catcher [and roommate], Brad Gulden, in the crotch, in the nuts. Jerry Narron came in to replace Gulden—both were my catchers in the minors—and Thompson grounded to third."

Slagle returned to the dugout after retiring the Tigers in the seventh but didn't have time to reflect on his three-up and three-down performance. "I was glad to get past those three power-hitting lefties, although I seemed to pitch better to left-handed hitters. But between innings, I felt for my catcher," he says, "and that kind of took the edge off. I have to tell you that having catchers who know you is important. I felt comfortable with both Gulden and Narron because they knew what I could throw and what I did best. I remember back in 1977 when I was with West Haven, the Yankees called me up to pitch the Mayor's Trophy [exhibition] game. I had gone nine innings two days before. Fran Healy was the catcher, and he didn't know me. All he did was call for fastballs all day, and I got bombed. I also remember I got lost that day, trying to drive to Yankee Stadium," Slagle laughs.

For the Yankees in the top of the eighth, Narron, in his first at bat, singled to center, but was quickly erased when second baseman Willie Randolph hit into a double play. Murcer grounded out to end the inning, and Slagle returned to the mound for the bottom of the eighth.

"That next inning, I faced three right-handed batters," Slagle says. "I can't remember who the first batter was [Tigers rightfielder Jerry Morales]. I think he grounded to third. Next was [catcher] Lance Parrish. I threw four of my best pitches in perfect spots to strike him out. I don't recall if he swung or it was called. Last was [third baseman] Aurilio Rodriguez. He hit a bullet to right, and Reggie Jackson caught it running in.

"As I was coming off the field, I noticed a little boy above the dugout. I didn't think about the ball I had being from my first big-league game, and I rolled the ball across the top of the dugout to him. He was as happy as I was at the time. It wasn't until I got in the clubhouse that I realized I had given away my game ball. But I still feel good about giving that boy the ball to this day. I never dreamed that I wouldn't get the chance to pitch again."

In the top of the ninth, the Yankees did not score, and the game ended. In the clubhouse, Slagle told reporters, "It helped that it was late in the game. They were all pretty much swinging away. If the game had been a little bit closer they would have been taking more pitches."

Today Slagle says, "After the game, I was relieved that I had finally done it," he says. "I remember thinking, 'Now I've got my name in the record books. Now they won't be afraid to use me.' Little did I know they'd never use me again."

Four days after having pitched two perfect innings in his first game in the major leagues, the twenty-five-year-old Slagle was simply dropped from the Yankees' 40-man roster to make room for his best friend in professional ball, pitcher Rick Anderson. Slagle stayed with the team through the end of the season, however, pitching batting practice.

Of his Yankee teammates, Slagle says he was closest to Gossage. "Gossage was one of the best friends I had in baseball," he says. "We really hit it off, and I enjoyed being with him and his boys. As a matter of fact, if you read Billy Martin's book, *Number One*, it tells of a time when Martin and Gossage almost got into a fight over an argument Gossage had with [Yankees pitching coach] Art Fowler. It talks about Gossage being with an *unidentified* rookie pitcher. Well, I was the rookie pitcher. But Gossage wouldn't fight Martin. He had gotten into too much trouble earlier that year because of a fight with Cliff Johnson."

As for Martin, Slagle says, "I really liked him. I knew where I stood with him, and he was always up-front with me. Billy was under a lot of pressure, but I really enjoyed playing for him. He treated you fair. All he asked is that you bust your butt. After that time in Boston [the incident with Gossage], he apologized to me. He taught the game well."

Slagle also liked Sparky Lyle and Graig Nettles. "They were really nice. They used to wait on the rookies. We'd be on the plane and they used to bring us drinks so we wouldn't have to get up and have the manager see us," he laughs. "Nettles kind of watched out for me."

Slagle comments on Munson and Reggie Jackson: "Munson was a great guy. He was the leader of that team. Jackson was fairly outspoken. He liked me at first. One day, he gave me some advice about what I should do to improve myself in the off-season, but when I didn't take it or agree with it, he became cool to me."

Slagle also has fond memories of the Yankees' pitchers, including Catfish Hunter ("a class guy, friendly, cordial"); Tommy John ("He used to call me 'Lefty,' because I reminded him of [Steve] Carleton. I threw lefty for fun every once and a while"); and Luis Tiant. Slagle describes Tiant as "a lot of laughs. I remember him sitting in the whirlpool all the time, up to his neck, smoking those big cigars. He was always scared of flying. Every time we'd take off, he'd be screaming, '*Up! Up!*'"

As for his role on the team, Slagle says, "I thought I could make the team in 1980, but during that winter, I was supposedly traded to the Texas Rangers along with some other players. But the deal was screwed up because they announced the trade before we had cleared waivers."

So the Yankees sent him back to Columbus instead, where Joe Altobelli had taken over as manager from Gene Michael. "They wanted to make me a relief pitcher," Slagle says, "and I started off the season real well. But then they had me start again, and I hurt my arm."

He was sent to the Nashville Sounds. "Pat Dobson was the pitching coach there," Slagle says, "and he worked on my mechanics. He helped me a lot, and pretty soon I was throwing good and I did well. He was a great help.

"But then I got pinkeye. I wiped myself with a towel that had been used by somebody who had it, and I caught it from that. I couldn't see. I was pitching and I couldn't see the catcher's signs. The first guy up lined one back that hit me right in the face and crushed my nose. I wasn't knocked out. It just felt like a lot of bees on my face. But it affected my vision." And ended his season.

By the time spring training came in 1981, "I felt really good," Slagle says. With the Yankees that spring, he thought he threw fairly well. "I pitched 16 innings in training, but they sent me back [to Nashville]. I thought I was fixing to get buried."

In the first half of the season, Slagle's record with Nashville was 9–5, with a 3.02 earned run average, but then he suffered a torn rotator cuff, again abruptly ending his season early. "I didn't want to go through surgery, and I thought I'd rather rehabilitate it with weights," says.

He came back to pitch for Nashville in 1982, but the arm would not hold up. "I threw a slider one day and heard my arm snap," he recalls. "The doctor told me it was a bad one. He told me it was like a rubber band with a hole in it. When it's normal, you don't see the hole, but when you stretch it, you can see the hole and it becomes bigger. I went on the disabled list and became a pitching coach."

Slagle decided to retire after that year. "I didn't want to stay in baseball then," he says. "Now I wish I did. But I was tired of the travel. I saw how it affected married guys with families, and I thought if I had a family of my own, I wouldn't want to be away from them so long. Besides, I had sort of a bad taste in my mouth at that point. I didn't think I got a fair shake."

He remained in Nashville, where he helped paint houses and played on a local softball team. In September, Slagle joined the Davidson County Sheriff's Department, working in a pretrial release program. But in January 1984, he bought a friend's catering truck business in White House, Tennessee, about twenty-five miles north of Nashville. He operated that through mid-1986. From then until late 1992, he was in the steel erection business, serving as a safety director for the Cumberland Steel Company. He also took a month off in 1990 to join his old pitching coach, Pat Dobson, in Fort Meyers, Florida, for a stab at senior-league baseball, but the league folded.

At the end of 1984, Slagle married Sherry Nash, a school teacher and a women's basketball coach, to whom he was introduced by his Nashville softball friends. Together with their four children (two from Sherry's previous marriage), they reside in White House today and are the owners and operators of Sherry Babes Learning Center for preschoolers.

What effect did his major-league status have on his life? "None, really," Slagle says. "Maybe if I could have stayed in the big leagues longer, things would be different," he adds. "But it's always nice to say that I made it and was successful for one game."

Successful? For that one game he was perfect.

Robert Banks Davidson

NEW YORK YANKEES, 1989

Ten years after Roger Slagle (see Chapter 39) pitched in a game for the New York Yankees, so did Bobby Davidson. He is still bitter about the experience.

Slagle had pitched for a team in turmoil because of various feuds involving men of strong personalities—George Steinbrenner, Billy Martin, Reggie Jackson, Thurman Munson, and Goose Gossage, to name a few. When Davidson arrived a decade later, the turmoil was still going on. The principals this time, however, were Steinbrenner and his manager of the moment, Dallas Green.

Davidson, the older of two sons of a career army officer, first played baseball in a West German Little League. "I was born in Germany [in January 1963] and grew up there," he says. "I started playing tee ball at age six and didn't miss a year 'til age twenty-nine. I didn't come to the United States until junior high school when my father was transferred back to Fort Bragg, North Carolina. That was in 1976, actually on New Year's Eve, 1975. I remember we stayed in guest quarters."

In North Carolina, Davidson attended E. E. Smith High School in Fayetteville, where he was an all-around athlete. He pitched for the baseball team, played offensive tight end and defensive back on the football team, ran track, and played basketball. In both baseball and football, he was named to all-conference teams. "I only played basketball my freshman year 'cause I was always getting hurt," he says. "I never got hurt playing baseball. I never got hurt playing football. But in basketball, I got hurt *all* the time."

After graduation in 1981, the six-foot, 185-pounder enrolled at East

Bobby Davidson, credited with being in the major leagues for three days,
says it was really more like twenty-six hours.

Carolina University in Greenville, North Carolina, to major in computer science. For three years, he pitched on the school's baseball team. "All in all, I was mediocre," he says of his college play. "I had a good freshman year but a dismal sophomore year. I hurt my arm that year—a strained elbow—and didn't really get back on track until the tail end of my junior year.

"The [New York] Yankees had spoken to me in high school," Davidson says, "but when I got hurt in my sophomore year in college, they dropped me. Nobody was interested in me. I guess I got a tag for being hurt. And because I was hurt during my sophomore year, I wasn't in the starting rotation as a junior. I was a reliever. But then, at the end of the year, I had some good outings and was pitching my best. I remember pitching well against the University of Miami in the regional finals."

In June 1984, the Yankees selected the right-handed Davidson in the twenty-fourth round of the free-agent draft. "I was surprised to be drafted," he says. "I hadn't heard from anybody. You know, it was funny. After the draft, the teams had either eleven or sixteen days to get in touch with you, and the Yankees waited 'til the very last day. Finally a scout, Jim Gruzdis, came around, but he didn't sign me. He just had me sign a paper which said that they talked to me within the proper time frame and that they intended to make me an offer. But he said he wasn't sure yet what they were gonna offer. He said they'd watch me play for a couple of weeks and then decide. So, after I was drafted, I still had to try out."

At the time, Davidson was pitching in an amateur summer league in Virginia, and Gruzdis finally came by with a contract. "I got a [signing] bonus of $7,000," Davidson says, "and they sent me to Oneonta, New York [in the Class-A New York-Pennsylvania League], after the season had already started. I got there around the same time as Al Leiter, and we roomed together. Evidently, they had signed him late, too."

Davidson was used strictly as a reliever that first season and got into 24 games. He won 2, lost 5, saved 10, and had a 3.45 earned run average. Using his fastball and a quick-breaking slider, he recorded 26 strikeouts in twenty-eight and two-thirds innings.

"Right after the season, I played in the Instructional League the Yankees had," Davidson says. "It wasn't winter ball. They ran this for two months right after the season, in October and November. I think this was the last year they had it. It was by invitation, and I felt it was kind of an honor to be invited because they usually limited it to players who were drafted in the top five rounds. There were a number of major leaguers there, and managers and coaches. I enjoyed it."

In 1985, Davidson went to spring training at the Yankees' minor-league complex in Hollywood, Florida, and was assigned back to Oneonta for his first full season in professional ball. Between the end of spring training and the start of the season, he and Sherri Guerrero, his high school sweetheart, were married. "I went home to get married, and then we went up to Oneonta on our honeymoon," he laughs. "We got there three weeks before the season started and waited for the team to show up.

"That was a fantasy team that year," he says. "I think we broke the league record for most wins in a year, and we had a team ERA of under 3.00. The pitchers included Leiter and Troy Evers, and Ricky Balabon, who was the Yankees' number-one pick, was there. The manager was Buck Showalter. You keep an eye on him," Davidson says. "He's a good one."

At Oneonta that year, Davidson pitched primarily as the team's short reliever, coming in to close out the opposition in the final innings. In 29 games, he pitched 36 innings and struck out 44 batters. He was credited with five saves and compiled a 2.50 earned run average.

In 1986, Davidson was sent to Fort Lauderdale in the Florida State

League under manager Bucky Dent. "I had a dismal first part of the year," Davidson recalls, "and Bucky called me into his office one day, and I thought I was gonna be released. But, instead, he told me I was going up to Albany [in the Double-A Eastern League].

"You know, it's funny, but being married, it's different. I moved a lot during the middle of a lot of seasons, and each time the first thought you have is about how you're gonna move your wife and family," Davidson continues. "Another thing I found is that each time I moved up, I would come back a different player—a better, more mature player.

"This time, I was going up to replace Steve Fry, who got injured or something, and I was supposed to come back in two weeks. So Sherri just stayed in Fort Lauderdale. When I got to Albany, I pitched well, so when Fry came back, I stayed and they sent someone else out," Davidson recalls. "But finally, they sent me back to Fort Lauderdale for the last four weeks in August."

In 24 games at Albany that year, Davidson was used strictly in relief and was credited with five saves. In his split time with Fort Lauderdale, he started 7 of the 16 games he was in, winning 4 and losing 2.

During the off-season, Davidson took a part-time job as a chimney cleaner. "The Yankees had a policy then of not sending their pitchers to play winter ball," he says. "I think they had a prospect who got hurt once, so they wouldn't do it anymore."

The following year was, according to Davidson, "my biggest growth year. It was a good learning year for me." At Prince William in the Carolina League, manager Wally Moon turned him into a starting pitcher. Davidson's won-lost record with Prince William that year was only 3–10, but he got to start 16 times and pitched 124 innings, by far the most he ever pitched in a season.

"I'd be in situations that year where I had to pitch, not just relieve. It was the turning point for me," Davidson says. "I was twenty-four, and kind of old for that league, but we had a pitching coach—I wish I could remember his name—who was a young fellow and I could relate to him. He was trying to teach me to throw a sinker. Now I always wanted to throw *hard*. If I got three balls on a batter, normally I'd go back to the fastball. But that year, I decided I would keep throwing the sinker, no matter what. I said I'd sink or swim with the sinker—no pun intended. I'd go with it. If I walked him, I walked him. But my control got better the more I threw it, and I had a good year." He was named to the league's All-Star team. "That was something," he laughs. "I was voted to the All-Star team, and I think at the time I had won only one game."

In the latter part of the season, Davidson was again promoted to Albany, where he started six more times that season and pitched an additional 60 innings. While winning one and losing two, he had an impressive 2.41 earned run average. "There was a new guy to the organization who was managing there that year," Davidson says, "Tommy Jones. He was

a fireball. One time he got thrown out of six games in a row! He used to turn red as a beet."

In 1988, Davidson was plucked out of the Yankees' minor-league spring training complex to accompany the major-league squad on its visit to play teams on Florida's west coast. "They just wanted some extra arms around in case they needed them," he says, "but I never got to pitch."

At the start of the season, he was sent to the Yankee's Triple-A Columbus team in the International League, where Dent was managing. "That was another season where I started in Columbus, went to Albany in midyear, and then came back to Columbus at the end of the year," Davidson says.

Most of his pitching that year was done in Albany. He appeared there in 34 games, but started only three and pitched 93 innings. He won six, lost three, saved six, and had a 2.72 earned run average. In his time with Columbus, he relieved six times, pitched 19 innings, got one save, and ended up with an earned run average of 2.37. At that point, he was twenty-five years old.

But the following year, in 1989, Davidson finally got to the major leagues. He started the season back in Albany, under manager Showalter, and was 2–0 with a 2.87 earned run average, before being shifted to Columbus. Then suddenly, on July 15, 1989, Davidson was summoned to come up to the Yankees.

"I'm credited with being in the big leagues three days," Davidson says, "but it was really more like twenty-six hours. I got to New York on a Saturday, around noon, got to the ballpark, and got dressed in time for the game. I stayed over for Sunday's game, which was called off early because of rain, and then I was told I was going back to Columbus.

"They told me I was brought up because somebody was supposed go on the DL [disabled list], but then they changed their minds and said he wasn't. They asked me if I wanted to stay overnight, but I was so angry, I just wanted to get out of there, so I left Sunday afternoon."

As Davidson recounts his experience, he arrived at Yankee Stadium that Saturday, the fifteenth, shortly before game time. It was Old-Timers Day, and more than 50,000 fans were on hand. "The locker room was a madhouse," he says. "I got there and I didn't know who was who. I never met [manager Dallas] Green or [pitching coach Billy] Connors. I didn't know who were the coaches or who were the players. I didn't know any of the old-timers and I wasn't about to ask anybody for an autograph. I saw [pitcher] Dave Eiland there, whom I knew from the minors. He was being sent back that day because of the DL situation, but he had not been told yet that he was going.

"I'm there with my suitcase," he continues, "and I got dressed in the middle of the locker room, at the table they had in the middle. I put on my pants and a T-shirt. Then the stirrups would show up. Finally, I was

assigned a locker. I looked around and saw I knew some of the guys, like [catcher Bob] Geren and [outfielder] Roberto Kelly.

"It was almost game time. The Old-Timers game had ended. I didn't see any of it 'cause I was finishing getting dressed. Then I got lost going from the clubhouse out to the field. I almost ended up in the other team's locker room. See, while the Yankee dugout is on the first base side, the locker room is actually on the third base side, and I couldn't find the way to get to the field. There's also a shortcut to the bullpen, but I ended up going out and walking across the field, going *in* the fence in the bullpen that you usually come *out* of. I saw Geren in the bullpen and also Lee Guetterman, whom I knew. I was jittery just getting there. It was chaos," he says.

Chaos was not uncommon with the Yankees. The team had undergone twelve managerial changes starting from 1979, with Bob Lemon and Billy Martin, to 1989, with Dallas Green.

When Davidson came to play in Yankee Stadium in 1989, Dallas Green was the current winner in the Yankees' managerial musical chair game.

With Davidson finally in the bullpen, Green still in the dugout, and 50,124 in the stands, the regular game between the Yankees and the Kansas City Royals finally got under way. It soon turned into a pitchers' duel between Luis Aquino of the Royals and Chuck Cary of the Yankees.

Cary lasted through seven innings. With the game was tied, 1–1, Green brought in Guetterman to pitch. The Royals' center fielder, Willie Wilson, led off the top of the eighth with his third hit of the game, but was forced at second on an attempted sacrifice by third baseman Kevin Seitzer. The Royals then got six more hits in a row off Guetterman and his successor, Dale Mohorcic, including a three-run homer by right fielder Danny Tartabull, as they batted around and scored four runs to take a 5–1 lead.

"I was warming up," Davidson says, "and we got a phone call in the bullpen in the middle of the inning that said, 'If we don't score, he's in.' We didn't score in the bottom of the eighth, so I came in to pitch the ninth. I felt kind of numb. It was like sensory overload. I remember coming in across the outfield and I saw the faces of the second baseman [Tom Brookens] and the shortstop [Alvaro Espinoza] looking at me and they were grinning. Nobody said a word. Sluggo [catcher Don Slaught] didn't even give me any signs. At that point, it was just pitch and catch."

The first batter up was Wilson, who already had three hits. "I knew him by name, and I knew he had some speed," Davidson says, "but that's about all. As I was pitching to him, I began to settle in. I began to hear sounds around me. Before that, it was all kind of isolated."

Wilson grounded out to Brookens. "I remember that when he [Wilson] was going back to the dugout, he crossed by the mound and said something like, 'I didn't think you'd throw me another one.' That's about when I realized it was still just baseball," Davidson says.

The next batter was Seitzer, who had led the American League in base hits two years earlier. Davidson walked him on four pitches. "They were all sinkers," Davidson says, "and in the International League, some of them would have been strikes."

George Brett, playing first base, came to the plate. Brett had been the league's leading batter twice already and would do it a third time the following year. "I started him out with a curve," Davidson says, "and I thought it was a strike. The catcher thought it was a strike. But not the umpire. He called it a ball. As a rookie against Brett, I wasn't gonna get the call. The next pitch was a sinker over the outside corner. Sluggo held his glove right there for a long time, but the umpire [Eugene "Ted" Hendry] called it ball two.

"Now, having walked a guy on four pitches and going 0-2 on the next batter," he continues, "there was no way I wasn't gonna throw a strike this next pitch. So I took a lot off it. I took so much off it, it was a bad pitch, inside. I thought Brett literally came out of his shoes to hit it. It was so slow I thought sure he'd hook it foul. I had thrown pitches like that before, and guys had always hit them foul. In fact, I sometimes threw them on purpose to get lefty guys to hook them foul. But this time, it stayed straight. There was no bend in it. He lined it straight down the line into the right field stands for a home run.

"After he hit it, I was embarrassed, but I thought to myself, 'Get over it.' I got angry at myself. I said, 'Stop being like a young rookie and get the job done!' I remember thinking of a guy I knew who had come to the majors and gave up three home runs in his debut [see Chapter 17]. I didn't want to repeat that debut. I remember hearing about a number of pitchers who had given up home runs in their first game," Davidson says.

The next batter was the cleanup hitter Tartabull, who had homered his last time up. "Bo [Jackson] was not playing that day," Davidson recalls, "and right after Brett homered, Tartabull swung so hard at my first pitch that it made me angry. He was showing me no respect. I started to pitch. I told myself, 'I'm *not* nervous. I'm *not* gonna be embarrassed. Now I go on the offense.'"

Tartabull grounded to Espinoza, and left fielder Jim Eisenreich, playing that day instead of Jackson, ended the inning by grounding out to Brookens. "I still felt embarrassed when I walked off," Davidson says. "I said to myself, 'I'm better than this.'"

But when the game ended, Davidson admits, "I was relieved it was over. But let me tell you something, I still had a lot of anxiety after the game. After I took a shower and got dressed, I had to wait around the locker until they told me what to do. I had no place to go and no money. I had about ten bucks with me.

"Finally, somebody came down and told me I was staying at a hotel, but I didn't get the name, and that they were getting a cab to take me there. They gave the cab driver a chit or something, so I didn't have to pay. But

when I got in the cab, the driver could hardly talk English and turned around and asked, 'So where we going?' I said, 'Don't you know? Didn't they tell you?' So finally he drives me to a Holiday Inn. I said, 'Are you sure this is the right place?' I told him not to move while I went inside to see if it was the right hotel. I was afraid if he took off, I'd really be stuck. I was totally confused." Fortunately, it was the right place.

The next day, Sunday, July 16, Davidson returned to the Stadium, where the Yankees were again hosting the Royals. This time it was far from a pitchers' duel. The Yankees scored in each of the first four innings and, at the end of six, had pounded out 14 hits to lead 10–0.

"That day," Davidson says. "I sat in the bullpen and watched, and they got me up to throw twice. I don't remember the inning, but one time Green went out to the mound to talk to the pitcher [Greg Cadaret] while I was getting loose. Then the bullpen coach yelled over, 'All right. You're in.' So I picked up my jacket and walked out of the bullpen onto the field and started walking in toward the mound with my head down. I got past the outfielder and was nearing the infield when I heard the right fielder [Jesse Barfield] saying, 'Go back!' I looked up and saw Dallas Green going back into the dugout. He hadn't taken the pitcher out! I turned around and went back to the bullpen. The fans were yelling and laughing. When I got back, the coach said, 'I'm sorry. Dallas Green *never* goes out to the mound without taking the pitcher out. That's the first time that's ever happened.'

"Well, I just wanted to hide. Later they got me up to throw again, and the fans were all yelling at me and having fun," Davidson says. In the top of the seventh, the Royals scored a run. "We got a phone call again, and they said, 'Next inning, he's in.' So I was all set to go in to pitch the eighth inning, but the rains came and the game was called. I never got another chance."

After the game, Davidson was told he was being returned to Columbus. "Dallas told me in his office," Davidson says. "He didn't say much. He said, 'One day you'll understand the way the numbers work.' He said the game I pitched had nothing to do with it. He said he talked to Sluggo, and Sluggo said I pitched fine. 'You'll be back at the end of the year,' he said. He said I could stay the night in New York, if I wanted. But I was perturbed. I just wanted out. I was kind of sick. I was feeling really ill. You know how it is when you're happy, and then all of a sudden, it's like your guts were ripped out. I was really down.

"Somebody came down from the front office and gave me my travel money," Davidson says. "They gave it to me all at once, coming and going. The guy, I think his name was Jamieson, said he couldn't believe what they were doing to me. He sounded real angry. 'If you got any expense receipts,' he said, 'you send them to me and I'll double them. Any receipts at all.' I don't know if he meant it or not. I just wanted out. I got out so fast I beat Dave Eiland back to Columbus—and he had left before me. In fact, I played in Columbus the next night.

"When I got back, Bucky [Dent] told me not to let it get to me, but I was upset. In fact, I didn't do well the next couple of times I pitched. But Bucky told me, 'You can't go back like this,' and I settled down. He let me start, and I always wanted to start. I remember I pitched 21 straight shutout innings," Davidson says. He ended the season with eight wins, five losses, and an exceptional 1.83 earned run average.

As the International League season wound to its end, Dent was called up to manage the Yankees, succeeding Green. "I remember Green telling me I'd go back up at the end of the year," Davidson says. "At that time, my wife was pregnant and she was due in October. So we moved her to Connecticut, where I had family, so she would be close to New York, where I expected I'd be.

"But when the rosters expanded, the only players they took up were veterans," Davidson says. "Somebody told me that Dent didn't want young players. But one day when I was in Toledo, Bucky called and explained. He said that wasn't true. He told me there were more people than him that made the decisions. I believed him. He didn't *have* to call me, but he did. I thought I had an enemy up there I didn't know about. It was peculiar."

Davidson spent the following season at Columbus where, he says, "I had a very un–Bobby-like year. I was 3 and 3, mediocre." At year end, he opted for free agency and was signed by the Minnesota Twins, only to be released during spring training in 1991.

"St. Louis picked me up three days later and sent me to Louisville that year," Davidson says. "It was a weird year. I was bad and good. I just had lost a lot of drive. The Yanks had messed with my mind. My wife and I were dragging, we were drained, and I just wasn't pitching aggressively. I lost it mentally, and near the end of the 1991 season, we decided to wrap it up. I finished the year at Louisville, but that was it."

At twenty-eight, Davidson retired from professional baseball, and he and his family moved back to North Carolina, where they settled in Raleigh. He went back to work in the chimney-sweeping business and also returned to school at night, resuming his studies in computer science at North Carolina Wesleyan.

In late 1993, his wife, working for a consulting firm, was transferred to Cincinnati, Ohio, and the Davidson family, including their young daughter, Hannah, moved again. He and his wife have since had twins, Maria and Antonio. Today, Davidson continues in the chimney-cleaning and restoration business there and also attends the University of Cincinnati, where he expects to receive his degree in the near future.

"I like the construction and restoration business," Davidson says. "But I'm good at computers as well as with my hands. I think there should be some way I can blend the two after I get my degree. We'll see."

Of his one brief time in the major leagues, Davidson says, "I remember I flew first-class coming up and coach going back. I thought that was symbolic."